PRACTICAL COLLEGE READING

Strategies for Comprehension and Vocabulary

Gene Wintner

Northern Essex Community College

IRWIN
CAREER
EDUCATION
DIVISION

Chicago • Bogota • Boston • Buenos Aires • Caracas
London • Madrid • Mexico City • Sydney • Toronto

IRWIN
Concerned About Our Environment
In recognition of the fact that our company is a large end-user of fragile yet replenishable resources, we at IRWIN can assure you that every effort is made to meet or exceed Environmental Protection Agency (EPA) recommendations and requirements for a "greener" workplace.
To preserve these natural assets, a number of environmental policies, both companywide and department-specific, have been implemented. From the use of 50% recycled paper in our textbooks to the printing of promotional materials with recycled stock and soy inks to our office paper recycling program, we are committed to reducing waste and replacing environmentally unsafe products with safer alternatives.

Senior developmental editor: Jean Roberts
Senior marketing manager: Lynn M. Kalanik
Production supervisor: Ann Cassady
Project editor: Amy E. Lund
Designer: Michael Warrell
Cover designer: Jamie O'Neil
Cover illustrator: Cathleen Toelke
Art manager: Kim Meriwether
Art studio: Electra Graphics
Compositor: BookMasters, Inc.
Typeface: 10/12 Times Roman
Printer: R. R. Donnelley & Sons Company

Library of Congress Cataloging-in-Publication Data

Wintner, Gene.
    Practical college reading / Gene Wintner.
        p.   cm.
    Includes index.
    ISBN 0-256-15451-1
    1. Reading (Higher education)   I. Title.
LB2365.R4W56   1995
428.4'071'1—dc20   94–9321

Printed in the United States of America
1 2 3 4 5 6 7 8 9 0 DO 1 0 9 8 7 6 5 4

PREFACE

Practical College Reading is a student-centered text intended for developmental readers in two- and four-year colleges and career schools. The book may be used successfully by ESL, bilingual, and learning-disabled students, as well as more typical developmental students who have come to college with little reading experience and perhaps little interest in reading.

The text uses an integrative approach. After the first chapter, which is introductory, each chapter begins with an engaging reading selection accompanied by comprehension and vocabulary exercises. Then the chapter introduces one or two new strategies for improving comprehension and/or vocabulary, with practice exercises. Integrative exercises follow that provide additional practice and reinforcement for the new skills and for skills taught in previous chapters. Each chapter ends with a journal entry that evokes a written response to concepts that have been presented in the chapter.

Practical College Reading incorporates some of the principles of whole language learning. Students learn to see reading as a process in which they actively engage and that they themselves monitor. The text provides extensive opportunity for the application of strategies and for monitoring their effectiveness. Reading is approached as a meaning-oriented process in which the student's own experience and knowledge play a pivotal role.

Special Features

The following features make *Practical College Reading* an especially effective textbook for developmental students:

- High-interest reading selections begin each chapter, representing a variety of college disciplines. The selections increase in difficulty as the text progresses. The exercises accompanying the reading selections provide a meaningful practice context for the strategies and skills taught in the text.

- Extensive instruction and practice are provided in the use of key vocabulary strategies, including context, dictionary, word associations, prefixes, roots, and suffixes.
- Extensive instruction and practice are also provided in the use of key comprehension strategies, including pre-reading, monitoring, questioning, recognizing main ideas, recognizing patterns of organization, underlining and notetaking, inference, and critical reading.
- Written responses on comprehension exercises and journal assignments are a regular part of each chapter.
- Ten additional reading selections provide alternative or supplementary practice.
- Six appendixes augment the text instruction in both comprehension and vocabulary strategies. Word pronunciation strategies and test-taking tips are included in the appendixed material.

Organization of the Text

Chapter 1 shows students how to establish good study habits and become more aware of their own learning styles. Chapters 2 to 8 introduce the fundamental vocabulary and comprehension strategies, as follows:

Chapter 2   Presents a process model for vocabulary building and introduces use of context clues.

Chapter 3   Presents a process model for study reading and introduces pre-reading strategies, including previewing and pre-thinking.

Chapter 4   Focuses on the effective use of the dictionary and the relation of context and dictionary. Also shows students how to use index cards to study vocabulary.

Chapter 5   Teaches students how to monitor their comprehension and use corrective strategies.

Chapter 6   Teaches students how to use goal questions to guide their reading, and begins work on prefixes.

Chapter 7   Begins work on reading for main ideas, and continues work on prefixes.

Chapter 8   Continues work on reading for main ideas, and reviews word roots.

Chapter 8 is followed by a Strategies Check, which reviews the skills and strategies discussed in Chapters 1 to 8. Chapters 9 to 13 emphasize higher-level strategies, as follows:

Chapter 9   Reviews suffixes, shows students how to use word associations to remember word meanings, and shows how vocabulary strategies are interrelated.

Chapter 10   Shows students how to recognize the organization of articles and textbook material.

Chapter 11   Teaches students how to mark in their textbooks and how to take effective notes from reading assignments.

Chapter 12   Practices with inference skills.

Chapter 13   Teaches students how to use after-reading strategies to review and evaluate what they read.

Chapter 14   Reviews the skills and strategies taught throughout the text and asks students to apply their skills to several reading selections.

The supplementary material following Chapter 14 includes 10 additional practice readings and six appendixes. The appendixes include a reading habits inventory, book preview instruction, expanded prefix and root tables, phonics instruction, and tips for taking tests.

Special Pedagogical Characteristics

- Each reading selection is preceded by pre-reading exercises. The pre-reading exercises become less structured in the second half of the text to encourage greater student independence in their use.

- Students are asked to rate the interest level and difficulty level of each main selection. The use of these ratings encourages self-monitoring.

- All comprehension exercises include multiple-choice and written response questions.

- Vocabulary work is context-based. Students learn to judge when context is sufficient and when the dictionary is necessary.

- The exercises that accompany each main reading selection incorporate the skills and strategies taught in previous chapters. This ensures that the strategies will be retained.

- In the second half of the textbook, an essay question is included with each main reading selection (the journal-writing practice in the first half of the textbook has prepared students to write essays in an unthreatening manner).

- Integrative exercises make additional practice available and provide reinforcement for skills learned in previous chapters.

- Journal entries allow for open-ended writing practice in each chapter.

- A skills and strategies review is provided in the middle and end of the book.

Using the Text

Practical College Reading is intended to be a flexible tool that each instructor can adapt to his or her particular program, course, and student needs. The text has been organized to allow the instructor maximum flexibility in choice of content, skills/strategies, and degree of practice. The Instructor's Manual includes guidelines for a variety of text adaptations.

The Selections.   The reading selections in *Practical College Reading* have been placed at the beginning of each chapter (with the exception of Chapter 1). This placement affords several advantages. First, the student is confronted immediately with reading content from an academic subject, rather than didactic instructional material. Second, the selection and its accompanying exercises provide immediate practice with skills and strategies learned in the previous chapter. Third, material from the selection is used for modeling the new strategies presented later in the chapter.

　　Some instructors may wish to have their students reread the selection after completing the chapter exercises.

The Ratings.   The interest and difficulty ratings following each selection act as a first-line metacognitive strategy for the student. By consciously assessing these factors, students will learn about the dynamic role they play in their reading experiences. Journal entries in the text and exercises provided in the Instructor's Manual will help students further explore these variables. At the same time, instructors may learn something helpful about their students from their ratings.

Selection Exercises.   Pre-reading exercises ensure that students will employ these strategies before reading the chapter selection and encourage the habit of using them in their other courses as well. "While You Read" suggestions remind students to apply the strategies taught in previous chapters to the current selection. Comprehension exercises provide ongoing practice with literal and inferential levels of comprehension, as well as reinforcement of the specific skills and strategies taught in preceding chapters. Essay questions (in the second half of the text) provide a more formal writing exercise than the journal entries located at the end of each chapter. The simple format of the vocabulary exercises accompanying the selections reinforces the use of context and dictionary skills throughout the text. The Instructor's Manual includes the vocabulary list for each chapter and suggestions for a variety of supplemental vocabulary exercises.

Skills and Strategies Instruction.   Each chapter introduces one or two new strategies for comprehension and/or vocabulary development. For the most part, didactic material is kept as simple and practical as possible and is followed immediately by practice exercises. In general, it is best for the instructor to model strategies in class before having students do independent practice. See the Instructor's Manual for elaboration on this point.

Integrative Exercises.   The integrative exercises offer opportunities for reinforcement and integration of the strategies taught in the text. Some of the integrative exercises ask students to apply the strategies in a new way or in a new context. They may be assigned to the class as a whole or to individuals on a prescriptive basis. They may be skipped without loss of continuity in proceeding from chapter to chapter.

Journal Entries. The journal entries provide open-ended writing practice at the conclusion of each chapter. The journal questions invite students to respond to the chapter's reading selection and instructional material. They encourage metacognition in that they ask students to assess their work in the chapter and their reading and vocabulary habits in general. See the Instructor's Manual for additional and alternative uses of the journal entries.

Additional Readings. The 10 additional readings following Chapter 14 may be used as supplementary exercises or as alternatives to the regular chapter selections. They follow a progression similar to that of the regular chapter selections, increasing in difficulty and sophistication as they go along.

Acknowledgments

I am sincerely grateful to the many people who have supported me in this project and helped make this book a reality. Special thanks are owed to the following reviewers for their suggestions and feedback:

Stefanie Allen	Tacoma Community College
Dorothy Barth	Catherine College
L. Jacquelene Burnett	Southern Illinois University at Edwardsville
Ruth Ellis	Cooke County College
Judy Lipke	Brookdale Community College
Esther M. Tremblay	Duff's Business Institute

I would like to thank Carol Long for her confidence and collegiality and Rachel Snyder for her suggestions and corrections. Special thanks go to Jean Roberts, my developmental editor, whose support, humor, and practical wisdom have been invaluable. And thanks to my production team—project editor Amy Lund, designer Michael Warrell, art coordinator Kim Meriwether, and production supervisor Ann Cassady.

I would also like to thank my colleagues at Northern Essex, Patricia McDermott and Mary Roche, for all that I have learned from them and for their encouragement on this project. Finally, I would like to thank my family—my wife Sharon, my daughters Merissa and Rachel, and my sister Susan—for their support and encouragement and for helping me with all those little things that needed to be done.

Gene Wintner

To the Student

You are well aware of the importance of good reading skills in today's complex, information-oriented world. You also know, more immediately, that as a college or career school student you need good reading and vocabulary skills to be successful in your classes. *Practical College Reading* will help you develop the reading and vocabulary skills needed for success in school and work.

There is no real mystery to reading improvement. As with most learning, it requires practice and instruction. If you wanted to learn to play tennis well, you would practice frequently and would take some lessons. Improving your reading is similar. *Practical College Reading* will teach you the most important reading and vocabulary strategies and provide you with plenty of practice to sharpen your skills.

Using This Book

There are a few things you should know about the organization of this textbook before you begin working in Chapter 1:

• *General organization.* Chapter 1 will provide guidelines for getting off to a good start this term. The chapter contains several exercises that will help you evaluate your current study habits and set goals for improvement. Chapters 2 to 8 introduce basic vocabulary and comprehension strategies. A brief review section follows Chapter 8. Chapters 9 to 13 introduce more advanced strategies. Chapter 14 provides and end-of-term review. Chapter 14 is followed by 10 additional reading selections and 6 appendixes.

• *Reading selections.* Except for the first chapter, each chapter of the text begins with a reading selection drawn from a traditional college subject. The selections are intended to stimulate your interest and expose you to new concepts. After reading each selection, you will be asked to rate its interest level and difficulty level. These ratings will help you become more aware of your own reading habits and interests. Each selection is accompanied by comprehension and vocabulary exercises to help you develop your skills in these areas.

• *Vocabulary.* Vocabulary instruction in *Practical College Reading* is context-based. This means that the vocabulary words you are expected to learn will be contained within the reading selections. You will learn how to use context clues to determine the meaning of unfamiliar words and how to use the dictionary to locate and understand definitions that apply to the context of what you are reading. To help you locate vocabulary words more easily within the reading selections, every fifth line of each selection is numbered, and the line location for each vocabulary word is indicated.

• *Comprehension strategies.* Comprehension strategies will be introduced chapter by chapter. Each strategy will be carefully explained and accompanied by practice exercises. It is important that you use the strategies not only in this textbook but in your reading assignments in other textbooks as well.

• *Journal entries.* Each chapter ends with a journal entry. Unless otherwise directed by your instructor, you should write a half-page response to each question in each entry. The journal entries offer you an opportunity to react to what you've read in each chapter and to evaluate your use of the strategies taught.

I hope you enjoy using this book. I know that if you apply yourself, you will be pleased with your improvement.

CONTENTS

1   Getting Started   1

How College Is Different from High School   1
Plan to Succeed   3
   Attitudes   3
   Habits   4
   Setting Goals   6
Selection 1: Goals Get You Going   6
     Exercise 1-1. Self-Assessment   8
     Exercise 1-2. Individual Interests and Learning Styles   9
     Exercise 1-3. Planning Your Time   10
Journal Entry   13

2   Using the Context   15

Selection 2: Sleep and Dreams   15
The Vocabulary Building Process   20
Context Clues   22
     Exercise 2-1. Using Context Clues   22
   Types of Context Clues   23
     Exercise 2-2. Direct Context Clues   24
     Exercise 2-3. Indirect Context Clues   26
     Exercise 2-4. Mixed Practice   27
Integrative Exercises   29
     Exercise 2-5. Goal Setting   29
     Exercise 2-6. Reading Habits Questionnaire   29
Journal Entry   30

3   Pre-reading Strategies   31

Selection 3: Interpreting Your Dreams   31
The Study-Reading Process   38
Pre-reading Strategies   39
   Previewing   39
      Exercise 3-1. Previewing Practice   40
      Exercise 3-2. Previewing Practice   41
   Pre-thinking   41
      Exercise 3-3. Pre-thinking Practice   43
      Exercise 3-4. Pre-thinking Practice   43
Integrative Exercises   45
      Exercise 3-5. Using the Context   45
      Exercise 3-6. Book Preview   45
Journal Entry   47

4   Using the Dictionary   49

Selection 4: Take the Sting Out of Criticism   49
Using the Dictionary   54
   When to Use the Dictionary   55
   Which Dictionary Should You Use?   55
   Understanding the Entry   56
   If You Can't Find the Word   62
   Remembering Definitions   63
      Exercise 4-1. Dictionary Practice   64
      Exercise 4-2. Dictionary Practice   67
      Exercise 4-3. Practice with Your Own Dictionary   68
      Exercise 4-4. Practice with Your Own Dictionary   69
Integrative Exercises   71
      Exercise 4-5. Previewing   71
      Exercise 4-6. Previewing in Another Textbook   71
Journal Entry   72

5   Monitoring Comprehension   73

Selection 5: Names and Identity   73
Simplifying Definitions   80
      Exercise 5-1. Simplifying Definitions   81
      Exercise 5-2. Simplifying Definitions   82
Monitoring Comprehension   82
      Exercise 5-3. Monitoring Comprehension   83
Integrative Exercises   87
      Exercise 5-4. Dictionary Practice   87
      Exercise 5-5. Context and Dictionary   88
Journal Entry   90

6   Using Goal Questions and Learning Prefixes   91

Selection 6: Maslow's Theory of Human Needs   91
Goal Questions   98
       Exercise 6-1. Raising Goal Questions   99
       Exercise 6-2. Raising Goal Questions   102
Analyzing Word Structure   104
   Prefix, Root, and Suffix   104
Prefixes   105
   Negative Prefixes   105
       Exercises 6-3–6-8. Negative Prefixes   106
   Number Prefixes   108
       Exercises 6-9–6-15. Number Prefixes   108
Integrative Exercises   113
       Exercise 6-16. Formulating Goal Questions   113
       Exercise 6-17. Monitoring Comprehension and Raising Goal
       Questions   113
Journal Entry   116

7   Reading for Main Ideas and Learning More Prefixes   117

Selection 7: Hypnosis   117
Reading for Main Ideas   124
   What Is a Main Idea?   124
   Topic Sentences   127
       Exercise 7-1. Topic and Topic Sentence   127
   Locating the Topic Sentence   129
       Exercise 7-2. Locating the Topic Sentence   130
       Exercise 7-3. Paragraph Writing   131
Prefixes Continued   132
   Common Prefixes   132
       Exercises 7-4–7-16. Commonly Used Prefixes   133
   Applications   138
Integrative Exercises   139
       Exercise 7-17. Goal Questions   139
       Exercise 7-18. Paragraph Practice   140
       Exercise 7-19. Prefix Review   141
Journal Entry   143

8   More on Reading for Main Ideas and Learning Roots   145

Selection 8: Work and Personal Adjustment   145
Main Ideas and Details   154
       Exercise 8-1. Main Ideas and Details   157
Implied Main Ideas   162

Exercise 8-2. Implied Paragraphs   163
Roots   164
Common Roots   165
Exercise 8-3. Practice with Roots   166
Exercise 8-4. Practice with Roots   168
Exercise 8-5. Matching   169
Exercise 8-6. Practice with Roots   171
Exercise 8-7. Practice with Roots   173
Exercise 8-8. Matching   173
Integrative Exercise   175
Exercise 8-9. Topic and Topic Sentence   175
Journal Entry   177

Strategies Check   179

Exercise 1. Time Management Revisited   179
Exercise 2. Self-Evaluation: Time Management   180
Other Suggestions   182
Exercise 3. Self-Assessment Revisited   183
Exercise 4. Learning Style   184
Exercise 5. Comprehension and Vocabulary Strategies   185
Exercise 6. Self-Evaluation: Use of Strategies   185
Applying Your Skills   186

9   Integrating Vocabulary Strategies   189

Selection 9: Love Is Never Enough   189
Suffixes   197
Exercise 9-1. Recognizing Base Words   198
Learning Suffixes   199
Exercise 9-2. Suffixes   199
Exercise 9-3. Suffixes   199
Word Associations   201
Integrating Vocabulary Strategies   202
Exercise 9-4. Integrating Vocabulary Strategies   203
Exercise 9-5. Integrating Vocabulary Strategies   203
Integrative Exercises   205
Exercise 9-6. Implied Paragraphs   205
Exercise 9-7. Remembering Your Roots   206
Journal Entry   207

10   Recognizing Organization   209

Selection 10. A Brief History of Drug Addiction in America   209
Recognizing Organization   215

The Introduction   215
      Exercise 10-1. Practice with Introductions   217
The Body   219
   Supporting Material   219
   Patterns of Organization   220
      Exercise 10-2. Supporting Material and Patterns of
         Organization   222
Summaries and Conclusions   228
      Exercise 10-3. Understanding the Summary   229
Integrative Exercise   229
      Exercise 10-4. Base Words and Suffixes   229
Journal Entry   231

11   Underlining and Notetaking   233

Selection 11: Are Women Better Cops?   233
Underlining and Notetaking   240
   Underlining   240
   Tips for Effective Underlining and Marking   240
      Exercise 11-1. Underlining   242
      Exercise 11-2. Underlining   243
   Notetaking   244
   Tips for Notetaking from Text   245
      Exercise 11-3. Notetaking   246
      Exercise 11-4. Notetaking   246
   Mapping   249
      Exercise 11-5. Mapping   252
      Exercise 11-6. Mapping   253
      Exercise 11-7. Underlining and Notetaking   254
Integrative Exercise   257
      Exercise 11-8. Recognizing Organization   257
Journal Entry   263

12   Inference   265

Selection 12: Nonverbal Communication   265
Inference   274
   Inference and Humor   274
   Inference and Poetry   275
   Inference in Nonfiction Reading   276
      Exercise 12-1. Inference in Short Passages   277
Integrative Exercise   285
      Exercise 12-2. Underlining and Notetaking   285
Journal Entry   288

13 Strategies Used after Reading 289

Selection 13: In the Barrios of the City of Angels   289
Strategies to Use after Reading   296
  Reviewing   296
    Exercise 13-1. Self-Testing   298
    Exercise 13-2. Summarizing   298
    Exercise 13-3. Reviewing   299
    Exercise 13-4. Reviewing   302
  Reacting   307
    Exercise 13-5. Reacting   307
  Evaluating   308
    Exercise 13-6. Fact or Opinion   310
    Exercise 13-7. Reacting and Evaluating   311
Integrative Exercise   317
    Exercise 13-8. Critical Reading   317
Journal Entry   323

14 Applying Your Skills 325

Selection 14: Biting the Bullet   325
Strategies Review   335
    Exercise 14-1. Review of Comprehension Strategies   335
    Exercise 14-2. Review of Vocabulary Strategies   337
    Exercise 14-3. Review, React, and Evaluate   337
Journal Entry   342

ADDITIONAL READINGS

Reading 1: Psychology of Self-Awareness   345

Reading 2: The Power to Change   353

Reading 3: All Stressed Out   359

Reading 4: What Is Business?   367

Reading 5: Appealing to Buying Motives   373

Reading 6: A Nutritional Challenge to Eat at Home   383

Reading 7: Education Myths   391

Reading 8: Mrs. Cassadore and Apache Students   399

Reading 9: The Nature of Love   407

Reading 10: Norms   413

APPENDIXES

Appendix A: Reading Habits Questionnaire 423

Appendix B: How to Preview a Book 427

Appendix C: Pronouncing Unfamiliar Words 429

Syllabication 429
   What Is a Syllable? 429
      Exercise C-1. Syllable Count 430
   Syllabication Rules 430
      Exercise C-2. Syllabication 431
      Exercise C-3. Syllabication 431
      Exercise C-4. Syllabication 432
      Exercise C-5. Syllabication 433
Recognizing Vowel Sounds 434
   English Vowel Sounds 434
   Vowel Rules 435
      Exercise C-6. Marking Vowel Sounds 437
Using the Dictionary's Pronunciation Key 437
      Exercise C-7. Recognizing Phonetic Spellings 439
      Exercise C-8. Phonetic Writing 440
      Exercise C-9. Jokes in Phonetic Writing 440
      Exercise C-10. Quotes in Phonetic Writing 441

Appendix D: Expanded Prefix List 443

Appendix E: Expanded List of Roots 445

Appendix F: Test-Taking Tips 447

Preparing for Tests 447
Taking Tests 448
Reducing Test Anxiety 449

Acknowledgments 451

1

GETTING STARTED

In Chapter 1, you will:

1. Learn what college will be like.
2. Learn what habits and attitudes will help you succeed as a college or career school student.
3. Learn about the importance of goal setting.
4. Assess your current study habits, academic interests, and learning style and set goals for improvement.
5. Develop a weekly study schedule to help plan your time.

Welcome to college!

You've probably been wondering what college is going to be like. If you are a recent high school graduate, you may want to know how college will be different from high school. If you are an older student who has been out of school for a long time, you may be wondering how difficult it will be for you to adjust to student life again.

This chapter will answer some of your questions. It will also provide some suggestions to help you get off to a good start and exercises to help you evaluate your current study habits. Good study habits will help you read with better concentration and a clearer sense of purpose.

How College Is Different from High School

One of the first things new college and career school students notice is that they have more freedom than they did in high school. As a college student, you choose your own major and have a greater choice regarding what courses you take. You have more control over your schedule, and there are fewer hours when you must be in class. If you are an adult returning to school, however, you may have an opposite reaction. Perhaps for you college is an addition to an already busy schedule, and you are feeling that you now have less control over your time.

In any case, as a college student, you must be self-directed. Your instructors are interested in you and want you to succeed, but they won't chase after you as some of your high school teachers did. It's all up to you.

In the following excerpt, a Massachusetts community college student discusses the transition from high school to college. Read the excerpt to learn about some of the adjustments new college students face.

Students Must Apply Themselves to Succeed
As the first semester for new NECC [Northern Essex Community College] students comes to a close, some are realizing college life isn't what they thought it would be.

Many new students first enter college with the illusion that they are entering the land of freedom, opportunity and good times; but soon find themselves face to face with reality.

Reality Crashes In
The transition from high school to college is hard. Most students spend their high school years longing for responsibility, and then have plenty of it at their feet.

No longer do teachers chase down students for homework or keep after them to get things done. Suddenly, there are tests, reports, books, jobs, and bills. There is very little free time for social lives, talking on the phone, watching TV, or going out with friends.

Often times, after about two months of college, many students wish they could return to high school, something they swore they'd never say.

Suddenly, it's understood what people meant by, "Don't rush out of high school, enjoy it while you can."

Humbling Experience
The first semester can be a real ego-buster. Some students don't meet anyone, and may feel unimportant or alone. They go from being a talented artist or football player in high school, to a college full of talented artists and football players. They must start from the bottom and establish themselves all over again.

The ones who stick with it, however, learn many valuable lessons. Students must have a goal or ambition to keep them in school. They must realize early that it is important to get an education now, rather than to wait. College pulls everything together and gives life both a foundation and a focus.

Learning the Ropes
Eventually, students learn to budget their time, and the routine becomes easier. They learn how to do their own work, not to slack off and leave assignments for the last minute. They also learn how to promote their own self-confidence.[1]

We can see from this student's comments that college is a time of stimulation and growth. Though most students enjoy their college years, starting college also involves some stress. The word *stress,* by the way, is often misunderstood. Most people think of stress as a bad thing, to be avoided whenever possible. But stress is a normal part of life and only becomes a problem when there's too much of it. Properly defined, stress is simply a demand placed on people to adapt and respond to changes in their lives. Both happy events (getting married or starting college) and unhappy events (losing a pet or failing a course) can produce stress.

The point is that as a new college student, it will be valuable for you to become aware of the changes that are now occurring in your life. How is your life different from last year, or last month, or even last week? How do you feel about these changes?

New students often worry about how difficult college work will be. One important difference between high school and college course work is the pace. College courses are more concentrated and proceed much faster than high school classes. Another important difference is that college work involves greater use of higher-level thinking skills. You will not only be asked to learn and remember information, you will also be expected to analyze and interpret information—in short, to become a critical thinker. Don't be intimidated! You are well capable of meeting the challenge. If you are an adult returning to school, your maturity and motivation are great assets.

Also different will be the subjects you study. While you will continue with some of the same subjects you had in high school, you will have a chance to study some new subjects as well, such as psychology and sociology. Most students enjoy these subjects. They help them better understand themselves, other people, and the world around them.

How much work will there be? Though you are in class for fewer hours than in high school, the amount of work expected of you outside class is greater. The standard rule of thumb for college course work is to expect two hours of homework for every hour in class. For a typical three-credit course, you should expect six hours of homework each week. The time will be used for reading, writing papers, studying, and completing assigned exercises. You can see why it's advantageous to enjoy your studies.

What are college teachers like? Most of your instructors are eager to get to know you and work with you. These men and women have become teachers for two main reasons. The first is that they have a strong and genuine interest in the discipline (subject) they teach. The second is that they want to share their enthusiasm and help others learn about their subject. Don't be afraid to approach your instructors after class or during office hours; most will be glad to have the opportunity to talk with you.

Plan to Succeed

By now you've realized that you will need to develop good study habits if you are to enjoy your courses and be a successful student. Good study habits will help you become an independent student and an independent thinker. They will be valuable to you now and in the future.

Here are some suggestions that can help you enjoy your classes more and earn better grades. These suggestions are based on research findings and describe the attitudes and habits that characterize effective students. Habits and attitudes are closely related. A habit is simply a way we are used to doing something. An attitude is a mental habit, a way we are used to thinking.

Attitudes

Attitudes play an important role in our lives. Some psychologists believe that the best way to change your life is to change your thinking. In other words, to become a successful student, start thinking like a successful student! The most important attitude you can have is a good, positive attitude about yourself.

Have Confidence in Yourself.   Self-confidence will help you succeed. You need confidence to face the challenges that lie ahead. Some students quit school in their first semester because they lack confidence. If they receive a bad grade on a test or paper, they think, "I'm not smart enough. I guess college is not for me." This is unfortunate, because most of these students are quite capable of doing college work.

Difficulties and problems are a normal part of the college experience. If you believe that you can cope with the challenges you face, you won't give up. Believing in yourself will help you succeed in meeting your goals in the long run.

Don't Be Afraid to Make Mistakes.   Everyone makes mistakes. Look at mistakes as learning opportunities. Benefit from your errors.

Learn from Everyone.   Chances are you will like most of your college instructors, but you may not like all of them. That's OK. You can respect all your teachers, and you can learn something from all your teachers—even the ones you don't like. Remember, you are in charge of your own learning. View your instructors as guides to your learning process. Don't be afraid to ask questions.

Overcome Boredom.   Some classes will naturally be more interesting to you than others, but you can develop an interest in all of your subjects. View boredom as a problem to be overcome. Every course offers unique learning opportunities; discover how you can benefit from each one. Sometimes it is helpful to take a businesslike attitude and view your less interesting courses as something you simply must do in order to meet your long-range goals.

View Each Assignment as a Chance to Learn Something New.   If you look at assignments only as obligations, your schoolwork will become drudgery. Enjoy the work and be sure you understand the purpose of each assignment.

Habits

Attend All Your Classes.   Attendance is critical to your success in college. Every class is important. Studies at various schools have discovered that there is a strong correlation between attendance and grades. The students who get the best grades tend to have the best attendance records, and the students with poor attendance records are likely to earn poor grades.

Come to Class Prepared.   Get to class a few minutes early and find a good seat. Studies show that it is better to sit toward the front of the class. Be ready to start when the instructor starts.

Do All Assigned Work. Look over all assignments as soon as they're given. If you have questions about the directions, or if you need help, ask right away. Don't wait until the last minute to get started.

Have a Regular Time and Place for Study. Ideally, you should have your own desk in a quiet room (the kitchen and your bed are not the best places to do your homework). Having regular times for study will not only help you manage your time effectively but will also improve your concentration.

Plan Your Time. In today's world, everyone needs time management skills. Time management is especially important for college students who usually have a substantial amount of unscheduled time and a substantial amount of responsibility. Plan your time on a weekly and daily basis. Exercise 1–3, at the end of this chapter, will help you develop some time management strategies.

Turn in Attractive Work. The appearance of your work makes an impression on your instructor. Read over your completed assignments before turning them in. Prepare assignments on a typewriter or word processor when possible. Assignments that are handwritten should be legible and neat.

Don't Wait until the Last Minute to Study for a Test. Spend a few minutes each day reviewing your notes. Frequent, intermittent study has been proven superior to cramming.

Take Breaks. Pace yourself. No one can maintain a high level of concentration for an indefinite period of time. Work for a half hour to an hour and then take a 5- to 10-minute break. Distribute your study time evenly over the week, avoiding unrealistic amounts of study in a single day.

Don't Take on Too Much. Don't take more courses than you can handle successfully. If you have a job, discuss your schedule with your advisor.

Don't Be Afraid to Ask for Help. It is often the better students who ask the most questions. If you've made a reasonable effort on an assignment without success, ask for help.

Discover Your Own Learning Style. Everyone needs good study habits, but we do not all learn in exactly the same fashion. For example, some people are auditory learners: they learn information best by hearing it. Visual learners, on the other hand, like to see what they're learning. Kinesthetic learners learn best by doing.

An auditory learner might benefit from using tapes for study; a visual learner would prefer visual aids—for example, charts and tables; and a kinesthetic learner benefits from activity—for example, writing down the information to be learned. Discover which study methods work best for you. Vary your strategies and notice what is most effective.

Reward Yourself. Give yourself a mental pat on the back, or a more tangible reward, when you do a good job on an assignment. Avoid the "all work and no play" syndrome.

Setting Goals

Successful students are usually good goal setters, and goal setting is an important part of study reading. Goals motivate us and help us assess our progress. It is useful to set both long-range and short-range goals.

Long-range goals give us direction. Where would you like to be five years from now? What would you like to be doing? It is not necessary for you to have a specific career in mind when you start college, but thinking about your personal, educational, and professional goals will allow you to plan your college program more effectively.

Short-range goals provide us with targets to aim for on a daily and weekly basis. Defining your short-term goals will help you establish priorities for planning and managing your time.

Directions. Try writing some short-term goals right now. In the space below, list three goals for tomorrow and three goals for the coming week.

Goals for Tomorrow

1. _____

2. _____

3. _____

Goals for the Coming Week (Starting Tomorrow)

1. _____

2. _____

3. _____

SELECTION 1
GOALS GET YOU GOING

Les Brown

Les Brown grew up in the poorest sections of Miami, Florida. Guided by his mother and one of his high school teachers, he developed a strong personal philosophy. He went on to become a disc jockey and community activist and later served three terms in the Ohio state legislature. He is now a nationally known public speaker and a popular TV personality. Read Selection 1 to learn how Mr. Brown views the importance of setting goals.

Goals give you a purpose for taking life on. People who live without goals have no purpose and it is obvious even in their body language. They are on permanent idle, they slouch, they list from side to side. Their conversations dawdle. They telephone you: "Hey, I'm just calling. I wasn't doing anything, so I thought I'd call you." *Well,*
5   *don't call ME. I'VE got things to do.*

Many people just muddle through life. They don't read informational material, they don't even pay attention when they WATCH television. If you ask them what they are watching, they mumblemouth, "*Nothin', I'm just lookin'.*"

What are your goals for your career? For your relationships? For your spiritual
10   life? Develop a schedule for the next month, the next six months, the next year, five years, and ten years. Write it all out.

Your goals are the road maps that guide you and show you what is possible for your life. Life takes on meaning when you become motivated, set goals and charge after them in an unstoppable manner. Goals help you channel your energy into action.
15   They place you in charge of your life.

Solid Goals

You must see your goals clearly and specifically before you can set out for them. Hold them in your mind until they become second nature. Before you go to bed each night visualize yourself accomplishing your goal. Do the same while you brush your teeth or take a shower in the morning.
20   Goals are not dreamy, pie-in-the-sky ideals. They have everyday practical applications and they should be practical. Your goals should be:

- *Well-defined.* You won't know if you've reached them if you haven't established exactly what they are.
- *Realistic.* Not that you can't be president some day, but shooting for state
25   representative might be a wiser first step.
- *Exciting and meaningful to you.* Otherwise, where will your motivation come from?
- *Locked into your mind.*
- *Acted upon.* There is no sense in having a goal if you aren't going to go
30   after it.

How do you find your goals? We all have dreams of what we would like to be doing, what we would like to have, who we would like to be with. Think about your dreams. What goal would you go after if you knew you would not fail? If you had unlimited funds? If you had infinite wisdom and ability?
35   One of the most essential things you need to do for yourself is to choose a goal that is important to you. If you need to set goals for your career, find a job or profession that is important to you beyond the bills that it pays.[2]

Exercises

Exercise 1–1. Self-Assessment

Directions. The following exercise will help you assess your current study habits and set goals for improvement. To begin, place a check in front of each statement that is true for you. Answer honestly.

_____✓__ 1. I have confidence in myself as a student.

_____ 2. I tend to blame others when things go wrong.

_____ 3. I only do well in courses in which I'm interested.

_____✓__ 4. I enjoy learning something new.

_____✓__ 5. I attend all my classes.

_____✓__ 6. I need a better place to study.

_____✓__ 7. I study at regular times.

_____✓__ 8. I plan my study time.

_____ 9. I often wait until the last minute to study for a test.

_____10. I often have problems concentrating.

_____11. I worry a lot about passing my classes.

_____12. I don't like to read.

____✓__13. I am afraid or embarrassed to ask for help.

_____14. I know which learning strategies are most effective for me.

_____✓_15. I check over an assignment after I've completed it.

_____✓_16. I don't always complete my assignments on time.

_____17. It's often difficult for me to get started on assignments.

____✓__18. I am easily frustrated and give up when things go wrong.

_____19. I usually sit near the front of the class.

_____20. It's difficult for me to pay attention in class.

____✓_21. I have reliable transportation to school every day.

____✓_22. Sometimes there are reasons why I have to be absent or late to class.

_____23. I get very anxious when I have to take a test.

_____24. It is hard for me to study at home.

_____25. I do not have enough time to study.

Now, read the 25 statements again and circle the numbers of the three habits you would most like to change.

Finally, identify one or two specific steps you could take to start changing each of these three habits.

1. _____

_____

2. _____

_____

3. _____

_____

Discuss any serious concerns you have about your study habits with your instructor or advisor. We will return to your self-assessment later in the text.

Exercise 1–2. Individual Interests and Learning Styles

Directions. The following exercise will help you tune in to your learning style and subject preferences. Write your answer to each question in the space provided.

1. What subjects do you enjoy the most?

_____

_____

2. What subjects do you enjoy the least?

_____

_____

3. In which subjects do you usually earn your best grades?

_____

_____

4. Which subjects are most difficult for you?

_____

_____

5. List five things you really enjoy doing.

_____

_____

6. List three things you are good at or know more about than the average person.

_____

_____

7. What are your chief strengths as a student?

_____

_____

8. What are your chief weaknesses as a student?

_____

_____

9. Do you prefer to learn information by (*a*) hearing it, (*b*), seeing it, or (*c*) no preference?

_____

10. What would be the easiest way for you to learn a new telephone number?

_____

_____

11. If you had to memorize the following list of words, what strategies would you use?
    Horse, table, justice, friendly, spell, remind, radio, magazine, yellow, convince

_____

_____

12. Is it easier for you to follow a teacher who (*a*) writes information on the board, (*b*) leads informal talks and discussions, or (*c*) no preference?

_____

Exercise 1–3. Planning Your Time

Directions. Use this exercise to develop a study schedule. Carefully follow each instruction.

1. Use the accompanying block schedule. It shows the days of the week at the top and the hours of the day on the left. Start by filling in the hours of your classes. Place an X in each block when you have a class, or write in the course names.

2. If you have a job, fill in your scheduled job hours. The schedule showing class and job hours is your base schedule. Make several copies of it.

3. Calculate the number of study hours you should plan for a typical week. You can do this by multiplying by two the number of credits you are carrying this semester. For example, if you are carrying 12 credits, you should be planning 24 hours of study time per week. As the semester goes on, you can adjust this estimate from week to week according to your actual assignments. Your estimate should include all time needed for completing assignments, reviewing notes, and studying for tests.

	MON	TUES	WED	THURS	FRI	SAT	SUN
7							
8							
9							
10							
11							
12							
1							
2							
3							
4							
5							
6							
7							
8							
9							
10							
11							
12							

4. Decide how to distribute your study time over the week and mark in your planned study hours on the base schedule. Divide the time as evenly as possible, avoiding too many study hours on any given day. (A general rule is not to plan more than five hours of study for any given day.) Also, avoid more than three consecutive study hours anywhere in your base schedule.

At the beginning of each week, make a list of all assignments for the week with their due dates. Fill in your base schedule accordingly.

Follow your schedule closely, at least until you have established good study routines. Once you are used to studying at regular times, you can be more flexible about implementing your plans.

If your schedule is too crowded or if you are unable to plan your time effectively, meet with your advisor or instructor.

Journal Entry

Directions. You will conclude your work in each chapter of *Practical College Reading* with a journal entry. (Note that after this chapter, each entry will include two questions). The journal entries offer you an opportunity to respond to the chapter material and express your own ideas about what you've read. They will also help you assess your progress as you work through the text.

Unless otherwise directed by your instructor, write a one-half page response to each journal question. When a question consists of several parts, you are not expected to respond to each part. Rather, you should focus your answer on that part of the question that is of greatest interest to you.

Discuss your goals for coming to college. Why have you decided to continue your education? What personal goals will college help you to achieve? What are you most interested in studying? What are your career goals and how will college help you achieve them?

_____

_____

_____

_____

_____

_____

_____

_____

_____

_____

_____

_____

_____

_____

_____

_____

_____

_____

2 USING THE CONTEXT

In Chapter 2, you will:

1. Read a selection from a psychology textbook to learn how modern psychologists approach the subject of sleep and dreams.
2. Answer comprehension questions on the selection to check your understanding.
3. Learn the process for building an effective vocabulary.
4. Learn how to use context clues to determine the meanings of unfamiliar words.

SELECTION 2
SLEEP AND DREAMS

Jerome Kagan and Ernest Havemann

In this selection, you'll learn how modern psychologists approach the subject of sleep and dreams and what they have discovered about the stages of sleep. Before you read, answer the following questions.

Pre-reading Questions

1. How much do you sleep each night?

   _____

2. How do you feel when you don't sleep enough?

   _____

3. Do you remember your dreams?

_____

4. Have you ever had a dream that seemed important to you?

_____

Directions.   Read the selection carefully. When you feel you have understood what you have read, complete the accompanying exercises.

Dreams presumably have always fascinated humanity, for they seem to free us from all limitations of space or time. Our early ancestors must have been baffled by dreams in which they seemed to move about in distant places and to talk to people long dead. The line between dream and reality must have been difficult to draw—and must have
5   hinted at all sorts of mysteries of the human spirit and of a world beyond ordinary human understanding.

Dreams have often been regarded as portents of the future, for dreams sometimes come true. To a statistician, this fact is not surprising. There are more than four billion people in the world. The average adult, it has been found, dreams for nearly two
10   hours a night. Thus there are bound to be numerous occasions when somebody dreams of the death of a friend and the friend actually does die soon afterward—or when a dream seems to accurately predict the receipt of an important letter, the result of a sports event, or a train wreck. Such coincidences are startling and memorable. The great majority of dreams that turn out to be mistaken go unnoticed.
15   Since the time of Sigmund Freud, a different kind of meaning has been attached to dreams. Freud believed that dreams were an expression of wishes prohibited by the dreamer's conscience. Forbidden sexual desires in particular, he thought, were likely to crop up.

Many psychoanalysts and other therapists have followed Freud's lead. They try
20   to analyze their patients' dreams in search of clues to hidden conflicts. Although different therapists use different methods of interpreting dreams, enough successes have been reported to indicate that the content of a dream may indeed reflect the dreamer's unconscious wishes at times. An interesting sidelight is the fact that there seem to be some sex differences in dreams. One study found that American men tend to dream
25   about such matters as achievement, hostility, and aggression. Women's dreams were found to be emotional and friendly, often taking place in indoor settings and relating to home and family life. This may be due to the different roles men and women have traditionally been taught to play in our society.

Ordinary and Paradoxical Sleep

As for how sleep differs from the waking state of consciousness, some clues have
30   been provided by studies of brain waves and muscle activity, measured by electrodes attached to people sleeping through the night in laboratories. The studies have shown quite clearly that sleep is by no means a state of suspended animation in which body

and brain are shut down for a time. Sleep is not just a slowing down but a kind of
activity in its own right. The brain continues to be highly active—though in a differ-
35   ent way. Moreover it has been found that there are several different kinds of sleep.

   Most of the night is spent in what is called *ordinary sleep.* As can be seen in
Figure 2–1, the brain's activity during ordinary sleep differs considerably from the
pattern during waking hours, and the muscles of the body are considerably more
relaxed. Four stages of ordinary sleep, ranging from light to very deep, can be dis-
40   tinguished from tracings of brain and muscle activity. We move back and forth
among these four stages during the night. Most people have three periods of the
deepest sleep, the first starting within an hour after dropping off, the last ending
after about three or four hours.

   About a quarter of the night is spent in *paradoxical sleep*—which gets its name
45   from the fact (also shown in Figure 2–1) that the brain's activity is very similar to the
waking state but the bodily muscles are almost totally relaxed. When subjects who
are in *paradoxical sleep* are awakened, about 80 to 85 percent of them report that they
have been dreaming. In fact, during paradoxical sleep the eyes dart quickly about as
if following a series of visual images. Thus this stage is also known as *REM sleep*—
50   REM standing for the *rapid eye movements* that can be observed.

How Much Sleep Do We Need?

Young adults sleep an average of 7 1/2 hours a night, but there are wide individual
differences. Some people prefer to sleep as long as ten hours or more, others only a
few hours. One woman was found to get along on 45 minutes of sleep a night. Why
these differences exist is not known. One study concluded that they were related to
55   personality. People who need a lot of sleep were found in general to be "worriers"
who brooded over their personal problems and the state of the world, whereas those
who got by on little sleep were energetic, efficient, hard-working, and self-satisfied.
But other studies have failed to show any significant personality differences. Whatever your own sleeping habits, you are stuck with them. They cannot be comfortably
60   changed. In one experiment some couples were asked to try to get along on less sleep

---

FIGURE 2–1   *Brain and Muscle Activity During Sleep*

**The tracings show typical patterns of brain waves and muscle activity during periods
of wakefulness, ordinary sleep, and paradoxical (or REM) sleep. Note that during
paradoxical sleep the brain waves resemble the pattern during wakefulness, but the
muscles are most relaxed of all.**

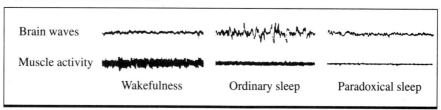

Brain waves	Wakefulness	Ordinary sleep	Paradoxical sleep
Muscle activity			

by cutting down slowly—a half a hour a week. None of them ever got below five hours a night and all of them eventually gave up the attempt.

65

Many people are occasionally troubled by insomnia, or the inability to fall asleep, and some people suffer from it chronically. In one large-scale survey 6 percent of adult men and 14 percent of women reported that they experienced insomnia often or fairly often—an indication that perhaps 10 million or more adult Americans spend many nights tossing and turning before they drop off to sleep. Among the people most likely to experience insomnia are those suffering from depression and those who have frequently used sleeping pills, which are occasionally helpful but can lead

70

to chronic sleep disturbances if used too often.[1]

After each reading selection in *Practical College Reading,* you will be asked to rate the interest level and difficulty level of the selection. Your interest rating will furnish your instructor with feedback about your reading interests and will help you become more aware of your reading preferences. Rating the difficulty of the passage will help you develop strategies for monitoring and improving your comprehension. You may also comment on your ratings if you wish.

Interest Rating.   Please rate the interest level of Selection 2 on the following 1–5 scale (circle one):

    5—Very interesting
    4—Fairly interesting
    3—Mildly interesting
    2—A little boring
    1—Very boring

Difficulty Rating.   Please indicate how difficult Selection 2 was for you to understand on the following 1–5 scale (circle one):

    5—Very difficult
    4—Fairly difficult
    3—Moderate
    2—Fairly easy
    1—Very easy

Comments: _____

_____

Warm-up Questions

    1. List three things you learned from this passage.

_____

_____

_____

2. Was there information in the selection that you had already known before you read the selection? If so, what was it?

_____

_____

Comprehension Questions

Directions. For questions 1–5, choose the answer that best completes the statement. For questions 6–10, write your response in the space provided. Base all answers on what you read in the selection (you may refer to the selection when you are not sure of an answer).

_____ 1. Our early ancestors viewed dreams:
   a. As meaningless.
   b. With fascination.
   c. As signs of mental illness.
   d. As expressions of forbidden wishes.

_____ 2. Most psychologists believe that dreams:
   a. Accurately predict the future.
   b. May reflect our unconscious wishes.
   c. Should not be analyzed.
   d. Are more important for women than for men.

_____ 3. The study of sleep reveals that:
   a. Not much goes on when we are sleeping.
   b. Sleeping is, in reality, a state of suspended animation.
   c. The brain functions the same way when we're asleep as when we're awake.
   d. The brain is active during sleep.

_____ 4. REM sleep is:
   a. When we usually dream.
   b. The shortest stage of sleep.
   c. 80 to 85 percent of our sleep time.
   d. The first stage of sleep.

_____ 5. According to the passage, the amount of sleep required:
   a. Is about the same for everybody.
   b. Increases with age.
   c. Cannot be easily changed.
   d. Can be reduced to a few hours a night with regular practice.

6. According to the author, why do dreams sometimes come true?

_____

_____

7. Refer to Figure 2–1 to answer the following questions.
   a. During which of the two periods shown are brain waves most similar?

   _____

   b. During which of the periods shown are muscles *least* relaxed?

   _____

8. According to the passage, how are men's dreams different from women's dreams? Why?

   _____

   _____

   _____

9. How is paradoxical sleep different from ordinary sleep?

   _____

   _____

   _____

10. Who is most likely to suffer from insomnia?

    _____

    _____

_____

The Vocabulary Building Process

What do you usually do when you encounter an unfamiliar word? What did you do when you came across words in Selection 2, "Sleep and Dreams," that you didn't know?

As a college student, you will be exposed to a wide range of new vocabulary words. Some of these will be technical terms—that is, words that belong to a specific subject—and some will be general vocabulary words that might appear in anything you read. Your ability to learn and remember new words is critical to your success as a college student.

Practical College Reading will teach you how to use several vocabulary strategies. When used together, these strategies form a powerful process that will enable you to approach new words with confidence. Over time, you will build a strong and extensive vocabulary.

Keep in mind that your goal is to really understand the new words you encounter. This involves more than just memorizing a definition. You have probably had the experience of memorizing definitions for a test, only to forget them as soon as the test was over. When you really understand a word, you can explain its meaning and understand how it is used. With proper reinforcement, the word will remain in your memory.

The process we will use for building vocabulary includes the following steps, illustrated in Figure 2–2:

1. *Exposure to new words through reading.* Reading exposes you to new vocabulary in a meaningful context. College students are required to do a great deal of reading. Reading on your own is a great way to accelerate your vocabulary growth.

2. *Using context clues.* When you encounter an unfamiliar word, study the context—the sentence or paragraph the word is in—looking for clues to the word's meaning.

3. *Recognizing word parts.* Recognizing the prefix, root, or suffix in a word makes it easier to learn and remember its meaning. *Practical College Reading* will introduce you to many of the common prefixes, roots, and suffixes used in English words.

4. *Consulting the dictionary.* Find the definition that best fits the context. Study the definition and how it fits into the sentence. The dictionary also provides other information helpful for learning and remembering the word.

5. *Mastering the pronunciation.* Pronouncing the word aloud makes it easier to remember. Use the dictionary's phonetic spelling to determine the correct pronunciation when you are unable to sound the word out yourself.

6. *Remembering the meaning.* Write down the word and its meaning. Associate the word with something familiar.

We will review these steps in detail from chapter to chapter, beginning in this chapter with a look at context clues.

FIGURE 2–2 *The Vocabulary Building Process*

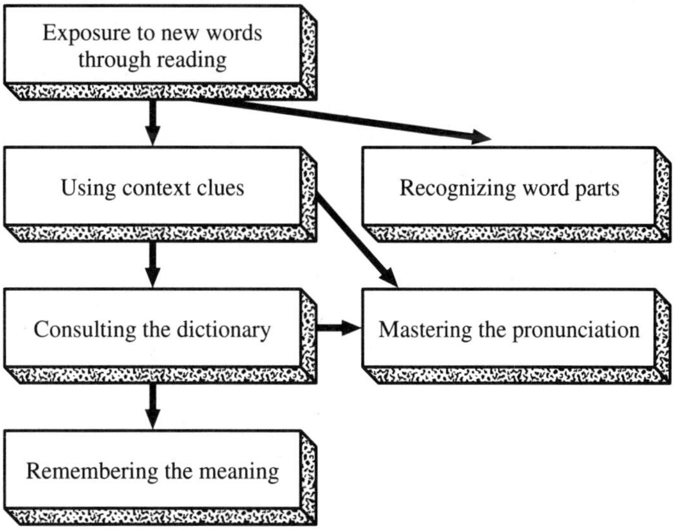

Context Clues

Webster's New World Dictionary defines context as "the parts of a sentence or paragraph immediately next to or surrounding a specified word." By taking a moment to study the context, we can often find clues to the meaning of an unfamiliar word.

Studying the context is a very important step. We should study the context both before and after we look up a word in the dictionary. The meaning of a word will become apparent only when we see how that word is used. This is true even for common words with which we are quite familiar. For example, consider the word *fence*. What does it mean? You probably have a picture in your mind of something people put around their yards. But you know that *fence* has other meanings as well. What does *fence* mean in the following sentence?

The jewel thieves were looking for a *fence* for their loot.

In this sentence, *fence* means "a person who deals in stolen goods." The meaning of a word, then, can only be determined in context.

Context clues can be strong or weak. Sometimes, the context makes the meaning of an unfamiliar word obvious. At other times, the context provides no real clue to the word's meaning. Usually we are able to get some sense of a word's meaning from context, but not its exact definition. Read the following sentences:

- The cause of the *conflagration* was unknown.
- The *conflagration* probably started in one of the buildings it destroyed.
- The *conflagration*, which destroyed several buildings, was probably started by children playing with matches.

Which sentence provides the strongest clues to the meaning of *conflagration*? Which sentence provides the weakest?

Look for context clues whenever you encounter an unfamiliar word. Carefully read over the sentence in which the word appears, looking for clues to the word's meaning. If the clues within the sentence are weak, see if the preceding or following sentence provides a stronger clue.

Exercise 2–1. Using Context Clues

Directions.   Each statement below, taken from Selection 2, "Sleep and Dreams," contains one or two underlined words. Try to determine the meaning of each of the underlined words from the context, and write your guess of the meaning in the space provided. You may write a synonym for the word (another word with the same meaning) or use several words to express the definition. (The numbers in parentheses indicate the words' line locations in the selection.)

1. Dreams presumably have always fascinated humanity. Our early <u>ancestors</u> must have been <u>baffled</u> by dreams in which they seemed to move about in distant places and to talk to people long dead. (2)

ancestors _____

baffled _____

2. Dreams have often been regarded as <u>portents</u> of the future, for dreams sometimes come true. (7)

   portents _____

3. Freud believed that dreams were an expression of wishes <u>prohibited</u> by the dreamer's conscience. Forbidden sexual desires in particular, he thought, were likely to crop up. (16)

   prohibited _____

4. The studies have shown quite clearly that sleep is by no means a state of <u>suspended animation</u> in which body and brain are shut down for a time. (32)

   suspended animation _____

5. Four stages of ordinary sleep, ranging from light to very deep, can be <u>distinguished</u> from tracings of brain and muscle activity. (39–40)

   distinguished _____

6. Many people are occasionally troubled by <u>insomnia,</u> or the inability to fall asleep, and some people suffer from it <u>chronically.</u> (63, 64)

   insomnia _____

   chronically _____

Types of Context Clues

Context clues may be classified as direct or indirect.

Direct Context Clues. Direct context clues include *definition clues* and *contrast clues.* A definition clue is an actual definition provided by the context. For example, did you notice in statement 6 above that the definition for *insomnia* was contained within the sentence? Let's look it again:

Most people are occasionally troubled by *insomnia,* or <u>the inability to sleep.</u>

The definition of *insomnia* comes right after the word itself. The comma, followed by the word *or*, leads us to the definition.

Punctuation marks (commas, dashes, and parentheses) are often used to set aside a definition clue. The reader must be alert to recognize these clues and then be sure she understands what the definition says. Definitions of terms in textbooks can be long and complicated.

Contrast clues are also very helpful to the alert reader. Contrast means difference. A contrast clue consists of a word or phrase that means the opposite of the unfamiliar word. Statement 6 provides a good example:

Most people are occasionally troubled by insomnia, and some people suffer from it *chronically.*

We can guess the meaning of the word *chronically* from the contrast clue *occasionally.* Chronically means the opposite of occasionally—so chronically, in this sentence, means regularly or frequently.

Let's look at another example:

I love volleyball, but I *abhor* tennis.

What do you think *abhor* means? The contrast clue is *love,* so abhor means the opposite of love: abhor means hate.

Contrast clues are often indicated by words such as *but, however,* and *although.*

Exercise 2–2. Direct Context Clues

Directions.   Use the context clues in the following sentences to determine the meanings of the underlined words. In the space provided, write the meaning of the underlined word and write whether a definition clue or a contrast clue was used. For definition clues, you may copy the definition or you may explain it in your own words.

Examples

I love volleyball, but I abhor tennis.

hate—contrast

Self-disclosure is the process of letting another person know what you think, feel, or want.

letting someone else know your thoughts and feelings—definition

1. All English majors must take a course in linguistics, the study of language.

    language

2. More crimes are committed in urban areas than in the country.

    city

3. An increase in taxes can have both beneficial and harmful effects on the nation's economy.

    useful

4. Anthropologists study human culture—the ideas, customs, skills, and arts of a people or group.

    typical refinement of a people or group

5. To multiply binomials (expressions made up of two terms), multiply each term of the first binomial times each term of the second binomial.

    expressions made up of two term

Nhu Tuyen Doan Dao

Integrative Exercises

Exercise 2–5. Goal Setting

1. List three important goals you'd like to achieve this semester.

   complete two classes in school

   study for TASP.

   Saving money to buy a car.

2. List three important goals you'd like to achieve this month (the next 30 days).

   write a letter for my friend.

   complete homework for this month,

   Decorate two   flowers for two friends

   of mine.

3. List three goals for the coming week.

   go to the dentist.

   do homework for next week.

   practise cooking a new food.

4. List three goals for tomorrow.

   pay for my car insurance.

   working.

   do homework for next thurday.

Exercise 2–6. Reading Habits Questionnaire

Please turn to Appendix A and complete the Reading Habits Questionnaire.

Journal Entry

1. Do you think dreams really can predict the future? Why or why not? Have you ever had a dream that came true?

_____

_____

_____

_____

_____

_____

_____

_____

_____

_____

_____

2. What do you usually do when you encounter a new word? How effectively do you use the context? How might your context skills be improved?

_____

_____

_____

_____

_____

_____

_____

_____

_____

_____

_____

_____

_____

3

PRE-READING STRATEGIES

In Chapter 3, you will:

1. Read a selection about dream interpretation, using context clues to determine the meaning of unfamiliar words.
2. Answer comprehension questions about the selection to check your understanding.
3. Learn the steps of the study reading process.
4. Learn how to use pre-reading strategies.

SELECTION 3
INTERPRETING YOUR DREAMS

Eugene Wintner

In Chapter 2, you read a selection about sleep and dreams. From the following selection, you will learn more about the study of dreams and dream interpretation. Before you read, answer the following questions.

Pre-reading Questions

1. What do you usually dream about?

_____

2. Do you think dreams are important?

_____

3. Have you ever tried to interpret your dreams?

Directions.   While reading the passage, underline unfamiliar words and look for context clues to help you guess the words' meanings. When you feel that you have understood the selection, complete the exercises that follow it.

Is all that we see or seem
But a dream within a dream?

Edgar Allan Poe

Every night we sleep, and every night we dream. Studies of REM (rapid eye move-
5   ment) sleep have determined not only that everyone dreams but that everyone
dreams every night. People who believe that they don't dream simply don't remember their dreams.

By awakening people during REM and non-REM stages of sleep, researchers
have discovered that dreaming occurs almost exclusively during REM sleep. In other
10   words, REM sleep is dream sleep. Typically, the first period of REM sleep occurs
after about an hour and a half of non-REM (ordinary) sleep and lasts for about 10
minutes. After that, the sleeper alternates between ordinary and REM sleep approximately on hour and a half cycles. The REM periods tend to increase in length, up to
30 to 45 minutes, as the night progresses. Most people enter dream sleep four to five
15   times each night.

These studies have also demonstrated that we need REM sleep. Subjects
deprived of REM sleep became grouchy and irritable and, when left alone, increased
their REM sleep, apparently to "catch up" on what they'd missed. It is clear from
these studies that REM sleep is needed. The question why is harder to answer. Do we
20   need to dream? If so, why? What functions might dreams serve?

Dream Interpretation Long Ago

In ancient times, people believed that dreams were very important. The Egyptians
and Romans viewed dreams as prophetic, considering them to be messages from the
gods. Because such dreams were highly desirable, priests and other diviners who
could interpret them were highly valued. The Old Testament records an excellent
25   example of a prophetic dream. Joseph had been sold into slavery in Egypt by his
brothers and was delivered into the court of the Egyptian Pharoah (king). The
Pharoah had a dream in which seven strong healthy cows appeared, followed by
seven thins cows that devoured the healthy cows. Then, seven fat sheaves of corn
appeared, followed and devoured by seven thin sheaves. None of Pharoah's advisors
30   could interpret the dream—none, that is, except Joseph. Joseph warned Pharoah that
the dream indicated that seven years of famine would follow seven years of plenty.
Pharoah heeded Joseph's warning and had food stored during the seven good years.
As Joseph had foretold, the seven years of famine followed the seven good years—
but the Egyptians were ready. Joseph was rewarded with a position of great power
35   in the Pharoah's court.

In some cultures, dreams have been taken quite literally. For example, if a man
dreamt about a dead uncle, it was believed that the spirit of the dead uncle had actually visited him that night. If he dreamed that a neighbor insulted him, he would treat
that neighbor as though the insult had occurred in waking life. We may laugh at such
40   "primitive" ideas, but many of us have similar reactions to our own dreams. If you
dreamt about a car accident, you might be a little nervous getting into your car the
next morning. If you dreamt about a number, mightn't you head down to the corner
store to play that number in the state lottery?

Psychology's Approach to Dreams

I believe it to be true that dreams are the true interpreters of our inclinations; but there is
45   art required to sort and understand them.

Montaigne

Modern psychology's approach to interpreting dreams was initiated by Sigmund
Freud. Freud was an Austrian physician who specialized in diseases of the nervous
system. He realized that many of his patients were suffering from emotional prob-
50   lems and theorized that his patients had repressed memories and feelings that were
causing their problems. He believed that these memories and feelings were stored in
the person's unconscious. He further believed that his patients needed to gain access
to this unconscious material in order to solve their problems and that dream interpretation was a way to gain this access.
55   Freud's central theory was that dreams expressed unconscious wishes. Since
these wishes might not be acceptable to the conscious mind, they are often disguised
in dream symbols. Thus, the language of the dream needs to be interpreted. A bear in
a dream, for example, might symbolize one of the dreamer's parents or another
important person in his life.
60   Carl Jung was a follower of Freud who later broke from him to develop his own
theories. Like Freud, Jung believed that dreams were messages from the unconscious
and were of extreme significance. Jung, however, believed that dreams did much
more than express unconscious wishes. One of the other important functions of
dreams, Jung suggested, was compensation. A compensatory dream would express
65   an unknown or hidden aspect of the personality. By reminding the dreamer of an unfamiliar part of himself, the compensatory dream could lead to increased balance and
growth. Consider the example of a poor girl who dreams she is a princess. Freud
would interpret this dream as wish fulfillment. Jung, on the other hand, might suggest that the dream expresses an unknown potential—the "princess within," waiting
70   to be discovered.
One modern psychologist has challenged the notion that dreams are in any way
meaningful. J Allan Hobson, a psychiatry professor at Harvard University, believes
that dreams are simply a by-product of the brain's activity during sleep. The brain is
activated during sleep, and this activity is translated into the visual images we call
75   dreams. Thus, according to Hobson, there is little point in looking for a secret meaning to our dreams, because there is none!

Most psychologists, however, tend to agree with Freud and Jung that dreams are significant. Perhaps we cannot or should not try to interpret all the elements of our dreams, but when a dream feels important to the individual, it probably is.

Types of Dreams

80   Based on the work of Freud, Jung, and many other psychologists, it is possible to recognize distinctly different types of dreams and to categorize them. The following list is by no means complete, but it represents some of the most interesting types of dreams.

Wish-Fulfilling Dreams.   Freud is probably right that at least some dreams express
85   unconscious wishes. For example, a woman who has repressed her anger at her boss is likely to vent that anger in a dream. It is clear that dreams also express desires of which we are perfectly conscious. A runner who dreams of a win in a big race is fulfilling a wish of which he is almost certainly aware.

Compensatory Dreams.   Jung is probably also right that dreams often reveal a hidden aspect of the personality. The accountant who dreams about playing the flute may
90   not have musical talent, but he may have creative energies that he has not tapped and has not recognized.

Recurring Dreams.   A recurring dream is one that occurs repeatedly. Dreams may recur frequently over a short period of time or sporadically over a long period of
95   time—even years. A recurring dream is almost certainly a message from the unconscious and deserves special attention. If you have a recurring dream, give it some thought. What issue in your life does the dream represent?

Telepathic or Prophetic Dreams.   There is little doubt that some people have had dreams that accurately anticipated future events. Abraham Lincoln, for example,
100   dreamed of his coffin in the White House surrounded by mourners just a few days before he was assassinated. It is difficult to provide a satisfactory explanation for such dreams.

The Nightmare.   Sooner or later, almost everyone experiences a nightmare. Nightmares can have a powerful emotional impact. Explanations for nightmares vary.
105   Some can be explained by physical causes such as overeating or drug use (including sleeping pills). Some nightmares, on the other hand, merit a psychological explanation. They express fear or represent a problem the individual has been avoiding. Like the recurring dream, this type of nightmare is a message sent by the unconscious, indicating a problem that needs to be faced or dealt with.

110   **Lucid Dreams.**   One of the most intriguing dream experiences is the lucid dream. A lucid dream is one in which the dreamer realizes she is dreaming. In other words, during the dream, she recognizes that it is "only a dream." People who experience

lucid dreams usually describe them as highly pleasurable and satisfying. The dreamer may feel that she can control what is going to take place in her dream.

115   In sum, a tremendous amount of progress has been made in the last hundred years towards a better understanding of dreams. Many questions, however, remain unanswered and perhaps will never be satisfactorily answered. It is likely that dreams will continue to fascinate us, no matter how much new information science may contribute to our understanding of them.

120   If you are interested in learning more about your own dreams, try keeping a dream journal. Keep a notebook and pen at your bedside and record your dreams as soon as you wake up. Over time, you will remember more of your dreams and become more familiar with your own dream symbols.

Pleasant dreams!

Interest Rating.   Please rate the interest level of Selection 3 on the following scale (circle one):

5—Very interesting
4—Fairly interesting
3—Mildly interesting
2—A little boring
1—Very boring

Difficulty Rating.   Please rate the difficulty level of the selection on the following scale (circle one):

5—Very difficult
4—Fairly difficult
3—Moderate
2—Fairly easy
1—Very easy

Comments: _____

_____

Comprehension Questions

Directions.   For questions 1–5, choose the answer that best completes the statement. For questions 6–10, write your response in the space provided. Base all answers on what you read in the selection (you may refer to the selection when you are not sure of an answer).

_____ 1. In ancient times, dream interpreters were:
   a. Respected.
   b. Feared.
   c. Considered to be strange and untrustworthy.
   d. Always priests.

_____ 2. Which of the following statements best summarizes Freud's approach to dreams?
   a. Dreams are literal expressions of unconscious problems.
   b. Dreams repress memories that are unpleasant.
   c. Dreams express unconscious wishes in symbolic form.
   d. Dreams express an unknown aspect of the personality, which leads to balance and growth.

_____ 3. Which of the following individuals views dreams as *least* significant?
   a. Montaigne.
   b. Freud.
   c. Jung.
   d. Hobson.

_____ 4. Maria is having a dream in which she is being chased by two large bears. While being chased, Maria realizes she is dreaming and doesn't need to be afraid. Maria's dream is an example of a:
   a. Compensatory dream.
   b. Recurring dream.
   c. Telepathic dream.
   d. Lucid dream.

_____ 5. The author suggests that:
   a. All dreams deserve careful analysis.
   b. Jung's approach to dreams is superior to Freud's.
   c. Hobson may be partially correct.
   d. Nightmares are usually due to overeating or drug abuse.

6. What were the most important findings of the REM sleep studies?

   _____

   _____

   _____

7. How is Jung's approach to dreams different from Freud's?

   _____

   _____

   _____

8. According to the passage, why do people have nightmares?

   _____

   _____

   _____

9. Which psychologist's view of dreams (Freud, Jung, or Hobson) do you most agree with? Why?

_____

_____

_____

10. Why does the author recommend keeping a dream journal? Do you think it is a good idea? Why or why not?

_____

_____

_____

_____

Vocabulary Exercise

Directions. Each statement below is taken from the selection. Use the context to determine the meaning of the underlined word in each statement. Write a synonym for the word (another word with the same meaning), or express the definition in several words.

1. By awakening people during REM and non-REM stages of sleep, researchers have discovered that dreaming occurs almost <u>exclusively</u> during REM sleep. (7)

   _____

2. The Egyptians and Romans viewed dreams as <u>prophetic,</u> considering them to be messages from the gods. (21)

   _____

3. As Joseph had <u>foretold,</u> the seven years of famine followed the seven good years—but the Egyptians were ready. (33)

   _____

4. We may laugh at such "<u>primitive</u>" ideas, but many of us have similar reactions to our own dreams. (39)

   _____

5. I believe that dreams are the true interpreters of our <u>inclinations;</u> but there is art required to sort and understand them. (44)

   _____

6. Modern psychology's approach to interpreting dreams was <u>initiated</u> by Sigmund Freud. (46)

   _____

7. He realized that many of his patients were suffering from emotional problems and <u>theorized</u> that his patients had repressed memories and feelings that were causing their problems. (50)

   _____

8. He realized that many of his patients were suffering from emotional problems and theorized that his patients had <u>repressed</u> memories and feelings that were causing their problems. (50)

   _____

9. The accountant who dreams about playing the flute may not have musical talent, but he may have creative energies that he has not <u>tapped</u> and has not recognized. (91)

   _____

10. A <u>recurring</u> dream is one that occurs repeatedly. (93)

    _____

11. Dreams may recur frequently over a short period of time or <u>sporadically</u> over a long period of time—even years. (94)

    _____

12. One of the most <u>intriguing</u> dream experiences is the lucid dream. (110)

    _____

The Study–Reading Process

Reading is a complex process. You read for a wide variety of purposes. For example, you read the newspaper to be informed of current events—or perhaps just to find out the sports results! You read magazine articles to learn more about an interesting subject. You read a mystery novel, a romance, or a best-seller to enjoy a good story.

Why do you read a textbook? Reading a textbook or an article assigned for class has a special purpose. Generally, the purpose of assigned readings is to learn and remember ideas and information. Reading of this type is called *study reading*.

It is important to realize that reading is a thinking process. Effective study reading is an active search for meaning. Experienced readers know that they must use spe-

FIGURE 3–1 *Simplified Process Model for Study Reading*

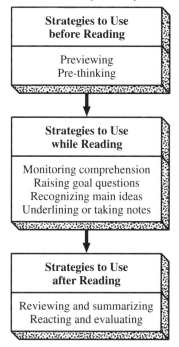

cial strategies when the goal of reading is to learn and remember. Study-reading strategies should be employed *before* you start reading an assignment, *while* you are reading the assignment, and *after* you finish reading the assignment. The use of study-reading strategies enables you to set goals for your reading, clarify and monitor your comprehension while you are reading, and identify and store the important ideas and information when you have finished.

A simplified process model for study reading is shown in Figure 3–1.

While the strategies in the process model can be applied to all reading, it is most important to use them when you are expected to remember the important points of what you've read.

We will practice with the various components of the process model throughout this text. Right now, let's focus on the pre-reading strategies—previewing and pre-thinking.

Pre-reading Strategies

Strategies that are used before reading are called pre-reading strategies. Pre-reading strategies are easy to use and highly effective. The use of pre-reading strategies enhances concentration, comprehension, and retention and leads to more efficient reading. Pre-reading strategies are especially valuable for textbook assignments, because they help you clarify your purpose for reading. There are two important pre-reading strategies: *previewing* and *pre-thinking.*

Previewing

Previewing involves looking over a chapter or article before starting to read it. The primary purpose of previewing is to gain a preliminary orientation, an overview of the material. Previewing enables us to discover the subject of the chapter or article, the main topics that will be covered, and the basic organization of the chapter or article. We may also get a sense of the author's attitude toward the subject, and perhaps even identify the central thesis (main idea) of the article. Previewing allows us to judge the interest level of the passage as well as its difficulty or familiarity, and enables us to budget our time more realistically. By previewing, we know what to look for when we actually read the chapter or article. Previewing is like looking over a map before starting on a journey.

To preview a chapter or article, follow these steps:

1. Read and think about *the title.* What clues does the title provide to the subject and theme of the passage?
2. Note the *author's name* and any *background* material about the author that may be provided.
3. Read any *introductory material* and the *first one or two paragraphs.* If *chapter objectives* are provided, be sure to study them.
4. Read each *heading* and *subheading* to determine the topic of each major section in the chapter or article. If the topic of a section is not clear from the heading, read the *first sentence or two under the heading.*

   If you are reading a short article with no headings, read the first sentence of each paragraph.
5. Notice any *visual aids* such as charts and graphs, *italicized print,* and anything else that stands out to the eye as you glance over the pages.
6. Read the *summary or conclusion* at the end of the chapter or article. If no summary or conclusion is provided, read the last paragraph.
7. Look over *end-of-chapter material.* Sometimes your text will provide a list of important terms or a set of study questions at the end of the chapter. Previewing them will help you know what to look for when you read the chapter.

Students sometimes object to previewing because they think it will add time to their reading assignment. In reality, previewing should not take more than a few minutes once you are used to doing it. Those few minutes will contribute substantially to your understanding and memory of what you read. In the long run, previewing may even save you time by enabling you to read with greater efficiency. Previewed material tends to be read faster.

Make previewing a habit. Preview every assignment you are given. You will quickly become a good previewer, and you will enjoy your reading more.

Exercise 3–1. Previewing Practice

Directions. Turn to page 373 and preview Reading 5, "Appealing to Buying Motives." When you have finished previewing the selection, answer the following questions.

1. What is the subject of the selection?

   _____

2. What are the three types of consumer buying motives?

   _____

3. List two or three industrial buying motives.

   _____

4. For whom is this passage written?

   _____

5. What is the difference between a rational motive and an emotional motive?

   _____

   _____

Exercise 3–2. Previewing Practice

Directions. Turn to page 345 and preview Reading 1, "Psychology of Self-Awareness." When you have finished previewing the selection, answer the following questions.

1. What is the subject of the selection?

   _____

2. What is self-awareness?

   _____

3. What types of self-awareness are discussed?

   _____

   _____

4. What else did you learn about the selection from your preview?

   _____

   _____

5. Does the selection look interesting? Why or why not?

_____

_____

Pre-thinking

Would you play a baseball game without first warming up? Probably not. Certainly no professional ballplayer would. He knows the body needs to be prepared before playing.

The mind, too, needs to warm up before becoming fully engaged. Very few of us can move instantly into a high level of concentration. Many people find that when they start reading, their concentration is poor and takes several minutes to improve.

Pre-thinking activities prepare the mind just as exercise prepares the body. They help us tune in to the subject at hand and become curious about it. By stimulating our interest and our thinking, pre-thinking activities prepare us to better comprehend what we read.

There are two primary pre-thinking strategies, *recalling prior knowledge* and *raising questions.*

Recalling Prior Knowledge.   To use this strategy, ask yourself:

What do I already know about the subject?

What have I previously learned about the subject?

What have I learned that I can relate to this subject?

What personal experiences have I had that relate to this subject?

Too often, students start a reading assignment with the feeling that they don't know anything about the subject. If you stop and think, you'll probably realize that you do have at least some knowledge or experience that you can relate to the subject matter.

For example, before reading Selection 3, you might have thought about your own dreams and your own ideas about dreams. Or, you could have recalled something else you'd read, heard, or learned about dreams and their interpretation.

Raising Questions.   To use this strategy, quickly raise 5 to 10 questions about the subject. Let the questions flow—do not pause to judge if they are "good" questions or "bad" questions. Raising questions will stimulate your curiosity and start you thinking about the subject.

For example, here are some questions that might have been raised for Selection 3:

How much do people dream?

What do most people dream about?

Why is it so hard to remember your dreams?

How do psychologists interpret dreams?

What do dreams mean?

How do we know if dreams are really important?

Do most people have similar dreams?

Note that when using this strategy, you are not limited to questions you expect to be answered in the passage. You are merely focusing your mind on the subject at hand.

Pre-thinking strategies go hand in hand with previewing. Previewing an article or chapter will stimulate the pre-thinking process. Pre-thinking strategies, however, may also be used without previewing. Because they are mental activities, they can be used almost anytime and anywhere (while driving a car, waiting for a bus, taking a shower, etc.).

If you make pre-thinking strategies a regular part of your approach to reading assignments, even apparently boring assignments will become interesting. Pre-thinking strategies not only aid comprehension and concentration, they also make reading more fun.

Exercise 3–3. Pre-thinking Practice

Directions. Apply the first pre-thinking strategy, recalling prior knowledge, to Reading 1, "Psychology of Self-Awareness," by answering the following questions:

1. Have you ever read or learned anything before on the subject of self-awareness or self-esteem?

   _____

   _____

2. In your opinion, why are some people more successful at meeting their goals than others?

   _____

   _____

3. Put yourself in the place of some of your friends or teachers. How would they describe you?

   _____

   _____

   _____

4. Describe a situation in which you felt stressed or angry and explain how you handled it.

   _____

   _____

_____

_____

Exercise 3–4. Pre-thinking Practice

Directions.   Apply the second pre-thinking strategy, raising questions, to Reading 5, "Appealing to Buying Motives." As quickly as you can, write any five questions about the subject of this selection in the space below. Two sample questions are provided.

Examples

What are rational motives?
_____

When I shop, are my motives usually rational?
_____

1. _____

2. _____

3. _____

4. _____

5. _____

Integrative Exercises

Exercise 3–5. Using the Context

Directions. The following passage is taken from the first chapter of a psychology textbook. Read through the entire passage once, then use the context clues to determine the meaning of each of the underlined words. Write the meanings of the words in the spaces provided following the passage. If a definition clue was given, underline it in the passage.

Psychology—which can be defined as the systematic study of behavior and all the factors that influence behavior—takes the scientific approach. It is skeptical and demands proof. It is based on controlled experiments and on observations made with the greatest possible precision and objectivity (meaning freedom from personal prejudices or preconceived notions).

The first psychologists were chiefly interested in studying human consciousness. Indeed, a textbook written by the most prominent of the early American psychologists, William James, began with the words: "Psychology is the study of mental life."

To make this study of "mental life," the early psychologists used as their tool the practice of introspection, or looking inward. They tried to analyze, as carefully and objectively as possible, the processes of their minds. They also asked their subjects to make the same kind of analysis. Among the interests of the early psychologists, as James defined them, were feelings, desires, thoughts, reasonings, and decisions—as well as people's struggles to attain their goals or to become reconciled to failure.[1]

1. psychology _____

2. skeptical _____

3. objectivity _____

4. preconceived _____

5. consciousness _____

6. prominent _____

7. introspection _____

8. analysis _____

9. attain _____

10. reconcile _____

Exercise 3–6. Book Preview

Directions. Turn to Appendix B. After reading the directions for previewing a textbook, select a textbook you are using for one of your other courses and preview it. Then answer the following questions.

1. What is the book's title?

   _____

2. Who is the author?

   _____

3. When was the book first published?

   _____

4. How many major sections does the text contain?

   _____

5. What are the subjects of the major sections?

   _____

6. Does the text contain a glossary?

   _____

7. Are any study aids provided at the beginning of the chapters?

   _____

8. What study aids are provided at the end of the chapters?

   _____

9. Does the text have any other special features?

   _____

10. Does the text look interesting? Why or why not?

   _____

Journal Entry

1. Explain your difficulty and interest ratings for Selection 3. What made the selection difficult (or easy) for you to understand? Why was the selection interesting or uninteresting to you?

_____

_____

_____

_____

_____

_____

_____

_____

_____

_____

2. Discuss the pre-reading strategies introduced in this chapter. Will you use them? Why or why not? How can they be helpful to you? Which ones seem most valuable?

_____

_____

_____

_____

_____

_____

_____

_____

_____

_____

_____

_____

4

USING THE DICTIONARY

In Chapter 4, you will:

1. Preview and read a selection about personal criticism and answer comprehension questions on the selection to check your understanding.
2. Learn to make effective use of the dictionary.
3. Learn to use context and dictionary strategies together.

SELECTION 4
TAKE THE STING OUT OF CRITICISM

Richard F Graber

Previewing Exercise

Directions. Preview Selection 4 by reading the first two paragraphs, the first sentence of every other paragraph, and the entire last paragraph. When you have completed your preview, answer the following questions.

1. What is the selection about?

   _____

2. What will you learn from reading this article?

   _____

3. What does the author's attitude toward criticism seem to be?

   _____

4. What are some of the suggestions the author makes regarding criticism?

_____

_____

Pre-thinking Exercise

1. How do you usually react when someone criticizes you?

_____

2. Do you ever criticize others? Why? What is your style of criticism?

_____

_____

3. Have you ever read or heard anything else on this subject?

_____

4. As quickly as you can, write five questions about criticism. Write *any* questions that come to mind, as long as they are related to the subject of criticism.

    1. _____

    2. _____

    3. _____

    4. _____

    5. _____

Now you are ready to read the passage.

Ask ten people what they think of criticism, and nine will call it frightening and destructive. They go to great lengths to avoid it. Only the tenth may see its positive side, which is growth.

Indeed, you can make criticism work for you. Here's how you can respond to criticism without losing your cool and making yourself and others miserable.

When you find yourself being criticized, determine if the criticism is valid, advises Margaret Verble, a communication consultant in Lexington, Ky. Tell yourself to consider the source. "Mothers have advised this for generations," Verble says. "It's maddening how often our studies prove them right." If the source is an expert, or is powerful—your boss, for instance—you'll be wise to listen. But not all things can be judged, psychologist Marsha Linehan of the University of Washington points out. Missing a scheduled appointment can be justifiably criticized, but the color of your walls cannot, because it is a matter of taste.

Next, ask yourself if you've heard this criticism before. "When we're criticized repeatedly for the same things, we probably should pay attention," Verble says. However, consider the critic's motive. Try to gauge the emotional climate. If your critic is visibly upset, he or she, rather than you, may have the problem.

What you do *not* say in response to criticism often is as important as what you do say. Destructive responses serve to cut off criticism, and you may miss

20 the point, because initial criticism is seldom right on target. Here are some responses to avoid:

Do not overgeneralize. If someone says your shoes do not go with your outfit, react only to that. Resist saying to yourself, "That means I have poor taste in everything, and I'm a clod and an awful person." When your superior asks you to be on

25 time for morning planning sessions, this does not mean he or she is about to fire you. Stay with the specific criticism.

Do not counterattack. This "topper" technique fosters nothing but ill feelings. Verble explains, "If I arrive home late and my husband greets me with 'You're late again,' it does no good for me to counter, 'What about *you?* You're *never* on time.'

30 It's hard for some of us to resist, but it's worth the effort."

Do not offer excuses or retreat into silence. Defensiveness leads nowhere, and silence in this context is far from passive. Both of these responses cut off further discussion.

Do not use dishonest "agreement." If you appear to agree with the criticism but

35 honestly do not, your critic will look for evidence of change. When nothing happens, it will seem to the critic as though you have been lying.

Behavior experts say we should avoid destructive responses like those above, and we should also *help* our critics. Here's how:

1. Be quiet and listen. Rein in your emotions and try to hear what your critic is

40 actually saying.

2. Ask for more information, if needed. A simple "Can you be more specific?" is a good way to start.

3. Ask for a solution, or for help in finding one. "What specifically would you like me to do?" often clears the air.

45 When you find a criticism valid, you then have three options:

Straightforward acceptance. "You're right—I see your point. I won't do that again."

Delay. Your critic has initiated this confrontation, which is to his or her advantage. But you seldom have to give an immediate answer. Something like "I need time to think about what you've said. Let's come back to it in the morning" is a reason-

50 able response and gives you some measure of control.

Disagreement. When you disagree, be diplomatic: "I can understand how you feel, but I'm sorry I can't feel the same." Or you can focus your disagreement, accepting part of the criticism. "If my husband says, 'You're late tonight; you're always late,' " Verble explains, "I can agree with the first part, which is true, but not

55 the second part, which is untrue. This response often helps both parties to better define the criticism."

Sometimes, standing up for yourself requires *you* to be the critic. The cardinal rule in giving criticism is never to do it publicly. Do it privately, give the person every opportunity to save face, and criticize when it will achieve the most good. Don't let

60 resentments build up.

"Because it takes so long to work up courage to criticize," Marsha Linehan says, "many of us match the criticism to the courage and make judgmental, all-encompassing accusations instead of sticking with the much smaller criticism we wanted to make."

65 Separate the deed from the person and be sure you know what the deed *is.* It's not enough to say, "He's driving me crazy." Zero in on the specific behavior prob-

lem you want to help correct. If it is a habit of constantly interrupting, stay with that. Since people usually change just one behavior pattern at a time, it's best to limit your criticism to a single goal.

70   Specifically, what does this behavior cause? Antagonism? Lost time? Be sure you *know,* because this is your basic reason for criticizing. Explain how you will help.

Empathize with the person you criticize. Use the pronoun "I" often. "It helps if you couch your criticism in terms of 'When do you X, I feel Y,' " Linehan says.

Select a good time and place. Sharp criticism the very minute a spouse walks in
75   the door from work or just before an employee leaves on vacation almost assuredly will be poorly received.

Follow your criticism with appreciation for positive characteristics. If you criticize someone for constantly interrupting, be sure you also explain how much you need his or her ideas and information.

80   Verble recommends that no criticism be longer than three or four sentences, beginning with a statement of desire: "I wish you'd call when you're going to be late (desire). When you don't call, I worry that something may have happened to you (effect). If you call when you know you're going to be late, I'll start dinner later (incentive and how the person will help)." Most of us will almost always react posi-
85   tively to something like that.

People who learn these basic techniques for improving the way they criticize and respond to criticism seem to go through life without the emotional upsets that plague so many of us. They believe that criticism can be a positive tool, and it works that way.[1]

Interest Rating.   Please rate the interest level of Selection 4 on the following 1–5 scale (circle one):

    5—Very interesting
    4—Fairly interesting
    3—Mildly interesting
    2—A little boring
    1—Very boring

Difficulty Rating.   Please indicate how difficult Selection 4 was for you to understand on the following 1–5 scale (circle one):

    5—Very difficult
    4—Fairly difficult
    3—Moderate
    2—Fairly easy
    1—Very easy

Comments: _____

_____

Pre-reading Follow-up

1. Did previewing the selection help you? In what way?

   _____

   _____

2. Look back at the questions you wrote in the pre-thinking exercise. Were some of them answered in the selection?

   _____

   _____

Comprehension Questions

Directions. For questions 1–5, choose the answer that best completes the statement. For questions 6–10, write your response in the space provided. Base all answers on what you read in the selection (you may refer to the selection when you are not sure of an answer).

_____ 1. According to the passage:
   a. Most people have a positive attitude toward criticism.
   b. Most people avoid criticism.
   c. One out of 10 people will go to great lengths to avoid criticism.
   d. Nine out of 10 people believe that criticism leads to growth.

_____ 2. When being criticized, the first thing to do is:
   a. Ask yourself if you've heard the criticism before.
   b. Consider the critic's motive.
   c. Avoid overgeneralizing.
   d. Determine if the criticism is valid.

_____ 3. When being criticized, you should not:
   a. Respond with a countercriticism.
   b. Ask questions.
   c. Ask for a solution.
   d. Consider the source of the criticism.

_____ 4. When giving criticism, it is important to do all of the following except:
   a. Be specific.
   b. Do it in private.
   c. Include some positive feedback.
   d. Make the criticism general and thorough.

_____ 5. The author implies that:
   a. Mothers' advice is always proved right.
   b. An emotional critic deserves special consideration.
   c. Matters of taste should not be criticized.
   d. It is sometimes best to pretend to agree with your critic.

6. In your opinion, why are people afraid of criticism?

_____

_____

7. According to the passage, what are our three options when we find a criticism to be valid? Briefly explain each.

_____

_____

_____

8. What are some of the suggestions Linehan makes for giving criticism?

_____

_____

_____

9. If you were to follow the author's advice, how would you respond to a classmate who accused you of always coming late to class?

_____

_____

10. In your opinion, which of the author's suggestions for responding to criticism is most valuable? Why?

_____

_____

Using the Dictionary

You have already learned that the first step when encountering a new word is studying the context. The second step, of course, is to look up the word in the dictionary and find the definition that best fits the sentence. Let's look at an example from Selection 4:

When you disagree, be *diplomatic.* "I can understand how you feel, but I'm sorry I can't feel the same way."

From the context, what do you think *diplomatic* means?

Now look at the dictionary entry below. Which definition best fits into the sentence?

> **dip•lo•mat•ic** (dĭp´lə-măt´ĭk) *adj.* **1.** *Abbr.* **dipl.** Of, relating to, or involving diplomacy or diplomats. **2.** Using or marked by tact and sensitivity in dealing with others. See Synonyms at **suave. 3.a.** Of or

relating to diplomatics. **b.** Being an exact copy of the original: *a diplomatic edition.* [French *diplomatique,* from New Latin *diplomaticus,* from
Latin *diplōma, diplōmat-,* letter of introduction. See DIPLOMA.] —
dip´lo•mat´i•cal•ly *adv.*

Definition 2 is the best choice: "Using or marked by tact and sensitivity in dealing with others."

When to Use the Dictionary

Should you look up every new word you come across? How do you decide whether
or not to look up a word?

Of course, it's never wrong to use the dictionary. There are times when it is
important to look up a word, and there are times when it may not be necessary. Consider the following:

- *How strong are the context clues?* If a definition clue is provided, it is probably unnecessary to consult the dictionary. In fact, if the word is a technical
  term in your textbook, the author (and your teacher) wants you to learn the
  definition provided by the text. In general, the weaker the context clues, the
  more important it is to use the dictionary.

- *Can you understand the sentence without looking up the word?* If so, perhaps
  you should simply read on. Conversely, if you cannot understand the
  author's point without knowing the word, look it up.

- *Do you need to remember the word?* If it is a word you are expected to know
  or that is important to remember for any reason, you had better look it up.

In short, consider the strength of the context clues, the importance of the word to
the meaning of the sentence, and your need or desire to learn the word before deciding whether or not to consult the dictionary.

Some people do not like to interrupt their reading to consult the dictionary. If it
is not critical to know the word's meaning immediately, you can simply mark the
word with a pencil and continue reading without interruption. Then you can look the
word up when you come to a better stopping point. It is also possible to spot new
words during your preview and look them up before you start reading.

Which Dictionary Should You Use?

Paperback dictionaries are convenient, but they are too small to contain all the definitions (and other information) you'll require. College students should use a college
dictionary, or a standard desk-size dictionary. Several good ones are available
(*American Heritage College Dictionary, Webster's New World Dictionary, Merriam Webster's Collegiate Dictionary, Random House Dictionary*), at prices lower
than what you will pay for a typical textbook. Look over a few of them in your local
or school bookstore and choose the one that most appeals to you. Keep the dictionary at your desk and use it frequently. A good dictionary is an indispensable aid for
a college student.

You may occasionally need to use an unabridged dictionary. The unabridged dictionary is the most complete dictionary available, containing more words, definitions, and entries than the standard desk-size dictionary. You probably don't need to own one, however. You can use your library's copy on those rare occasions when your college dictionary isn't sufficient.

You may wish to consider purchasing an electronic dictionary. An electronic dictionary is a handheld computer on which you type a word and are shown its definitions. If you misspell the word, the dictionary will try to find the correct spelling for you. Some electronic dictionaries have the capacity to pronounce words, too! Good models are fairly expensive, but since the cheaper models are not very good, if you are going to purchase an electronic dictionary, invest in a good one.

Understanding the Entry

Using the dictionary can be frustrating at times: You look for a word and can't find it, you find the word but can't find a definition that seems to fit what you're reading, or you find the word but can't understand the definition. These problems will occur less frequently, however, as you become more familiar with the dictionary and its format.

To use the dictionary effectively, you first need to understand how a dictionary entry is organized. Take a few minutes to preview your own dictionary. You will find a section in the beginning that explains how to use the dictionary. Refer to that section when you have questions about the information your dictionary is providing you.

Though there are slight differences in arrangement from dictionary to dictionary, most follow a similar format. Let's look at a typical entry:

The Entry Word

1. Each new entry begins at the left with the entry word in boldface print, divided into syllables. The syllabication indicates where a word is to be split (at the end of a line of writing) and furnishes a clue to the word's pronunciation.

2. If a word has more than one correct spelling, the alternative spelling will be shown.

the·a·ter or the·a·tre (thē′ə- tər) *n.*

Pronunciation. The pronunciation of each entry word is shown in parentheses immediately after the word. The word is spelled phonetically—that is, exactly as it is pronounced. Accented syllables are marked.

pa•ren•the|sis (pə- ren´thə- sis)

gauge (gāj)

If you don't recognize some of the phonetic symbols, refer to the pronunciation key, usually found at the bottom of each page. (Some dictionaries will place the key on a previous page—check your table of contents.) The key shows the phonetic symbols in alphabetical order with each symbol followed by a familiar word that contains its sound.

ă pat / ā pay / âr care / ä father / b bib / ch church / d deed / ĕ pet / ē be /
f fife / g gag / h hat / hw which / ĭ pit / ī pie / îr pier / j judge / k kick /
l lid, needle / m mum / n no, sudden / ng thing / ŏ pot / ō toe / ô paw, for /
oi noise / ou out / o͝o took / o͞o boot / p pop / r roar / s sauce / sh ship, dish /
t tight / th thin, path / *th* this, bathe / ŭ cut / ûr urge / v valve / w with / y
yes / z zebra, size / zh vision / ə about, item, edible, gallop, circus

For example, the vowel sound in *gauge* (gāj) is ā. We see from the pronunciation key that that sound is the same as the vowel sound in *pay* (long a). (See Appendix C for more information on using the pronunciation key.)

Parts of Speech. The part of speech labels tell you whether a word can be used as a noun, verb, adjective, or other part of speech. The dictionary lists definitions by parts of speech. If a word may be used as more than one part of speech, the definitions return to number 1 as each new part of speech is introduced.

lure (loor) *n.* ⟦ME < MFr *leurre* < OFr *loirre*, prob. < Frank or Goth *lōthr*, akin to MDu *loder*, lure, OE *lathian*, to invite⟧ **1** a device consisting of a bunch of feathers on the end of a long cord, often baited with food: it is used in falconry to recall the hawk **2** *a)* the power of attracting, tempting, or enticing [the *lure* of the stage] *b)* anything that so attracts or tempts **3** a bait for animals; esp., an artificial one used in fishing—*vt.* lured, **lur´ing 1** to recall (a falcon) with a lure. **2** to attract, tempt, or entice: often with *on*—**lur´|er *n.***

You can tell from the entry that *lure* can be used as a noun or a verb. How many noun definitions are listed? How many verb definitions?

Look back to the entry for *cardinal* (p. 56). What parts of speech can the word *cardinal* be?

Plurals and Verb Endings. The beginning of the entry will also show irregular plurals and verb forms.

ox (äks) *n., pl.* **ox´|en** or [Rare] **ox**

swim¹ (swim) *vi.* **swam, swum, swim´ming**

Etymology.   Most dictionary entries also include information about the word's etymology. The etymology explains the origin and history of the word. That is, the etymology tells us from where the word came. The etymology is enclosed in brackets.
Some dictionaries place the etymology before the definitions; some place it after.

al•li•ga•tor (ăl´ĭ-gā´tər) *n.* **1.** Either of two large, amphibious
reptiles, *Alligator mississipiensis,* of the southeastern United
States, or *A. sinensis,* of China, having sharp teeth and powerful
jaws, and differing from crocodiles in having a broader, shorter
snout. **2.** Leather made from the hide of an alligator. **3.** A tool or
fastener having strong, adjustable jaws often toothed. [< Sp. *el
lagarto,* the lizard : *el,* the (< Lat. *ille,* that) + *lagarto,* lizard <
Lat. *lacertus.*]

al•li•ga•tor (al´ə gāt´ər) *n., pl.* **-tors** or **-tor** ⟦Sp *el lagarto*
< *el,* the + L *lacerta, lacertus:* see LIZARD⟧ **1** any of a genus
(*Alligator*) of large crocodilian reptiles found in tropical rivers
and marshes of the U.S. and China: its snout is shorter and
blunter than the crocodile's, and its teeth do not protrude outside
its closed mouth

The etymology tells us that the English word *alligator* came from the Spanish *el
lagarto,* meaning the lizard.

Sometimes, the etymology of a word is interesting and amusing:

> **bi•ki|ni** (bi kē´nē) *n.* ⟦Fr, after *Bikini,* Marshall Islands atomic
> bomb testing site (1946); to suggest the explosive effect on the
> viewer⟧ **1** a very brief two-piece swimsuit for women **2** very
> brief, legless underpants or swimming trunks

Since most English words are derived from words of other languages, the typical etymology will indicate the language the word came from and explain the meaning of the foreign word:

> **val|id** (val´id) *adj.* ⟦Fr *valide* < L *validus,* strong, powerful (in
> ML, valid) < *valere,* to be strong: see VALUE⟧ **1** having legal
> force; properly executed and binding under the law **2** well-
> grounded on principles or evidence; able to withstand criticism
> or objection, as an argument; sound **3** effective, effectual,
> cogent, etc. **4** [Rare] robust;strong; healthy **5** *Logic* correctly
> derived or inferred according tothe rules of logic—**val´id|ly**
> *adv.*—**val´id•ness** *n.*

The English word *valid* came from a French word, which came from the Latin word
validus, meaning strong or powerful.

Commonly used abbreviations for languages used in the dictionary are L (Latin),
Gr (Greek), Fr (French), Sp (Spanish), ME (Middle English), and OE (Old English).

Refer again to the entry for *cardinal* on page 56. From what language did the
word *cardinal* come?

The etymology sometimes shows the prefix and root in a word:

> **an•tag|o•nize** (an tag´ə nīz´) *vt.* **-nized´, -niz´ing** ⟦Gr
> *antagōnizesthai,* to struggle against < *anti-,* against + *ago-
> nizesthai:* see AGONIZE⟧ **1** to oppose or counteract **2** to incur the
> dislike of; make an enemy of

The etymology shows that the prefix in *antagonize* is *anti,* which means against.

Usage Labels and Subject Labels. Some definitions are marked with usage labels. For example, the usage label *Obsolete* (Obs.) indicates that a word or definition is no longer used. The usage label *Slang* marks words or definitions that are not used in formal English.

> ☆**dude** (dōōd, dyōōd) *n.* ⟦< ?⟧ **1** a man too much concerned with his clothes and appearance; dandy; fop **2** [West Slang] a city fellow or tourist, esp. an Easterner who is vacationing on a ranch **3** [Slang] any man or boy—*vt.* **dud´ed, dud´ing** [Slang] **1** to dress up, esp. in showy or flashy clothes **2** to add showy ornamentation to. Usually used with *up*—*vi.* [Slang] to dress up, esp. in showy or flashy clothes: usually used with *up*—**dud´ish** *adj.*—**dud´ish•ly** *adv.*

Understanding the usage labels makes it easier to find the definitions you are looking for. For example, if you are reading something written in Modern English, you can ignore a definition that is marked *Obs.* On the other hand, you might need that definition if you are reading something written a long time ago.

Subject labels indicate that a definition applies to a particular subject. Examples are: *Psych.* (Psychology), *Naut.* (Nautical), *Mus.* (Music), and *Bus.* (Business). If you are reading a business passage, then, you might first check the definition labeled *Bus.* But you could ignore the definition labeled *Bus.* when reading in other subjects.

Subject
Labels

ra•tion•al•ize (rash´ən əl iz´) *vt.* **-ized´, -iz´ing 1** to make rational; make conform to reason **2** to explain or interpret on rational grounds **3** [Chiefly Brit.] to apply modern methods of efficiency to (an industry, agriculture, etc.) **4** *Math.* to remove the radical signs from (an expression) without changing the value **5** *Psychol.* to devise superficially rational, or plausible, explanations or excuses for (one's acts, beliefs, desires, etc.), usually without being aware that these are not the real motives—*vi.* **1** to think in a rational or rationalistic manner **2** to rationalize one's acts, beliefs, etc.—**ra´-tion•al•i•za´tion** *n.*—**ra´tion•al•iz´ er** *n.*

couch (kouch) *n.* ⟦ME & OFr *couche,* a bed, lair: see the *v.*⟧ **1** an article of furniture on which one may sit or lie down; sofa; divan **2** any resting place **3** [Old Poet.] a place for sleeping; bed **4** [Obs.] an animal's lair or den **5** *Brewing* a layer of grain spread to germinate **6** *Fine Arts* a priming layer or coat, as of paint or varnish—*vt.* ⟦ME *couchen* < OFr *coucher,* to lie down < L *collocare,* to lay < *com-,* together + *locare,* to place: see LOCAL⟧ **1** to lay or put on or as on a couch, as to sleep: now usually used reflexively or in the passive voice **2** to lower or bring down; esp., to lower (a spear, lance, etc.) to an attacking position **3** to put in specific or particular words; phrase; express [*couched* in veiled language] **4** to embroider with thread laid flat and fastened down with fine stitches **5** [Archaic] to put in a layer **6** [Obs.] to hide **7** *Brewing* to spread (grain) in a thin layer to germinate **8** *Surgery* to remove (a cataract) by using a needle to push down the crystalline lens of the eye—*vi.* **1** to lie down on a bed, as to sleep; recline **2** to lie in hiding or in ambush **3** to lie in a pile, as decomposing leaves—☆**on the couch** [Colloq.] undergoing psychoanalysis

Idioms. Idioms are commonly used expressions that have special meanings. For example, the idiomatic expression "down in the dumps" means depressed, in low spirits. Idioms are listed under one of the main words in the expression. "Down in the dumps," for example, is listed under the word *dump.* Look at the following entry and find out what it means to be "down and out":

down[1] (doun) *adv.* **1. a.** From a higher to a lower place or position. **b.** Toward, to, or on the ground, floor, or bottom. **2. a.** Into a lower posture. **b.** In or into a prostrate position. **3.** Toward or in the south or in a southerly direction. **4. a.** Toward or in a center of activity: *going down to the office.* **b.** Away from the present place: *down on the farm.* **5.** To the source: *tracking a rumor down.* **6.** Toward or at a low or lower point on a scale. **7.** To or in a quiescent or subdued state. **8.** To or in a low status, as of subjection or disgrace. **9.** To an extreme degree. **10.** Seriously or vigorously: *get down to work.* **11.** From earlier times or people. **12.** To a reduced or concentrated form: *boiling down maple syrup.* **13.** In writing; on paper: *taking a statement down.* **14.** In partial payment at the time of purchase: *five dollars down.*—*adj.* **1. a.** Moving or directed downward: *a down elevator.* **b.** In a low position. **c.** At a reduced level. **2. a.** Sick: *He is down with a cold.* **b.** Low in spirit; depressed: *feel down.* **3. a.** In games, trailing an opponent by a specified number of points, goals, or strokes: *down two.* **b.** *Football.* Not in play. Used of the ball. **c.** *Baseball.* Having been put out. **4.** Being the first installment.—*prep.* **1.** In a descending direction along, upon, into, or through. **2.** Along the course of. **3.** Toward the mouth of a river.—*n.* **1.** A downward movement; descent. **2.** *Football.* Any of a series of four plays during which a team must advance at least ten yards to retain possession of the ball.—*v.* **downed, down•ing, downs.**—*tr.* **1.** To bring, put, strike, or throw down. **2.** To swallow hastily; gulp. **3.** *Football.* To put (the ball) out of play by touching it to the ground.—*intr.* To go or come down; descend.—*idioms.* **down and out.** Lacking friends or resources; destitute. **down in the mouth.** Discouraged; sad. **down on.** *Informal.* Hostile or negative toward; out of patience with. [ME *doun* < OE *dūne* < *adūne*: *a-*, from (< *of*) + *dūn*, hill.]

Derived Forms.

A derived form is a word formed from another word by the addition of a suffix (*separately,* for instance, is a derived form of *separate*). Derived forms are listed at the end of the entry with their parts of speech indicated. Referring to the entry for *valid,* you see two derived forms. What is the adverb derived from *valid?* What part of speech is *validness?*

val|id (val´id) *adj.* ⟦Fr *valide* < L *validus,* strong, powerful (in ML, valid) < *valere,* to be strong: see VALUE⟧ **1** having legal force; properly executed and binding under the law **2** well-grounded on principles or evidence; able to withstand criticism or objection, as an argument; sound **3** effective, effectual, cogent, etc. **4** [Rare] robust; strong; healthy **5** *Logic* correctly derived or inferred according to the rules of logic— **val´id|ly** *adv.*—**val´id•ness** *n.*

Synonyms.

For some words, the dictionary will list and compare synonyms. Though synonyms have approximately the same meaning, there are usually slight differences in their definitions and usage. Synonyms are shown at the end of the entry.

crit|i•cize (krit´ə sīz´) *vi., vt.* **-cized´, -ciz´ing 1** to analyze and judge as a critic **2** to judge disapprovingly; find fault (with); censure— **crit´i•ciz´a|ble** *adj.*—**crit´i•ciz´|er** *n.*
SYN.—**criticize,** in this comparison, is the general term for finding fault with or disapproving of a person or thing; **reprehend** suggests sharp or

severe disapproval, generally of faults, errors, etc. rather than of persons; **blame** stresses the fixing of responsibility for an error, fault, etc.; **censure** implies the expression of severe criticism or disapproval by a person in authority or in a position to pass judgment; **condemn** and **denounce** both imply an emphatic pronouncement of blame or guilt, **condemn** suggesting the rendering of a judicial decision, and **denounce,** public accusation against persons of their acts—*ANT.* **praise**

Homographs.   Homographs are words that are spelled the same but have different meanings and origins. Homographs often have different pronunciations and are different parts of speech. Homographs are listed in the dictionary as separate entries with raised numbers after the words.

wind[1] (wīnd) *vt.* **wound** or [Rare] **wind´led, wind´ing** ⟦ME *winden* < OE *windan,* akin to ON *vinda,* Ger *winden* < IE base **wendh-,* to turn, wind, twist > Arm *gind,* a ring⟧ **1** *a)* to turn, or make revolve [to *wind* a crank] *b)* to move by or as if by cranking

wind[2] (wind; *for n., also poet.* wīnd) *n.* ⟦ME < OE, akin to ON *vindr,* Ger *wind* < IE **wentos* (> L *ventus*) < base **we-, *awe-,* to blow > WEATHER⟧ **1** air in motion; specif., *a)* any noticeable natural movement of air parallel to the earth's surface (see BEAUFORT SCALE) *b)* air artificially put in motion, as by an air pump or fan

When a word you are looking up is a homograph, quickly scan both entries to determine which fits the context of what you are reading.

Cross-References.   Sometimes the dictionary makes use of cross-references. That is, when we look up a word, we are referred to another entry.

go•losh or **go•loshe** (gə läsh´) *n. Brit. sp. of* GALOSH

Sometimes, a definition uses a different form of the word being defined, so that we must check the other definition:

em•pa•thize (em´pə thīz´) *vt.* **-thized´, -thiz´ing** ⟦< fol., after SYMPA-THIZE⟧ to undergo or feel empathy (*with* another or others)

To understand the meaning of *empathize,* we must refer to the definition of *empathy.*

em•pa•thy (em´pə thē) *n.* ⟦< Gr *empatheia,* affection, passion < *en-,* in + *pathos,* feeling: used to transl. Ger *einfühlung* (< *ein-,* in + *fühlung,* feeling⟧ **1** the projection of one's own personality into the personality of another in order to understand the person better; ability to share in another's emotions, thoughts, or feelings **2** the projection of one's own personality into an object, with the attribution to the object of one's own emotions, responses, etc.

Let's apply this process to the following sentence:

The *cardinal* rule in giving criticism is never to do it publicly.

By studying the context, you can guess that *cardinal* means something like

How to Choose the Best Definition

1. Don't be lazy and settle on the first definition. Look for the definition that best fits the context.
2. Use the subject and usage labels to locate probable definitions.
3. Use the part of speech labels. If you know that the word you are looking up is used as a verb, check only the verb definitions.
4. If the word you are looking up is a homograph (if it has a raised number after it), quickly look over all entries for that spelling to determine which one fits your context.
5. When you have found an appropriate definition, study the definition within the context. Try to understand how the definition you have selected relates to the sentence and paragraph.
6. To make sure you understand the definition, especially if it is long, rephrase the definition—explain it to yourself in your own words.

important. Now check the following dictionary entry:

> **car•di•nal** (kärd″n əl) *adj.* ⟦ME < OFr < L *cardinalis,* principal, chief < *cardo,* that on which something turns or depends, orig., door hinge: see SCHERZO⟧ **1** of main importance; principal; chief **2** bright-red, like the robe of a cardinal—*n.* ⟦ME < LL(Ec) *cardinalis,* chief presbyter, cardinal < the L *adj.*⟧ **1** one of the Roman Catholic officials appointed by the pope to his council (COLLEGE OF CARDINALS) **2** bright red **3** a woman's short cloak, originally red and usually hooded, fashionable in the 18th cent. ☆**4** ⟦so named because colored like a cardinal's robe⟧ any of various passerine birds (family Emberizidae); esp., a bright-red, crested American species *(Cardinalis cardinalis)* with a red bill **5** CARDINAL NUMBER

Since *cardinal* is used as an adjective in the above sentence, read just the two adjective definitions. You can easily see that the first definition is the one you want. Now study the definition for a moment and make sure that you understand how it fits the sentence. You can tell that the cardinal rule means the principal, main, or most important rule.

If You Can't Find the Word

We have all had the frustrating experience of looking up a word and not finding it. When this happens, here are some things you can do.

1. Check your spelling and alphabetization. It's especially easy to make an alphabetizing error in the middle of a word.

2. If the word you're looking up is a plural or a verb ending in -ed or -ing, it's probably not listed as an entry word. Drop the suffix and make sure you are spelling the base word correctly.

Find the word *harried* in the following entry:

> **har|ry** (har´ē) *vt.* **-ried, -ry•ing** ⟦ME *hergien* < OE *hergian* < base of *here,* army < IE **koryos,* army, var. of base **koros,* war > Lith *kāras,* war, MIr *cuire,* host⟧ **1** to raid, esp. repeatedly, and ravage or rob; pillage; plunder **2** to torment or worry; harass **3** to force or push along

3. Is the word you're looking up a derived form? If the word ends in -ly or another suffix, it may not be listed as an entry word. Try dropping the suffix and looking for the base word.

Find the word *criminological* in the following entry:

> **crim|i•nol•o|gy** (krim´ə näl´ə jē) *n.* ⟦< L *crimen,* gen. *criminis* (see CRIME) + -LOGY⟧ the scientific study and investigation of crime and criminals—**crim´i•no•log´|i•cal** (-nə läj´i kəl) *adj.*—**crim´|i•no•log´|i•cal|ly** *adv.*—**crim´|i•nol´|o•gist** *n.*

4. Does the word have a prefix attached to it? If so, you may need to drop the prefix and look up the base word.

Use the following entries to determine the meanings of the words *all-encompassing* and *overgeneralize:*

en•com•pass (en kum´pəs, in-) *vt.* **1** to shut in all around; surround; encircle **2** to contain; include **3** to bring about; achieve; contrive [*to encompass* its destruction]—**en•com´pass•ment** *n.*

gen•er•al•ize (jen´ər əl īz´; *often* jen´rəl īz´) *vt.* **-ized´, -iz´ing** ⟦ME *generalisen*⟧ to make general; esp., *a)* to state in terms of a general law or precept *b)* to infer or derive (a general law or precept) from (particular instances) *c)* to emphasize the general character rather than specific details of *d)* to cause to be widely known or used; popularize—*vi.* **1** to formulate general principles or inferences from particulars **2** to talk in generalities **3** to become general or spread throughout a body or area

5. If you are looking up a proper noun (a capitalized word, the name of a person or place), or an abbreviation, it may be listed in a separate section. Some dictionaries have special sections for biographical entries (famous people) and geographical entries (places) as well as abbreviations.

6. If you still cannot find the word, it's time to try another dictionary!

Remembering Definitions

We will talk in a later chapter about some special techniques for remembering word meanings. A good starting point is to get into the habit of writing down new words in a special section of your notebook or on index cards. Copy the word, the definition, and the sentence in which you found the word. If you use index cards, write the word on the front of the card and its definition on the back (see Figure 4–1). Use your index cards like flash cards to study for vocabulary tests.

FIGURE 4–1   *Index Cards*

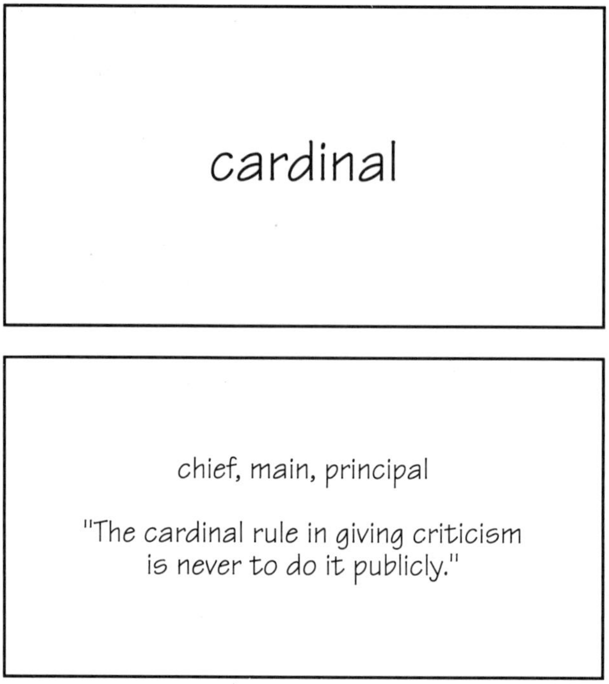

cardinal

chief, main, principal

"The cardinal rule in giving criticism
is never to do it publicly."

Exercise 4–1. Dictionary Practice

Directions.   Each of the sentences below is taken from Selection 4. First, use the context clues to guess at the meaning of the underlined word and write down your guess in the space provided. Then study the dictionary entry and underline the definition that best fits the sentence.

1. When you find yourself being criticized, determine if the criticism is <u>valid</u>. (6)

   Guess from context: _____

   > **val|id** (val′id) *adj.* [Fr *valide* < L *validus,* strong, powerful (in ML, valid) < *valere,* to be strong: see VALUE] **1** having legal force; properly executed and binding under the law **2** well-grounded on principles or evidence; able to withstand criticism or objection, as an argument; sound **3** effective, effectual, cogent, etc. **4** [Rare] robust; strong; healthy **5** *Logic* correctly derived or inferred according to the rules of logic—**val′id|ly** *adv.*—**val′id•ness** *n.*

2. Consider the critic's <u>motive</u>. (16)

   Guess from context: _____

mo•tive (mōt´iv) *n.* [[ME *motif* < OFr *motif* (*adj.*) < ML *motivus,* moving < L *motus,* pp. of *movere,* to MOVE]] **1** some inner drive, impulse, intention, etc. that causes a person to do something or act in a certain way; incentive; goal **2** MOTIF (sense 1)—*adj.* [[ML *motivus*]] **1** of, causing, or tending to cause motion **2** [Rare] of, or having the nature of, a motive or motives—*vt.* **-tived, -tiv•ing** to supply a motive for; motivate—*SYN.* CAUSE—**mo´tive•less** *adj.*

3. Try to <u>gauge</u> the emotional climate. (16)

   Guess from context: _____

   gauge (gāj) *n.* [[ME < NormFr: see the *v.*]] **1** a standard measure or scale of measurement **2** dimensions, capacity, thickness, etc. **3** any device for measuring something, as the thickness of wire, the dimensions of a machined part, the amount of liquid in a container, steam pressure, etc. **4** any means of estimating or judging **5** the distance between the rails of a rail track: cf. STANDARD GAUGE, BROAD GAUGE, NARROW GAUGE **6** the distance between parallel wheels at opposite ends of an axle **7** the size of a bore, esp. of a shotgun, expressed in terms of the number per pound of round lead balls of a diameter equal to that of the bore **8** the thickness of sheet metal, diameter of wire, etc. **9** *a)* a measure of the fineness of a knitted or crocheted fabric *b)* the fineness of a machine-knitted fabric expressed in terms of the number of loops per 1 1/2 inches **10** *Naut.* the position of a ship in relation to another ship and the wind [a sailboat that has the weather *gauge* of another boat is to windward of it] **11** *Plastering* the amount of plaster of Paris used with common plaster to hasten its setting. Usually GAGE[1] in technical senses—*vt.* **gauged, gaug´ing** [[ME *gaugen* < NormFr *gaugier,* prob. < VL **gallicare* < ?]] **1** to measure accurately by means of a gauge **2** to measure the size, amount, extent, or capacity of **3** to estimate; judge; appraise **4** to bring to correct gauge; make conform with a standard **5** *Masonry* to cut or rub (bricks or stone) to a desired shape **6** *Plastering* to mix (plaster) in the proportions required for a specified setting time— *SYN.* STANDARD—**gauge´a|ble** *adj.*

4. Destructive responses serve to cut off criticism, and you may miss the point, because <u>initial</u> criticism is seldom right on target. (20)

   Guess from context: _____

   in|i•tial (i nish´əl) *adj.* [[< Fr or L: Fr < L *initialis* < *initium,* a beginning < *inire,* to go into, enter upon, begin < *in-,* into, in + *ire,* to go < IE base **ei-* > Goth *iddja*]] having to do with, indicating, or occurring at the beginning [the *initial* stage of a disease, the *initial* letter of a word]— *n.* **1** a capital, or uppercase, letter; specif., *a)* an extra-large capital letter at the start of a printed paragraph, chapter, etc. *b)* the first letter of a name **2** *Biol.* a primordial cell that determines the basic pattern of derived tissues; specif., a meristematic cell —*vt.* **-tialed** or **-tialled, -tial•ing** or **-tial•ling** to mark or sign with an initial or initials.

5. "That means I have poor taste in everything, and I'm a <u>clod</u> and an awful person." (24)

   Guess from context: _____

clod (kläd) *n.* ⟦ME & OE < IE *g(e)leu- < base *gel-, to make round
> CLIMB⟧ **1** a lump, esp. a lump of earth, clay, loam, etc. **2** earth; soil
3 a dull, stupid person; dolt **4** the part of a neck of beef nearest the
shoulder—**clod′dish** *adj.*—**clod′dish|ly** *adv.*—**clod′dish•ness** *n.*—
clod′|dy *adj.*

6. Your critic has initiated this <u>confrontation</u>, which is to his or her advantage. (47)

   Guess from context: _____

   con•front (kən frunt′) *vt.* ⟦Fr *confronter* < ML *confrontare* < L *com-*,
   together + *frons,* forehead: see FRONT⟧ **1** to face; stand or meet face to
   face **2** to face or oppose boldly, defiantly, or antagonistically **3** to bring
   face to face (*with*) [to *confront* one with the facts] **4** to set side by side
   to compare—**con•fron•ta•tion** (kän′frən tā′shən) or **con•front′|al** *n.*—
   con′fron•ta′tion•al *adj.*

7. "Because it takes so long to work up courage to criticize," Marsha Linehan
   says, "many of us match the criticism to the courage and make <u>judgmental</u>,
   all-encompassing accusations instead of sticking with the much smaller
   criticism we wanted to make." (62)

   Guess from context: _____

   judg•men•tal (juj ment″l) *adj.* **1** of or having to do with the exercise of
   judgment **2** making or tending to make judgments as to value, importance, etc., often specif., judgments considered to be lacking in toler-
   ance, compassion, objectivity, etc.

8. Specifically, what does this behavior cause? <u>Antagonism</u>? Lost time? (70)

   Guess from context: _____

   an•tag|o•nism (an tag′ə niz′əm) *n.* ⟦Gr *antagōnisma* < *antagōnizes-*
   thai: see ANTAGONIZE⟧ **1** the state of being opposed or hostile to another
   or to each other; opposition or hostility **2** an opposing force, principle,
   etc.; specif., a mutually opposing action that can take place between
   organisms, muscles, drugs, etc.—*SYN.* ENMITY

9. It helps if you <u>couch</u> your criticism in terms of "When you do X, I feel Y,"
   Linehan says. (73)

   Guess from context: _____

   couch (kouch) *n.* ⟦ME & OFr *couche,* a bed, lair: see the *v.*⟧ **1** an article
   of furniture on which one may sit or lie down; sofa; divan **2** any resting
   place **3** [Old Poet.] a place for sleeping; bed **4** [Obs.] an animal's lair or
   den **5** *Brewing* a layer of grain spread to germinate **6** *Fine Arts* a priming layer or coat, as of paint or varnish— *vt.* ⟦ME *couchen* < OFr
   coucher, to lie down < L *collocare,* to lay < *com-*, together + *locare,* to
   place: see LOCAL⟧ **1** to lay or put on or as on a couch, as to sleep: now
   usually used reflexively or in the passive voice **2** to lower or bring down;
   esp., to lower (a spear, lance, etc.) to an attacking position **3** to put in specific or particular words; phrase; express [*couched* to veiled language] **4**

to embroider with thread laid flat and fastened down with fine stitches **5** [Archaic] to put in a layer **6** [Obs.] to hide **7** *Brewing* to spread (grain) in a thin layer to germinate **8** *Surgery* to remove (a cataract) by using a needle to push down the crystalline lens of the eye —*vi.* **1** to lie down on a bed, as to sleep; recline **2** to lie in hiding or in ambush **3** to lie in a pile, as decomposing leaves—☆**on the couch** [Colloq.] undergoing psychoanalysis

10. "If you call when you're going to be late, I'll start dinner later (<u>incentive</u> and how the person will help)." (84)

Guess from context: _____

in•cen•tive (in sent´iv) *adj.* ⟦ME < LL *incentivum* < neut. pp. of L *incinere*, to sing < *in-*, in, on + *canere*, to sing: see CHANT⟧ stimulating one to take action, work harder, etc.; encouraging; motivating—*n.* something that stimulates one to take action, work harder, etc.; stimulus, encouragement

Exercise 4–2. Dictionary Practice

Directions. Refer to the dictionary entries in Exercise 4–1 to answer the following questions.

1. *a.* <u>Motive</u> is derived from a Latin word meaning _____
   b. What parts of speech can <u>motive</u> be?

   _____

   c. What word is a synonym for <u>motive</u>?

   _____

2. Which definitions of <u>gauge</u> have subject labels?

   _____

3. *a.* How many adjective definitions are shown for <u>initial</u>? _____
   b. How many verb definitions? _____
   c. How many noun definitions? _____

4. *a.* How many derived forms are listed under <u>clod</u>? _____
   b. What are they? _____
   c. Choose one of them and use it in a sentence.

   _____

   _____

5. What part of speech is <u>confrontation</u>?

   _____

6. Which definition of <u>couch</u> is now obsolete?

_____

7. Explain the etymology of the word <u>incentive</u>.

_____

_____

8. How many definitions are shown for <u>incentive</u>? _____

Exercise 4–3. Practice with Your Own Dictionary

Directions.   Use a hardbound college dictionary to answer the following questions.

1. What is the plural of <u>crisis</u>?

   _____

2. Look up <u>circadian</u> and study the phonetic spellings. How many pronunciations are shown? Copy them below and pronounce each one to yourself.

   _____

   _____

3. What is another way to spell <u>cigarette</u>?

   _____

4. Look up the homographs refuse¹ and refuse², and study both entries.
   a. Is the pronunciation of refuse¹ the same as the pronunciation of refuse², or are they different?

   _____

   b. What part of speech is shown for each entry?

   _____

   _____

   c. Explain the difference in meaning between the two words.

   _____

   _____

   d. Write a sentence to illustrate each definition.

   _____

   _____

   _____

5. *a.* What parts of speech can the word <u>extreme</u> be?

_____

b. Write a sentence to illustrate each.

_____

_____

_____

6. What does the expression "take it on the lam" mean?

_____

7. What does <u>extract</u> mean when used in math?

_____

8. Explain the etymology of the word <u>lunatic</u>.

_____

9. What is the colloquial meaning of <u>chisel</u>? (Hint: look for the label *Col.*)

_____

10. What does a <u>pathologist</u> study?

_____

Exercise 4–4. Practice with Your Own Dictionary

Directions. Using a college dictionary, look up the underlined word in each of the following sentences. Find the definition that best fits the context and copy that definition in the space provided.

1. Most of the <u>exploits</u> of Sherlock Holmes are narrated by his friend Dr. John Watson.

_____

2. Law and government practices have often separated men and women into distinct roles—and <u>subordinated</u> women.

_____

3. With the adoption of the 13th amendment, the right of citizens to vote could no longer be <u>abridged</u> on account of sex.

_____

4. Fuel costs are expected to increase as the nation's <u>domestic</u> supplies continue to shrink.

_____

5. Most Americans do not favor a <u>radical</u> change in government.

   _____

6. Rude behavior will not be <u>countenanced</u> at the Halloween party.

   _____

7. From society's point of view, an important responsibility of parents is the <u>socialization</u> of their children.

   _____

8. Despite the evidence against him, John <u>contended</u> that he was innocent.

   _____

9. Traveling by longboat up the Baram River in northern Sarawak, I watched the rainforest of Borneo <u>wash</u> by.

   _____

10. The suspect was arrested and charged with assault and <u>battery</u>.

    _____

Integrative Exercises

Exercise 4–5. Previewing

1. Preview any selection from the back of the text that you have not already read. When you have completed your preview, write a summary of what you learned.

_____

_____

_____

_____

2. What is your prior knowledge of the subject of this selection?

_____

_____

_____

Exercise 4–6. Previewing in Another Textbook

1. Preview a chapter from a textbook you are using in another course or an article you have been assigned to read. Then write a summary of what you learned. Indicate the subject of the chapter and the main topics covered.

_____

_____

_____

_____

_____

2. Write any five questions about the subject of the chapter you've just previewed.

1. _____

2. _____

3. _____

4. _____

5. _____

Journal Entry

1. Discuss a time when someone criticized you or discuss a time when you criticized someone else. How did you feel? How did you respond? Was there a better way to handle your situation?

_____

_____

_____

_____

_____

_____

_____

_____

_____

_____

_____

_____

2. Discuss your dictionary habits. How often do you look up words? Do you like using the dictionary? What problems have you had? Do your dictionary skills need improvement?

_____

_____

_____

_____

_____

_____

_____

_____

_____

_____

_____

_____

5

MONITORING COMPREHENSION

In Chapter 5, you will:

1. Preview and read a selection about names and answer comprehension questions on the selection to check your understanding.

2. Continue practice with context and dictionary strategies and learn to simplify dictionary definitions.

3. Learn to monitor your comprehension.

SELECTION 5
NAMES AND IDENTITY

Muriel James and Dorothy Jongeward

Previewing Exercise

Directions. Preview the selection now. When you have completed your preview, answer the following questions:

1. What is the passage about?

_____

2. How many sections does the passage contain? _____
What do you think will be discussed in each?

_____

_____

3. What main points do the authors wish to make about names?

_____

_____

4. Does the article seem interesting? Why or why not?

_____

_____

Pre-thinking Exercise

1. How do you feel about your own name? Do you like it or dislike it? Why? Would you change your name if you could?

_____

_____

2. What does your name mean?

_____

3. Do you think names are important? Do they influence our personalities and behavior?

_____

_____

4. Do you know people with unusual names or nicknames? How do their names affect them?

_____

_____

What's in a Name?

Paramount to a person's identity is his or her name. Even though this name should not change one's character, it often contributes to the person's identity, either negatively or positively, because of the message it sends to the child.

On a birth certificate, a boy's name could read James William Stone. However,
5   he might be called:

Jim (by a friend).

James (by his father).

Jimmy (by his mother when pleased).

James William Stone (by his mother when displeased).

10   Each of these variations on the boy's name reflects an emotional feeling of the person using them. Each gives the boy a different message to live up to. Each activates a different response in him.

Egbert, now a banker, relates that at age seven he decided to change his name to Butch. This successfully stopped the other children from picking on him

15 and calling him sissy. Another man reported that he had to defend himself continually because of his family name of Francis. Bertha, an attractive housewife, changed her name to Maria because of the images of an elephant that always came to mind when she heard the name Bertha. Some people indicate their dislike for the identity their first name holds for them by choosing to use their middle name
20 or initials.

Many children labeled Junior or the "III" assume that they should follow in their father's footsteps. The same can occur with designations such as "Big" Bill and "Little" Bill for a father and a son. In either case there is a risk the son will feel he can never measure up to dad. In addition, he may feel like a carbon copy rather than an
25 original, confusing his own identity with his father's.

Many children are given symbolic names from literature, family genealogy, or history and are expected to live up to them. For example, children with biblical names such as David or Solomon, Martha or Mary may learn to identify with, or choose to fight against, the implied expectations. A Solomon may assume he is wiser than he
30 really is. A Martha may resent the implication that her interests lie in the kitchen rather than "in things of the spirit."

Foreign-sounding names, as well as symbolic names, are often burdensome. In both World Wars many families with German names were persecuted or rejected. Throughout history many Jewish families have suffered the same fate. It is common
35 for families with difficult foreign names to shorten or anglicize them as a way of fitting into a new culture. However, in disowning their identity based on traditions they often end up with a sense of rootlessness and with a generation split between those of the "old" country and those born on new soil.

Surnames

Surnames usually reflect the family heritage and give some clues—pleasant or
40 unpleasant—to a person's cultural identity. Some people are so closely identified with their family name that they use it almost exclusively.

Traditionally, it has been a common American practice for a woman, when marrying, to drop the use of her surname and take on that of her husband. Spanish cultures, in contrast, add the mother's maiden name to surnames, recognizing both lines
45 of descent instead of the father's alone.

Although a practice similar to that used by the Spanish was common in early America, today it is infrequent. Consequently, many married women—often without their awareness—lose the sense of the early identity associated with their maiden name. As one woman recounted, "One day when home alone and bored, I took out
50 my college photo albums and turned the pages. I was amazed at the dynamic young woman pictured there—receiving scholarships, being politically active, debating on the team. This was *me*! What happened along the way? Did becoming Mrs. Roberts make me a different person?"

Nicknames

Although both given names and surnames affect the sense of identity and destiny,
55 nicknames, pet names, and being called names have even more influence on some

people. These names are descriptive, and may be affectionate or demeaning, and their effect either positive or negative.

Some nicknames conjure up physical images. Fatso, Stringbean, Freckles, Venus, Blondie, Piano-legs, Shortie, Fish-face, and Dimples, all focus on appearance.

60 Some nicknames imply behavioral characteristics. Stupid, Sweetie-pie, Monster, Knuckle-head, The Clod, Angel, Red-the-Hothead, all give a child "permission" to act in specific ways.

Case Illustration

"Kicker" was the nickname of a four-year-old boy. It was given to him by his father, who had had a strong frog kick as a swimmer on a college team and was proud of the
65 strength in his infant son's legs. He continually commented, "He's a real kicker." In nursery school the boy frequently kicked other children to get what he wanted and even attacked the teacher. When she tried to correct him, he bragged, "but I'm a real kicker, just ask my daddy."

In a sense Kicker was acting out his nickname, but in an aggressive way, not
70 related to the original, constructive, "good" meaning. He was making life miserable for his family, friends, and schoolmates. In counseling, his parents became aware of the implications of his nickname. They had unintentionally given him "permission" to act aggressively toward others. It had become part of his identity to "kick up a fuss." They dropped the use of this nickname and used only his given name, Alan,
75 and they asked others to do the same. The child's behavior soon began to improve, and he eventually gave up being The Kicker.

Some children are summoned or scolded with derogatory names. This name-calling is a vicious form of discounting.* Some children are almost totally ignored or are called "Hey you" or "Kid." Some children enter kindergarten without even
80 knowing their name. Lacking a sense of identity, such children feel unreal or like a nothing.

When a name gives a child unnecessary pain, perhaps the old jingle "Sticks and stones can break my bones, but names can never hurt me" is less true than the proverb that says, "The hurt of a stick dies away, but words hurt forever."[1]

Interest Rating.   Please rate the interest level of Selection 5 on the following 1–5 scale (circle one):

5—Very interesting
4—Fairly interesting
3—Mildly interesting
2—A little boring
1—Very boring

---

*Discounting means lack of attention or negative attention that hurts emotionally or physically.

Difficulty Rating. Please indicate how difficult Selection 5 was for you to understand on the following 1–5 scale (circle one):

5—Very difficult

4—Fairly difficult

3—Moderate

2—Fairly easy

1—Very easy

Comments: _____

_____

Comprehension Questions

Directions. For questions 1–5, choose the answer that best completes the statement. For questions 6–10, write your response in the space provided. Base all answers on what you read in the selection (you may refer to the selection when you are not sure of an answer).

_____ 1. When Egbert changed his name to Butch:
   a. He lost his friends.
   b. Other children stopped bullying him.
   c. He became a good fighter.
   d. His teachers treated him better.

_____ 2. According to the authors, foreign-sounding names:
   a. Are troublesome.
   b. Are unusual and distinctive.
   c. Create a favorable impression.
   d. Are always changed in a new culture.

_____ 3. The authors feel that nicknames:
   a. Can be more important than given names.
   b. Are unimportant.
   c. Should not be used.
   d. Must reflect physical images or behavioral characteristics.

_____ 4. According to the passage, a boy named Junior or the "III":
   a. Is likely to be picked on by other boys.
   b. Will be proud of having the same name as his dad.
   c. May feel inadequate because he can't measure up to his father.
   d. Will probably try to establish his own identity by being different from his father.

_____ 5. The authors feel that:
   a. People should not change their names.
   b. Names can hurt you, but only temporarily.
   c. Symbolic names are desirable.
   d. Names can cause more hurt than physical pain.

6. How do people's names affect their identities?

_____

_____

7. Why did Bertha change her name?

_____

_____

8. Why do people with foreign-sounding names change their names? What problems may result from this name change?

_____

_____

9. According to the passage, how might a woman's change of surnames when marrying affect her identity?

_____

_____

10. What problem was caused by the nickname Kicker? How was the problem solved?

_____

_____

Vocabulary Exercise

Part I. Use the context clues to guess at the meaning of each underlined word and write your guess in the space provided. Then study the dictionary entry and underline the definition that best fits the context.

1. Paramount to a person's identity is his or her name. (1)

_____

> **par|a•mount** (par´ə mount´) *adj.* ⟦ Anglo-Fr *paramont* < OFr *par* (L *per*), by + *amont, à mont* (< L *ad montem,* to the hill), uphill ⟧ ranking higher than any other, as in power or importance; chief; supreme —*n.* supreme ruler; overlord —*SYN.* DOMINANT —**par´|a•mount´|cy** (-sē) *n.* —**par´|a•mount´|ly** *adv.*

2. Many children labeled Junior or the "III" assume that they should follow in their father's footsteps. The same can occur with underlined designations such as "Big" Bill and "Little" Bill for a father and son. (22)

_____

des•ig•na•tion (dez´ig nā´shən) *n.* ⟦ ME *designacioun* < L *designatio*: see DESIGNATE ⟧ **1** a pointing out or marking out; indication **2** a naming or being named for an office, post, or duty **3** a distinguishing name, title, etc.

3. In both World Wars many families with German names were persecuted or rejected. (33)

per•se|cute (pʉr´si kyo͞ot´) *vt.* -|**cut´|ed**, -|**cut´ing** ⟦ LME *persecuten* < MFr *persécuter*, back-form. < *persécuteur* < L *persecutor* < *persequi,* to pursue < *per,* through + *sequi,* to follow: see SEQUENT ⟧ **1** to afflict or harass constantly so as to injure or distress; oppress cruelly, esp. for reasons of religion, politics, or race **2** to trouble or annoy constantly [*persecuted* by mosquitoes] —*SYN.* WRONG —**per´se|cu´-tive** or **per•se|cu•to|ry** (pʉr´si kyo͞o tôr´ē, pər sek´yo͞o-) *adj.* —**per´-se|cu´tor** *n.*

4. Surnames usually reflect the family heritage and give some clues—pleasant or unpleasant—to a person's cultural identity. (39)

sur•name (sʉr´nām´; *for v., also* sʉr´nām´) *n.* ⟦ ME < *sur-* (see SUR-¹) + *name,* infl. by earlier *surnoun* < OFr *surnom* < *sur-* + *nom* < L *nomen,* name ⟧ **1** the family name, or last name, as distinguished from a given name **2** a name or epithet added to a person's given name (Ex.: *Ivan the Terrible)* —*vt.* -**named´, -nam´ing** to give a surname to

5. These names are descriptive and may be affectionate or demeaning, and their effect either positive or negative. (56)

de•mean¹ (dē mēn´, di-) *vt.* ⟦ DE- + MEAN², after DEBASE ⟧ to lower in status or character; degrade; humble [to *demean* oneself by taking a bribe]
de•mean² (dē mēn´, di-) *vt.* ⟦ see fol. ⟧ to behave, conduct, or comport (oneself) —*SYN.* BEHAVE

6. Some nicknames conjure up physical images. (58)

con•jure (kun´jər, kän´-; *for vi.1 & vt.1* kən joor´) *vi.* -**jured, -jur•ing** ⟦ME *conjuren* < OFr *conjurer* < L *conjurare,* to swear together, conspire < *com-,* together + *jurare,* to swear: see JURY¹ ⟧ **1** orig., to be sworn in a conspiracy **2** in primitve or superstitious rites, to summon a demon or spirit as by a magic spell **3** to practice magic or legerdemain —*vt.* **1** to call upon or entreat solemnly, esp. by some oath **2** in primitive or superstitious rites, to summon (a demon or spirit) as by a magic spell **3** to bring about by conjuration —**conjure up 1** to cause to be or appear as by magic or legerdemain **2** to call to mind [the music *conjured up* memories]

7. Some children are <u>summoned</u> or scolded with derogatory names. (77)

---

sum•mon (sum´ən) *vt.* ⟦ ME *somonen* < OFr *somondre* < VL *submonere*, for L *summonere*, to remind privily < *sub-*, under, secretly + *monere*, to advise, warn: see MONITOR ⟧ **1** to call together; order to meet or convene **2** to order to come or appear; call for or send for with authority or urgency **3** to order, as by a summons, to appear in court **4** to call upon to do something **5** to call forth; rouse; gather; collect; often with *up* [to *summon* up one's strength] —*SYN.* CALL— **sum´mon|er** *n.*

8. When a name gives a child unnecessary pain, perhaps the old jingle "Sticks and stones can break my bones but names can never hurt me" is less true than the <u>proverb</u> that says, "The hurt of a stick dies away, but words hurt forever." (83)

---

prov•erb (präv´ɛrb´) *n.* ⟦OFr *proverbe* < L *proverbium* < *pro-*, PRO-[2] + *verbum*, word: see verb⟧ **1** a short, traditional saying that expresses some obvious truth or familiar experience; adage; maxim **2** a person or thing that has become commonly recognized as a type of specified characteristics, byword **3** *Bible* an enigmatic saying in which a profound truth is cloaked —*vt.* ⟦ME *prouerben*⟧ [Archaic] to make a proverb or byword of —*SYN.* SAYING

Part II. Use the dictionary entries in Part I to answer the following questions.

1. What parts of speech can the word <u>paramount</u> be?

---

2. Explain the etymology of the word <u>conjure</u>.

---

3. How many different pronunciations are shown for <u>conjure</u>?

---

4. What noun is derived from the word <u>persecute</u>?

---

5. What word is a synonym for <u>proverb</u>?

Simplifying Definitions

Unless you are learning a technical term, you should not usually try to memorize an exact definition from the dictionary. Instead, you should simplify the definition by shortening it, rephrasing it, or thinking of a synonym that could replace the word in context. In this way, you can be sure that you are understanding the definition and not just memorizing it.

For example, *Webster's New World Dictionary* provides the following definition for *paramount:* "ranking higher than any other, as in power or importance; chief, supreme." After studying the definition, you might simplify it as "ranking high in importance" or "very important."

Exercise 5–1. Simplifying Definitions

Directions. After studying the context clues and dictionary entry, write a simplified definition (1–3 words) for the underlined word in each sentence.

1. Many children are given symbolic names from literature, family genealogy, or history and are expected to live up to them.

   ge•ne|al•ol•gy (jē´nē al´ə jē; *often,* -äl´-; *also* jen´ē-) *n., pl.* **-gies** ⟦ ME *genelogi* < OFr *genealogie* < LL *genealogia* < Gr < *genea,* race, descent (akin to *genos:* see GENUS) + *-logia,* -LOGY ⟧ **1** a chart or recorded history of the descent of a person or family from an ancestor or ancestors **2** the science or study of family descent **3** descent from an ancestor; pedigree; lineage —**ge´ne|al´|o•gist** *n.*

2. A Martha may resent the implication that her interests lie in the kitchen rather than "in things of the spirit."

   im•pli•ca•tion (im´pli kā´shən) *n.* ⟦ ME *implicacioun* < L *implicatio* ⟧ **1** an implicating or being implicated **2** an implying or being implied **3** *a)* something implied, from which an inference may be drawn *b) Logic* a formal relationship between two propositions such that if the first is true then the second is necessarily or logically true

3. It is common for families with difficult foreign names to shorten or anglicize them as a way of fitting into a new culture.

   An•gli•cize (an´glə sīz´) *vt., vi.* **-cized´, -ciz´ing** ⟦ < ML *Anglicus* (see ANGLICAN + -IZE ⟧ [*also* **a-**] to change to English idiom, pronunciation, customs, manner, etc. —**An´gli•ci•za´tion** (-si zā´shən) *n.*

4. Some nicknames imply behavioral characteristics.

   be•hav•ior (bē hāv´yər, bi-) *n.* ⟦ < prec. by analogy with ME *havior,* property < OFr *aveir* < *avoir,* to have ⟧ **1** the way a person behaves or acts; conduct; manners **2** an organism's responses to stimulation or environment, esp. those responses that can be observed **3** the way a machine, element, etc., acts or functions —**be•hav´ior|al** *adj.* —**be•hav´ior•al|ly** *adv.*

5. Some children are summoned or scolded with <u>derogatory</u> names.

> **de•rog|a•to|ry** (di räg′ə tôr´ē) *adj.* ⟦ L *derogatorius*: see DEROGATE ⟧ **1** tending to lessen or impair; detracting **2** disparaging; belittling Also **de•rog´la•tive** —**de•rog´la•to´ri|ly** *adv.*

Exercise 5–2. Simplifying Definitions

Directions.   Using the dictionary entries provided on pages 79 and 80, write a simplified definition (1–3 words) for each of the following words.

1. surname

_____

2. designation

_____

3. demeaning

_____

4. proverb

_____

5. summon

_____

Monitoring Comprehension

The pre-reading strategies you have learned help you start to read with concentration and interest. *While* reading, there are additional strategies to use that will enable you not only to sustain your concentration but also to read with better comprehension and memory. One of these important strategies is *monitoring comprehension.*

Monitoring comprehension includes two steps: judging how well you've understood the material, and clarifying your understanding when necessary. To judge your understanding, you must interrupt your reading from time to time. Too often, we tend to read steadily along whether or not we are understanding—or even paying attention to—the material. Instead, make a habit of pausing at the end of each section in your textbook, or after any difficult paragraph, to make sure you've understood what you've just read.

If you are not confident that you've understood the material, try explaining it to yourself. If you cannot summarize adequately, assume you did not achieve satisfactory comprehension and go back to the paragraph or section to clarify your understanding. You may want to reread part or all of the passage, or you may need to look up some words. It is often helpful to locate difficult sentences, analyze them, and try to simplify their points (some readers find it helpful to read difficult sentences aloud). Paraphrase the sentence—that is, try explaining it to yourself using different words than the author's. Sometimes you just need an extra minute to think over what you've read. Try to picture what the author is saying or relate the author's ideas to something in your own experience or prior knowledge.

Of course, it will take longer to read in this manner, but keep in mind that if you do not have satisfactory understanding, your study-reading time is poorly spent. There is a joke about an airplane pilot who gets on the intercom to talk to his passengers. He says, "I have some good news and some bad news to tell you. The bad news is that we're lost. The good news is that we're making record time!" So decide—is your priority to read quickly or to read with understanding?

Exercise 5–3. Monitoring Comprehension

Directions.   After reading each passage below, rate your comprehension on a 1–5 scale (with 5 the highest rating). If your rating is 1, 2 or 3, use one or more of the strategies listed below to clarify your understanding. Then, write a brief summary of what you've read. Finally, indicate which of the strategies you used to clarify your comprehension.

Re-reading.

Using the dictionary.

Analyzing difficult sentences/paraphrasing.

Reading aloud.

Visualizing or relating.

Example

Rumors frequently touch on our important fears and anxieties. Where food shortages exist, individuals circulate stories about the supply and distribution of provisions; where access to economic resources depends on tracing descent through uncertain genealogies, they gossip about one another's ancestors; where witchcraft is a cultural belief, they spread tales about who is and is not a witch; and when economic times are bad, workers depend on the office grapevine to forecast management changes.[2]

Comprehension rating ___3___

Summary: Rumors reflect our important fears. For example, if the economy is bad, employees will listen for rumors about management's plans.

Strategies used: re-reading, analyzing sentences

1. **Stress**
    One of the main causes of stress, experts agree, is a lack of control. In order to withstand tension, says cardiologist Robert S. Eliot, M.D., director of the Institute of Stress Medicine in Denver, a person must feel that she is in charge of the events in her life. "The problem is, this society increasingly gives people less control," he says.[3]

Comprehension rating: _____

Summary: _____

_____

_____

_____

_____

Strategies used: _____

2. **Faster than Light?**
    For experimentalists studying quantum mechanics, the fantastic often turns into reality. A recent example emerges from the study of a phenomenon known as nonlocality, or "action at a distance." This concept calls into question one of the most fundamental tenets of modern physics, the proposition that nothing travels faster than the speed of light.

    An apparent violation of this proposition occurs when a particle at a wall vanishes, only to reappear—almost instantaneously—on the other side. A reference to Lewis Carroll may help here. When Alice stepped through the looking glass, her movement constituted in some sense action at a distance, or nonlocality: her effortless passage through a solid object was instantaneous. The particle's behavior is equally odd. If we attempted to calculate the particle's average velocity, we would find that it exceeded the speed of light.[4]

Comprehension rating: _____

Summary: _____

_____

_____

_____

_____

Strategies used: _____

3. **Monetary Policy**
    In learning about monetary policy, the first thing one must understand is the role of the Federal Reserve Bank (the Fed). The Fed is one of the sources of money; it can add or subtract money from the economy as it sees fit. For example, the Fed can simply produce more dollars or cut the amount it lends to banks, if it thinks one of those actions is warranted.

    Managing the money supply is the responsibility of the Federal Reserve System. It operates independently of the president or Congress and has the goal of keeping the economy growing without causing inflation. It does that by trying to manage the money supply and interest rates. This process is called monetary policy.

A nation's monetary policy is the management of the money placed into the economy and the management of interest rates. As you know, inflation is sometimes caused by having too much money in the economy. When that happens, the Fed cuts the money supply and increases interest rates. That makes less money available for spending and discourages businesses and consumers from borrowing money (because of high interest rates). When businesses find it hard to borrow money, they often cut back on production and lay off workers. This slows the economy and lowers inflation.[5]

Comprehension rating: _____

Summary: _____

_____

_____

_____

_____

Strategies used: _____

4. Wake Up, America!

On March 24, 1989, the giant oil tanker *Exxon Valdez* slammed into Blythe Reef off the coast of Alaska in Prince William Sound. Two hundred fifty-eight thousand barrels of crude oil spilled onto one of the most beautiful unspoiled coastlines in the world. The environmental damage of this catastrophe will never be accurately assessed, but the cost of the subsequent clean-up effort was estimated at about $2 billion. In a July 1990 report, the National Transportation Safety Board identified the primary cause of the accident as the third mate's failure to maneuver the vessel properly. The description of the third mate's behavior on the bridge minutes before the accident is both sad and dramatic: he was simply so sleepy he could not perform.[6]

Comprehension rating: _____

Summary: _____

_____

_____

_____

_____

Strategies used: _____

5. Indian Removal

Indian Removal, as it has been politely called, cleared the land for white occupancy between the Appalachians and the Mississippi, cleared it for cotton in the South and grain in the North, for expansion, immigration, canals, railroads, new cities, and the building of a huge continental empire clear across to the Pacific Ocean. The cost in human life cannot be accurately measured, in suffering not even roughly measured. Most of the history books given to children pass quickly over it.

Statistics tell the story. In 1820, 120,000 Indians lived east of the Mississippi. By 1844, fewer than 30,000 were left. Most of them had been forced to migrate westward. But the word "force" cannot convey what happened.[7]

Comprehension rating: _____

Summary: _____

_____

_____

_____

_____

Strategies used: _____

Integrative Exercises

Exercise 5–4. Dictionary Practice

Part I. Use a standard-size, hardbound college dictionary to answer the following questions.

1. What parts of speech may the word <u>lure</u> be?

   _____

2. How many syllables are in <u>lutetium</u>?

   _____

3. The third syllable in <u>lutetium</u> sounds like the word: _____
   a. Tie.
   b. Tea.
   c. She.
   d. Shy.

4. What noun is derived from the word <u>lurid</u>?

   _____

5. What meaning for <u>lust</u> is now <u>obsolete</u>?

   _____

6. What is a <u>lutenist</u>?

   _____

7. Explain the etymology of the word <u>lurid</u>.

   _____

8. What does the expression "leave in the lurch" mean?

   _____

9. What does the abbreviation <u>Lux.</u> stand for?

   _____

10. Lush[1] and lush[2] are homographs.

    a. Are they pronounced the same? _____
    b. Are they used as the same part of speech? _____
    c. Write a sentence illustrating any definition for lush[1]. Then write a second sentence illustrating any definition for lush[2].

    _____

    _____

    _____

Part II.   Find the definition that best fits the underlined word in each sentence. Copy or simplify the definition in the space provided.

1. The new *Dracula* movie is a <u>lurid</u> film.

   _____

2. Chocolate lovers find it hard to resist the <u>lure</u> of a hot fudge sundae.

   _____

3. Thieves <u>lurked</u> in the forest, waiting for innocent victims to pass by.

   _____

4. Travelers through Brazil's rain forest are impressed by the forest's <u>lushness</u>.

   _____

5. Seal the hole with <u>lute.</u>

   _____

Exercise 5–5. Context and Dictionary

Directions.   Read the following excerpt from the article "Sticks and Stones May Break . . . In Reality, Names May Indeed Hurt You," by Jack Levin. Using your own dictionary, find the definition that best fits the context for each underlined word. Write the definition in the space provided following the passage, simplifying the definition whenever possible.

What's in a name? Plenty, if you happen to be political spokesperson Larry Speakes, professor Robert Smart, psychiatrist Ronald Bliss or Dorchester District Court Judge Darrel Outlaw. Whether or not such names <u>inspired</u> career choices, they undoubtedly have provided material for countless after-dinner conversations.

According to psychologist Rom Harre and his associates at SUNY [State University of New York] at Binghamton and <u>confirmed</u> in countless other studies, the influence of names begins in childhood. Names that we are familiar with—common names such as John and Michael—are associated with images of strength and competence, whereas unusual names like Ivan and Horace conjure up weakness and <u>passivity.</u> Consequently, those kids who are unfortunate enough to have been given <u>bizarre</u> or unpopular names are sometimes poorly adjusted and <u>pessimistic</u> about their <u>prospects</u> of being successful in the future; they tend to score lower on achievement tests and get lower grades in school.

This <u>phenomenon</u> extends into adulthood. Men who have strange or unusual names are more likely to suffer from mental illness or to have criminal records. In many cases, a self-fulfilling <u>prophecy</u> may operate. A child is ridiculed because of his name. As a result, he develops a negative attitude toward himself which influences his behavior in the classroom and on the playground. And teachers and <u>peers</u> notice this poor behavior. They assume that kids with unusual names aren't very competent or skillful. So very little is seen; very little is expected; and very little is obtained.

The importance of names is nowhere more important than in Hollywood. Consider all the celebrities who weren't born with the right name for the image they want to <u>portray.</u>

The former Elliot Goldstein is now Elliot Gould; Alphonso D'Abrusso is Alan Alda; Robert Zimmerman calls himself Bob Dylan; Frances Gumm's stage name was Judy Garland; and Patricia Andrzejewski is better known as rock singer Pat Benetar.

The flip side of this is that uncommon names sometimes imply <u>uniqueness.</u> Thus one might <u>speculate</u> that Zsa Zsa Gabor, Yahoo Serious, River Phoenix, Moon Unit Zappa, Pee Wee Herman, Yakov Smirnoff, Rip Torn, Mr. T., Whoopie Goldberg, and Minnie Pearl owe at least part of their celebrity status to their names.[8]

1. inspired

   _____

2. confirmed

   _____

3. passivity

   _____

4. bizarre

   _____

5. pessimistic

   _____

6. prospects

   _____

7. phenomenon

   _____

8. prophecy

   _____

9. peers

   _____

10. portray

    _____

11. uniqueness

    _____

12. speculate

    _____

Journal Entry

1. Do you agree with the authors' statement that name-calling can be as hurtful as physical pain? Why or why not? If possible, support your answer with examples from your own experience.

_____

_____

_____

_____

_____

_____

_____

_____

_____

_____

2. Review your difficulty ratings for the last four reading selections ("Sleep and Dreams," "Interpreting Your Dreams," "Take the Sting Out of Criticism," and "Names and Identity"). Which was the most difficult for you to understand? Why? Which was the easiest? Why?

_____

_____

_____

_____

_____

_____

_____

_____

_____

_____

6 USING GOAL QUESTIONS AND LEARNING PREFIXES

In Chapter 6, you will:

1. Preview and read a difficult selection from a psychology textbook, monitoring your comprehension as you read.
2. Answer comprehension questions on the selection to check your understanding.
3. Learn to use goal questions to establish purposes for reading.
4. Learn the meanings of common negative prefixes and common number prefixes.

SELECTION 6
MASLOW'S THEORY OF HUMAN NEEDS

Valerian J Derlega and Louis H Janda

Previewing Exercise

Directions. Preview the selection and answer the following questions.

   1. What is the selection about?

_____

   2. What are the five levels of needs?

_____

_____

_____

_____

3. What is the subject of the last section?

_____

4. How are self-actualized people different from others?

_____

_____

Pre-thinking Exercise

1. Selection 6 explains Maslow's theory of human motivation. A theory is an idea that is not completely proved or accepted by everyone. Psychologists propose theories based on evidence they have gathered and then seek additional evidence to confirm their theories. What other theories of motivation have you studied or read about?

_____

_____

2. What needs seem most important in your own life? What needs seem most important in the lives of your family and friends?

_____

_____

While-You-Read

Directions.   Pause at the end of each section to monitor your comprehension and summarize what you've read. When necessary, use the strategies discussed in Chapter 5 to clarify your comprehension:

Rereading
Using the dictionary
Analyzing difficult sentences/paraphrasing
Reading aloud
Visualizing or relating

Abraham Maslow was interested in why people have differing motivations. For instance, one person may be motivated by money, while for another person, money has little or no value. To resolve this puzzle, Maslow suggested that motivational states, or needs, vary, depending on the circumstances of an individual's life and that
5   the lower-order needs must be satisfied before a person would be motivated by higher needs. He named five needs in a hierarchy of importance (see Figure 6–1).

Figure 6–1 *Maslow's Hierarchy of Needs*

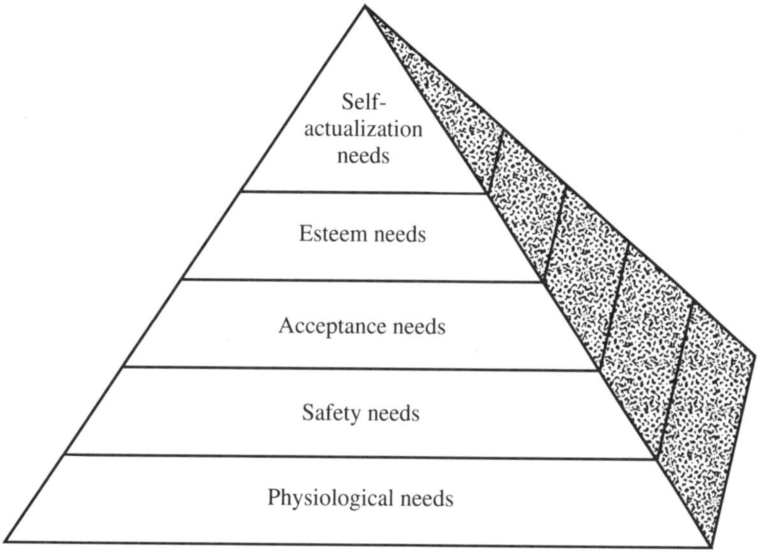

Physiological Needs

Maslow's lowest level of needs—physiological needs—are the ones for water, food, warmth, and, during adulthood, sex. These needs must be satisfied before the individual will be concerned about anything else. The power these needs can exert over
10 human behavior can be seen in the book *Alive,* which vividly describes the plight of airplane-crash victims who resorted to eating the flesh of nonsurvivors in order to stay alive. A majority of the people living in our society are able to satisfy their physiological needs adequately. Such individuals can move on to higher-order needs.

It has been suggested that one reason children of lower socioeconomic status fail
15 in school is that their physiological needs are not being met; they are hungry. Therefore, some school systems have free breakfast and lunch programs. Only children who have had enough to eat can benefit from classroom experiences.

Safety Needs

After physiological needs are satisfied, the individual seeks to satisfy safety needs, according to Maslow. Safety needs include freedom from physical harm, such as the
20 need to be protected from injury, illness, and physical abuse. The adult who was a battered child will probably have difficulty in progressing past this level. Adults must provide children with feelings of safety and security. Another example of a physical safety need might be the need for decent housing.

Safety needs also include freedom from psychological harm. As people mature,
25 they generally move to the next level in Maslow's hierarchy. But the behavior of

many adults can be seen as a means of protecting themselves from psychological harm. The student who cannot tolerate any form of criticism, the professor who cannot have his or her opinions questioned, or the boss who demands that employees respect his or her authority and status are all operating at the safety level of self-
30   preservation. These individuals are continually searching for security.

Acceptance Needs

Once safety needs have been adequately met, one can move up to the level of needing to be accepted, to be loved, and to belong. This need also originates in childhood. Parents must accept their children for what they are, not for what they do. Acceptance and love for the child should not be conditional. If children receive acceptance and
35   warmth from parents, they can begin to give love to others. Adults who have not had satisfying acceptance and affection may chronically seek love from others, but never seem to get enough.

Esteem Needs

Once people feel that others accept them, they become concerned with feelings about themselves—esteem needs. Are they adequate, competent, strong, and useful?
40   Individuals who are functioning at this level have the ability to care for and to be concerned with others. The teacher who is interested in what students learn is operating at the esteem level. The teacher who wants to entertain and be liked by students or who will not tolerate differences of opinion is operating at lower-need levels.

Self-Actualization Needs

45   Self-actualization is the highest level of motivation one can attain. It involves a "need" for personal growth. Individuals who reach this stage are actualizing their potential, according to Maslow.
     Maslow became interested in studying self-actualized people because he felt his scientific training in psychology did little to help him understand life or other people.
50   In his study of self-actualized people, both living and historical, Maslow discussed a number of characteristics.

Maslow's Self-Actualized Individual

Self-actualized individuals, according to Maslow, have an efficient perception of reality. That is, they have an unusual ability to detect the fake and the unreal in other people. They can judge others quite efficiently and correctly. This ability extends
55   itself to other areas, such as scientific matters, politics, and public affairs. Given a set of facts, these people can make more accurate predictions of the future than others can. This is possible because their perceptions are not influenced by anxieties, fears, or defenses.

60 Self-actualized persons accept their own human natures, as well as those of others. They can recognize the shortcomings of people and view them uncritically.

These individuals have an affinity for solitude. They are not dependent on outside satisfactions, according to Maslow. They do not derive their greatest pleasures in life from other people, things, or culture. Their main sources of satisfaction stem from individual development and growth. In order to grow they may want to spend
65 more time alone than most people do.

Self-actualized people have a continuing yet fresh appreciation for life. Even ordinary experiences—such as a sunset, a casual workday, or the touch of a child—can generate awe and pleasure. Maslow reported that many of the self-actualized had mystic or peak experiences. Such feelings are almost impossible to describe because
70 they are private experiences. But imagine the special feeling one might have when he or she walks through a forest or hears a particular musical passage. It's as if this event were being experienced for the first time. At such a moment one might feel particularly content about life and the world.

Self-actualized persons may have reached a high level of adjustment, but they
75 are not perfect. Like all of us, they have their faults.

They too are equipped with silly, wasteful, or thoughtless habits. They can be boring, stubborn, irritating. They are by no means free from a rather superficial vanity, pride, particularly to their own productions, family, friends, and children. Temper outbursts are not rare. Our subjects are occasionally capable of an extraordinary and
80 unexpected ruthlessness. It must be remembered that they are very strong people. This makes it possible for them to display a surgical coldness when this is called for, beyond the power of the average man. The man who found that a long-trusted acquaintance was dishonest cut himself off from this friendship sharply and abruptly and without any pangs whatsoever. Another woman who was married to someone she did not love,
85 when she decided on divorce, did it with a decisiveness that looked almost like ruthlessness. Some of them recover so quickly from the death of people close to them as to seem heartless.

To summarize, self-actualized people are generally free from threat and anxiety. This enables them to behave in ways that are consistent with their own values and
90 self-concepts. They like and accept others, but require time by themselves to pursue their personal development. They are not without faults. Although they have reached a high level of psychological development, they can exhibit the same shortcomings as others, but accept these as well as other aspects of themselves.[1]

Interest Rating.   Please rate the interest level of Selection 6 on the following 1–5 scale (circle one):

5—Very interesting

4—Fairly interesting

3—Mildly interesting

2—A little boring

1—Very boring

Difficulty Rating. Please indicate how difficult Selection 6 was for you to understand on the following 1–5 scale (circle one):

      5—Very difficult

      4—Fairly difficult

      3—Moderate

      2—Fairly easy

      1—Very easy

Comments: _____

_____

Monitoring Questions

1. What parts of the selection were most difficult for you to understand? Why?

      _____

      _____

2. What strategies did you use to clarify your comprehension on those sections? How effective were those strategies?

      _____

      _____

Comprehension Questions

Directions. For questions 1–5, choose the answer that best completes the statement. For questions 6–10, write your response in the space provided. Base all answers on what you read in the selection (you may refer to the selection when you are not sure of an answer).

_____ 1. Maslow became interested in studying self-actualized people because:

      a. He needed a research topic.

      b. He valued his scientific training.

      c. He wanted to better understand other people.

      d. He did not want to follow the scientific method.

_____ 2. According to Maslow:

      a. An individual must satisfy lower needs before moving on to higher needs.

      b. Physiological needs are always the most important.

      c. Safety needs are the most difficult to satisfy.

      d. Most adults are self-actualized.

_____ 3. Which of the following is *not* an example of a safety need:

      a. A child's need for a good breakfast.

      b. The need for freedom from injury.

      c. The need for psychological security.

      d. The need for decent housing.

_____ 4. The teacher who is most concerned with being liked by her students is operating at which needs level?

    a. Safety.

    b. Acceptance.

    c. Esteem.

    d. Self-actualization.

_____ 5. Self-actualized people can be:

    a. Perfect.

    b. Very fearful.

    c. Ruthless.

    d. Overly concerned with the opinions of others.

6. List the five levels of needs and give an example of each.

_____

_____

_____

_____

_____

7. List three characteristics of self-actualized people.

_____

_____

_____

8. Why is it important to meet lower-level needs? What happens when these needs are not met?

_____

_____

9. Give an example of a time when you were being motivated by your self-actualization needs.

_____

_____

10. Name a person you know or a public figure who you think fits Maslow's description of a self-actualized person.

_____

Vocabulary Exercise

Directions. Use the line numbers to locate each of the following words in the passage. Study the context clues and use your own dictionary to choose the definition that best fits the context. Write an accurate definition for each word in the space provided. Write simplified definitions or synonyms whenever possible.

1. motivations (1) _____

2. hierarchy (6) _____

3. physiological (7) _____

4. plight (10) _____

5. socioeconomic (14) _____

6. status (29) _____

7. conditional (34) _____

8. short comings (60) _____

9. affinity (61) _____

10. mystic (69) _____

11. peak (69) _____

12. ruthlessness (80) _____

Goal Questions

In Chapter 5, you learned how to monitor your comprehension. It is also important when reading assignments to set goals. Having a defined purpose for reading strengthens your motivation and increases your concentration.

Study reading is a purposeful activity. It is an active search for meaning. When you read an assignment, you should know why you are reading it—that is, what you are trying to learn and remember.

Previewing enables you to define a general goal for reading a chapter or article. For example, after previewing Selection 6, you could define your goal as "to understand how different needs motivate us," or, more simply, "to understand Maslow's theory of motivation." For Selection 5, you might have defined your goal in this way—"to find out how names influence people's identity."

It is usually best to express reading goals in question form. A good goal question makes your purpose clear and definite. For example, a goal question for Selection 6 might be: "What are the five different levels of needs, and how do they motivate our behavior?"

You can raise more specific goal questions while reading as you come to new headings and subheadings. For example, in Selection 6, when you come to the heading "Physiological Needs," you could raise the question, "What are physiological needs, and how do they motivate us?" What question might we ask at the heading "Maslow's Self-Actualized Individual"?

Sometimes a new goal question may be stimulated by a sentence within a paragraph. For example, in paragraph 1, after reading the sentence, "He [Maslow] named five needs in a hierarchy of importance," you might raise the question, "What were the five needs named by Maslow?"

Notice that using questions to set goals is very different from using questions as a pre-thinking strategy. When pre-thinking, any and all questions are helpful to stimulate curiosity and interest. When setting goals, you wish to raise only questions that will be answered in the passage. In short, you raise goal questions to help you know what to look for while reading.

Exercise 6–1. Raising Goal Questions

Directions.   Use the following headings to form a goal question for each of the accompanying passages. After reading each passage, write a brief answer to your question. An example is provided.

Example

Professional Crime

Goal question: <u>What is professional crime?</u>

> Although the adage "crime doesn't pay" is familiar, many people do make a career of illegal activities. A professional criminal is a person who pursues crime as a day-by-day occupation, developing skilled techniques and enjoying a certain degree of status among other criminals. Some professional criminals specialize in safecracking, hijacking of cargo, pickpocketing, and shoplifting. Such persons can reduce the likelihood of arrest, conviction, and imprisonment through their skill. As a result, they may have long careers in their chosen "professions."
>
> Edwin Sutherland (1937) offered pioneering insights regarding professional criminals by publishing an annotated account written by a professional thief. Unlike the person who engages in crime only once or twice, professional thieves make a business of stealing. These criminals devote their entire working time to planning and executing crimes and sometimes travel across the nation to pursue their "professional duties."[2]*

Answer: <u>Professional crime is the use of crime as a</u>

<u>career or business. The professional criminal</u>

<u>often develops special skills to use in his</u>

<u>particular line of crime and engages in crime regularly.</u>

1.   **The Food Value of Milk**

Goal question: _____

---

*Richard Schaeffer, *Sociology,* 2nd ed. (New York: McGraw-Hill, 1985), p. 176. Used with permission of McGraw-Hill.

Cow's milk is about 87 percent water and 13 percent solids. The solids contain the nutrients in milk. The body needs five kinds of nutrients for energy, growth, and the replacement of worn-out tissue. These nutrients are (1) carbohydrates, (2) fats, (3) minerals, (4) proteins, and (5) vitamins. Milk has been called "the most nearly perfect food" because it is an outstanding source of these nutrients. But milk is not "the perfect food" because it lacks enough iron and does not provide all vitamins.[3]

Answer: _____

_____

_____

_____

2. Printing Paper Money

Goal question: _____

The production of a new bill begins when artists sketch their designs for it. The secretary of the treasury must approve the final design. Engravers cut the design into a steel plate. A machine called a *transfer press* squeezes the engraving against a soft steel roller, making a raised design on the roller's surface. After the roller is heat-treated to harden it, another transfer press reproduces the design from the roller 32 times on a printing plate. Each plate prints a sheet of 32 bills. Separate plates print the front and back of the bills.

Many people believe that the paper used for money is made by a secret process. However, the government publishes a detailed description of the paper so that private companies can compete for the contracts to manufacture it. Federal law forbids unauthorized persons to manufacture any paper similar to that used for money.

The Bureau of Engraving and Printing uses high-speed presses to print sheets of paper currency. The design is printed first. Then the seals, serial numbers and signatures are added in a separate operation. The sheets are cut into stacks of bills. Imperfect bills are replaced with new ones called *star notes*. Each star note has the same serial number as the bill it replaces, but a star after the number shows that it is a replacement bill. The bills are shipped to Reserve Banks, which distribute them to commercial banks.

Most $1 bills wear out after 18 months in circulation. Larger denominations last for years because they are handled less often. Banks collect worn-out bills and ship them to Federal Reserve banks for replacement. The Reserve Banks destroy worn-out money in shredding machines.[4]

Answer: _____

_____

_____

_____

_____

_____

3. **Circadian Rhythms**

Goal question: _____

> Every plant seems to follow a cycle that includes sleep. Some flowers close their petals at night and open them again in the morning, as if they were aware of the transition between night and day. Scientists call these cycles *circadian rhythms,* which are daily fluctuations comprising a 24-hour period. These cycles are presumed to be present in every living cell.[5]

Answer: _____

_____

_____

_____

4. **Other-Imposed Discipline versus Self-Discipline**

Goal question: _____

> Now let's distinguish between two radically different kinds of control-type discipline. One is externally administered or "other-imposed"; the other is internally administered or self-imposed. Discipline by others versus discipline of oneself; control by others as opposed to self-control.
> Everyone is familiar with the term *self-discipline,* but what does it actually mean? Psychologists use the term *locus of control,* which I think is helpful here. Their investigations show that some people tend to have the locus of control *inside* themselves. With self-discipline, the locus of control is inside the person, but with discipline enforced by others, the locus of control is outside the person—actually inside the controller.[6]

Answer: _____

_____

_____

_____

5. **Principles of Criminal Law**

Goal question: _____

> Our system of justice operates on two key principles of criminal law. The first is the presumption of innocence. This means that those accused of crimes are considered innocent until proved guilty. The second principle is the burden of proof, which in criminal cases means that guilt must be proved beyond a reasonable doubt.

Theoretically, determining guilt is a process involving arguing the issues of fact or law in the particular case; in actual practice, however, this seldom happens. In many cases, the existence of guilt is supported by sufficient evidence; in others, where the issues of fact are such that the accused may or may not be found guilty beyond a reasonable doubt, concessions are worked out that may result in a reduced charge if the accused agrees to plead guilty.[7]*

Answer: _____

_____

_____

_____

_____

Exercise 6–2. Raising Goal Questions

The first sentence has been separated from each of the following passages. After reading the first sentence, write a goal question in the space provided. Remember to raise a question that you expect to be answered by the passage. When you have finished reading the passage, write a brief answer to your question (if your question was not answered by the passage, you may change your question and write an answer to the new question). An example is provided.

Example

Most of the night is spent in what is called *ordinary sleep*.

Goal question: _What happens during ordinary sleep?_____

The brain's activity during ordinary sleep differs considerably from the pattern during waking hours, and the muscles of the body are considerably more relaxed. Four stages of ordinary sleep, ranging from light to very deep, can be distinguished from tracings of brain and muscle activity. We move back and forth among these four stages during the night. Most people have three periods of the deepest sleep, the first starting within an hour after dropping off, the last ending after about three or four hours.[8]

Answer: _Muscles are more relaxed. We go back and forth_____

_____between 4 stages, varying in depth. Usually there_____

_____are 3 periods of the deepest sleep._____

_____

1. Last year was the most wonderful—and worrisome—of times for Mike and Angie Rooney, of St. Louis, Missouri.

_____

*Reprinted with the permission of Macmillan College Publishing Company from INTRODUCTION TO CRIMINAL JUSTICE, Third Edition by Robert D. Pursley. Copyright © 1984 by Macmillan College Publishing Company, Inc.

Goal question: _____

> The Rooneys, both twenty-nine, were thrilled to learn they were expecting their first child. But when Angie, an accountant, was four months pregnant, her firm laid her off. "I'd worked sixty- and seventy-hour weeks during tax time and was up for a promotion," she recalls. "My boss told me I was laid off for economic reasons, but I think it was because they found out I was pregnant."[9]

Answer: _____

_____

_____

_____

2. Almost everything people do with their cars causes some form of pollution.

Goal question: _____

> Driving creates auto exhaust, which spews out chemicals and poisons the air. Oil spills and the dumping of auto-related refuse pollute the water supply. Auto "graveyards" and tire dumps deface the landscape, and highway runoff is a major source of soil pollution. Making and using cars may be one of humankind's most polluting activities.[10]

Answer: _____

_____

_____

_____

3. When people become parents, something strange and unfortunate happens.

Goal question: _____

> They begin to assume a role or act a part and forget that they are persons. Now that they have entered the sacred realm of parenthood, they feel they must take up the mantle of "parents." Now they earnestly try to behave in certain ways because they think that is how parents should behave. Frank and Helen Bates, two human beings, suddenly became transformed into Mr. and Mrs. Bates, Parents.[11]

Answer: _____

_____

_____

_____

4. Psychologists have found it useful to identify several levels of consciousness.

Goal question: _____

> The *conscious* level contains thoughts and memories of which we are fully aware. Information found in the *preconscious* level may be brought to awareness, but otherwise it remains out of consciousness. For example, your memories of your first day at college will remain at the preconscious level until you stop to think of them. The *unconscious* level contains

memories, feelings, and impulses that are difficult to bring to awareness. Such information, however, may become available through dreams, hypnosis, and other special means.[12]

Answer: _____

_____

_____

_____

5. When the alcoholic stops drinking and seeks help, good things begin to happen quickly.

Goal question: _____

He looks better and feels better. He is healthier and happier. His self-confidence and self-esteem begin to return. He begins to look at himself and the world around him differently. As time goes on, he feels more comfortable in sobriety than in drunkenness. As life continues, the alcoholic chooses not to drink because life is better than it was in his drinking days. But the sober alcoholic must forever be on guard against the temptation to drink again. At the beginning it will be a battle. New patterns and habits must be put into place, but the alcoholic is on the road to a new life.[13]

Answer: _____

_____

_____

_____

_____

Analyzing Word Structure

You have learned how to use context clues and the dictionary to determine the meaning of new words, and you have learned a strategy for remembering them. The focus of our vocabulary work will now shift to the study of meaningful word elements—prefixes, roots, and suffixes.

The study of word parts has several benefits. First, when encountering a new word, recognizing its prefix, root, or suffix gives you a clue to its meaning. When context clues are also available, you may be able to make a good guess at the word's meaning. Second, knowing the prefix, root, or suffix in a word makes it easier to remember the word and its meaning. Third, building your knowledge of word parts is a shortcut to expanding vocabulary; many prefixes, roots, and suffixes are common, appearing in tens and even hundreds of words.

Prefix, Root, and Suffix

All words contain a main element, referred to as the root of the word. A part attached at the beginning of a root is called a prefix; a part attached at the end of a root is called a suffix. A word may have no prefix or suffix, or a word may have more than one prefix, root, or suffix.

Examples

predict	pre (prefix) + dict (root)
predictable	pre (prefix) + dict (root) + able (suffix)
unpredictable	un (prefix) + pre (prefix) + dict (root) + able (suffix)

Prefixes

The English language uses hundreds of prefixes. This section will begin a review of 30 common prefixes that will be completed in Chapter 7 (an expanded table of prefixes can be found in Appendix D). In this chapter, we will study negative prefixes and number prefixes; Chapter 7 will review other common prefixes. The information and exercises that are provided will help you learn the prefixes quickly and efficiently.

There are a few considerations to bear in mind before you continue:

• Some prefixes have more than one meaning.

• Some prefixes change their form (spelling and pronunciation). For example, the prefix *in* changes to *ir* before roots beginning with *r* (example: *in* + responsible becomes irresponsible).

• In some words, the meaning of the prefix will not be obvious. For example, the word *prevent* contains the prefix *pre,* though it may not be obvious how the meaning *before* is part of the meaning of the word *prevent* (you can check your dictionary when unsure).

Directions. Study each prefix as it is presented in the box. Look over the examples and learn the prefix's meaning. Complete each exercise as you come to it.

Negative Prefixes

Several prefixes mean no or not or reverse the meaning of the base word to which they are attached.

The most common negative prefix is *un.*

---

1. un	1. not	1. unhappy, unfinished
	2. reverses the action	2. unplug

Additional Comments. Un is a very common prefix. If you look in your dictionary, you will see hundreds of words with this prefix. You can probably think of many of them yourself.

Exercise 6–3

Directions. List five words that begin with the prefix *un*. Don't use any of the example words already provided.

_____

_____

<table>
<tr><td>2. in, il, ir, im</td><td>not</td><td>inactive, insecure,
illegal, irregular,
impossible</td></tr>
</table>

Additional Comments. In is another common negative prefix. The prefix changes to:

    il when the base word begins with *l* (illegal)

    ir when the base word begins with *r* (irregular)

    im when the base word begins with *m, b,* or *p* (immodest, imbalance, impossible)

Exercise 6–4

Directions. List two words under each spelling of this prefix. Be sure you choose words where the prefix means not (this prefix has a second meaning, which will be introduced in Chapter 7).

in	**il**	**ir**	**im**
_____	_____	_____	_____
_____	_____	_____	_____

<table>
<tr><td>3. dis</td><td>1. not
2. reverses the action
3. away, apart</td><td>1. dissatisfied
2. dismount
3. dismiss, distant</td></tr>
</table>

Additional Comments. Dis is a negative prefix with several meanings. Notice how the prefix works in the verb *dismount:* It reverses the action of the base word *mount.* In *dismiss, dis* means away (*dismiss* means to send away).

Exercise 6–5

Directions.   Write five words that begin with the prefix *dis*. After each word, write which of the three meanings is correct for that word.

_____

_____

_____

_____

_____

4. mis	wrong	misinterpret, misspell

Exercise 6–6

Directions.   Write three words that begin with the prefix *mis*.

_____

5. a, an	not, without	<u>a</u>typical, atheist, anarchy, anesthesia

Additional Comments. The prefix *a* is a less common negative prefix. It becomes *an* when the base word begins with a vowel. Note that in some words, the prefix *a* or *an* means without or lacking. For example, anarchy means lack of order, or without government. The word *apathy* means not caring or without feeling.

Exercise 6–7

Directions.   Complete each sentence by writing in the correct meaning of the prefix in the underlined word.

1. An <u>unintentional</u> error is one that was _____ done intentionally.

2. To <u>dispel</u> a child's fear is to help the child push her fear _____.

3. <u>Irreconcilable</u> differences can _____ be made up.

4. A politician who <u>misuses</u> the power of his office uses his power in the _____ way.

5. An <u>asymmetrical</u> design is one that is _____ symmetry.

Exercise 6–8

Directions. Complete each sentence by writing in the missing prefix.

1. The benefits of a college education are _____*calculable.*

2. It is a _____*carriage* of justice when an innocent person is found guilty.

3. Do not _____*regard* this wise advice.

4. The effects of drug abuse are long lasting and _____*reversible.*

5. Many people consider it _____*moral* to have an _____*licit* love affair.

Number Prefixes

English has prefixes for the numbers 1 to 10, and for some of the larger numbers as well. We will review a few of the more common number prefixes.

There are two prefixes that mean one. They are *uni* and *mono.*

6.	uni	one	unicycle
7.	mono	one	monotheism

Additional Comments. A unicycle has one wheel. Monotheism is the belief that there is one God.

Note: In some words, *uni* may also function as the root: unique, union, unite

Exercise 6–9

Directions. Complete each sentence by filling in the prefix or the meaning of the prefix as appropriate.

1. A _____*poly* is when one company controls an entire industry.

2. Monogamy is the practice of having _____ husband or wife (at the same time, that is!).

3. The _____*verse* is one world.

4. A unicorn is a mythical creature with _____ horn.

5. A _____*archy* is a country ruled by one person (e.g., a king or queen).

8. bi	two	bicycle, biceps

Exercise 6–10

Directions. List three words beginning with the prefix *bi.*

9. tri	three	tricycle, trimester

Exercise 6–11

Directions. List three words beginning with the prefix *tri.*

10. deci, deca	ten	decade

Exercise 6–12

Directions. List three words beginning with the prefix *deci* or *deca.*

11. cent, centi	hundred	centimeter

Exercise 6–13

Directions. List three words beginning with the prefix *cent.*

| 12. | poly | many, several | polygon |
| 13. | multi | many, several | multivitamin |

Additional Comments. Poly and multi both indicate an inexact quantity that is more than one. We don't know how many vitamins are in a multivitamin; we just know it contains several, or many, vitamins.

Exercise 6–14

Directions. Complete each sentence by filling in the prefix or the meaning of the prefix as appropriate.

1. To be multilingual is to be able to speak __many__ languages.

2. A polytheist is a person who believes there are __many__ gods.

3. A __poly__ *graph* test is administered to people whose honesty is suspect.

4. If you play Megabucks, you could become a __multi__*millionaire.*

5. The practice of having more than one husband or wife is called __poly__ *gamy.*

| 14. | semi | half, partly | semicircle, semidressed |

Exercise 6–15

Directions. Complete each sentence by filling in the prefix or the meaning of the prefix as appropriate (use prefixes 6–14 and their meanings.)

1. A talk or speech given by one person is a _____*logue.*

2. Bigamy is having __bi__ husband(s) or wive(s).

3. The decathlon is an Olympic contest consisting of __ten__ event(s).

4. A semester is __semi__ of an academic year.

5. A monomial is a mathematical expression consisting of __mono__ term(s). A mathematical expression consisting of more than one term is called a __poly__*nomial.*

6. A centennial is a period of ___*cent*___ years.

7. A ___*bi*___ *ped* is an animal that has two legs. A decapod is an animal that has _____ legs.

8. A ___*uni*___ *lateral* withdrawal of troops is when only one side withdraws. When ___*bi*___ side(s) withdraw(s), it is a bilateral withdrawal.

9. A three-legged stand for a camera is a ___*tri*___ *pod.*

10. A bicameral legislature consists of ___*bi*___ houses.

Use Table 6–1 to review the meanings of prefixes 1–14.

TABLE 6–1   **Common Negative and Number Prefixes**

Prefix	*Meaning*	*Example*
Negative Prefixes		
1. un	not, reverses the action	unfinished
2. in, il, ir, im	not,	inactive, illegal, irregular, impossible
3. dis	not, reverses the action	dissatisfied
	away, apart	dismiss
4. mis	wrong	misinterpret
5. a, an	not, without	atypical, anarchy
Number Prefixes		
6. uni	one	unicycle
7. mono	one	monotheism
8. bi	two	bicycle
9. tri	three	tricycle
10. deci, deca	ten	decade
11. cent, centi	hundred	centimeter
12. poly	many, several	polygon
13. multi	many, several	multivitamin
14. semi	half, partly	semicircle, semidressed

Integrative Exercises

Exercise 6–16. Formulating Goal Questions

Directions. Preview Reading 9, "The Nature of Love" (p. 407), and write three or four goal questions for the passage.

_____

_____

_____

_____

Exercise 6–17. Monitoring Comprehension and Raising Goal Questions

Directions. The following passage consists of an introduction and four other sections.

1. Form a goal question from the title and each subheading as you come to it.
2. After reading each section, rate your comprehension on a 1–5 scale (with 5 the highest) and clarify your understanding, if necessary.
3. Then write a brief summary of the section before continuing to the next one.

The Four Features of a Close Friendship

Goal question: _____

> A close relationship provides the give and take between friends that enable them to grow as individuals. Friendship, in other words, can help us fulfill our needs for independence and self-actualization. Critical to personal growth in a friendship is the development of mutual acceptance and a mutual willingness to explore and understand one another's feelings and experiences.
>
> Carl Rogers identifies four features of a healthy relationship—genuineness, warmth, empathy, and self-disclosure. These features were used by Rogers to refer to a therapist's responsibility toward a patient. But they seem equally appropriate characterizing the relationship between personal friends.

Comprehension rating: _____

Summary: _____

_____

_____

_____

_____

1. *Genuineness*

Goal question: _____

Individuals should be honest about their feelings in a relationship and should not deny how they feel. There should be no effort to hide feelings. A relationship will deepen only if both persons are honest in what they say and feel toward one another.

Comprehension rating: _____

Summary: _____

_____

_____

_____

_____

2. *Warmth*

Goal question: _____

Individuals must display a warm acceptance of each other. This can be called *unconditional positive regard.* Individuals do not impose any conditions on acceptance. They don't say to one another, "I will like you if you do such and such a thing." Unconditional acceptance means accepting both good and bad qualities in a friend. It means seeing the other individual as a unique person, with his or her own thoughts, feelings, and experiences.

Comprehension rating: _____

Summary: _____

_____

_____

_____

_____

3. *Empathy*

Goal question: _____

Healthy friendships also depend on individuals' efforts to understand the nature of their friends' private worlds. Friends who experience growth in their relationships are able to understand and know what the friend is feeling. Individuals can only help one another if they understand the emotions and experiences that each undergoes. Empathy depends on listening carefully to what the other person says and on understanding the other person. Through sharing, experiences can be seen as realistic or not realistic, and steps to explain events can be taken. Empathy means showing that you care.

Comprehension rating: _____

Summary: _____

_____

_____

_____

_____

4. *Self-disclosure*

Goal question: _____

The development of a relationship depends on how much individuals are willing to disclose about themselves. Persons who are unable to reveal their innermost thoughts to anyone will find themselves isolated. Those who are able to reveal their thoughts to people they trust are more likely to have friends. Friendship depends on one's willingness to risk being hurt and to trust other persons. When a person trusts a friend with an intimate disclosure, the hearer may feel warmer toward the person for this act of trust. As persons exchange intimate information, a powerful basis for trust and friendship is built up.

It is easy to see that these four qualities do not occur in every relationship in everyday life. But friends should try to achieve these goals in their relationships. Such conditions for friendships provide a framework in which individuals may behave nondefensively and help one another to grow. Unfortunately, many friendships are only able to maintain these qualities for a brief time. A long, close friendship truly depends on working at the relationship.[14]

Comprehension rating: _____

Summary: _____

_____

_____

_____

_____

Journal Entry

1. How can an understanding of Maslow's theory help you lead a more satisfying life?

_____

_____

_____

_____

_____

_____

_____

_____

_____

_____

2. How can the use of goal questions help you read with better concentration and retention?

_____

_____

_____

_____

_____

_____

_____

_____

_____

_____

_____

_____

7

READING FOR MAIN IDEAS AND LEARNING MORE PREFIXES

In Chapter 7, you will:

1. Preview and read a selection about hypnosis, using goal questions and monitoring strategies.
2. Answer comprehension questions on the selection to check your understanding.
3. Begin work on reading for main ideas by learning to identify paragraph topics and topic sentences.
4. Learn the meanings of 16 additional prefixes.

SELECTION 7
HYPNOSIS

Zick Rubin and Elton B McNeil

Previewing Exercise

Directions.   Preview the article and answer the following questions.

  1. How many sections does the article contain?

  _____

  2. What is the subject of each section?

  _____

  _____

3. How difficult does the selection seem? Why?

_____

_____

Pre-thinking Exercise

1. Have you ever been hypnotized or witnessed someone else being hypnotized? If so, describe what happened.

_____

_____

2. Do you know anyone who has seen a hypnotist to stop smoking or to change another bad habit? If so, what was the experience like? Was it successful?

_____

_____

3. What else have you learned or heard about hypnosis?

_____

_____

4. Would you like to be hypnotized? Why or why not?

_____

_____

While You Read

Directions.   You may have noticed from your preview of Selection 7 that the heading for each section is in the form of a question. Use these questions as goal questions for your reading. At the end of each section, monitor and clarify your comprehension as needed. In the space marked "Notes," write a brief answer to the question expressed in the heading.

Don't look up while you're reading this. There may be someone nearby whose piercing eyes are waiting to catch your attention, hypnotize you, destroy your willpower, and make you a slave. At least, that's what you might believe if you watch too many old movies. The mystery surrounding hypnosis was inevitable, because it can produce so many unusual phenomena. Although there is still some controversy about it, hypnosis can be considered an altered state of consciousness, in which the hypnotized subject can be influenced to behave and to experience things differently than she would in the ordinary waking state. Whereas drugs can induce changes in consciousness chemically, hypnosis is a non-chemically-induced altered state. Naturally you have some questions about this unusual state of consciousness, and we will try to answer a few of them for you.

What Is Hypnosis?

Hypnosis is a state of increased suggestibility (or willingness to comply with another person's directions) that is brought about through the use of certain procedures by another person, the hypnotist. The hypnotist usually begins by asking the person to
15 focus on an object or by telling the person that she is getting sleepy. The point is to get the subject to relax, to use her imagination, to attend closely to what is said, and to stop fighting it. The rest is up to the subject and her willingness to go along with the hypnotist's suggestions.

The hypnotist might then suggest that the subject perform certain behaviors, such
20 as hopping on one foot or singing a song in the style of Elvis Presley. Or the suggestion might be to hallucinate or imagine something that isn't really there, such as a fly buzzing around the subject's head. A subject may be told to forget specific material, such as her boyfriend's name; this type of suggestion, when it works, creates *hypnotic amnesia.* Or the subject may be instructed to perform certain behaviors on a signal
25 after she is back in the waking state; this is termed *posthypnotic suggestion.* For example, the suggestion might be for the subject to stand up whenever the hypnotist says the word *day.* After the subject comes out of the trance she is not aware of this posthypnotic suggestion and is baffled by the fact that she stands up when the hypnotist says, "This sure is a beautiful day."

Notes: _____

_____

_____

Who Can Be Hypnotized?

30 Most people are susceptible to hypnosis to some degree, but some people are much more susceptible than others. Ernest Hilgard and his colleagues developed the Stanford Hypnotic Susceptibility Scale to measure how easily a person can be hypnotized. After a short attempted hypnotic induction, the subject is given a series of suggestions— to sway, to close his eyes, to imagine a buzzing fly, and so on. The more items that the
35 subject "passes"—for example, by swaying when asked to or by grimacing to acknowledge the buzzing fly—the higher his susceptibility score. This score provides a good indication of how susceptible subjects will be to full-fledged hypnotic inductions.

In general, men and women are equally hypnotizable. People who have vivid imaginations and who feel comfortable accepting the commands of others tend to be
40 hypnotized more easily. Susceptibility to hypnosis rises during childhood to a maximum at age 8 to 10, then declines slowly after that. Josephine Hilgard has also found a clear link between children's involvement in imaginative activities such as reading and fantasy play and their later hypnotizability as adults.

Notes: _____

_____

_____

Can Hypnosis Reduce Pain?

There is no question that some people can free themselves from even severe pain
45   through hypnosis. Dental patients, burn victims, women in childbirth, and terminal
cancer patients have all been relieved of pain through hypnosis. One method of studying pain in the laboratory uses the *cold pressor response,* which is the pain experienced when the hand and forearm are placed in circulating ice water. The pain is quite
severe for most people and increases very rapidly over 30 to 45 seconds. But hypno-
50   tized subjects placed in this situation and given suggestions to the effect that the experience is not painful report very little pain. Instead they may describe what they feel
as "a slight tingle" or "like a cold wind blowing on my arm."

While subjects in this situation report very little pain, physiological measures such as heart rate and blood pressure are extremely high. Ernest Hilgard views
55   this phenomenon as a *dissociation,* or separation between different aspects of
consciousness. Hilgard considers pain to be a complex state with at least two sepa-
rable components: the sensory aspect (such as the sensation of extreme cold) and
the emotional aspect (the feeling of suffering that commonly accompanies the
sensation). Hilgard concludes that the hypnotic suggestion primarily affects the
60   emotional component and not the sensory component. This type of dissociation
is very different from the mechanism of pain reduction found with certain pain-
reducing drugs. The drugs appear to act by blocking the transmission of pain signals to the brain, especially to the areas that control thought and emotion. Hypnosis
apparently does not cause this sort of blocking. Instead, the pain information
65   does reach the brain but the emotions that are produced are kept from conscious
awareness.

Notes: _____

_____

_____

_____

How Does Hypnosis Work?

No one really knows how the hypnotic state is produced. As noted above, hypnosis
has not yet been clearly related to physiological or chemical events. This vagueness
has led some researchers to doubt whether a unique condition called the "hypnotic
70   trance" even exists. Theodore X. Barber is the leading advocate of the viewpoint that
it does not. For instance, hypnotized subjects do not exhibit an EEG pattern different
from that found in the ordinary waking state. Barber believes that the "hypnotized"
person is simply someone who is highly motivated to cooperate with the hypnotist's
suggestions and who is good at "playing the role" of hypnotized subject, much as a
75   good stage actor can display a wide range of emotions and behavior when the director calls for it. Barber's research suggests that anything you can do while "hypnotized" you can do in a wide-awake state.

80   Although hypnosis does rely heavily on cooperativeness and role playing, other researchers believe that such hypnotic phenomena as the reduction of severe pain indicate that hypnosis is a special state of consciousness. To help establish this point, Martin Orne has conducted experiments to show that hypnotized subjects are likely to behave quite differently from subjects who are pretending to be hypnotized. In a typical experiment, two hypnotists are involved. The first one hypnotizes one group of subjects and instructs another group of subjects to "simulate" hypno-

85   sis—to act as if they have been hypnotized. A second hypnotist, who does not know which subjects are hypnotized and which are simulators, then gives them various suggestions.

Can we tell the difference between the two groups of subjects? In fact, subjects in the two groups behave quite similarly, but there are also intriguing differences. For

90   example, in one experiment the subjects were told that a helium balloon was tied to a finger on their right hand and that the balloon was pulling their arm up. All the subjects complied by raising their right arms. Suddenly the lights went out in a fake power failure. Infrared videotapes later revealed that in the dark most of the simulators had put their arms down, while the real subjects continued to hold their arms up.

95   These results suggest that being hypnotized is more than simply trying to be a "good subject."

As with the nature of consciousness in general, the nature of hypnosis remains largely uncharted. But there has been a great deal of recent research on hypnosis, and it seems certain that our understanding of this mysterious phenomenon will continue

100   to expand. The same can be said for our understanding of consciousness generally— of attention and fantasy, sleep and dreams, and drug-induced states. From a domain that was not long ago viewed as inappropriate for psychological study, consciousness has become perhaps the most exciting frontier of current psychological research.[1]

Notes: _____

_____

_____

_____

_____

_____

Interest Rating.   Please rate the interest level of Selection 7 on the following 1–5 scale (circle one):

5 — Very interesting

4 — Fairly interesting

3 — Mildly interesting

2 — A little boring

1 — Very boring

Difficulty Rating.   Please indicate how difficult Selection 7 was for you to understand on the following 1–5 scale (circle one):

   5—Very difficult

   4—Fairly difficult

   3—Moderate

   2—Fairly easy

   1—Very easy

Comments: _____

_____

Comprehension Questions

Directions.   For questions 1–5, choose the answer that best completes the statement.
For questions 6–10, write your response in the space provided. Base all answers on
what you read in the selection (you may refer to the selection when you are not sure
of an answer).

_____   1. The passage suggests that:
   a. It is possible to predict which people are easier to hypnotize.
   b. Men are harder to hypnotize than women.
   c. It is not possible to predict which people are easier to hypnotize.
   d. More imaginative children are harder to hypnotize.

_____   2. Hypnotized subjects feel very little pain because:
   a. Pain signals are not transmitted to the brain.
   b. They do not sense the pain.
   c. They are pretending not to feel pain.
   d. Emotions associated with pain do not reach the conscious level.

_____   3. Which researcher is most skeptical (doubtful) about hypnosis?
   a. Hilgard.
   b. Barber.
   c. Orne.
   d. Presley.

_____   4. The experiment with the helium balloon revealed that:
   a. Hypnotic trance does not really exist.
   b. Hypnotized subjects are not merely acting out a role.
   c. Most hypnotized subjects are faking it.
   d. It is not possible to distinguish simulators from those truly
       hypnotized.

_____   5. The author believes that:
   a. There is a lot more to be learned about hypnosis.
   b. Hypnosis is interesting but of little use.
   c. Everyone should be hypnotized.
   d. We will never really understand hypnosis.

6. What is hypnotic amnesia?

   _____

   _____

7. Explain how the cold pressor response is used to study pain.

   _____

   _____

   _____

8. Give an example of a posthypnotic suggestion.

   _____

   _____

9. Explain how psychologists predict which people will be easier to hypnotize.

   _____

   _____

10. Has your opinion about hypnosis been changed by reading this article? Why or why not?

    _____

    _____

    _____

Vocabulary Exercise

Directions. Use the line numbers to locate each of the following words in the passage. Study the context clues and use your own dictionary to choose the definition that best fits the context. Write an accurate definition for each word in the space provided. Write simplified definitions or synonyms whenever possible.

1. inevitable (4) _____

2. induce (8) _____

3. comply (12) _____

4. susceptible (30) _____

5. grimacing (35) _____

6. components (57) _____

7. sensory (57) _____

8. transmission (62) _____

9. vagueness (68) _____

10. unique (69) _____

11. advocate (70) _____

12. simulate (84) _____

Reading for Main Ideas

In Chapter 6, you learned how to use goal questions to direct your reading. Using goal questions is an important comprehension strategy, but it is only a first step. The college reader must look for all the important ideas and information while reading an assignment.

Recognizing main ideas, however, is not always an easy task. One of the most common complaints students make is that they are unable to distinguish the more important ideas from the less important; when reading texts, everything seems important. This makes for a problem when underlining, taking notes, or studying.

Recognizing main ideas is a very practical skill. Remembering the main ideas is usually the bottom line when reading assignments. Given the amount of reading required and the difficulty of the material, it is not realistic to think you will understand everything you read. And, unless you have a photographic memory, you will certainly not remember everything. Recognizing main ideas is the starting point for separating the more important ideas from the less important.

The ability to recognize main ideas has other benefits as well. It helps the reader understand the relationship of ideas within a paragraph and thus makes it easier to remember the important details. Recognizing the main ideas also helps you see how ideas are related from one paragraph to the next. Finally, looking for the main idea is a simple and effective monitoring strategy. You can check your comprehension of a paragraph by seeing if you can explain the main idea.

What Is a Main Idea?

Almost everything you read is organized in paragraphs. You learned in high school that a paragraph is a group of sentences dealing with the same topic. In discussing the topic, the author presents several details—specific ideas or information about the topic. Usually, in expository writing, whose main purpose is to explain ideas and give information (most textbook writing is expository writing), a paragraph develops one general point about the topic. This general point is the paragraph's main idea. When we refer to the main idea of a paragraph, then, we mean the one general point developed by the entire paragraph about the topic. The main idea summarizes, or generalizes, all of the details in the paragraph.

Let's look at an example from Selection 7:

There is no question that some people can free themselves from even severe pain through hypnosis. Dental patients, burn victims, women in childbirth, and terminal cancer patients have all been relieved of pain through hypnosis. One method of studying pain in the laboratory uses the *cold pressor response,* which is the pain experienced when the hand and forearm are placed in circulating ice water. The pain is quite severe for most people and increases very rapidly over 30 to 45 seconds. But hypnotized subjects placed in this situ-

ation and given suggestions to the effect that the experience is not painful report very little pain. Instead they may describe what they feel as "a slight tingle" or "like a cold wind
blowing on my arm."

The *topic* of the paragraph is "relieving pain through hypnosis." The *details* of
the paragraph provide examples of cases where hypnosis was used to relieve pain and
explain a method used for studying pain. The *main idea,* or general point, of the paragraph is "hypnosis can free people of pain."

Let's consider another paragraph from the selection. Read the paragraph below
and answer the questions about topic, main idea, and details that follow it.

No one really knows how the hypnotic state is produced. As noted above, hypnosis has
not yet been clearly related to physiological or chemical events. This vagueness has led
some researchers to doubt whether a unique condition called the "hypnotic trance" even
exists. Theodore X. Barber is the leading advocate of the viewpoint that it does not. For
instance, hypnotized subjects do not exhibit an EEG pattern different from that found in
the ordinary waking state. Barber believes that the "hypnotized" person is simply someone who is highly motivated to cooperate with the hypnotist's suggestions and who is
good at "playing the role" of hypnotized subject, much as a good stage actor can display
a wide range of emotions and behavior when the director calls for it. Barber's research
suggests that anything you can do while "hypnotized" you can do in a wide-awake state.

1. What is the topic of the paragraph?

_____ 2. Which statement best expresses the main idea of the paragraph?
    a. Hypnosis has not yet been clearly related to physiological or chemical
       events.
    b. Hypnotized subjects' EEGs are not different from those found in the
       ordinary waking state.
    c. The hypnotic trance does not exist.
    d. Theodore X. Barber is one of several researchers who believe that the
       hypnotized state is not a special state, but just a kind of role-playing.

_____ 3. The details in this paragraph:
    a. Explain how the hypnotic state is produced.
    b. List several researchers who do not believe in hypnosis.
    c. Explain Barber's beliefs about hypnosis.
    d. Give examples of hypnotized subjects who were only pretending.

Answers

1. The topic of this paragraph might be expressed "doubts about hypnosis."
   (You may have expressed the topic differently but correctly—check with
   your instructor if you are not sure of your answer.)
2. Statement *d* best expresses the main idea. The paragraph states that some
   researchers do not believe that hypnosis is a special state; they believe that
   hypnotized subjects are acting a role. Notice that the whole paragraph
   focuses on this point. Statements *a* and *b* are correct statements but are

details, because they are not what the whole paragraph discusses. Statement *c* is not an accurate statement. The author's point is not that the hypnotic state does not exist but that this is a theory held by some researchers.

3. Statement *c* is the best answer since most of the paragraph is devoted to explaining Barber's theories and the evidence that supports his point of view. Statements *a, b,* and *d* are not accurate statements regarding the details of this paragraph.

Let's analyze one more paragraph from Selection 7. Read the paragraph below and answer the questions about topic, main idea, and details that follow it.

Most people are susceptible to hypnosis to some degree, but some are much more susceptible than others. Ernest Hilgard and his colleagues developed the Stanford Hypnotic Susceptibility Scale to measure how easily a person can be hypnotized. After a short attempted hypnotic induction, the subject is given a series of suggestions—to sway, to close his eyes, to imagine a buzzing fly, and so on. The more items that the subject "passes"—for example, by swaying when asked to or by grimacing to acknowledge the buzzing fly—the higher his susceptibility score. This score provides a good indication of how susceptible subjects will be to full-fledged hypnotic inductions.

1. What is the topic of the paragraph?

2. Which statement best expresses the main idea of the paragraph?
   a. Not everyone can be hypnotized.
   b. People's susceptibility to hypnosis varies, and this susceptibility can be tested.
   c. There are always differences between people.
   d. The Stanford Hypnotic Susceptibility Scale was developed by Ernest Hilgard.

3. The details in this paragraph:
   a. Explain why the Stanford Hypnotic Susceptibility Scale is used.
   b. Explain how the Stanford Hypnotic Susceptibility Scale is used.
   c. Give examples of people who are not easily hypnotized.
   d. Explain when the scale should and should not be used.

Answers

1. The topic of this paragraph is "susceptibility to hypnosis."

2. Statement *b* best expresses the main idea. The whole paragraph is about people's susceptibility to hypnosis and how it can be measured. Statement *a* might be inferred from the paragraph, but is not a point that is discussed or developed in the paragraph. Statement *c* is too broad an answer (not specific enough). Statement *d* is an important detail but not the point developed by the whole paragraph.

3. Statement *b* is the best choice. The details are concerned with how the Stanford Hypnotic Susceptibility Scale is used to predict susceptibility to hypnosis. They do not tell us why the test is used or when it should be used. Statement *c* is incorrect because no examples are provided.

Topic Sentences

It is common in expository writing for the author to express the main point of a paragraph in one or two of the sentences within the paragraph. The sentence that expresses the main idea is called the topic sentence. Most often, the topic sentence is the first sentence of the paragraph. However, it is sometimes placed later in the paragraph, and some paragraphs do not contain a topic sentence at all.

To identify the topic sentence, look for the sentence that seems to summarize or generalize for the rest of the paragraph. In some way, the topic sentence will be supported or developed by every other sentence in the paragraph. It is usually the most general statement in the paragraph.

Look back at the paragraph about hypnosis and pain on pages 124–125. Notice that the first sentence of the paragraph states the main idea, which is then supported and developed by the rest of the paragraph. In sentence 2, the author provides examples of people who have been helped by hypnosis. The rest of the paragraph supports the main idea by explaining how pain is studied in the laboratory and stating that hypnotized subjects don't experience pain under these conditions.

Exercise 7–1. Topic and Topic Sentence

Directions.   This exercise consists of five groups of sentences. Each group was once a paragraph, but the sentences have been rearranged so that they are no longer in their original order. For each group of sentences:

- *Write the topic.* Tell who or what the paragraph is about in one word or a short phrase.
- *Write the number of the topic sentence*—the sentence that states the main idea for the group.

Example

1. Most important of all, friendships can help us to grow and develop as individuals.
2. The most basic of these is survival—friendships provide mutual protection.
3. Friendships serve many human needs.
4. In addition to that need, friendships also help us to avoid loneliness, gain approval for ourselves, and increase our certainty about our own behavior.[2]

Topic: _Friendship_____

Topic sentence: _3_____

1.
    1. Notice that two co-workers sit closer to each other than do the employee and the "boss."
    2. You will discover that, the closer an individual chooses to sit to another, the more comfortable that person feels about the relationship.
    3. In business, the more confident a person is, the closer he or she will decide, even subconsciously, to sit to a partner or associate.[3]

Topic: _sitting close (or: how close people sit)_

Topic sentence: _2_

2.
    1. It is an issue that captured the attention of the president and has been debated in the highest court of our land and in Congress.
    2. It is the most frequent cause of disputes between spouses.
    3. Strict discipline, including the right (and duty) of parents to punish their children, is a critical plank in the platform of the Moral Majority and so-called family life advocates.
    4. Discipline has recently surfaced as a very important issue in our nation—in fact, throughout the world.
    5. And it has shown up in opinion polls as the number one concern of parents.
    6. It is the subject of spirited debates in PTA chapters, at school faculty meetings and within boards of education.[4]

Topic: _Discipline_

Topic sentence: _4_

3.
    1. More than eight million cars take to L.A.'s roads each day.
    2. Los Angeles is the smog capital of the nation.
    3. Nearly 60% of the city center is devoted to freeways, streets and parking lots.
    4. According to the American Lung Association, airborne particulates (air pollution) are responsible for more than 1,600 deaths in the L.A. basin each year.
    5. In 1989, the city experienced 213 days in which the Pollution Standards Index rose above 100.[5]

Topic: _smog in L.A_

Topic sentence: _2_

4.
    1. In my relationships with people I have found that it does not help, in the long run, to act as though I were something that I am not.
    2. It does not help to act calm and pleasant, when actually I am angry and critical.
    3. It does not help to act as though I know the answers when I do not.
    4. It does not help for me to act as though I were full of assurance, if actually I am frightened and unsure.[6]

Topic: _____

Topic sentence: _1_

5.   1. In some cases, if the loss of sleep continues, the person begins to develop marked paranoid symptoms.

2. He also feels lightheaded and often hears a buzzing sound in his ears.

3. After three nights without sleep, the average person complains of itchy eyes and begins to see double.

4. He is unable to count past 15, and cannot concentrate on any subject for longer than a few minutes.

5. Actual sleep deprivation, where a person loses more than one night's sleep, does tend to affect the organism, impairing several faculties of the body.[7]

Topic: _sleep deprivation_

Topic sentence: _____5_____

Locating the Topic Sentence

The topic sentence is a great aid to the alert reader. It provides a clear and recognizable statement of the writer's main point and helps the reader know what to look for as he continues reading.

The topic sentence is most often the first sentence of the paragraph. The rest of the paragraph provides details to support, explain, or develop the main point. It is easiest for the reader to identify the topic sentence when it is at the beginning of the paragraph.

Example 1

Although hypnosis does rely on cooperativeness and role playing, other researchers believe that such hypnotic phenomena as the reduction of severe pain indicate that hypnosis is a special state of consciousness. To help establish this point, Martin Orne has conducted experiments to show that hypnotized subjects are likely to behave quite differently from subjects who are pretending to be hypnotized. In a typical experiment, two hypnotists are involved. The first one hypnotizes one group of subjects and instructs another group of subjects to "simulate" hypnosis—to act as if they have been hypnotized. A second hypnotist, who does not know which subjects are hypnotized and which are simulators, then gives them various suggestions.

Sometimes the main idea is stated at the end of the paragraph. The details are provided first, leading up to a conclusion or generalization in the last sentence.

Example 2

Can we tell the difference between the two groups of subjects? In fact, subjects in the two groups behave quite similarly, but there are also intriguing differences. For example, in one experiment the subjects were told that a helium balloon was tied to a finger on their right hand and that the balloon was pulling their arm up. All the subjects complied by raising their right arms. Suddenly the lights went out in a fake power failure. Infrared videotapes later revealed that in the dark most of the simulators had put their arms down, while the real subjects continued to hold their arms up. These results suggest that being hypnotized is more than simply trying to be a "good subject."

Occasionally, the main idea may be stated in one of the sentences in the middle of the paragraph. This makes the main idea more difficult for the reader to detect. The alert reader, however, may notice a shift in a middle sentence to a general point, often signaled by a transition word or phrase (e.g., "however," "although").

Example 3

Don't look up while you're reading this. There may be someone nearby whose piercing eyes are waiting to catch your attention, hypnotize you, destroy your willpower, and make you a slave. At least, that's what you might believe if you watch too many old movies. The mystery surrounding hypnosis was inevitable, because it can produce so many unusual phenomena. Although there is still some controversy about it, hypnosis can be considered an altered state of consciousness, in which the hypnotized subject can be influenced to behave and to experience things differently than she would in the ordinary waking state. Whereas drugs can induce changes in consciousness chemically, hypnosis is a non-chemically-induced altered state. Naturally you have some questions about this unusual state of consciousness, and we will try to answer a few of them for you.

Exercise 7–2. Locating the Topic Sentence

Directions.

1. Read each paragraph carefully, looking up any unfamiliar words.
2. Under each paragraph, write the topic, in one word or a short phrase.
3. Then, return to the paragraph to underline the topic sentence.

1. Hypnosis is a state of increased suggestibility (or willingness to comply with another person's directions) that is brought about through the use of certain procedures by another person, the hypnotist. The hypnotist usually begins by asking the person to focus on an object or by telling the person that she is getting sleepy. The point is to get the subject to relax, to use her imagination, to attend closely to what is said, and to stop fighting it. The rest is up to the subject and her willingness to go along with the hypnotist's suggestions.[8]

   Topic: _Hypnosis_

2. When casual users were asked about their current reasons for marijuana use, two answers—"to feel good" and "to have a good time"—prevailed overwhelmingly. In contrast, while regular marijuana users all continued to cite these two reasons, large numbers additionally responded, "to get away from my problems" (37%) or "to help me get through the day" (29%). Using marijuana as a means of escaping or coping with problems thus strongly distinguishes the regular daily user of marijuana from the casual user.[9]

   Topic: _marijuana   ues_

3. After physiological needs are satisfied, the individual seeks to satisfy safety needs, according to Maslow. Safety needs include freedom from physical harm, such as the need

to be protected from injury, illness, and physical abuse. The adult who was a battered child will probably have difficulty in progressing past this level. Adults must provide children with feelings of safety and security. Another example of a physical safety need might be the need for decent housing.[10]

Topic: _____ *physical safety needing*

4. Some social scientists believe that society still operates more smoothly when the sexes specialize in different roles—the male as breadwinner and link between the family and the outside world; the female as the source of affection and support within the family. Many observers, however, have concluded that there is no longer any need in our modern society for men to be masculine and women to be feminine. They point out that physical strength is no longer important. There are very few jobs in the industrial system that cannot be performed as well by a woman as by a man. In a world of nuclear weapons, aggressiveness of the kind that can lead to warfare is disastrous. The population explosion has turned large families into a liability instead of an asset—and women, in the age of birth control, have fewer children and more years to live after the last of them has gone to school or left home. Because they are not necessarily immobilized by children and are free to enter the work force, they're no longer dependent on men to support them.[11]

Topic: _____

5. Newborn babies sleep an average of 17–18 hours a day. Adolescents sleep approximately 10–11 hours in a 24-hour period, while young adults spend an average of eight hours a night sleeping. Elderly people, on the other hand, seldom sleep more than six hours during the night. This seems to indicate that we require less sleep as we grow older, but still, on the whole, we spend approximately one-third of our lives sleeping.[12]

Topic: _____ *Sleeping required*

Exercise 7–3. Paragraph Writing

Directions.   Write two different paragraphs about the same topic. In your first paragraph, place the topic sentence at the beginning. In your second paragraph, place the topic sentence at the end. You may write about one of the following suggested topics or any other topic you wish. Each of your paragraphs should contain four to six sentences.

Suggested Topics

Your current job.
Problems with the US economy.
The police.
One of your high school teachers.

1. _____

_____

_____

_____

_____

_____

_____

_____

_____

_____

2. _____

_____

_____

_____

_____

_____

_____

_____

_____

Prefixes Continued

In Chapter 6, you learned the meaning of 14 important negative and number prefixes. We will now review 16 other commonly used prefixes.

Directions. Study the prefixes, examples, and comments in the boxes and complete each exercise as you come to it.

Common Prefixes

15. in, il, ir, im	in, into	inhale, illustrate, irritate, import

Additional Comments. Remember that you have seen this prefix before! Do you remember its other meaning?

| 16. ex, e | out | exhale, export, emit, eject |

Additional Comments. Note that the prefix *ex* has a second meaning with which you are probably familiar. In words like *ex-president* and *ex-husband, ex* means former.

Exercise 7–4

Directions

1. List three words beginning with the prefix *in* or *im* where the prefix means in or into.

2. List three words beginning with the prefix *ex* or *e* where the prefix means out.

| 17. pre | before | predict, prepare |
| 18. post | after | postwar, postpone |

Additional Comments. Pre and *post* are opposites. A *pretest* is given before instruction begins; a *posttest* is given after instruction is completed. Do not confuse the prefix *post* with the word *post* (as in post office).

Exercise 7–5

Directions. List three words beginning with the prefix *pre.* Can you think of any words that begin with the prefix *post?*

| 19. inter | between | intercept |
| 20. intra | within | intrastate |

Additional Comments. Inter and *intra* are opposites. Interstate commerce occurs between two or more different states. Intrastate commerce occurs within one and the same state. *Inter* is a much more commonly used prefix than *intra.*

Exercise 7–6

Directions. Complete each sentence by filling in the prefix or the meaning of the prefix as appropriate.

1. Travel from one city to another is _____*city* travel; travel within the same city is _____*city* travel.

2. To intervene in an argument is to come _____ the people arguing.

3. Intramural sports are played by teams that are all _____ the same school.

4. An interim is a time period _____ events.

5. Tubes that go into, or within, a vein, to supply medication or nutrition are called _____*venous*.

21.	bene	good, well	benefit
22.	male, mal	bad	malevolent, malodorous

Additional Comments. *Bene* and *male* are opposites. A *benefactor* is someone who does something good for you; a *malefactor* is someone who does you harm.

Exercise 7–7

Directions. Complete each sentence by filling in the prefix or the meaning of the prefix as appropriate (use prefixes 15–22).

1. A _____*volent* person is kindly, or goodwilled. A person who is ill willed is _____*volent*.

2. A premonition is a feeling about something _____ it happens.

3. If you don't pay your rent you may get _____*victed* from your home.

4. Postwar elections occur _____ a war.

5. In areas where there is not enough rainfall, the soil must be _____*rigated*.

6. Intracellular activities occur _____ a cell.

7. The time period between semesters is an _____*session*.

8. A benediction is a blessing; a _____*diction* is a curse.

9. A person moving into a country is an _____*migrant.* An emigrant is a person moving _____ of a country.

10. Malicious remarks are remarks that say _____ things about someone.

23.	anti	against	antiwar, antidote

Exercise 7–8

Directions.   List three words beginning with the prefix *anti.*

_____

24.	con, com, col, cor, co	with, together	connect, company, colleague, correspond, co-owner

Additional Comments.   The prefix *con* is a very common one. It changes to *col* when the root begins with *l, cor* when the root begins with *r,* and *com* when the root begins with *m, b,* or *p. Co* is used when the root begins with a vowel (cooperate), *h* (cohabit) or when a hyphen is used (co-owner).

Exercise 7–9

Directions.   List any five words that use the prefix *con, com, cor, col,* or *co,* where the prefix means with or together.

_____

25.	de	1. down, away from 2. reverses the action	1. descend, deprive 2. deemphasize

Additional Comments.   To *descend* is to go down, to deprive is to take away, to *deemphasize* is the reverse of *emphasize.*

Exercise 7–10

Directions. List five words that begin with the prefix *de*. Next to each word, write which meaning of the prefix is correct for that word.

_____

_____

26. re

        1. again   1. repeat

        2. back   2. reverse

Additional Comments.   *Re* has two different meanings. In words like *repeat* and *rearrange, re* means again. In words like *reverse* and *retract, re* means back (to retract a statement, for example, is to take back what you've said.)

Exercise 7–11

Directions. List five words that begin with the prefix *re*. Next to each word, indicate whether the prefix means again or back in that word.

_____

_____

27. sub   under   submarine

Exercise 7–12

Directions. List three words that begin with the prefix *sub*.

_____

28. super

        1. above, over   1. supervise

        2. greater, extra   2. superfluous

Additional Comments.   The prefix *super* is not always complimentary. In some words, it suggests too much of something. For example, *superfluous* means "using too many words" or "more than is necessary."

Journal Entry

1. If you wanted to stop smoking or change another bad habit, would you try hypnosis? Why or why not?

_____

_____

_____

_____

_____

_____

_____

_____

_____

_____

_____

2. How effective were the headings in Selection 7 as goal questions? Would you have been better off making up your own questions? Explain your answer.

_____

_____

_____

_____

_____

_____

_____

_____

_____

_____

_____

8

MORE ON READING FOR MAIN IDEAS AND LEARNING ROOTS

In Chapter 8, you will:

1. Preview and read a selection about work, using goal questions and monitoring strategies, and looking for main ideas.
2. Answer comprehension questions on the selection to check your understanding.
3. Learn to diagram a paragraph's main idea and details.
4. Learn to determine the main idea of an implied paragraph.
5. Learn the meaning of 20 common word roots.

SELECTION 8
WORK AND PERSONAL ADJUSTMENT

Valerian Derlega and Louis H Janda

Previewing Exercise

Directions. Preview the selection and answer the following questions.

1. How many sections does the passage contain?

   _____

2. What are some of the subjects that will be discussed?

   _____

   _____

   _____

3. What will be most important to learn and remember from this passage?

_____

_____

_____

Pre-thinking Exercise

1. Discuss the pros and cons of your current job, or a job you've held recently.

_____

_____

_____

_____

2. In your opinion, what are the most important considerations when deciding on a career?

_____

_____

_____

_____

While You Read

1. Monitor and clarify your comprehension as necessary. Write a goal question for each heading (you can write your questions in the margin). Look for the main ideas as you go from paragraph to paragraph.

2. When you finish each section, in the space marked "Notes," answer your goal question and briefly summarize any other important points you found in that section.

A person's work is an important factor in determining personal identity and satisfaction in life. Personal worth and self-identity are heavily influenced by the opportunity to work and by the type of work one chooses to do. Work experiences, then, are closely related to personal adjustment.

Decisions about a Career

5   Consider the case of Mike:

In the first month of college, Mike had an interview with an academic counselor. The counselor asked Mike what he wanted to major in. Mike said he wasn't sure but he thought that the physical sciences sounded interesting. The counselor said that they had to put something down on the advisement form and it was never too early to con-

10 sider a major. The counselor suggested trying chemistry and so Mike went along. He was assigned to an advisor in the chemistry department who explained the requirements for majoring in chemistry. The advisor indicated what courses Mike should start taking.

In Mike's junior year, he came to the counseling center because he was feeling
15 depressed and uninterested in his courses. Though he had been taking chemistry courses for almost 3 years, chemistry did not interest him and he had difficulty in it. He took an interest inventory and it revealed that his interests were like those of students majoring in business administration. He is wondering now why he spent so much time majoring in a field that held so little interest for him.

20 Making a decision about a career is one of the most important and difficult tasks confronting individuals. For many, this decision seems almost ominous. Many, particularly students preparing for a career, are afraid of being trapped in a vocation from which they might not be able to escape. A career choice is to them a "moment of truth" that will determine how they will live for most of their adult lives. For young people,
25 and persons who are in the midst of a major life change (such as women whose children are almost grown up), this decision poses considerable anxiety and stress. Faced by social pressures to make a choice, they feel it is important that the decision be made carefully. In addition, college graduates, especially those with majors in the humanities, have found that a college degree no longer assures them of a job in their chosen
30 field. Competition is fierce for the new job openings available, and many have to take unskilled jobs just to make a living.

Along with thinking about what one might be best suited for, a person must also consider how important needs may be satisfied by an occupation. The following points, developed by psychologist David Matteson, illustrate important personal con-
35 siderations in selecting a career:

1. What is the relationship between my own needs and the needs of others? How much do I owe to each?
2. How much security do I demand in life? How much creative insecurity can I tolerate or do I desire?
40 3. What level of material goods provides a base from which I can function well?
4. What kinds of rewards do I need? Am I rewarded by prestige through things, prestige through status, aesthetic experience, intimate personal experience, the possession of power, or others?

Various measures of vocational interest have been developed to determine the
45 relationship between personal goals and professional choice. These are not tests of ability but of interest. Such tests assume that persons in different occupations differ in the kinds of activities or interests they prefer.

Though vocational interest tests may have some value in helping individuals choose a career, they also have drawbacks. They depend on individuals' guesses and
50 fantasies of what they think they might like to do. Often these preferences are not based on realistic experiences or expectations of an occupational role. It may sound glamorous to be a lawyer or a biologist, but young people may not realize the tedious aspects of education and training required for these occupations.

Perhaps more useful than any test would be the chance to sample different job
55   experiences so that an occupation is not chosen without some concrete knowledge.
Many college students, for instance, have been frustrated by educational experiences
that confront them with books and ideas but very little actual involvement in meaningful work experiences. Education has frequently been separated from the jobs for
which individuals are being prepared. Some students drop out for a while in order to
60   obtain everyday experiences in the world of work. A student wrote this note indicating his frustration:

> Here I am taking all these courses that are supposed to teach me all I need to know about
> a profession. And these courses are also supposed to introduce me to new ideas, to think
> logically, to be rational and deliberate. But it's all so theoretical. I can't see how the
65 > courses are related to real life.
>   I'm thinking of dropping out of college for a while—maybe a semester or for a year.
> If I work for a while, maybe I'll figure out what kind of ideas I want to study so I can be
> more prepared.

Individuals should have a wide range of work experiences in order to make a
70   decision about a career. Vocational preparation should combine project interests with
actual practice in different fields. College-level courses, on the other hand, may also
provide useful training for a satisfying life. Persons are taught to think logically in
solving problems and are exposed to experiences (including courses in philosophy,
literature, and history) that help them identify and develop their attitudes toward var-
75   ious careers.

Notes: _____

_____

_____

_____

Sources of Job Satisfaction

There are a number of assumptions about what satisfies workers. At one extreme,
workers may be viewed as "economic creatures" who are interested in earning
money, having comfortable working conditions and putting in little effort. At the
other extreme, workers may be viewed as self-actualizers who are interested in find-
80   ing personal fulfillment on the job. A more accurate view would be to describe workers as having both economic and noneconomic goals.

The results of a national survey of workers identified five conditions as being
important in evaluating job satisfaction.

1. *Resources.* Workers feel they should have the resources available, such as
85   help and equipment, to perform their jobs well. Typical questionnaire items from the
survey included "I receive enough help and equipment to get the job done." "My
responsibilities are clearly defined." "My supervisor is competent in doing his job."

2. *Financial reward.* This includes pay, job security, and fringe benefits. Typical items included "The pay is good." "The job security is good." "My fringe bene-
90   fits are good."

3. *Challenge.* This condition reflects the workers' concern for meaningful work. Typical items included "The work is interesting." "I am given a chance to do things I do best." "I have an opportunity to develop my special abilities."

95 4. *Relations with coworkers.* Workers desire friendship and helpfulness among coworkers. Typical items included "My coworkers are friendly and helpful." "I am given a lot of chances to make friends."

5. *Comfort.* This represents workers' interest in a relatively problem-free job and in physical comforts. Typical items included "The hours are good." "Travel to and from work is convenient." "Physical surroundings are pleasant." "I am free from

100 conflicting demands that other people make of me." "I am not asked to do excessive amounts of work."

Each of these factors is important. Workers want to be adequately paid for their jobs, and they want adequate resources to do the job well. There is a tendency to rate a challenging job (which requires considerable effort) as more important than a com-

105 fortable job. American workers seem to want financially rewarding work that will also be challenging.

There are, however, some social-class differences in the importance of these factors to workers. White-collar workers rate the challenge of a job as more important. Blue-collar workers rate financial rewards as most important. Adequacy of resources

110 to do a job is second in importance for both groups. Comfort is rated lowest in importance by both white- and blue-collar workers.

Notes: _____

_____

_____

_____

Sources of Job Dissatisfaction

Though most Americans have jobs, many white-collar and blue-collar workers report considerable dissatisfaction. Many persons identify themselves not in terms of their employment, but by how they spend their time outside of the office or factory. Many

115 seem resigned to their jobs, spending the time at work waiting for the next holiday, 3-day weekend, or vacation period. As an indication of this dissatisfaction, the number of absentee workers in automobile factories is particularly high. On an ordinary day in such factories, about 5 percent of the work force may be absent. On a typical Monday or Friday, the absentee rate may jump to about 15 percent.

120 Many are not satisfied with their jobs, but the problem can be much worse for the majority of American youth who have little or no college education. College students frequently choose educational training that will prepare them for professional or managerial careers. These professions can provide college graduates with economic security, as well as an opportunity for self-fulfillment. Those who do not go to

125 college, who are in the majority, may have a narrower choice of jobs. These persons often have to take jobs with good pay at the start but little opportunity for advancement or psychological growth. Individuals in "dead end" jobs may become more interested in fringe benefits—such as shorter working hours, longer vacations, early

retirement, and more leisure time. Work may lose much of its meaning for individu-
130 als who cannot find satisfaction on the job. Often, these persons make a sharp distinction between work and the rest of life.

Notes: _____

_____

_____

_____

Unemployment and Mental Health

Research data show a relationship between joblessness and a variety of mental-health
problems. Unemployed persons not only don't get paid, but they pay as well. Joblessness has been associated with frequency of suicides, mental hospital admission,
135 deaths from cirrhosis of the liver (due to alcoholism), and death due to cardiovascular and kidney disease.

Between 1922 and 1968, whenever joblessness increased, admissions to mental
hospitals also increased. This suggests that economic problems may lead to increased
rates of mental illness. Economic problems (such as unemployment and inflation)
140 have their greatest effect on middle-aged persons. Men between 35 and 54 are most
vulnerable psychologically to an economic slump. Women in the age group between
25 and 44 are also vulnerable. These persons are in their peak period for earnings and
for providing for their families. Thus, when such persons lose their jobs, they are
placed under great psychological stress.
145 Joblessness may produce emotional problems, as we have seen. But the reverse
may also be true. In other words, persons who have emotional problems may be unable
to cope and therefore may lose their jobs repeatedly until they remain unemployed.

Notes: _____

_____

_____

_____

Computers and the Workplace

Computer technology is influencing every aspect of life, and the computer is becoming a standard feature in many large and small organizations. In the past, familiarity
150 with computers was required only for certain technical positions, but every one of us
will probably need to have some knowledge of computers in the future.

The use of computers will have an enormous impact on working conditions, both
for low-level clerks and high-level executives. Unfortunately, the computer can
sometimes be a mixed blessing. Word processors, for instance, are replacing type-
155 writers in secretarial pools. Word processors can produce miracles with written texts

that require a good deal of revision, editing, and copying, but they also can produce boredom and alienation for operators who may spend the whole day doing nothing but typing. These impersonal working conditions can create enormous stress, causing worker alienation and absenteeism. Organizations will have to consider carefully
160   the consequences for people that occur from computerizing the workplace. Computer systems will have to be designed to produce interesting and meaningful work, which would help guarantee high performance from workers.

Notes: _____

_____

_____

_____

Improving the Quality of Work

For most of us, our identities and degree of life satisfaction are linked to the extent that career choices fulfill personal goals. To help persons fulfill such goals, a number of
165   programs have been developed to improve job satisfaction. Some programs have emphasized the suitability between workers and jobs. For instance, information about job openings and the specific skills, interests, and educations of persons seeking employment can be fed into a computer. This information can then be distributed to various community agencies and offices in a city. Other programs combine counseling
170   and on-the-job training, so that persons have a realistic view of their job opportunities.
       Many efforts to make work more meaningful are based on the idea of giving workers more responsibility and control over working conditions. According to this view, job reform involves treating workers as unique human beings rather than as impersonal objects or machines. When workers take part in deciding the nature of
175   working conditions, methods of doing the job, and even their salaries, this involvement can have beneficial effects both for workers and management.[1]

Notes: _____

_____

_____

_____

Interest Rating.   Please rate the interest level of Selection 8 on the following 1–5 scale (circle one):

   5—Very interesting
   4—Fairly interesting
   3—Mildly interesting
   2—A little boring
   1—Very boring

Difficulty Rating.   Please indicate how difficult Selection 8 was for you to under-stand on the following 1–5 scale (circle one):

>   5 — Very difficult
>
>   4 — Fairly difficult
>
>   3 — Moderate
>
>   2 — Fairly easy
>
>   1 — Very easy

Comments: _____

_____

Comprehension Questions

Directions.   For question 1, return to the passage to mark the topic sentences as indicated. For questions 2–6, choose the answer that best completes the statement. For questions 7–10, write your response in the space provided. Base all answers on what you read in the passage (you may refer to the selection when you are not sure of an answer).

_____   1. Underline the topic sentence in each of the following paragraphs:
   a. P. 147, last paragraph (lines 48–53).
   b. P. 149, fifth paragraph (lines 107–111).
   c. P. 150, second paragraph (lines 137–144).
   d. P. 150, last paragraph (lines 152–162).
   e. P. 151, first paragraph (lines 163–170).

_____   2. The point of Mike's story is that:
   a. Mike's parents and teachers should have advised him better about a career decision.
   b. Students should know what they want to major in when they start college.
   c. Colleges should have better advising systems.
   d. Choosing a career direction is important but difficult.

_____   3. The main point of the section, "Sources of Job Satisfaction," on pages 148 to 149 is that:
   a. Social class differences affect job satisfaction.
   b. Pay and job security are most important.
   c. A variety of factors influence job satisfaction.
   d. Workers may be viewed as self-actualizers who are interested in find-ing personal fulfillment on the job.

_____   4. The author feels that:
   a. Everyone should take a vocational interest test.
   b. It is important to have a variety of job experiences.
   c. Vocational interest tests are a waste of time.
   d. Students should drop out of school to gain job experience.

_____ 5. Which is *not* true of programs intended to improve the quality of work?

    a. They often aim to give workers more control and responsibility.

    b. They are costly for employers.

    c. They match employees' skills and interests with job openings.

    d. They may involve counseling and on-the-job training.

_____ 6. The authors believe that:

    a. Job satisfaction is important to most people.

    b. It is impossible to avoid job dissatisfaction.

    c. Pay is the most important factor to job satisfaction.

    d. A knowledge of computers is essential to job satisfaction.

    7. List the five factors identified as important to job satisfaction.

    _____

    _____

    8. Of the four personal considerations listed on page 147, which seems most important to you? Why?

    _____

    _____

    9. According to the last paragraph on page 149 (lines 120–131), why are individuals who have not gone to college more likely to experience job dissatisfaction?

    _____

    _____

    10. The author states that "college courses . . . provide useful training for a satisfying life." Do you agree with this statement? Why or why not?

    _____

    _____

    _____

Vocabulary Exercise

Directions. Use the line numbers to locate each of the following words in the passage. Study the context clues and use your own dictionary to choose the definition that best fits the context. Write an accurate definition for each word in the space provided. Write simplified definitions or synonyms whenever possible.

    1. ominous (21) _____

    2. humanities (28) _____

    3. prestige (41) _____

4. aesthetic (42) _____

5. tedious (52) _____

6. white-collar (108) _____

7. blue-collar (109) _____

8. data (132) _____

9. cardiovascular (135) _____

10. vulnerable (141) _____

11. alienation (157) _____

12. suitability (166) _____

Main Ideas and Details

In Chapter 7, you learned that the main idea of a paragraph is the one general point developed by the whole paragraph and that the main idea is often stated in a topic sentence within the paragraph. The rest of the paragraph consists of details that support and develop the main idea (see Figure 8–1).

In some paragraphs, there are two levels of details. Major details directly support the main idea. Minor details usually expand on the major details by explaining them further or giving examples (see Figure 8–2).

You should not make a habit of ignoring details or assume they are unimportant. On the contrary, some details may be as important to learn and remember as the main idea. You must use your judgment to determine which details are most significant. Knowing your goals for reading an assignment will help you determine which details to remember. Good goal questions can be very helpful in this regard.

Example 1. Let's look at an example. Read the following paragraph from Selection 8:

> Though vocational interest tests may have some value in helping individuals choose a career, they also have drawbacks. They depend on individuals' guesses and fantasies of what they think they might like to do. Often these preferences are not based on realistic experiences or expectations of an occupational role. It may sound glamorous to be a lawyer or a biologist, but young people may not realize the tedious aspects of education and training required for these occupations.

Notice that in the above paragraph, the main idea is stated in the first sentence, which tells us that vocational interest tests have drawbacks. Next, we want to learn from the paragraph what those drawbacks are. If we were to raise a goal question after reading the first sentence, it might be "What are some of the drawbacks of vocational interest tests?" Which sentences answer the question?

FIGURE 8–1
Main Ideas and Details

FIGURE 8–2
Major and Minor Details

FIGURE 8–3
Paragraph Diagram— Example 1

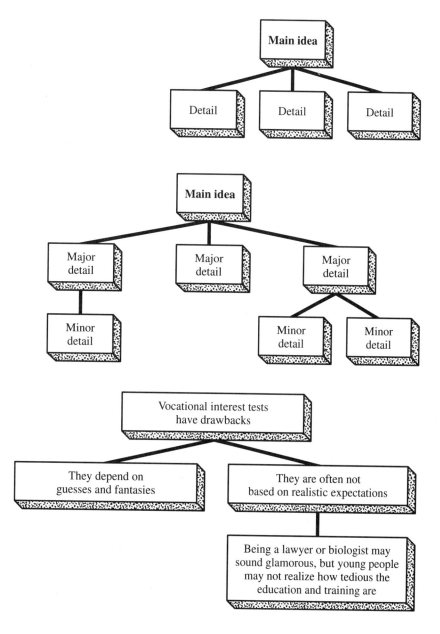

The second and third sentences explain the drawbacks—that the tests may depend on guesses or wishes, and that these preferences are not based on real experience and realistic expectations. So we consider sentences 2 and 3 as expressing the major details of the paragraph. Sentence 4, on the other hand, expresses a minor detail, in that it provides us with an example (see Figure 8–3).

Example 2.   Let's look at another paragraph:

> Between 1922 and 1968, whenever joblessness increased, admissions to mental hospitals also increased. This suggests that economic problems may lead to increased rates of mental illness. Economic problems (such as unemployment and inflation) have their greatest effect on middle-aged persons. Men between 35 and 54 are most vulnerable psychologically to an economic slump. Women in the age group between 25 and 44 are also vulnerable. These persons are in their peak period for earnings and for providing for their families. Thus, when such persons lose their jobs, they are placed under great psychological stress.

The main idea is expressed in the second sentence of the paragraph—that economic problems may lead to mental problems. Which details are most important to remember?

_____

_____

Although we probably would not need to remember the dates, we might regard the first sentence as an important detail in that it provides direct support (evidence) for the main idea. The most important detail in the paragraph is stated in sentence 3, which tells us that middle-aged people are most affected by economic problems. Notice that the rest of the paragraph expands on this point. Thus, we can consider sentences 4, 5, and 6 as minor details, because they further explain the point made in sentence 3 (see Figure 8–4).

FIGURE 8–4
Paragraph Diagram—Example 2

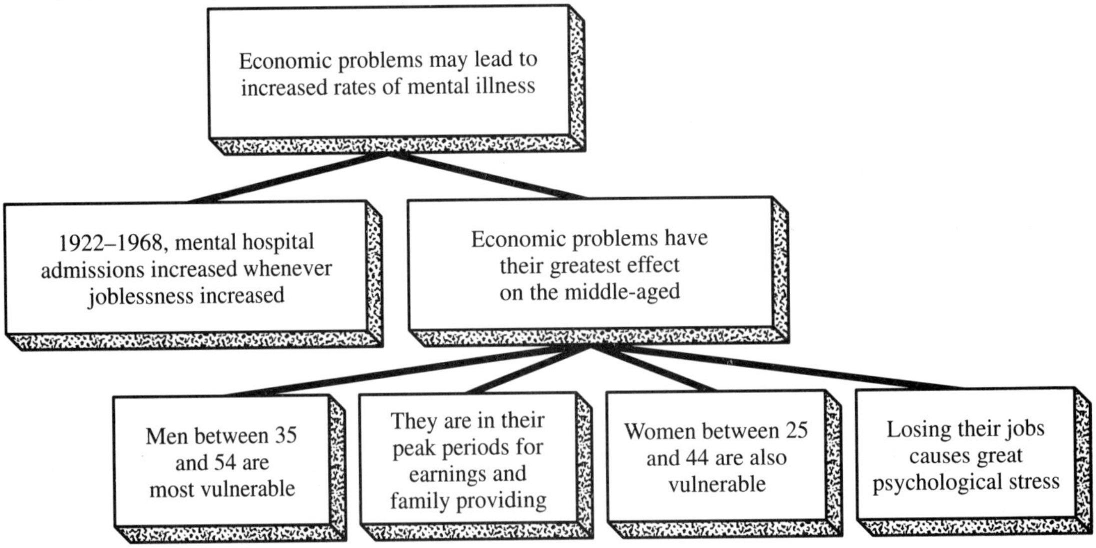

Exercise 8–1. Main Ideas and Details

Directions. After reading each paragraph, complete the paragraph diagram by inserting the main idea, major details, and minor details in the appropriate boxes.

1. A sociologist who made a large-scale study of housewives in the Chicage area found that many of them regarded their roles as "self-expressive and creative"—a chance to build a richer and more varied way of life than they could attain in most jobs available in the business world. They enjoyed the freedom and challenge of being their own bosses. They saw their relationships with their husbands as a matter not of domination and submission but of developing a deep intimacy "suited to the unique needs of both personalities." They found motherhood to be a stimulating challenge demanding skill, creativity, and leadership.[2]

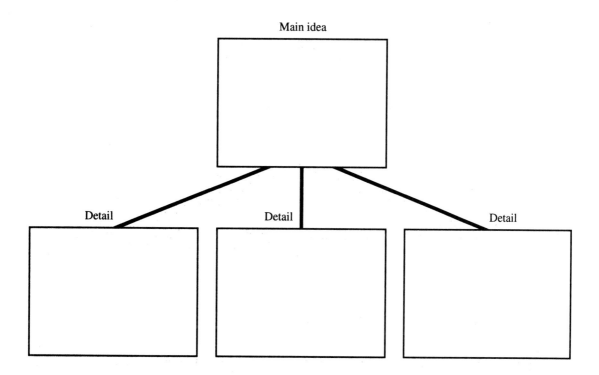

2. Though most Americans have jobs, many white-collar and blue-collar workers report considerable dissatisfaction. Many persons identify themselves not in terms of their employment, but by how they spend their time outside of the office or factory. Many seem resigned to their jobs, spending the time at work waiting for the next holiday, 3-day weekend, or vacation period. As an indication of this dissatisfaction, the number of absentee workers in automobile factories is particularly high. On an ordinary day in such factories, about 5 percent of the work force may be absent. On a typical Monday or Friday, the absentee rate may jump to about 15 percent.[3]

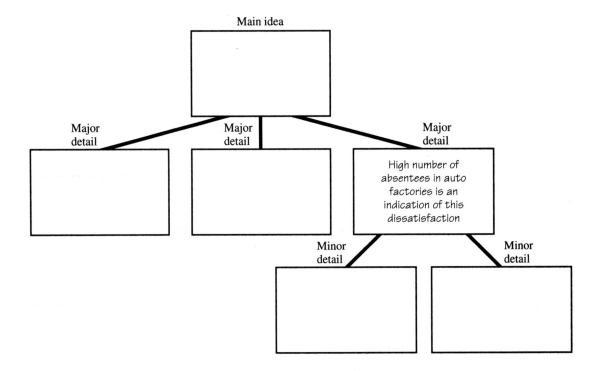

Main idea

Major detail

Major detail

Major detail

High number of absentees in auto factories is an indication of this dissatisfaction

Minor detail

Minor detail

3. For most consumers, price is always an important consideration. So, too, is the quality of the product—the consumer wants to know that she is buying a well-made product which will last. The attractiveness of the product may also play a part in the consumer's decision. In short, a variety of factors influence the consumer's decision to buy, perhaps even on the simplest purchase.

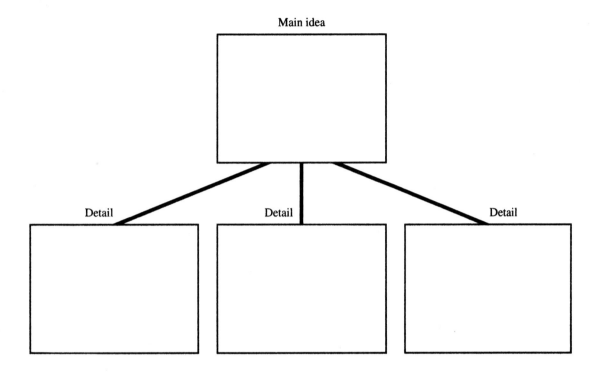

4. During the decade of the 1960s, a vast civil rights movement emerged, with many competing factions and strategies for change. The Southern Christian Leadership Conference (SCLC), founded by Dr. Martin Luther King, Jr., used tactics of nonviolent civil disobedience to oppose segregation. The National Association for the Advancement of Colored People (NAACP) favored use of the courts to press for legal equality for blacks. But many younger black leaders, most notably Malcom X, turned toward an ideology of black power. Proponents of black power rejected the goal of assimilation into white, middle-class society. They defended the beauty and dignity of black and African cultures and supported the creation of black-controlled political and economic institutions.[4]

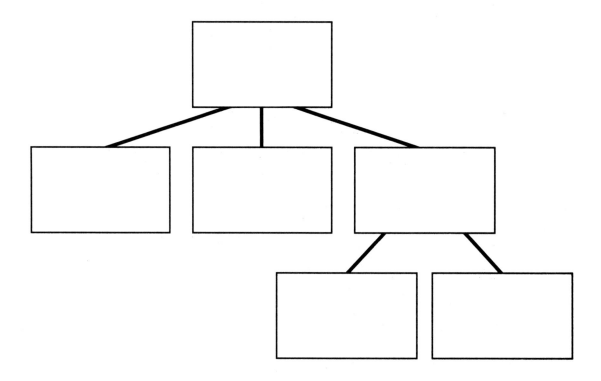

5. Making a decision about a career is one of the most important and difficult tasks confronting individuals. For many, this decision seems almost ominous. Many, particularly students preparing for a career, are afraid of being trapped in a vocation from which they might not be able to escape. A career choice is to them a "moment of truth" that will determine how they will live for most of their adult lives. For young people, and persons who are in the midst of a major life change (such as women whose children are almost grown up), this decision poses considerable anxiety and stress. Faced by social pressures to make a choice, they feel it is important that the decision be made carefully. In addition, college graduates, especially those with majors in the humanities, have found that a college degree no longer assures them of a job in their chosen field. Competition is fierce for the new job openings available, and many have to take unskilled jobs just to make a living.[5]

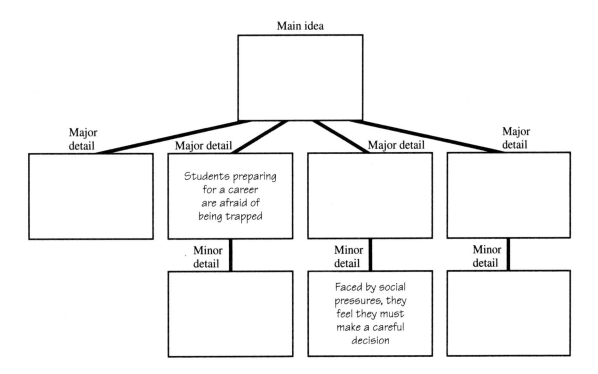

Implied Main Ideas

You have now learned how to analyze paragraphs in which the main idea is stated. Some paragraphs, however, consist only of details. In these paragraphs, the main idea is not stated but only implied (suggested) by the details. Such a paragraph is called an implied paragraph. An implied paragraph, in other words, is one in which there is no topic sentence. Each sentence expresses a detail, and no sentence summarizes or generalizes for the entire paragraph. Implied paragraphs tend to be more difficult for the reader because an extra mental step must be taken. You must arrive at the main idea yourself by formulating a generalization from all the details.

Let's look at an example from Selection 8:

> Individuals should have a wide range of work experiences in order to make a decision about a career. Vocational preparation should combine project interests with actual practice in different fields. College-level courses, on the other hand, may also provide useful training for a satisfying life. Persons are taught to think logically in solving problems and are exposed to experiences (including courses in philosophy, literature, and history) that help them identify and develop their attitudes toward various careers.

Notice that the first sentence is not a topic sentence, because the whole paragraph is not about work experiences or their importance in making a career decision. If you examine the paragraph sentence by sentence, you will come to the conclusion that no sentence in the paragraph adequately summarizes for the rest of the paragraph.

What is the main idea of the paragraph? Let's list the details:

- It's important to have a variety of work experiences.
- Vocational programs should include real experience.
- College courses also can provide useful experiences.

What general point do these details suggest? We might express the main idea in this way: "A variety of experience gained through work, vocational training, and college courses can help an individual make a career decision."

When analyzing an implied paragraph, it is important that you start by identifying the topic. Ask yourself, "Who or what is the paragraph about?" and answer in one word or a short phrase. (In the example above, the topic might have been expressed as "career decisions.") After identifying the topic, ask yourself, "What is the general point developed by the paragraph about the topic?" and answer in a complete sentence. *Always express the main idea in a complete sentence,* so that the point is clear and definite.

Let's look at another example, this one from Selection 7:

> The hypnotist might then suggest that the subject perform certain behaviors, such as hopping on one foot or singing a song in the style of Elvis Presley. Or the suggestion might be to hallucinate or imagine something that isn't really there, such as a fly buzzing around the subject's head. A subject may be told to forget specific material, such as her boyfriend's name; this type of suggestion, when it works, creates *hypnotic amnesia.* Or the subject may be instructed to perform certain behaviors on a signal after she is back in the waking state; this is termed *posthypnotic suggestion.* For example, the suggestion might be for the subject to stand up whenever the hypnotist says the word *day.* After the

subject comes out of the trance she is not aware of this posthypnotic suggestion and is baffled by the fact that she stands up when the hypnotist says, "This sure is a beautiful day."[6]

1. What is the topic of the paragraph? Answer in one word or a short phrase.

   _____

2. What is the main idea (general point) developed by the paragraph about the topic? Write one complete sentence to express the paragraph's main idea.

   _____

   _____

   _____

Read over your answers. Did you write a complete sentence for the main idea? Is your statement of the main idea general enough to include all the details in the paragraph? Here are possible answers:

Topic: _Hypnotic suggestion_ _____

Main idea: _Hypnotic suggestion may cause a subject to_ _____

_____ _behave in unusual ways. Or, people will do strange_ _____

_____ _things when hypnotized._ _____

Exercise 8–2. Implied Paragraphs

Directions

1. Read each paragraph.
2. Write the topic of the paragraph in one word or a short phrase.
3. Write the main idea of the paragraph in a complete sentence of your own wording.

1. Good study skills will not only allow you to learn material thoroughly and permanently. If you must look to someone else for an interpretation or an explanation, you cannot be an intellectually free person. To become an independent student, you must have the desire and the courage to open a textbook, and to read it, study it, and think about it.[7]

Topic: _Good study skills_ _____

Main idea: _Good study skills will help you_ _____

become a good student. _____

_____

2. Some activities are more rewarding than others in helping us meet our needs. The wise person will try to spend his or her time doing those things that are most rewarding. That's one reason why it's so important to make a good occupational choice. If you make a poor occupational choice, you will have to do a lot of things that really are not satisfying. And in the end, your total life will be less rewarding than it might have been.[8]

Topic: _____

Main idea: _____

_____

_____

3. The fact is that physically active people seem to feel and look healthier. Studies show they live longer. They appear to have better-regulated appetites. They eat more, but because exercise increases metabolism—the process of converting food into energy—they burn calories faster and don't gain weight.[9]

Topic: _____*physically active people*_____

Main idea: *physically active people (or: heathy)*

_____

4. Sometimes eye contact is a clue as to whether someone is lying. The liar tends not to make eye contact. Also the direction of a person's gaze is an important clue as to whether information or instructions are being absorbed. A wandering gaze plus a shifting posture usually are evidence that the individual has stopped listening.[10]

Topic: _____*eye contact*_____

Main idea: *Eye contact can tell you many thing about a person.*

_____

5. Unlike African slaves and American Indians, the Chinese were initially encouraged to immigrate to America. From 1850 to 1880, over 200,000 Chinese immigrated to this country, lured by job opportunities created by the discovery of gold. As employment possibilities decreased and competition for mining grew, the Chinese became the target of a bitter campaign to limit their numbers and restrict their rights. Chinese laborers were exploited, then discarded.[11]

Topic: _____

Main idea: _____

_____

_____

Roots

Roots are the base parts of words. The roots of many English words derive from Latin and Greek. Recognizing the root in a word gives you a valuable clue to its meaning. For example, if you know that the root *somn* means sleep, you will have no trouble learning and remembering that *insomnia* means inability to sleep. Thus, a knowledge of common roots is a valuable aid to vocabulary growth.

Studying roots is similar to studying prefixes with a few noteworthy differences:

- It is sometimes harder to identify the root of a word because the root may appear anywhere in the word—the beginning, middle, or end.
- Some roots have several spellings.
- Most roots cannot be looked up in the dictionary as prefixes can.

In this chapter, we will review 20 common word roots.* Study the meaning of the root in each of the following boxes and note the accompanying example words. After each box, you will be asked to list two other words containing that root. Review exercises are provided after every five roots.

Common Roots

1. aud, audit	hear	audible, auditorium

Audible means capable of being *heard*.
An *auditorium* is a place where people *hear* someone speak, sing, and so on.

List two other words using the root *aud* or *audit:*

_____

2. bio	life	biology, antibiotic

Biology is the science of *living* things and *life* processes.
An *antibiotic* kills the *living* bacteria causing illness.

List two other words using the root *bio:*

_____

_____

*See Appendix E for an expanded list of roots.

3.   cess, cede   go   proceed, procession

To *proceed* is to *go* forward.

A *procession* is a group of people *going* forward.

List two other words using the root *cess* or *cede:*

_____

4.   chron   time   synchronize, chronology

To *synchronize* is to set at the same *time.*

A *chronology* is a record of events in *time* order.

List two other words using the root *chron:*

_____

5.   cred   belief   credible, discredit

Credible means *believ*able.

To *discredit* is to negate *belief* in someone or something.

List two other words using the root *cred:*

_____

Exercise 8–3. Practice with Roots

Directions.   Use the meaning of the root in the word in italics to complete the sentences:

1. A *credulous* person will _____ anything you tell him.

2. When a doctor tests your *audition,* he is testing your _____.

3. The *biosphere* is that part of our planet where _____ is found.

4. When flood waters *recede,* they _____ back.

5. A *chronic* illness is one that lasts a long _____.

Fill in the missing root:

6. Dogs can hear sounds that are *in*_____*ible* to humans.

7. A new _____*graphy* of Elvis Presley will be published next year.

8. A _____*meter* is an instrument that measures time.

9. In the astrological cycle, the sign Aries *pre*_____ the sign Taurus.

10. The attorney challenged the witness's _____*ibility.*

---

6. dict   speak, say   predict, dictaphone

      To *predict* is to *say* that an event will occur.

      A *dictaphone* is a machine you *speak* into.

List two other words using the root *dict:*

---

7. duct, duce   lead, carry   conductor, introduce

      The *conductor leads* the orchestra.

      To *introduce* is to *lead* to, or *lead* into.

List two other words using the root *duct* or *duce:*

---

8. fact, fic(t),   do, make   factory, fiction

      A *factory* is a place where goods are *made.*

      Fiction is literature *made* up by the author.

List two other words using the root *fact* or *fic(t):*

_____

---

9. graph   write, draw   biography, graphics

A *biography* is a *written* account of someone's life.
Computer *graphics* involves *drawing* on the computer.

List two other words using the root *graph:*

_____

---

10. miss, mit   send   mission, transmit

A *mission* is something one is *sent* on to do.
To *transmit* a message is to *send* it.

List two other words using the root *miss* or *mit:*

_____

Exercise 8–4. Practice with Roots

Directions. Use the meaning of the root in the word in italics to complete the sentence:

1. The root *manu* means hand. The word *manufacture* originally meant
    _____make_____ by hand.

2. To *remit* payment on a bill is to _____sent_____ the payment in.

3. The root *ver* means truth. We hope that when a jury delivers its *verdict,* it
    will _____say_____ the truth.

4. To *seduce* is to _____lead_____ someone on sexually.

5. A *graphologist* analyzes your hand _drawing_

Fill in the missing root:

6. Nothing could in_duce_ Mike to go to the party.

7. Many parents do not like to be *contra_dict_ed* by their children.

8. Have you ever considered writing your *autobio_graphy_?*

9. The rocket ship was e_go_ting strange signals.

10. Many foods today use *arti_fic_ial* sweeteners.

Exercise 8–5. Matching

Directions.   Using the roots as clues, match the words on the left with their meanings on the right. Do not consult a dictionary.

_C_ 1. auditory   *a.* carry off, kidnap

_f_ 2. symbiosis (sủ cộngsinh)   *b.* historical record

_d_ 3. intercede   *c.* having to do with hearing

_j_ 4. credence   *d.* go between

_b_ 5. chronicle   *e.* creating a mental picture

_i_ 6. diction   *f.* interdependent living

_a_ 7. abduct   *g.* one who does good

_g_ 8. benefactor   *h.* one sent as an ambassador

_e_ 9. graphic   *i.* speech

_h_ 10. emissary (một sứ)   *j.* belief

11.	mor(t)	die, death	immortal, mortician

Immortal means never *dying.*
A *mortician* is someone who prepares *dead* bodies for their funerals.

List two other words using the root *mor(t):*

_____

---

12.   path   1. feeling   1. sympathy
                                            2. disease   2. pathology

To have *sympathy* is to have *feelings* for someone.
Pathology is the study of *disease* and its causes.

List two other words using the root *path:*

_____

---

13.   phon(o), phone   sound   phonics, symphony

Phonics is the study of the *sounds* used in a language.
In a *symphony,* the sounds of many instruments are *heard.*

List two other words using the root *phon(o)* or *phone:*

_____

---

14.   port   carry   transport, portable

To *transport* goods is to *carry* them from one place to another.
A *portable* object is one that can be *carried.*

List two other words using the root *port:*

_____

---

15.   scrib(e), script   write   inscription, scribble

An *inscription* is something *written.*
Scribble is careless *writing.*

List two other words using the root *scrib(e)* or *script:*

_____

Exercise 8–6. Practice with Roots

Directions. Use the meaning of the root in the word in italics to complete the sentence:

1. A *psychopath* is someone with a __crazy__ mind.

2. On a canoe trip, the distance you must __carry__ your canoe is called your *portage.*

3. *Mortality* rates are __death__ rates.

4. The *scriptures* are holy __writting__

5. A *dictaphone* records the __Tone__ of your voice.

Fill in the missing root:

6. Another word for the military draft is *con__scrip__ion* (in the past, the names of the young men to be drafted were written down).

7. A post *__mort__em* examination was needed to determine the exact cause of death.

8. When we got off our plane, we were unable to find a __port__*er* to help us with our luggage.

9. As a former alcoholic, John felt a great deal of *em__path__y* for others still struggling with their drinking.

10. Before CDs and cassette tapes, people listened to music on __phono__*graphs.*

---

16. spect, spic   look, see   spectacle, conspicuous

A *spectacle* is an event worth *seeing.*
Conspicuous means easily *seen* or obvious.

List two other words using the root *spect* or *spic:*

_____

---

17. tract   pull, draw   tractor, retract

A *tractor* pulls.
To *retract* is to draw back.

List two other words using the root *tract:*

_____

> 18. ven(t), vene　　　　　　　come　　　　　　　convene, invent
>
> To *convene* is to *come* together or meet.
> When something is *invented* it *comes* into being.

List two other words using the root *ven(t)* or *vene:*

_____

> 19. viv, vit　　　　　　　live, life　　　　　　survive, vital
>
> To *survive* is to continue to *live.*
> *Vital* means necessary for *life.*

List two other words using the root *viv* or *vit:*

_____

> 20. voc, voke　　　　　　　call, voice　　　　　　vocal, revoke
>
> *Vocal* means using the *voice.*
> To *revoke* is to *call* back.

List two other words using the root *voc* or *voke:*

_____

Exercise 8–7. Practice with Roots

Directions.   Use the meaning of the root in the word in italics to complete the sentence:

1. A *convivial* person is someone who is _live_ly.

2. When you are *attracted* to someone you are _drawn_ toward them.

3. To *evoke* a memory is to _bring_ it forth.

4. *Introspection* is _beginning_ within yourself.

5. People _come_ together for a *convention*.

Fill in the missing root:

6. Someone who watches events is a _spect_ator.

7. A bad tooth may need to be *ex_tract_ed*.

8. Who *pro_voke_d* the argument?

9. When his best hitter started to argue with the umpire, the manager *inter_vene_d*.

10. It is important to eat foods rich in essential *_vita_mins*.

Exercise 8–8. Matching

Directions.   Using the roots as clues, match the words on the left with their meanings on the right. Do not consult a dictionary.

_d_	1. vitality		*a.* expel, carry away
_f_	2. spectrum		*b.* tighten, pull together
_b_	3. contract		*c.* strong dislike
_e_	4. vociferous		*d.* health
_g_	5. advent		*e.* noisy
_i_	6. morgue		*f.* range of visible light
_c_	7. antipathy		*g.* beginning, coming into being
_j_	8. phonology		*h.* note at end of a letter
_a_	9. deport		*i.* place where bodies are kept
_h_	10. postscript		*j.* study of sounds of a language

Use Table 8–1 as a review of common roots.

TABLE 8–1   Common Roots

	Root	*Meaning*	*Example*
1.	aud, audit	hear	audible
2.	bio	life	biology
3.	cess, cede	go	proceed
4.	chron	time	synchronize
5.	cred	belief	credible
6.	dict	speak, say	predict
7.	duct, duce	lead, carry	conductor
8.	fact, fic(t)	do, make	factory
9.	graph	write, draw	biography
10.	miss, mit	send	mission
11.	mor(t)	die, death	immortal
12.	path	feeling, disease	sympathy, pathology
13.	phon	sound	phonics
14.	port	carry	transport
15.	scrib, script	write	inscription
16.	spect, spic	look, see	spectacle
17.	tract	draw, pull	tractor
18.	ven	come	convene
19.	viv, vit	life	survive
20.	voc, voke	call, voice	vocal

Journal Entry

1. Discuss your career goals. What would your ideal job be like?

_____

_____

_____

_____

_____

_____

_____

_____

_____

_____

_____

_____

_____

2. Did reading for the main idea help your comprehension in Selection 8? Why or why not?

_____

_____

_____

_____

_____

_____

_____

_____

_____

_____

_____

_____

_____

STRATEGIES CHECK

You have now studied several of the key strategies needed for successful college reading and vocabulary building. You are approximately halfway through this textbook and probably halfway through your current term. Before continuing to Chapter 9, please take a few minutes to complete the exercises on the following pages. This review will enable you and your instructor to reexamine your study habits and assess your understanding of the skills and strategies taught in Chapters 1 to 8.

Keep in mind that the review exercises in this chapter will *not* be used by your instructor to grade you or formally evaluate you. Their purpose is to help you analyze your current strengths and weaknesses so that you can continue to improve your reading and study habits.

Exercise 1. Time Management Revisited

Following the directions below, please fill in your *current* weekly schedule on the block schedule on page 181.

1. *Committed time.* First, place an X in the blocks when you have classes. If you have a job, X out the hours you work.
2. *Study time.* Next, indicate the hours that you are using for study purposes (study time includes time used for homework exercises, assigned reading, and compositions as well as studying for tests). Once you have identified your study hours, count them up.
3. Fill in any other routine activities that are part of your week. This may include meal times, travel time to and from school and work, regular exercise time, regular social time, or even TV shows you watch every week.
4. Compare the new schedule you have just filled out with your original schedule on page 11. Take note of any differences; then answer the following questions:

a. Have there been any changes in your class schedule or job schedule? If so, why were those changes made? Has the total of your committed time been increased or decreased?

No, I haven't

b. Have there been any changes in your study hours? If so, why?

_No, ..._

c. Compare the number of study hours you actually need now to the number you planned in your original schedule. Do you need more or fewer hours than originally planned?

Yes, I do

d. Have there been any other significant changes in your schedule since the beginning of the semester?

_No._

Exercise 2. Self–Evaluation: Time Management

The following questions will help you evaluate how effectively you have been managing your time. Answer honestly.

1. How successfully have you been budgeting your time this semester? What problems have you encountered? What do you feel could help you overcome any difficulties you may have experienced?

- I am not successful about that. I had tried to do Hw and study as well as i can.
- work too much → very tired some time.
- should do Hw whenever have free time.

	MON	TUES	WED	THURS	FRI	SAT	SUN
7							
8		X		X			
9	go → wrk	X	go → work	X	go → work	go work	
10	work	X	work	X	Work	work	
11	"	X	Wort	X	work	"	
12	lunch	go work eat	lunch	go work eat	lnch	"	
1	"	work	work	work	work	"	
2	"	"	"	"	"	"	
3	"	"	"	"	"	"	
4	"	"	"	"	"	"	
5	"	"	"	"	"	"	
6	"	"	"	"	"	"	
7	"	"	"	"	"	"	
8	"	"	"	"	"	"	
9	go home wash, eat	G.W. E	G.W. E	G.W. E	G.W.	G.W.	
10	study	study	study	study	Date	Date	
11	"	"	"	"			
12	"	"	"	"			

2. Do you need more time to study? Before answering, indicate which, if any, of the following problems you have experienced this semester.

_____ *(a.)* I am sometimes unable to complete assignments on time.

_____ *b.* At times I sacrifice the quality of my work, because I lack the time to do a high-quality job.

_____ *(c.)* I sometimes sacrifice sleep or skip meals to get schoolwork done.

_____ *(d.)* I sometimes procrastinate on assignments and studying.

_____ *e.* I do not always have enough time to adequately prepare for my tests.

_____ *f.* I have experienced a high degree of stress due to lack of time; I often work just to get things done and don't enjoy the work.

If you have experienced any of the problems just mentioned, take a closer look at your schedule. How might you modify your schedule to ensure that you will have adequate time for your assignments and studies? Take the following points into consideration:

• It is typical for students to underestimate the amount of work required for college classes. Students with time management problems are often those with jobs who are simply trying to do too much.

• College is not meant to be all work. A healthy weekly schedule includes some time for relaxation and recreation.

• You may need to think creatively about your time and make some difficult choices. Sometimes students must drop a course or cut back on job hours in order to have a successful term. Remember that you are the one who has to live with your decisions and schedule.

• If you are having time management problems, you may find it helpful to discuss your schedule with your instructor, advisor, or counselor.

Other Suggestions

As you plan your study time from week to week over the rest of the semester, here are some helpful hints:

• It is better to overestimate the amount of time you will need for assignments and study than to underestimate. Planning a little extra time reduces the stress associated with meeting an assignment deadline. It also allows you to feel like you can get ahead of your schedule instead of always staying behind it.

• Plan to have assignments completed a day early. Then, if you have an unexpected problem, you will not be forced to turn your work in late.

• When you have an assignment that involves more than one sitting (writing a paper, studying for a test), think concretely about the steps involved. Plan each specific step in the process. For example, on a composition assignment, the plan might be:

Tuesday	Outline and write first draft.
Wednesday	Read and revise first draft.
Thursday	Write second draft and edit.
Friday	Write final draft and proofread.

đánh giá

Exercise 3. Self-Assessment Revisited

Has college been different from what you expected? Are you meeting the goals you set for yourself at the beginning of the term?

Let's return to the self-assessment of your study habits on page 8. In the space below, please copy the three habits you selected as most important for you to change.

1. *I study regular time*
2. *I am afraid or embarrassed to ask for help*
3. *I don't always completed my assignment on time*

1. Which of the above habits have you successfully changed?

   (1) *(hoàn thành)*

2. What steps did you take to accomplish these changes?

   study when have free time at work.

3. Which habits do you still need to improve on?

   I enjoy learning something new.
   (phương hướng)

4. What new approaches might you take to their <u>improvement</u>? *(Sự traceđổi, cải thiện)*

   ask someone's help

5. Are there any other changes in your study habits that you would like to make? Before answering, indicate whether you have experienced any of the following problems this semester:

   ___✓___ *a.* I have missed classes or come late to class.

   _____ *b.* I have difficulty paying attention in class.

   ___✓___ *c.* I have not completed some of my assignments (for reasons other than lack of time).

   _____ *d.* I have earned low grades on assignments or tests.

   _____ *e.* I frequently lack motivation and don't enjoy my classes.

   _____ *f.* I have been very anxious about taking tests or passing my classes.

If you have experienced any of these problems, try to determine the cause. How might a change of habit or attitude help you avoid similar problems in the future?

6. What are your primary goals for the remainder of this term?

_____

_____

7. What obstacles to accomplishing these goals do you anticipate?

_____

_____

8. How will you deal with these obstacles if and when you encounter them?

_____

_____

Exercise 4. Learning Style

Answer the following questions:

1. What have you discovered about your learning style this semester?

_____

_____

2. Under what conditions do you concentrate best? What conditions are unfavorable for your concentration?

_____

_____

3. Have you noticed any differences in your ability to study at different times of day? Do you study better in the morning, afternoon, or evening?

_____

_____

4. Are you having more success in some subjects than others? Why?

_____

_____

5. When you have to remember definitions and other information for a test, what strategies are most helpful? How effective are your notes? Have you made any use of a tape recorder? Index cards?

_____

_____

_____

6. Has your self-confidence increased since the beginning of the semester? Why or why not?

_____

_____

Exercise 5. Comprehension and Vocabulary Strategies

Please complete the following miniquiz on the strategies you have been learning.

1. What two strategies should be used on a study-reading assignment *before* starting to read? Why are they used?

   _____

   _____

2. What strategies should be used on a study-reading assignment *while* reading? Why are they used?

   _____

   _____

   _____

3. The first step to take when encountering a new word is:

   _____

4. The second step is to: _____

5. Why is it helpful to learn prefixes and roots?

   _____

   _____

Exercise 6. Self-Evaluation: Use of Strategies

1. Please indicate how much you've been using each of the following strategies by checking the column *Frequently, Occasionally,* or *Rarely.*

	Frequently	*Occasionally*	*Rarely*
Previewing			
Pre-thinking—prior knowledge			
Pre-thinking—raising questions			
Monitoring comprehension			
Goal questions			
Reading for main ideas			

If you checked *Rarely* for any of the above strategies, explain why you haven't been using that strategy more:

_____

_____

_____

2. Please indicate how helpful the use of these strategies has been by checking the column *Very Helpful, Somewhat Helpful,* or *Of Little Help.*

	Very Helpful	Somewhat Helpful	Of Little Help
Previewing			
Pre-thinking—prior knowledge			
Pre-thinking—raising questions			
Monitoring comprehension			
Goal questions			
Reading for main ideas			

3. Please rate your skill with the following vocabulary strategies by checking the column *Poor, Fair, Good,* or *Very Good.*

	Poor	Fair	Good	Very Good
Using the context				
Using the dictionary				
Recognizing prefixes and roots				

Would you like more help with any of these skills?

_____

Please consult with your instructor if you would like further clarification on any of the strategies you have studied.

Applying Your Skills

On the reading selections in the remaining chapters, you will be asked to apply your skills more independently. Independent practice will increase your skill and confidence, making it easier for you to apply your skills and strategies when you read assignments for other classes.

1. Remember to start your work with each new selection by previewing. In the space marked "Preview Notes," summarize what you have learned about the passage from your preview.

2. After previewing, use one or both of the pre-thinking strategies—recalling prior knowledge and raising questions. In the space marked "Pre-thinking Notes," (*a*) indicate what you already know about the subject or discuss your own experiences that relate to the subject; or (*b*) jot down several questions that come to mind about the subject.

3. While reading, monitor your comprehension. Interrupt your reading from time to time to judge how well you are understanding the material. Clarify your comprehension when necessary.

4. Raise goal questions from the headings in the selection, or at any other time when a suitable question comes to mind.

5. Look for the answers to your goal questions and any other important points. Underline topic sentences and important details whenever you recognize them.

6. If you have been successful with the comprehensive exercises, try answering the questions without looking back at the selection.

7. Use context clues, your dictionary, and prefixes and roots to determine the meaning of unfamiliar words.

Note: An essay question will be added to the exercises for the remaining reading selections. For the essay question, you are to compose a well-written, half-page response.

9

INTEGRATING VOCABULARY STRATEGIES

In Chapter 9, you will:

1. Preview and read a selection about male-female communication, using all the strategies you have learned thus far.
2. Answer comprehension questions on the selection to check your understanding.
3. Learn to identify suffixes and base words.
4. Learn to use word associations to remember word meanings.
5. Learn to use the various vocabulary strategies in combination.

SELECTION 9
LOVE IS NEVER ENOUGH

Aaron Beck

Directions. Preview the passage and use the space below to write your preview and pre-thinking notes.

Preview Notes

_____

_____

_____

_____

_____

Pre-thinking Notes

_____

_____

_____

_____

While You Read

1. Monitor and clarify comprehension.
2. Raise goal questions.
3. Underline main ideas and important details.

- "My husband is deaf. He never hears what I say."
- "She talks every subject to death."
- "He always gets defensive when I ask him something."
- "She makes everything into an argument."
5 - "He is stubborn . . . he won't even consider what I have to say."
- "He never says what he means."
- "That's not what I meant."

Such statements are typical of troubled relationships. While they may simply reflect inadequate communication, they may also point to profound problems.
10 Even couples with only mild difficulties in communicating can have important misunderstandings.

Marjorie, for example, wanted Ken to invite her to a favorite cocktail lounge overlooking a bay to celebrate their anniversary. She archly asked him, "Ken, do you feel like going out for a drink tonight?" Ken, who was feeling tired, missed the hid-
15 den message contained in her question. He responded, "No, I'm too tired." Marjorie was extremely disappointed. Only after feeling hurt and sorry for herself did she realize that she had not communicated to Ken her real desire—to celebrate their anniversary. When she later made clear her true wish, he readily agreed to celebrate.

The important point about conversational styles is that they are *learned*—and if
20 they interfere with effective communication, they can be *unlearned*. Many people believe that their own style is the natural one but find that they can "unlearn" it and assume a more adaptive style.

Differences between the Sexes

Daniel Maltz and Ruth Borker summarize a number of findings that shed light on why
marital partners have problems communicating. One reason is that men and women
25 tend to have different conversational styles. Although a given person may have essentially the same style as the spouse, in most instances where there is a difference in

style, the wife adopts a culturally defined, "feminine" conversational style; the husband, a "masculine" style.

Characteristically, women show a greater tendency to ask questions. In observations of female-male conversations, a question-answer pattern was found, with the females asking most of the questions. Some researchers believe that women's propensity for question asking indicates their investment in maintaining routine interactions between people. Their questioning is a sign they take responsibility for facilitating and sustaining the flow of conversation. This conversational device may also represent their greater involvement in personal relations.

Men are less likely than women to ask personal questions. Men are prone to think, "*If she wants to tell me something, she'll tell me without my asking.*" A woman might reflect, "*If I don't ask, he'll think that I don't care.*" For men, questions may represent intrusive meddling and an invasion of privacy; for women, however, they are a sign of intimacy and an expression of caring.

Women use more utterances to encourage responses from the other person. . . . they are more likely than men to use listening signals like "mm-hmm" to indicate that they are paying attention. A man, typically, will use this response only when he is agreeing with what his wife is saying, whereas his wife will use it simply to indicate she is listening. Thus, a husband may interpret his wife's listening signals as signs that his wife agrees with him. Later, he may feel betrayed when he discovers that she was not agreeing with him at all. He does not realize that she was simply indicating her interest in what he was saying and "keeping the conversational ball in the air." The wife, on the other hand, may feel ignored and let down because her husband is not making any of these listening sounds, which she then interprets as his lack of interest.

Men are more likely than women to make comments throughout the stream of conversation rather than wait until the other person finishes speaking. Women appear to be more troubled—and apt to make a "silent protest"—after they have been interrupted or have failed to evoke a listening response. This difference lies behind the complaint of many wives that "My husband always interrupts me" or "He never listens." Women also show a greater use of the pronouns *you* and *we*, which acknowledge the other speaker. This conversational style promotes a sense of unity.

Drawing on these research findings, a couple might keep in mind the following observation about the husband's conversational habits. First, as indicated earlier, men are more likely to interrupt their conversational partners—male or female. Second, they are less likely to respond to the comments of the other speaker; frequently they make no response or acknowledgement at all, give a delayed response at the end of their partner's statement, or show a minimum degree of enthusiasm. Third, they are more likely to challenge or dispute statements made by their partners, which explains why a husband may seem to be eternally argumentative. Finally, men make more declarations of fact or opinion than do women. Some wives resent the "voice of authority"—not realizing that their husband's assertions may represent a masculine style rather than a sense of superiority.

Given the contrast between conversational styles among men and women, the conditions are ripe for conflicts to arise. A wife, for example, could easily perceive

her husband as uninterested, controlling, or unresponsive when his way of speaking simply reflects the style that he has learned to use with everyone, not just her. Judg-
75 ments such as "My husband never listens" or "My husband disagrees with everything I say" most often reflect the husband's habits of speech rather than any insensitivity or ill will toward his wife. Knowing that such differences between the sexes exist and that they are not caused by bad faith, lack of respect, or lack of interest can help couples to note their partner's style without taking offense, and to provide a safeguard against misinterpretation.

80   Despite these differences in communication styles, there is no question that husbands and wives can improve their relationships by learning to synchronize their styles. In view of the important symbolic meaning of his speaking style, a husband could facilitate communication if he, for instance, became more active in listening and interrupted or disputed his wife less. It would also help for him to pay more atten-
85 tion to the spirit of the conversation and recognize that signals of his attention (such as active listening signals or gestures) are often just as powerful as the words themselves—if not more so. Finally, he has to recognize that his dogmatic statements are "conversation stoppers."

Rules of Conversational Etiquette

There are guidelines that can make your conversations more enjoyable as well as
90 more effective. By following these suggestions, you will be able to prevent the kinds of glitches that impede many discussions.

- Tune In to Your Partner's Channel.
- Give Listening Signals.
- Don't Interrupt.
95 - Ask Questions Skillfully.
- Use Diplomacy and Tact.

Rule 1: Tune In to Your Partner's Channel
Having a fruitful talk demands that a husband and wife be tuned in to each other, that they connect with each other. Although they may be talking about the same topic, their approach can be so different that they fail to make meaningful contact.
100   Sometimes a spouse, in trying to relieve a partner's distress, accomplishes just the opposite. Judy is an artist. One evening she was quite upset by her problems in getting ready for a show, and she started to tell her husband, Cliff, about them. She wanted his support, encouragement, and sympathy. But Cliff instead fired off a barrage of instructions: "One, you've got to get all the people together in the group. Two,
105 you have to call anyone else who is involved. Three, you want to get your accountant in on it—check with the bank to see how much money you still have. Four, you could contact the PR people. Five, call the gallery and see about the time."
     Judy felt rejected by Cliff and thought, *"He doesn't care about how I feel. He just wants to get me off his back."* But in his eyes, Cliff thought that he was filling the
110 bill. He had given her his best advice—he thought that he *was* being supportive. To

Judy, however, Cliff was being controlling, not supportive. She was seeking sympathy and emotional rapport, while he was tuned in to problem solving.

How can you find the appropriate channel? One point to keep in mind is that the approach that works in impersonal or business relations may backfire in an intimate
115 relationship. If a husband, for example, discovers that his advice only stirs up his wife, he should resist his temptation to instruct her and, instead, try another strategy, such as showing he understands her feelings. Further, the next time his wife tells him her problems, he can keep in mind that he need not plunge in with advice giving unless she clearly wants it—that she may just need to talk over her feelings.
120 How could Judy have acted differently, and avoided the "He doesn't understand me" trap? For one thing, she could have anticipated his tendency to give pragmatic, didactic advice and said, "I've got a problem. I think I know the answers, but I'd like to talk it out—how I *feel,* not what to do. Is that okay?" Presenting the problem in these terms would help prepare Cliff to explore her feelings rather than to construct
125 a game plan for her.

Rule 2: Give Listening Signals

Sometimes a wife will complain that her husband never listens to her, while he protests that he has heard every word she says. Studies have shown a real sex-linked difference: while listening, women are much more prone to make sounds like "mhm, uh-huh," and "yeah," which indicate they are following what is being said, whereas
130 men are more prone to silence. Other signals, such as facial expressions and subtle gestures, inform your partner that you are tuned in.

People sometimes forget that conversation means a *mutual* exchange of information and ideas. Speaking without getting feedback is like talking to a wall. If you are the silent type, it may be helpful to get into the habit of giving nonverbal feed-
135 back and not leaving your mate wondering whether you are really listening.

Rule 3: Don't Interrupt

Interruptions may feel very natural to the offender but can evoke a number of negative thoughts in the person being cut off: *"He's not listening to me," "She doesn't think much of what I have to say," "He's only interested in hearing himself talk."*

As with other speech habits, interruptions may be part of a person's conversa-
140 tional style rather than an expression of egocentricity or disagreement—although this habit is frequently interpreted as such by the interrupted speaker. Here, too, we have a gender difference. Men tend to interrupt more than women do. They interrupt other men as much as they do women. Hence, the wife who thinks of negative explanations for her husband's interruptions should bear in mind that they may simply represent
145 his conversational style. Nonetheless, an interrupter would do well to refrain from voicing his or her ideas until the conversational partner has finished.

Rule 4: Ask Questions Skillfully

Asking questions can initiate a conversation and keep it going—or stop it prematurely. Some people are naturally reticent or inhibited, and they need to be nudged in order to be drawn into a conversation. A well-phrased question can sometimes work

150   magic in getting your mate to talk. But a question that is poorly timed, too probing, or irrelevant can stop the flow.

Many people unwittingly stop further conversation because of their style of talking. Len, for example, habitually responded to questions with one- or two-word answers such as "yes," "no," or "nothing much." Until this habit was pointed out to

155   him, he unintentionally thwarted most of his wife's attempts to engage him in conversation. For instance, after he came home one evening, his wife, Harriet, asked about his night out.

> *Harriet:* How was your poker game?
> *Len:* Okay.
160
> *Harriet:* Who was there?
> *Len:* The usual.
> *Harriet:* Did you talk about anything?
> *Len:* Nothing much.
> *Harriet:* Did you win or lose?
165
> *Len:* Neither.

In a case like this, instead of endlessly—and fruitlessly—plying her husband with questions, Harriet could have made a general but pointed observation, followed by a question: "I'm having trouble starting a conversation with you. Do you prefer not to

170   talk, or is something wrong?"

On another occasion, Harriet used her ingenuity to get Len talking.

> *Harriet:* What happened at the hospital today?
> *Len:* The same old thing.
> *Harriet:* You said you were going to discuss your research project with your
175
> chief. How did it turn out?
> *Len:* Oh, he actually had some good ideas . . . [goes on to discuss this at some length].

Rule 5: Use Diplomacy and Tact

This rule might seem out of place in intimate relationships, yet practically everybody has sensitive areas—and even a loving, well-intentioned spouse can injure

180   them. For example, some people are sensitive about their appearance, or the way they speak, or certain members of their family. If, for instance, in the course of conversation a wife implies that her husband is overweight, or his sister is immature, or his grammar is incorrect, she may put an end to pleasant conversation. This rule does not mean that you have to walk on eggshells—it merely calls for awareness

185   and judgment.

Most of the advice in this chapter applies to casual conversations, not to more serious discussions about such issues as resolving conflicts and making decisions. I have found that unless couples make an effort to keep light conversations separate, they drift into more serious discussions that take much of the lightness out of the relationship.[1]

Interest Rating. Please rate the interest level of Selection 9 on the following 1–5 scale (circle one):

5—Very interesting

4—Fairly interesting

3—Mildly interesting

2—A little boring

1—Very boring

Difficulty Rating. Please indicate how difficult Selection 9 was for you to understand on the following 1–5 scale (circle one):

5—Very difficult

4—Fairly difficult

3—Moderate

2—Fairly easy

1—Very easy

Comments: _____

_____

Comprehension Questions

Directions. For questions 1–4, choose the answer that best completes the statement. For questions 5–10, write your response in the space provided. Base all answers on what you read in the selection (you may refer back to the selection when necessary).

_____ 1. The author uses Judy and Cliff's difficulties (lines 100–125) to show that:
   a. Men and women can't get along.
   b. It is important to tune in to your partner's channel.
   c. Cliff was insensitive to Judy.
   d. People don't communicate effectively.

_____ 2. In male–female conversation, women ask more questions because:
   a. Women naturally talk more than men.
   b. Men are less curious than women.
   c. Women feel that questions show caring.
   d. Women believe that questions are the best way to get information.

_____ 3. If a woman brings up a problem, a man would be most likely to:
   a. Try to find a quick solution.
   b. Ask questions.
   c. Refuse to discuss the problem.
   d. Provide sympathy and express oneness.

_____ 4. The main point of the paragraph beginning "Given the contrast . . ."
(lines 70–79) is that:

     a. Men and women have different conversational styles.

     b. Most wives believe that their husbands don't pay attention to them.

     c. Misunderstanding is common in marriages.

     d. Recognizing the differences in conversational style can help couples
avoid misunderstandings.

5. What is most important to learn and remember from this passage?

_____

_____

6. What key point does the writer make in the passage's third paragraph
(lines 19–22)?

_____

_____

7. Briefly explain some of the important differences in the conversational
styles of men and women.

_____

_____

_____

_____

_____

_____

_____

8. In your own words, briefly explain the author's five suggestions for more
effective communication between men and women.

_____

_____

_____

_____

_____

_____

_____

9. Which of the suggestions do you feel is most valuable? Why?

_____

_____

_____

10. Explain the title. What does the author mean when he says "Love is never enough"?

_____

_____

Vocabulary Exercise

Directions. Use the context clues and your dictionary to determine the meaning of each of the following words. Write your definition in the space provided.

1. propensity (32) _____
2. facilitating (33) _____
3. intimacy (40) _____
4. rapport (112) _____
5. pragmatic (121) _____
6. egocentricity (140) _____
7. gender (142) _____
8. reticent (148) _____
9. ingenuity (170) _____
10. diplomacy (177) _____

Essay Question

Directions. On a separate sheet of paper, write a well-developed, half-page response to the following question:

Explain why you agree or disagree with this statement: "As long as two people love each other, their relationship is bound to work out."

Suffixes

A suffix is a word ending. Many words are formed by joining a suffix to a root.

diction   dict (root) + ion (suffix)

Often, suffixes are added to base words (a base word is a word that can stand independently) to form new words.

government   govern (base word) + ment (suffix)

Most suffixes add little meaning to the base words to which they are attached; their main function is to change the word's grammatical form (part of speech). For example, the suffix *ment* changes the verb *govern* to the noun *government*. The common suffix *ly* usually changes an adjective to an adverb—for example, *rapid* to *rapidly*. There is no substantial difference in meaning between *rapid* and *rapidly; rapid* is an adjective, and *rapidly* is an adverb:

> Please give a rapid response.
> Please respond rapidly.

Suffixes do have definitions—you can look them up in the dictionary. But these definitions are usually vague and abstract. The suffix *ion,* for example, is defined as "the act or condition of." *Communication* is the act of *communicating;* the suffix *ion* changes a verb—*communicate*—into a noun—*communication.*

Knowledge of suffixes is useful for a few practical reasons. Sometimes, an apparently unfamiliar word may become familiar when we recognize its base word and suffix. Familiarity with suffixes is also sometimes an aid to the pronunciation of new words. In the dictionary, words with suffixes are often listed as derived forms under their base words. We must remove the suffix to identify and locate the base word.

Exercise 9–1. Recognizing Base Words

Directions.   Identify the base word and suffix for each word.

Example

rarity	*rare*	*ity*
	Base Word	**Suffix**
1. perilous	_____	_____
2. skepticism	_____	_____
3. disposal	_____	_____
4. refreshments	_____	_____
5. expiration	_____	_____
6. dispensable	_____	_____
7. diplomacy	_____	_____
8. derivative	_____	_____
9. endurance	_____	_____
10. prescription	_____	_____
11. severity	_____	_____

12. resemblance   _____   _____

13. egocentricity   _____   _____

14. practical   _____   _____

15. perception   _____   _____

16. intrusive   _____   _____

17. mysterious   _____   _____

18. sympathize   _____   _____

19. carriage   _____   _____

20. pronunciation   _____   _____

Learning Suffixes

You will recognize and analyze words more easily if you are familiar with the more common suffixes. Review the suffixes listed in Table 9–1 on page 200 and then complete Exercises 9–2 and 9–3.

Exercise 9–2. Suffixes

Directions. Add a suffix to the underlined word in each of the following sentences to make the sentence grammatically correct. Make all necessary spelling changes when adding the suffix.

Example

Fish are *plent___iful___* in this stream.

1. Many illnesses that could not be cured in the past are *treat_____* today.

2. Teenage gangs can *terror_____* a *neighbor_____*.

3. The district attorney was waiting for a report from the lab *pathology_____*.

4. She is poor but not *penny_____*.

5. The *ship_____* of medical supplies was delayed by poor weather conditions.

6. Periods of study will help you *solid_____* your knowledge.

7. My uncle Leroy is a *reside_____* of California

8. To *simple_____* a long and complex paragraph, the first step is to determine the main idea.

9. Cigarette smoke in a restaurant is an *annoy_____* to nonsmokers.

10. A *skill_____* businessperson learns when to use *discreet_____*.

TABLE 9–1   Common Suffixes

Suffix	Meaning	Example Word
Adjective Suffixes		
1. able, ible	able to, capable of	desirable, responsible
2. ous	full of, containing	famous
3. ful	full of, having	skillful
4. al	pertaining to	withdrawal
5. ical	pertaining to	sociological
6. less	lacking	homeless
7. ive	tending to	creative
Noun Suffixes		
8. ion	act or state of	comprehension, hesitation
9. ity	quality or condition of	electricity
10. ment	state or condition of	commitment
11. hood	state or condition of	sisterhood
12. ness	state or quality of	wilderness
13. logy	study of	biology
14. er, or	person who	governor, player
15. ee	person who (receives)	employee
16. ist	person who	anthropologist
17. ence, ance	act or condition of	credence, hindrance
18. age	act or condition of	marriage
19. ism	belief in, philosophy of	communism
Verb Suffixes		
20. ize	cause, become, make	actualize
21. ify	cause, become, make	glorify
22. en	cause, become, make	frighten
23. ate	cause, become, provide, have	originate
Adverb Suffixes		
24. ly	in a specified manner or direction	happily
25. ward	in the direction of	homeward

Exercise 9–3. Suffixes

Directions.   List one example word (other than the one already provided) for each suffix listed in Table 12–1.

_____	_____	_____
_____	_____	_____
_____	_____	_____
_____	_____	_____

_____ _____ _____

_____ _____ _____

_____ _____ _____

_____ _____ _____

_____ _____ _____

_____

Word Associations

Studying the context clues, using the dictionary, and learning word parts are the basic strategies for building a powerful vocabulary. Sometimes, however, we learn new words but fail to retain their meanings in our long-term memory. We have all had the frustrating experience of looking up a word in the dictionary only to find that by the next time we encounter the word we have forgotten what it means. Special strategies can and should be used to avoid these problems and help us remember word meanings. The use of memory strategies is especially important with *low-frequency* words, which are words that are not used often. Because these words are encountered least frequently, they are the ones we are most likely to forget.

In Chapter 3, a simple technique was recommended for studying vocabulary—using index cards. Have you tried it? How did it work? What other strategies have you used when you want to remember the meaning of a new word?

One of the best memory techniques is *association.* Association simply means linking the new material you are learning with something you already know. Essentially, we acquire most of our knowledge in this way—linking the unknown to the known—but the process is often subconscious. Individuals with good memory skills, however, make frequent, conscious use of association techniques. Associations are easy to use and often fun. They provide an opportunity for creative thinking. Most importantly, they are powerful memory aids.

There are many ways to form vocabulary associations. The basic idea is to associate the new word and its meaning with something familiar. Associations may be personal, contextual, or based on the sound or spelling of the word.

Personal associations are drawn from your own experience. For example, let's take the word *rapport.* Do you remember the meaning? Rapport means "harmonious relationship." To remember this, you might think of someone with whom you have a great deal of rapport. When you come across the word *rapport,* think of that person. You can reinforce the association with a sentence: "I have a great deal of rapport with _____." For another example, let's imagine you were learning the word *loquacious,* which means talkative. You could associate the word with someone you know who talks a lot—someone who is loquacious. Or you might think of a time when you found yourself in a talkative mood—more loquacious than you usually are. Any example from your own experience can work as an association. You may also use people in the news or fictional characters (e.g., characters from TV shows).

Associations, of course, need not be personal. A second kind of association is *contextual*. For this kind of association, simply use the context of what you're reading to form an association. For example, to remember that *pragmatic* means practical, we could use the context of our passage, which said that men have a tendency to give pragmatic advice. Remember a short phrase—"men give pragmatic advice"—and visualize the situation if possible.

A third type of association uses the word's sound or spelling. Many words sound or look like other words; some words contain smaller words within them. You can create an association by linking the sound or spelling of a word, or part of a word, with its meaning. For example, let's consider the word *rapport* again. What do you see in it? The first syllable spells "rap." Rap can mean to talk, and people who have rapport like to talk to each other. We associate: You like to *rap* with people with whom you have *rapport*. When you next come across the word *rapport,* you will think of *rap* and remember your association. You can also add visualization to this type of association: You can form a picture in your mind of two people who have *rapport* sitting close to each other and rapping.

Can you think of any other ways to use the sound or spelling of rapport to form an association?

If you have never used association before, you may find the technique a bit strange at first. With a little practice, however, you will find association a natural way to help remember new information.

Right now, please make up an association for each of the following vocabulary words from Selection 9. Check your definitions from the vocabulary exercise or the dictionary before writing your association. After each association, indicate whether it was a personal, contextual, or sound/spelling association. An example is provided.

Example

pragmatic (121) _my father—personal_____

1. facilitating (33) _____

2. intimacy (40) _____

3. egocentricity (140) _____

4. gender (142) _____

5. reticent (148) _____

6. ingenuity (170) _____

Integrating Vocabulary Strategies

Now that you have learned the essential strategies for developing an effective vocabulary, let's focus for a moment on how these strategies are used together.

FIGURE 9–1

The Vocabulary Building Process

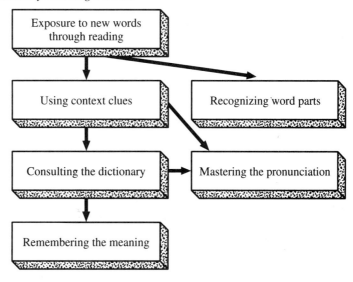

Figure 9–1 repeats the vocabulary building process model you studied in Chapter 2. As the model suggests, when you encounter a new word, you usually follow these steps:

1. Look for context clues.
2. Look for *structural* clues (prefix, root, and suffix).
3. Consult the dictionary.
4. Use a memory strategy.

Of course, you will not necessarily use all of these strategies with every new word you encounter. Sometimes the context clues are strong, and sometimes they are weak. The prefix, root, or suffix in a word may be obvious or not at all apparent. Sometimes the dictionary will be very helpful and, at other times, of little use. You, as a reader, must determine which strategies will be most effective as you approach each new word.

Nevertheless, with most words you will want to employ a combination of at least two strategies. A multistrategy approach enhances word learning and provides the reinforcement needed for remembering word meanings.

Exercise 9–4. Integrating Vocabulary Strategies

Directions. Five vocabulary words from Selection 9 are listed below. Next to each word, name the two strategies that most helped you learn the word.

1. propensity _____

2. facilitating _____

3. pragmatic _____

4. ingenuity _____

5. diplomacy _____

Exercise 9–5. Integrating Vocabulary Strategies

Directions.   Use a combination of strategies to learn the meaning of the underlined word in each of the following sentences. In the spaces provided, write the meaning of the word and list the strategies you used.

Example

"Cheating on a test is <u>contemptible!</u>" declared Professor Smiley.

Meaning: *low; deserving scorn* _____

Strategies used: *context, dictionary, suffix* _____

   1. Good study skills are a <u>prerequisite</u> for success in any college program.

Meaning: _____

Strategies used: _____

   2. Nancy approached her math assignments with <u>alacrity.</u>

Meaning: _____

Strategies used: _____

   3. The US Constitution protects the rights of every American citizen, regardless of race, <u>creed</u>, color, or religion.

Meaning: _____

Strategies used: _____

   4. "Our product contains only <u>biodegradable</u> ingredients," claimed the label.

Meaning: _____

Strategies used: _____

   5. Not even the President of the United States has the right to <u>abrogate</u> the law.

Meaning: _____

Strategies used: _____

Integrative Exercises

Exercise 9–6. Implied Paragraphs

Directions. For each paragraph, state the topic, in one word or a short phrase, and write one complete sentence of your own wording to express the main idea of the paragraph.

1. Altogether, every year Americans throw out 160 million tons of commercial and residential trash—that's 25 pounds per person per week—more than enough to bury 2,700 football fields in a layer ten stories high. That's twice as much trash as Japan or Europe generates. Add in all the industrial nonhazardous waste and the oil, natural gas, and mining wastes, and it comes out to a total of 11 billion tons of nonhazardous solid waste a year—in the U.S. alone. Industry generates the greatest portion of what environmentalists call the waste stream, an estimated 7.6 billions tons.[2]

    Topic: _____

    Main idea: _____

    _____

2. Research done by Lyman Steil, an authority on communications, indicates that people on the average listen effectively to only about 25 percent of what they hear. He states further that the ability to listen well is not an inherent trait. It is a learned behavior. When we come into this world, we don't have a built-in knowledge of how to listen well. That skill must be developed. Unfortunately, it is not developed well systematically in our school systems. We teach reading, writing, speaking, and numerous other abilities, but not listening. In the business world Steil has found that, as one advances in management, listening ability becomes increasingly critical.[3]

    Topic: _____

    Main idea: _____

    _____

3. What fun is walking a dog? With a cat, all you have to do is change her litter box once a week. Neither do cats need to be housebroken; their instincts tell them where to go. Cats eat less than dogs, and you don't have to worry about them drooling on your nice new clothes or chewing up your favorite pair of shoes.

    Topic: _____

    Main idea: _____

    _____

4. Drug use is now as much a scandal in professional athletics as it has been for many years among professional entertainers. Joining such stars as Janis Joplin, Elvis Presley, Judy Garland, and John Belushi, all of whom died from drug overdoses, are star athletes Len Bias and Don Rogers. Ben Johnson, the world record holder in the 100 meters, had his Olympic gold medal taken away because of the presence of drugs in his body, found

when he was tested after his victory. Alcohol-induced public rowdiness is rampant in stadiums in both the United States and Europe, often resulting in serious injuries and death. Accidents involving drunk driving are the second most frequent cause of death among teenagers.[4]

Topic: _____

Main idea: _____

_____

5. To the outsiders who came to the United States—European settlers and their descendants—the native people came to be known as American Indians. By the time that the Bureau of Indian Affairs (BIA) was organized as part of the War Department in 1824, Indian-white relations had already included three centuries of mutual misunderstanding. As we saw earlier, many bloody wars took place during the nineteenth century, and a significant part of the nation's Indian population was wiped out. By the end of the nineteenth century, schools for Indians operated by the BIA or church missions, often segregated, prohibited the practice of Indian cultures. Yet such schools did little to make the children effective competitors in white society.[5]

Topic: _____

Main idea: _____

_____

Exercise 9–7. Remembering Your Roots

Directions. For each word below, identify the root in the word and write the meaning of the root. The first one is done as an example.

	Root	**Meaning of Root**
1. prediction	dict	speak, say
2. concede	_____	_____
3. pathetic	_____	_____
4. monograph	_____	_____
5. factotum	_____	_____
6. morbid	_____	_____
7. conducive	_____	_____
8. missionary	_____	_____
9. prescribe	_____	_____
10. anachronism	_____	_____

Journal Entry

1. In what ways has college been different from what you expected? How has it been similar to what you expected?

_____

_____

_____

_____

_____

_____

_____

_____

_____

_____

2. Can the suggestions made in Selection 9 for better communication between men and women be helpful for communication between two people of the same sex? Why or why not?

_____

_____

_____

_____

_____

_____

_____

_____

_____

_____

10

RECOGNIZING
ORGANIZATION

In Chapter 10, you will:

1. Preview and read a selection about drug addiction and answer comprehension questions on the selection to check your understanding.
2. Use a multistrategy approach with the unfamiliar vocabulary in the selection.
3. Learn to recognize the primary organizational features of textbook chapters and articles.
4. Learn to recognize common patterns of organization and types of supporting material.

SELECTION 10
A BRIEF HISTORY OF DRUG ADDICTION IN AMERICA

Eugene Wintner

Directions. Preview the passage and use the space below to write your preview and pre-thinking notes.

Preview Notes

_____

_____

_____

_____

Pre-thinking Notes

_____

_____

_____

_____

> Cocaine's for horses, not for men,
> They say it'll kill you but they don't say when;
> Cocaine, round my brain.
>
> *Cocaine Blues*

5   Almost all Americans today are aware of the awful menace of drugs in our society. In fact, in the minds of many Americans, the drug problem is the most serious problem our society faces. A week cannot go by without a drug-related tragedy making its way into the news, whether it be the horrific account of a street murder or the pathetic tale of a newborn afflicted with an addiction to cocaine or heroin.

10   What many Americans do not realize, however, is that drug addiction, with its related social problems, is by no means a new phenomenon. The use of drugs on our planet goes back to pre-Biblical and, almost certainly, prehistoric times. And addiction to narcotic drugs in America can be traced back to the early nineteenth century.

Drug Addiction in Early America

Opium is derived from the innocent-looking poppy plant. During the nineteenth cen-
15   tury, opium was misused in parts of Europe and the Orient, where addicts would eat or smoke the drug for the high it provided. Some would visit squalid opium dens where the drug was smoked. However, most addictions in nineteenth century America were inadvertent. Doctors made wide use of opium-containing drugs for pain relief and for treatment of a variety of other ailments. In the absence of more modern
20   drugs, the opiates were among the most effective drugs available at that time. Patent medicines containing opium were also popular. One in particular, laudanum, was the source of many addictions.

Another widely used opium derivative was morphine, known for its potency as a pain reliever (it is still used today). Morphine was used to treat many wounded Civil
25   War soldiers. Ironically, when morphine was first isolated from opium, it was touted as a cure for opium addiction. The unfortunate individuals who were thus treated soon found themselves the victims of a new addiction. It is estimated that about a quarter of a million Americans—many of them soldiers and housewives—were addicted to a narcotic drug by the end of the nineteenth century.

Heroin and Cocaine

30   Heroin, derived from morphine, was first marketed by the Bayer Company at the turn of the century. Promoted as a new wonder drug, heroin appeared to relieve the with-

drawal symptoms of morphine and was hailed as a cure for morphine addicts. Once again, a new narcotic addiction was created. Initially, heroin sale was unregulated, and the drug soon began to be abused. By the 1950s and 1960s, heroin use had
35 reached epidemic proportions, ruining the lives of countless American men, women, and children.

What about cocaine, the scourge of the 1980s and 1990s? Though crack is a new form of the drug, cocaine use and addiction can be documented in America at least as early as the late nineteenth century. For example, cocaine was used by dockwork-
40 ers who discovered that the drug could increase their strength and endurance. It is also true that the original formula for Coca-Cola contained small amounts of cocaine.

Attempts to Regulate Drug Abuse

The first attempts of the US government to regulate the use of addictive drugs came in the early twentieth century. In 1906, the first Pure Food and Drug Act was passed. Though the law merely required that the active ingredients in a product be identified
45 on its label, it represented a first step toward discouraging the sale and use of addictive drugs.

In 1914, the first major antidrug legislation was enacted in the form of the Harrison Act. The intent of the law was to limit the use of addictive drugs to medicinal purposes. The law did not prevent doctors and pharmacists from supplying
50 drugs to addicts. In 1919, however, the Supreme Court reinterpreted the Harrison Act, prohibiting the supply of drugs to addicts. Since that time, a substantial number of drug laws have been enacted, primarily aimed at those who sell and distribute addictive drugs.

In recent times, the government's fight against drugs has shifted to an increased
55 emphasis on enforcement, with huge amounts of tax dollars funneled into the war on drugs (in 1991, $24 billion was spent on this "war"). Attempts have been made to interrupt the flow of drugs to the United States, including attacks on the drug lords in those South American countries where cocaine is harvested. Efforts to apprehend drug dealers have been increased, and prison terms for those convicted have been
60 lengthened. Rehabilitation programs for drug addicts have also been established, though in comparison to the monies allocated for enforcement, these programs are woefully underfunded.

It has been argued that drug laws are ineffective and that legalizing drugs would make it easier to solve America's drug problems. Proponents of this point of view
65 point out that laws have not stopped drug abuse and that, in fact, drug abuse has continued to increase over the years while more drug laws continue to be enacted. They argue that, just as Prohibition left alcohol sale in the hands of gangsters, laws against drugs force drug traffic into the criminal underworld. Some assert that our drug enforcement agencies are not part of the solution but part of the problem. They
70 believe that legalizing drugs would make it easier to control the spread of drugs and treat those addicted. On the other hand, opponents of drug legalization argue that legalizing drugs would not only condone their use but would also encourage their spread through increased availability.

75   The sad and simple fact is that drug addiction continues to destroy the lives of millions of Americans of all ages and races. Perhaps the real issue is not so much whether drugs should be legalized but rather how we can eradicate the underlying causes of drug addiction in our society. Education is only part of the answer. We must decrease and ultimately eliminate the motivations for drug use in our culture, especially among those most vulnerable—adolescents and the poor. This will be no easy

80   task, but may prove to be the only real hope for a drug-free America.

Interest Rating.   Please rate the interest level of Selection 10 on the following 1–5 scale (circle one):

5—Very interesting
4—Fairly interesting
3—Mildly interesting
2—A little boring
1—Very boring

Difficulty Rating.   Please indicate how difficult Selection 10 was for you to understand on the following 1–5 scale (circle one):

5—Very difficult
4—Fairly difficult
3—Moderate
2—Fairly easy
1—Very easy

Comments: _____

_____

Comprehension Questions

Directions.   For questions 1–5, choose the answer that best completes the statement. For questions 6–10, write your response in the space provided. Base all answers on what you read in the selection (you may refer to the selection when necessary).

_____ 1. The author suggests that Americans:
   a. Are incapable of solving the drug problem.
   b. Are unaware of the use of addictive drugs in our nation's past.
   c. Would like the media to give drug stories less publicity.
   d. Need a better understanding of the arguments in favor of drug legalization.

_____ 2. Opium addiction in early America:
   a. Resulted primarily from abuse of the drug in opium dens.
   b. Was often accidental.
   c. Was restricted to soldiers and housewives.
   d. Usually led to morphine addiction.

_____ 3. In summarizing government efforts to control the use of addictive drugs, the author mentions *all* of the following *except:*
   a. Labeling ingredients.
   b. Longer prison terms.
   c. Rehabilitation programs.
   d. Public education.

_____ 4. The main idea of the passage's sixth paragraph (lines 37–41) is:
   a. Cocaine is the most dangerous drug of the 1980s and 1990s.
   b. Cocaine use in the United States is not new.
   c. Coca-Cola once contained cocaine.
   d. Cocaine was used because it could increase strength and endurance.

_____ 5. The author believes that:
   a. Rehabilitation programs have not been adequately funded.
   b. Americans would not use addictive drugs if they were better educated.
   c. More money should be spent on enforcement.
   d. Harsher penalties for selling drugs should be imposed.

6. Why were opium-derived drugs used in the nineteenth century?

   _____

   _____

7. What were the main provisions of the Harrison Act?

   _____

   _____

   _____

8. Write a complete sentence of your own wording to express the main idea of paragraph 5 (lines 30–36).

   _____

   _____

9. What are some of the arguments for legalizing addictive drugs?

   _____

   _____

   _____

10. In your opinion, would legalizing addictive drugs make it easier to control them? Why or why not?

   _____

   _____

   _____

Vocabulary Exercise

Directions. Use a multistrategy approach to determine the meaning of each of the following words. Write your definition in the space provided.

1. afflicted (9) _____

2. squalid (16) _____

3. inadvertent (18) _____

4. potency (23) _____

5. ironically (25) _____

6. touted (25) _____

7. scourge (37) _____

8. apprehend (58) _____

9. allocated (61) _____

10. proponents (64) _____

11. condone (72) _____

12. eradicate (76) _____

Directions. In the space below, write your associations for any five of the above words:

Word   **Association**

_____   _____

_____   _____

_____   _____

_____   _____

_____   _____

Essay Question

Directions. On a separate sheet of paper, write a well-developed, half-page response to the following question:

How can the use of addictive drugs in our society be more effectively controlled? Why haven't previous efforts to control the use of addictive drugs been more successful?

Recognizing Organization

Good reading comprehension involves more than just identifying the important ideas—it also involves understanding how the ideas are related. The relationship and order of the ideas and information in a chapter or article form its organization. All written material is organized in some way.

Recognizing organization is an important part of study reading. Besides strengthening comprehension, recognizing organization has several other benefits:

- It makes it easier to *remember* the important points.
- It enables you to raise more useful goal questions.
- It encourages more effective underlining and notetaking.

You can learn a great deal about the organization of a chapter or article from your preview, especially if the material is divided into sections by headings and subheadings. In any case, the organization will become more apparent as you read through the chapter or article. Finally, you can analyze the organization after you finish the reading. This will enable you to lock the important points into your memory.

Most textbook chapters and essays are organized into three main segments: (1) an introduction, (2) a body, and (3) a summary or conclusion. Each will be discussed separately.

The Introduction

If there is no section headed "Introduction," consider all the material between the title and the first heading as the reading's introduction. If you are reading an article that has no headings, you can usually consider the first one or two paragraphs to be its introduction.

Introduction

> Think of all the people you see and meet every day—your neighbors, classmates at school, fellow commuters, coworkers at the office, and your family. We know by sight perhaps several hundred people, and we say hello to many of them. However, the number of persons we call our friends is small, and some of us cannot claim to have even a few friends.
>
> Human beings usually do not want to be isolated. We want friends—people around us who provide physical comforts and the social communication that adds to our appreciation of life. In this chapter, we will discuss several aspects of friendship: the factors that influence our choice of friends, how friendships develop, and some of the problems people may have in making friends. First, however, we will look at the various reasons why human beings need friends.
>
> **Why Do We Need Friends?**
> Friendships serve many human needs. The most basic of these is survival—friendships provide mutual protection. In addition to that need, friendships also help us to avoid loneliness, gain approval for ourselves, and . . .

The main function of the introduction is to introduce the topic of the chapter or article. Sometimes, useful background information on the topic is also furnished. In addition, you may be able to discern from the introduction the author's attitude toward the subject. In textbooks, the introduction will often indicate what subtopics will be addressed within the chapter. In some articles, the introduction contains a statement of the author's thesis—the main point that is developed in the article. Just as paragraphs have main ideas, an article or essay usually has one central theme the author wishes to communicate, and that central theme is called a thesis. An author will often state the thesis within the essay's introduction.

Another important function of the introduction is to arouse the reader's interest. Skilled writers use a variety of techniques to stimulate the reader's curiosity at the beginning of a chapter or article. Often, personal examples are used:

> Last year was the most wonderful—and worrisome—of times for Mike and Angie Rooney, of St. Louis, Missouri. The Rooneys, both twenty-nine, were thrilled to learn they were expecting their first child. But when Angie, an accountant, was four months pregnant, her firm laid her off.[2]

Sometimes quotes are used:

> Is all that we see or seem
> But a dream within a dream?[3]

Sometimes questions are used:

> Where is the traditional family meal heading?[4]

And sometimes the author uses humor or suspense:

> Don't look up while you're reading this. There may be someone nearby whose piercing eyes are waiting to catch your attention, hypnotize you, destroy your willpower, and make you a slave. At least, that's what you might believe if you watch too many old movies.[5]

The following is the beginning of Selection 9. How does the author arouse the reader's interest? What technique is used?

> - "My husband is deaf. He never hears what I say."
> - "She talks every subject to death."
> - "He always gets defensive when I ask him something."
> - "She makes everything into an argument."
> - "He is stubborn . . . he won't even consider what I have to say."
> - "He never says what he means."
> - "That's not what I meant."
>
> Such statements are typical of troubled relationships. While they may simply reflect inadequate communication, they may also point to profound problems. Even couples with only mild difficulties in communicating can have important misunderstandings.[6]

Note how the author uses a series of quotes to draw the reader in. He then follows with a general discussion of problems in relationships that we all experience at times.

Look back to the introduction for Selection 10. What techniques did the author use to stimulate your interest?

_____

_____

Exercise 10–1. Practice with Introductions

Part I. The following is an introduction to a chapter on race and ethnicity from a sociology textbook. Read the introduction and answer the questions that follow it.

What happens to a dream
deferred?

Does it dry up
like a raisin in the sun?
Or fester like a sore—
And then run?
Does it stink like rotten meat?
Or crust and sugar over—
like a syrupy sweet?

Maybe it just sags
like a heavy load

Or does it explode?

>   Langston Hughes
>   Harlem, 1951

Historically, Harlem has been the intellectual, cultural, and political center of New York City's (and America's) black community. It has served as a focal point for the hopes, dreams, frustrations, and anger of black writers, artists, and activists. As Langston Hughes suggests in his poem, many black Americans have had to put off their dreams, perhaps forever. But what happens to such unfulfilled dreams? Hughes observes that they may dry up within people's minds, weigh heavily on them, or eat away painfully at them. He ends by warning that the frustrations of black Americans may ultimately explode.

The portrait of Harlem drawn by Langston Hughes is, in a wider sense, a vision of the neighborhoods of many racial and ethnic minorities of the United States. Similar statements could describe the lives of American Indians on reservations or Chicanos (Mexican Americans) in the inner cities of the southwest. These and other minorities have experienced the often bitter contrast between the American dream of freedom, equality, and success and the grim realities of poverty, prejudice, and discrimination.

The social definitions of race and ethnicity, like that of class, affect people's place and status in a society's stratification system. Sociologists use such factors to define patterns of behavior—where one lives, whom one marries, what occupations one pursues. This chapter examines the meaning of race and ethnicity within American life. It will begin by identifying the basic characteristics of a minority group and distinguishing between racial and ethnic groups. The next part of the chapter will examine the dynamics of prejudice and discrimination and their impact on intergroup relations. Particular attention will be given to the experiences of America's racial and ethnic minorities. Finally, the social policy section will explore governmental policy in an area that has been of great concern to minority groups in the United States: affirmative action.[7]

1. How does the writer arouse the reader's interest?

    _____

    _____

2. Why did the author start the chapter with a poem?

    _____

    _____

3. What point is made by the poem?

    _____

    _____

4. What is the purpose of paragraph 3?

    _____

    _____

5. List some of the topics that will be addressed in this chapter.

    _____

    _____

Part II.   The introduction below is from the first chapter of a book on hypnosis. Read the introduction and answer the questions that follow it.

What Is Hypnosis?
Hypnosis has long been associated with the strange and mysterious, with sideshows and faith healers. But the truth is that hypnosis isn't the least bit mysterious or supernatural. In fact, you have been in an hypnotic state literally thousands of times. You didn't notice it because it seemed such a natural state of mind. And the hypnotic state *is* natural for all humans and many animals.

Chances are, at one time or another, you have found yourself driving along a familiar freeway *past* your exit, or perhaps you suddenly became aware of yourself behind the wheel and wondered where you were going. Occurrences such as these are common. Let's take a look at what makes them possible.

Everything you have learned is stored in your subconscious. Because you have already learned to drive, your driving skill is stored in your subconscious. As you begin your journey, you get in your car, maneuver out onto the freeway, move into a continuous flow of traffic, and reach a consistent speed. Now your conscious mind is free. That is, because the knowledge required for driving exists in your subconscious, your conscious mind drifts off, allowing your subconscious to become more active. You may become so engrossed in your thoughts that you drive in the direction of your office when your actual destination is the grocery store or the movie theater. When your attention is needed to change lanes, avoid something in the road, stop at a toll gate, or slow for an offramp, your conscious mind comes into play again. You may even arrive at your destination and wonder how you got there so quickly.

Driving is only one automatic activity. Whenever you do anything automatic, your conscious mind is diverted from your subconscious and you are more likely to go into an hypnotic state, such as the one described. Some of your automatic activities are more apt than others to allow or provide daydreaming. For example, your mind might drift when you are dining alone, taking a shower, mowing your lawn, or jogging. These activities, like driving, are stored in your subconscious. While you are functioning in this automatic mode, it is quite easy to drift from an alert state into a different level of consciousness. Daydreaming is the first of the levels in a trance state.[8]

1. How does the writer arouse the reader's interest?

   _____

   _____

2. What background information does the author provide about hypnosis?

   _____

   _____

   _____

3. What is the author's attitude toward hypnosis?

   _____

   _____

4. What do you think the next section will discuss?

   _____

   _____

The Body

The body of a chapter or article includes all the material between the introduction and the summary or conclusion. In other words, the body is the main part of the chapter, comprised of all its main sections. The body contains the ideas and information that develop the topic and provide support for the author's thesis. Most of the work in a typical reading assignment lies in learning the important points from the body of the chapter. When you read through the body of a chapter, it is helpful to identify the nature of the author's supporting material and to recognize the patterns of organization that are used to develop and present ideas and information.

Supporting Material

The supporting material in a chapter or essay consists of all the ideas and information used by the writer to develop his topic and support his thesis. Types of supporting material include:

   • **Facts.** A fact is a statement that can be proved true or is generally accepted as true. *Example:* The Harrison Act was passed in 1914.

   • **Statistics.** Statistics are number facts. *Example:* Between 45,000 and 50,000 civil war soldiers became addicted to narcotic drugs.

- **Examples.** Examples are often used as supporting material to clarify the author's main points. *Example:* Marjorie, for example, wanted Ken to invite her to a favorite cocktail lounge overlooking a bay to celebrate their anniversary.

- **Personal experience.** The writer may cite his own experiences to support and develop a point. *Example:* I will never forget the day the principal came into my fifth-grade classroom while we were clowning around.

- **Definitions of terms.** Key terms are often defined within the body of a text-book chapter. *Example: Norms* are established standards of behavior maintained by a society.

- **Explanations of theories.** The author may explain his own theory or the theories of others. *Example:* The *contact hypothesis* states that an interracial contact of people with equal status in cooperative circumstances will cause them to become less prejudiced and to abandon previously held stereotypes.

- **Quotes from experts or references to research studies.** The author may support her own ideas with the ideas of other writers or the results of her own or others' research. *Example:* Daniel Maltz and Ruth Borker summarize a number of findings that shed light on why marital partners have problems communicating.

- **Presentation of logical arguments.** An author may try to convince the reader of his opinion through logical argument. *Example:* Central to our understanding of environmental issues is the need to recognize the complexity of the problems we face and the relationships between environmental and other needs in our society.

- **Emotional appeal.** Sometimes an author will try to influence the reader by appealing to her emotions. *Example:* Recovery is a discovery; it is a joyful, happy, and positive experience, a discovery of self and of the world.

In Selection 10, the body of the passage consists primarily of factual information about drug use and drug regulation. Two statistical facts are included (the number of addictions at the end of the 19th century and the amount of money spent in 1991 on the war on drugs). The author also uses logical argument in discussing the issue of drug legalization.

Patterns of Organization

Have you ever had feedback like this from one of your English teachers: "The content of your paper was good, but it needs to be better organized"? All written material must be organized in some way. Organization allows the writer to communicate her ideas more effectively. Recognizing organizational patterns helps the reader to understand and remember the material better.

Writers use a wide variety of organizational patterns. The following four common patterns will be discussed in further detail:

- Chronological order — *Sequence*
- Listing or enumeration — *count*
- Comparison–contrast
- Cause–effect

Chronological Order.   Chronological order means time order. The material is presented in a time sequence—the order in which events actually occurred. Chronological order is common in history books, which usually trace sequences of events through time.

In Selection 10, the primary pattern of organization is chronological. The body of the passage begins with a discussion of drug use in early America and ends with a discussion of current efforts to curb drug abuse.

Listing or Enumeration.   Listing or enumeration is a simple and commonly used pattern that you will find in readings for virtually any college subject. In the listing pattern, the author lists related points of information. When the points are numbered, the pattern is called enumeration. Selection 9 relies heavily on listing and enumeration. The author lists the key differences in the communication styles of men and women. He then *enumerates,* or numbers, five suggestions for improving communication:

1. Tune in to your partner's channel.
2. Give listening signals.
3. Don't interrupt.
4. Ask questions skillfully.
5. Use diplomacy.

Comparison–Contrast.   In comparison–contrast, another commonly used pattern, the author shows the similarities and differences between two or more people, places, groups, theories, and so on. The comparison–contrast pattern is often used in social science readings, as well as other subjects. Selection 9 made frequent use of comparison–contrast. The author compared and contrasted the communication styles of men and women:

> Men are less likely than women to ask personal questions . . . For men, questions may represent intrusive meddling and an invasion of privacy; for women, however, they are a sign of intimacy and an expression of caring.

Cause–Effect.   The cause–effect pattern is used to show how one factor is the cause of another, or how one factor results from another. Cause–effect patterns are common in social science and science textbooks. Here is an example:

> China had a major opium addiction problem among its citizens. It sought to bar imports of opium, chiefly from Britain, which had damaged Chinese society and drained wealth overseas. Britain, seeking to end trade restrictions imposed by China, used this as an opportunity for war. In the first Opium War (1839–42), Britain forced China to expand trade and to cede Hong Kong. A second war (1856–58) opened more Chinese ports.
>
> With the loss to Britain, addiction in China increased. By the end of the century, there were nearly ninety million opium addicts in the country.[9]

The author explains the causes of the Opium Wars, as well as the unfortunate results of the wars for the Chinese.

It is not unusual to find more than one pattern of organization in a chapter, or even in a single paragraph. Generally, however, there is one dominant pattern you will recognize and use to help understand and remember the important points.

Exercise 10–2. Supporting Material and Patterns of Organization

Directions.   Read each passage and answer the questions that follow it.

1.   **Investigating Ozone**

For 30 years scientists have known about ozone. During the 1970's scientists began to study the effect of certain chemicals on ozone. They discovered that when a group of chemicals called "chlorofluorocarbons" (CFCs) enter the stratosphere, they undergo a chemical reaction that results in the release of the chemical chlorine. The chlorine in the stratosphere breaks up ozone molecules creating what we think of today as "ozone depletion." Since the mid-1980s, scientists have investigated the existence of ozone holes found both in Antarctica and the Arctic. Today, teams of researchers continue to study the problem of the disappearing ozone. Research projects include: (1) studies of the effects of other chemicals on ozone; (2) studies of the dynamic properties of global atmospheric circulation and how it affects the ozone layer; (3) direct measurements of the chemicals in the ozone layer; and (4) studies of the effects of ozone depletion on another important environmental problem, global warming. The emphasis of most of these studies is to understand why the ozone layer is disappearing.[10]

_c_ 1. The main idea of the passage is:
   a. Chlorofluorocarbons are environmental hazards.
   b. Chlorine causes ozone depletion.
   c. Scientists have been studying the problem of ozone depletion.
   d. Scientists are studying the effects of chemicals on ozone.

_a_ 2. The supporting material in this passage consists mainly of:
   a. Facts.
   b. Personal experience.
   c. Definition.
   d. Logical arguments to support the author's opinions.

_d_ 3. The patterns of organization used in this passage are:
   a. Chronological order and comparison–contrast.
   b. Comparison–contrast and cause–effect.
   c. Comparison–contrast and enumeration.
   d. Chronological order and enumeration. (cause - effect)

4. Explain your answer for question 3. (For example, if the passage used comparison–contrast, explain what was being compared or contrasted.)

_____

_____

2. **Fitness Isn't Health**

Health, fitness and performance are three separate and poorly correlated phenomena.

Health is generally defined as the freedom from disease.

Fitness strictly relates to your ability to meet the demands of your environment.

Performance is how well you accomplish a task.

You can be healthy without being fit. You can be in poor health and perform superbly. Sick athletes break records all the time. Every Olympic competition is populated by athletes with colds, fevers, infections and diarrhea. They invariably compete, and perform to their level.

The idea that sports make you healthy is a shibboleth. Sports can actually hurt you. They're not unhealthy *per se,* but they can be.

You don't have to be fit to be healthy. If health is defined as lack of disease, then fitness is not health. Only when your definition of health includes functional wellness—meaning the ability to cope with your environment—do health, fitness and performance coincide.

I was at a faculty picnic a few years back, swimming with a colleague of mine, John Sellwood. He was dying of lung cancer. One lung had been removed; the other was infected. He was to go into the hospital the next day. Both of us had been college swimmers. We'd been swimming for a while when he said, "I'll race you fifty yards."

"You've already given me my handicap," I said, and I thought it gave me an unfair advantage. We started off even. I didn't deliberately let him beat me, but he did. The next day he entered the hospital, and a month later he was dead. I can think of no better illustration of the lack of correlation between health and performance.[11]

_____ 1. The main idea of the passage is:
  a. Health, performance, and fitness are not the same.
  b. Health is more important than fitness.
  c. Performance is not the same as fitness.
  d. You can be healthy without being fit.

_____ 2. The supporting material in this passage includes:
  a. Statistics.
  b. Personal experience.
  c. Explanations of theories.
  d. Appeals to the reader's emotions.

_____ 3. The primary pattern of organization used in this passage is:
  a. Chronological order.
  b. Listing/enumeration.
  c. Comparison–contrast.
  d. Cause–effect.

4. Explain your answer for question 3.

_____

_____

3.   **American Feminism**

Many people believe that the feminist movement is a new and recent development in American history. But, in fact, the fight for women's rights dates back at least as far as colonial times. On March 31, 1776, months before the signing of the Declaration of Independence, Abigail Adams wrote to her husband John Adams, later the nation's second president:

history of American Feminism

> I desire you would Remember the Ladies, and be more favourable and generous to them than your ancestors. Do not put such unlimited power in the hands of Husbands. Remember all Men would be tyrants if they could. If particular care and attention is not paid to the Ladies, we are determined to foment a Rebellion, and will not hold ourselves bound by any Laws in which we have no voice, or representation.

In a formal sense, the American feminist movement was born in upstate New York, in a town called Seneca Falls, in the summer of 1848. On July 19, the first women's rights convention began, attended by Elizabeth Cady Stanton, Lucretia Mott, and other pioneers in the struggle for women's rights. This first wave of *feminists,* as they are currently known, battled ridicule and scorn as they fought for legal and political equality for women. They were not afraid to risk controversy on behalf of their cause; in 1872 Susan B. Anthony was arrested for attempting to vote in that year's presidential election.

Ultimately, the early feminists won many victories, among them the passage and ratification of the Nineteenth Amendment to the Constitution, which granted women the right to vote in national elections beginning in 1920. But suffrage did not lead to other reforms in women's social and economic position, and the women's movement became a much less powerful force for social change in the early and middle twentieth century.

The second wave of American feminism emerged in the 1960s and came into full force in the 1970s. In part, the movement was inspired by the publication of two pioneering arguments for women's rights: Simone de Beauvoir's book *The Second Sex* and Betty Friedan's book *The Feminine Mystique.* In addition, the general political activism of the 1960s led women—many of whom were working for black civil rights or against the war in Vietnam—to reexamine their own powerlessness as women. The sexism often found within allegedly progressive and radical political circles made many women decide that they needed to establish their own movement for "women's liberation."[12]

_C_ 1. The main idea of the passage is:
   a. The American feminist movement has faced many problems.
   b. The feminist movement is a recent development in American history.
   (c.) The American feminist movement has a long and interesting history.
   d. Women should have the same political rights as men.

_C_ 2. The supporting material in this passage consists mainly of:
   a. The writer's opinions.
   b. Explanation of a theory.
   (c.) Historical fact.
   d. Definitions.

_____ 3. The primary pattern of organization used in this passage is:
  a. Chronological order.
  b. Listing/enumeration.
  c. Comparison–contrast.
  d. Cause–effect.

4. Explain your answer for question 3.

_____

_____

4. **Pharmacological Effects of Alcohol**

It would be inaccurate to claim that the major mood-altering effects of alcohol are due only to the drinking environment. Clearly, if this were true, alcohol would not be used as widely as it is. In fact, alcohol has a number of pharmacologic properties that cause it to alter sensations, feelings, and abilities, regardless of the social setting.

Virtually all drugs have varied and increasingly stronger effects as they are used over a period of time and in greater doses. This is especially true for alcohol.

The dual nature of alcohol's effects has been known since alcohol was first used. Initially, alcohol is a stimulant and releaser of energy, but over time, and at larger doses, it acts as a strong depressant. One chemist, noting these contradictory characteristics, has called alcohol a "great deceiver."

Many studies have focused on alcohol's mood-changing qualities. The data are very clear. Using low doses of alcohol for short periods appears to liven spirits and produce greater happiness in normal people. Low doses also appear to reduce feelings of anxiety and depression in both normal and depressed people. High doses of alcohol, or moderate doses over longer periods, do not have mood-elevating effects on either of these groups of people. On the contrary, these higher doses can cause increased anxiety and depression in both normal and depressed people. Among alcoholics, the higher doses produce variable effects, none of them clearly positive.

Despite these findings, most people who use alcohol tend to remember only the light-use, low-dose, positive effects. They may recall how small amounts of alcohol helped lift their mood and relieve tension when a personal problem had made them depressed, frustrated, or insecure. Even heavy drinkers and alcoholics usually believe that using alcohol will raise their mood, decrease their anxiety, and improve their sleep.

These erroneous impressions have also been studied. Apparently, people in general, and heavy drinkers in particular, selectively remember the initial, low-dose, pleasant effects of alcohol and are generally less able to recall the later, high-dose, unpleasant effects. This phenomenon may be due to memory impairment caused by higher doses of alcohol, and is probably one of the reasons why heavy drinkers continue to abuse alcohol despite its adverse effects.[13]

_____ 1. The main idea of the passage is:
  a. People should consume less alcohol.
  b. Alcohol has a variety of pharmacologic effects, some of which are contradictory and deceiving.
  c. Most people who use alcohol tend to remember only the positive effects.
  d. Low doses of alcohol have positive effects, including reduction of anxiety and depression.

_____ 2. The supporting material in this passage includes:
   a. Research results.
   b. Statistical data.
   c. Definitions.
   d. Appeals to the reader's emotions.

_____ 3. The primary pattern of organization used in this passage is:
   a. Chronological order.
   b. Listing/enumeration.
   c. Comparison–contrast.
   d. Cause–effect.

   4. Explain your answer for question 3.

   _____

   _____

5. **The Contact Hypothesis**

A black woman is transferred from a job on an assembly line to a similar position working next to a white man. At first, he is patronizing, assuming she must be incompetent. She is cold and resentful; even when she needs assistance, she refuses to admit it. After a week, the growing tension between the two leads to a bitter quarrel. Yet, over time, each slowly comes to appreciate the other's strengths and talents. A year after they begin working together, these two workers become respectful friends. This is an example of what interactionists call the *contact hypothesis* in action.

The **contact hypothesis** states that an interracial contact of people with equal status in cooperative circumstances will cause them to become less prejudiced and to abandon previously held stereotypes. The factors of *equal status* and a *pleasant, noncompetitive atmosphere* must be underscored. In the example described above, if the two workers had been competing for one vacancy as a supervisor, the racial hostility between them might have worsened.

As blacks and other minorities slowly gain access to better-paying and more responsible jobs within American society, the contact hypothesis may take on even greater significance. The trend in our society is toward increasing contact between individuals from dominant and subordinate groups. This may be one hope of eliminating—or at least reducing—racial and ethnic stereotyping and prejudice.[14]

_____ 1. The main idea of the passage is:
   a. Prejudice can be reduced if people are open-minded.
   b. Contact between equal, cooperating members of different races reduces prejudice.
   c. The black woman and white man did not get along at first.
   d. The contact hypothesis explains why people of different races are unable to get along.

_____ 2. The supporting material in this passage includes:
   a. Research results.
   b. Example and explanation of theory.
   c. Definition and personal experience.
   d. Statistics and other facts.

_____ 3. The primary pattern of organization used in this passage is:
   a. Chronological order.
   b. Listing/enumeration.
   c. Comparison–contrast.
   d. Cause–effect.

4. Explain your answer for question 3.

---

6. **Index Crimes**

The term ***index crimes*** refers to the eight types of crimes that are reported annually by the Federal Bureau of Investigation (FBI) in its *Uniform Crime Report.* This category of criminal behavior generally consists of those serious offenses that people think of when they express concern about the nation's crime problem. Index crimes include murder, rape, robbery, and assault—all of which are violent crimes committed against people—as well as the property crimes of burglary, theft, motor vehicle theft, and arson.

In the United States, many index crimes involve the use of firearms. According to the FBI, in the year 1983, 21 percent of all reported assaults, 37 percent of reported robberies, and 58 percent of reported murders involved the use of a firearm. More than 11,000 Americans died in 1983 through homicides committed with a firearm. In addition, close to 1000 Americans die every year in accidents resulting from the improper use of handguns. Since 1963, guns have killed approximately 400,000 Americans, a figure which exceeds the number of our troops who died in World War II. While the general public has consistently favored gun control legislation in recent decades, the nation's major anti-gun control lobby, the National Rifle Association (NRA), has wielded impressive power in blocking or diluting such measures.

The prevalence of weapons and crime in a society can alter people's behavior in important ways. This is especially true in terms of common fears of index crimes. The majority of Americans never go out at night, avoid certain areas even during the day, never carry very much cash, and avoid wearing expensive jewelry. In addition, 44 percent keep a dog primarily for protection, and 48 percent have a gun or other weapon. Without question, the fear of crime against one's person or property has a dramatic effect on the lives of American citizens.[15]

_____ 1. The main idea of this passage is:
   a. The government should be more active in dealing with index crimes.
   b. We should not allow so many people to own guns.
   c. Index crimes are eight types of crimes reported annually to the FBI.
   d. Index crimes are serious crimes that cause many problems for our society.

_____ 2. The supporting material in this passage includes:
   a. Definition and statistics.
   b. Explanations of theories.
   c. Personal experience.
   d. Quotes from experts and other research findings.

_____ 3. The primary patterns of organization used in this passage are:
         a. Listing and cause–effect.
         b. Chronological order and comparison–contrast.
         c. Listing and chronological order.
         d. Cause–effect and comparison–contrast.
    4. Explain your answer for question 3.

_____

_____

Summaries and Conclusions

Most textbook chapters end with a summary. The summary is a convenience for the reader: It restates the important points from the chapter. Read the following summary from the chapter on race and ethnicity:

> The social dimensions of race and ethnicity are important factors in shaping people's lives in the United States and other countries. In this chapter, we examine the meaning of race and ethnicity and study the major racial and ethnic minorities of the United States.
>
> A *racial group* is set apart from others by obvious physical differences, whereas an *ethnic group* is set apart primarily because of national origin or distinctive cultural patterns.
>
> When sociologists define a *minority group,* they are primarily concerned with the economic and political power, or powerlessness, of the group.
>
> In a biological sense, there are no "pure races" and no physical traits that can be used to describe one group to the exclusion of all others.
>
> *Prejudice* is a negative attitude toward an entire category of people, often an ethnic or racial minority.
>
> Prejudiced attitudes often lead to discriminatory behavior, but the two are not identical, and each can be present without the other.
>
> *Institutional discrimination* results from the normal operations of a society.
>
> Four patterns describe typical intergroup relations in North America and elsewhere: *amalgamation, assimilation, segregation,* and *pluralism.*
>
> In the United States, the most highly rewarded pattern of intergroup relations is assimilation. Pluralism remains more of an ideal than a reality.
>
> Contemporary prejudice and discrimination against black Americans are rooted in the history of slavery in the United States.
>
> The various groups included under the general term *Hispanics* represent the largest ethnic minority in the United States.
>
> Despite recent *affirmative action* programs, white males continue to hold the overwhelming majority of prestigious and high-paying jobs in the United States.[16]

Unless it is very long, you should read the summary as part of your chapter preview. When you finish reading a chapter, you can reread the summary to remind yourself of what is important. Later, you can use the summary as a study aid.

Articles usually end with a conclusion rather than a summary. Instead of repeating what has already been stated, the conclusion leaves the reader with a final, or concluding, idea. The conclusion may tie together some of the points previously made, it may make a new point, or it may even ask a question, which will give the reader something new to think about. The following is the conclusion from Selection 10:

> The sad and simple fact is that drug addiction continues to destroy the lives of millions of Americans of all ages and races. Perhaps the real issue is not so much whether drugs should be legalized, but rather how we can eradicate the underlying causes of drug addiction in our society. Education is only part of the answer. We must decrease and ultimately eliminate the motivations for drug use in our culture, especially among those most vulnerable—adolescents and the poor. This will be no easy task, but may prove to be the only real hope for a drug-free America.

Instead of summarizing the information presented in the excerpt or offering his opinion on drug legalization, the author concludes by making a new point, suggesting that a different approach to the drug problem is needed.

Exercise 10–3. Understanding the Summary

Directions. Refer to the summary from the chapter on race and ethnicity (p. 228) to mark each of the following statements True or False.

_____ 1. The chapter provides a definition of prejudice.

_____ 2. The term *racial group* means the same thing as the term *ethnic group.*

_____ 3. Pluralism is common in the United States.

_____ 4. Prejudice is defined as a negative attitude toward particular individuals.

_____ 5. The chapter describes six patterns which typify intergroup relations.

Integrative Exercise

Exercise 10–4. Base Words and Suffixes

Directions.   The following words have been selected from the practice exercises within this chapter. Next to each word, write its base word and suffix. The first one is done as an example.

	Base Word	**Suffix**
1. performance	perform	ance
2. ethnicity		
3. global		
4. depletion		
5. ratification		
6. pharmacological		
7. depressant		
8. prevalence		
9. activism		
10. significance		
11. hostility		
12. interactionists		
13. pleasant		
14. erroneous		
15. variable		

Journal Entry

1. Why, in your opinion, do so many Americans use and abuse drugs?

_____

_____

_____

_____

_____

_____

_____

_____

_____

_____

_____

_____

2. Do you usually look for clues to the organization of what you read? How does recognizing organization help you read more effectively?

_____

_____

_____

_____

_____

_____

_____

_____

_____

_____

_____

_____

_____

11

UNDERLINING AND NOTETAKING

In Chapter 11, you will:

1. Preview and read a selection about female cops, trying to identify the patterns of organization and types of supporting material used in the selection.
2. Answer comprehension questions on the selection to check your understanding.
3. Learn strategies for underlining and marking in your textbooks and other reading assignments.
4. Learn strategies for taking notes from your textbooks and other reading assignments.

SELECTION 11
ARE WOMEN BETTER COPS?

Jeanne McDowell

Directions. Preview the passage and use the following space to write your preview and pre-thinking notes.

Preview Notes

_____

_____

_____

_____

Pre-thinking Notes

_____

_____

_____

_____

While You Read

1. Monitor your comprehension and look for the main ideas.
2. Try to recognize the types of supporting material and the patterns of organization used in the passage.

Among the residents, merchants, and criminals of Venice, Calif., officer Kelly Shea is as well known as the neighborhood gang leaders. The blond mane neatly tied back, slender figure and pink lipstick violate the stereotype of guardian of law and order; but Shea, 32, has managed to win the respect of street thugs who usually
5   answer more readily to the slam of a cop's billy club. She speaks softly, raising her voice only as needed. While her record of arrests during her 10 years on patrol is comparable to those of the men in her division, she has been involved in only two street fights, a small number by any cop's standard. Faced with hulking, 6-ft. 2-in. suspects, she admits that her physical strength cannot match theirs. "Coming across
10 aggressively doesn't work with gang members," says Shea. "If that first encounter is direct, knowledgeable and made with authority, they respond. It takes a few more words, but it works."

Hers is a far cry from the in-your-face style that has been the hallmark of mostly male police forces for years. But while women constitute only 9% of the nation's
15 523,262 police officers, they are bringing a distinctly different, and valuable, set of skills to the streets and the station house that may change the way the police are perceived in the community. Only on television is police work largely about high-speed heroics and gunfights in alleys. Experts estimate that 90% of an officer's day involves talking to citizens, doing paperwork and handling public relations. Many cops retire
20 after sterling careers never having drawn their gun.

As the job description expands beyond crime fighting into community service, the growing presence of women may help burnish the tarnished image of police officers, improve community relations and foster a more flexible, and less violent, approach to keeping the peace. "Policing today requires considerable intelligence,
25 communication, compassion and diplomacy," says Houston police chief Elizabeth Watson, the only female in the nation to head a major metropolitan force. "Women tend to rely more on intellectual than physical prowess. From that standpoint, policing is a natural match for them."

Such traits take on new value in police departments that have come under fire for
30 the brutal treatment of suspects in their custody. The videotaped beating of motorist

Rodney King by four Los Angeles cops last year threw a spotlight on the use of excessive force by police. The number of reports continues to remain high across the country after the furor that followed that attack. Female officers have been conspicuously absent from these charges: the independent Christopher commission, which investi-
35 gated the L.A.P.D.. in the aftermath of the King beating, found that the 120 officers with the most use-of-force reports were all men. Civilian complaints against women are also consistently lower. In San Francisco, for example, female officers account for only 5% of complaints although they make up 10% of the 1,839-person force. "And when you see a reference to a female," says Eileen Luna, former chief investi-
40 gator for the San Francisco citizen review board, "it's often the positive effect she has had in taking control in a different way from male officers."

Though much of the evidence is anecdotal, experts in policing say the verbal skills many women officers possess often have a calming effect that defuses potentially explosive situations. "As a rule, they tend to be much more likely to go in and
45 talk rather than try to get control in a way that makes everyone defensive," says Joanne Belknap, an associate professor of criminal justice at the University of Cincinnati. Women cops, she has found, perceive themselves as peacekeepers and negotiators. "We're like pacifiers in these situations," says Lieut. Helen DeWitte, a 21-year veteran of the Chicago force who was the first woman in the department to
50 be shot in the line of duty. Having women partners for 14 years taught San Francisco sergeant Tim Foley to use a softer touch with suspects, instead of always opening with a shove. "It's nonthreatening and disarming," he says, "and in the long run, it is easier than struggling."

Such a measured style is especially effective in handling rape and domestic-
55 violence calls, in which the victims are usually women. In 1985 a study of police officers' treatment of spousal-abuse cases by two University of Detroit professors concluded that female officers show more empathy and commitment to resolving these conflicts. While generalizations invite unfair stereotyping, male officers often tend not to take these calls as seriously, despite improved training and arrest policies in
60 almost half of all states. "Men tend to come on with a stronger approach to quiet a recalcitrant male suspect," notes Baltimore County police chief Cornelius Behan, whose 1,580-member force includes 143 women. "It gets his macho up, and he wants to take on the cop."

Despite the research, the notion of "female" and "male" policing styles remains
65 a controversial one. Individual temperament is more important than gender in the way cops perform, argues Edwin Delattre, author of *Character and Cops: Ethics in Policing.* Other experts contend that aggressiveness among officers is more a measure of a department's philosophy and the tone set by its top managers. "When cops are trained to think of themselves as fighters in a war against crime, they come to view
70 the public as the enemy," observes James Fyfe, a criminal-justice professor at The American University.

Some female officers have qualms as well about highlighting gender-based differences in police work, especially women who have struggled for years to achieve equity in mostly male departments. The women fear that emphasizing their "people
75 skills" will reinforce the charge that they don't have the heft or toughness to handle

a crisis on the street. But while women generally lack upper-body strength, studies consistently show that in situations in which force is needed, they perform as effectively as their male counterparts by using alternatives, such as karate, twist locks or a baton instead of their fists.

80   Yet the harassment that persists in many precinct houses tempts female cops to try to blend in and be one of the boys. All too often that means enduring the lewd jokes transmitted over police-car radios and the sexist remarks in the halls. In most places it means wearing an uncomfortable uniform designed for a man, including bulletproof vests that have not been adapted to women's figures. The atmosphere is made

85   worse because about 3% of supervisors over the rank of sergeant are women, in part owing to lack of seniority. Milwaukee police officer Kay Hanna remembers being reprimanded for going to the bathroom while on duty. Chicago Lieut. DeWitte found condoms and nude centerfolds in her mailbox when she started working patrol.

Women cops who have fought discrimination in court have fared well. Los

90   Angeles officer Fanchon Blake settled a memorable lawsuit in 1980 that opened up the ranks above sergeant to women. Last May, New York City detective Kathleen Burke won a settlement of $85,000 and a public promotion to detective first-grade. In her suit she had alleged that her supervisor's demeaning comments about her performance and his unwillingness to give her more responsible assignments impeded

95   her professional progress. He denied the charges. But many women still fear that complaining about such treatment carries its own risks. Beverly Harvard, deputy chief of administrative services in Atlanta, says a female officer would have to wonder "whether she would get a quick response to a call for backup later on."

Resistance toward women cops stems in part from the fact that they are still rel-

100   ative newcomers to the beat. In the years after 1910, when a Los Angeles social worker named Alice Stebbins Wells became the country's first full-fledged female police officer, women served mostly as radio dispatchers, matrons, and social workers for juveniles and female prison inmates. Not until 1968 did Indianapolis become the first force in the country to assign a woman to full-time field patrol. Since then,

105   the numbers of women in policing have risen steadily, thanks largely to changes in federal antidiscrimination laws. Madison, Wis., boasts a 25% female force, the highest percentage of any department in the country.

Because female cops are still relatively few in number, a woman answering a police call often evokes a mixed response. Reno officer Judy Holloday recalls arriv-

110   ing at the scene of a crime and being asked, "Where's the real cop?" Detective Burke, who stands 5 ft. 2 in. and has weighed 100 lbs. for most of her 23 years on the force, says she made 2,000 felony arrests and was never handicapped by a lack of physical strength. Burke recalls subduing a 6-ft. 4-in., 240-lb. robbery suspect who was wildly ranting about Jesus Christ. She pulled out her rosary beads and told him God had sent

115   her to make the arrest. "You use whatever you got," she says. When it looks as though a cop may be overpowered, the appropriate response for any officer—male or female—is to call for backup. "It's foolish for a cop of either sex to start dukin' it out," says Susan Martin, author of *On the Move: The Status of Women in Policing.*

A growing emphasis on other skills, especially communication, comes from a

120   movement in many police departments away from traditional law enforcement into a

community-oriented role. In major cities such as New York, Houston and Kansas City, the mark of a good officer is no longer simply responding to distress calls but working in partnership with citizens and local merchants to head off crime and improve the quality of life in neighborhoods. In Madison, which has been trans-
125   formed from a traditional, call-driven department into a community-oriented opera-
tion in the past 20 years, police chief David Couper says female officers have helped usher in a "kinder, gentler organization." Says Couper: "Police cooperation and a willingness to report domestic abuse and sexual assaults are all up. If a person is arrested, there is more of a feeling that he will be treated right instead of getting beat
130   up in the elevator."

In Los Angeles the city council is expected to pass a resolution next month that will lead to a 43% female force by the year 2000, up from 13.4% now. "We have so much to gain by achieving gender balance, we'd be nuts not to do it," says council-man Zev Yaroslavsky. Ideally, the solution in all cities and towns is a healthy mix of
135   male and female officers that reflects the constituency they serve and the changing demands of the job.[1]

Interest Rating.   Please rate the interest level of Selection 11 on the following 1–5 scale (circle one):

    5—Very interesting
    4—Fairly interesting
    3—Mildly interesting
    2—A little boring
    1—Very boring

Difficulty Rating.   Please indicate how difficult Selection 11 was for you to under-stand on the following 1–5 scale (circle one):

    5—Very difficult
    4—Fairly difficult
    3—Moderate
    2—Fairly easy
    1—Very easy

Comments: _____

_____

Comprehension Questions

Directions.   For questions 1–5, choose the answer that best completes the statement. For questions 6–10, write your response in the space provided. Base all answers on what you read in the selection (you may refer to the selection when necessary).

_____ 1. Supporting information in this article consists mainly of:
    a. Statistics and the author's personal experience.
    b. Quotes and examples.
    c. Theory and research.
    d. Historical fact and emotional appeal.

_____ 2. In the article's *conclusion,* the author suggests that:
    a. Females make better cops than males.
    b. Cops should avoid violent confrontations with offenders.
    c. People still don't trust female cops.
    d. A police force should contain an appropriate mix of female and male cops.

_____ 3. We can tell from the passage that most police work:
    a. Is exciting and heroic.
    b. Does not involve violent activity.
    c. Is dangerous.
    d. Is uninteresting.

_____ 4. According to the passage, female cops are especially effective in:
    a. Crimes against women.
    b. Crimes involving drugs.
    c. Undercover work.
    d. Disarming criminals.

_____ 5. The passage suggests that:
    a. Harassment of female cops has been steadily decreasing.
    b. Female cops are afraid of being beat up by male cops.
    c. Female cops are often unwilling to go to court to fight discrimination.
    d. It is unlikely that the attitude of male cops will ever change.

6. How does the author capture the reader's interest in the introductory paragraph?

_____

7. What is the primary pattern of organization used in this selection (chronological order, enumeration/listing, comparison–contrast, or cause–effect)? Explain your answer.

_____

8. Explain some of the advantages female cops have over male cops.

_____

_____

_____

9. In your opinion, what are some reasons why a male cop might harass a female cop?

   _____

   _____

10. In a complete sentence of your own wording, write the main idea of paragraph 5 (lines 42–53).

    _____

    _____

Vocabulary Exercise

Part I. Use a multistrategy approach to determine the meaning of each of the following words from the selection. Write your definition in the space provided.

1. stereotype (3) _____
2. sterling (20) _____
3. burnish (22) _____
4. tarnished (22) _____
5. metropolitan (26) _____
6. prowess (27) _____
7. conspicuously (33) _____
8. recalcitrant (61) _____
9. qualms (72) _____
10. equity (74) _____
11. reprimanded (87) _____
12. impeded (94) _____

Part II. In the following space, write your associations for any five of the above words.

Word	Association
1. _____	_____
2. _____	_____
3. _____	_____
4. _____	_____
5. _____	_____

Essay Question

Directions. On a separate sheet of paper, write a well-developed, half-page response to the following question:

Does the author believe that women are better cops? Support your answer.

Underlining and Notetaking

Good study reading is an active process, not a passive one. Marking in the text and taking notes are two commonly used strategies that will help you remain actively involved with the material you're reading.

Underlining

Most college students underline or highlight while reading assignments. Underlining is easy to do and allows the reader to reinforce important points. Unfortunately, most students do not mark their texts effectively. Often, they underline too much. Sometimes, upon rereading, they find that the underlined material is not clear. Sometimes students simply fail to capture the important points. The result is that the underlinings students make may not be valuable for later study.

Tips for Effective Underlining and Marking

The following tips will make your underlinings more useful:

• *Read before underlining.* If you underline as you read, everything may seem important, and you may underline material unnecessarily. Instead, read an entire section and then go back and decide what is important enough to be marked. If the section is long, you may prefer to stop at the end of every few paragraphs.

• *Do not underline too much.* Limit your underlining to main points and important details. A good rule of thumb is to underline no more than one-quarter to one-third of the material.

• *Underline complete thoughts.* Isolated words and phrases will not be meaningful when you reread them later. Underline enough of the words so that the point is clear when you read over what you have marked. It is usually best to underline whole sentences.

• *Avoid repetition.* Even though an idea may be important, there is no need to underline the same idea twice.

• *Use other annotations (markings).* Underlining alone will not show how the ideas in the passage are related. Enhance your underlinings with some other simple markings:

Use asterisks (*) to mark important terms and definitions.

Circle very important points.

Label examples "Ex" in the margin.

Write marginal notes to clarify what you've underlined.

Use numbers to show a listing and label other important patterns of organization (for example, if the author is using comparison–contrast, write "cc" in the margin).

Use a question mark (?) for information that needs clarification.

Use different color highlighters for visual reinforcement if you wish.

• *Read over what you have marked.* Doing this after you have finished each section will help you be sure that your underlinings and annotations are clear.

Effective Underlining

The following example illustrates effective underlining of the first five paragraphs of Selection 11.

"Ex"
Kelly Shea

Among the residents, merchants and criminals of Venice, Calif., officer Kelly Shea is as well known as the neighborhood gang leaders. The blond mane neatly tied back, slender figure and pink lipstick violate the stereotype of guardian of law and order; but Shea, 32, has managed to win the respect of street thugs who usually answer more readily to the slam of a cop's billy club. She speaks softly, raising her voice only as needed. While her record of arrests during her 10 years on patrol is comparable to those of the men in her division, she has been involved in only two street fights, a small number by any cop's standard. Faced with hulking, 6-ft. 2-in. suspects, she admits that her physical strength cannot match theirs. "Coming across aggressively doesn't work with gang members," says Shea. "If that first encounter is direct, knowledgeable and made with authority, they respond. It takes a few more words, but it works."

thesis

Hers is a far cry from the in-your-face style that has been the hallmark of mostly male police forces for years. But <u>while women constitute only 9% of the nation's 523,262 police officers,</u> they are bringing a distinctly different, and valuable, set of skills to the streets and the station house that may change the way the police are perceived in the community. Only on television is police work largely about high-speed heroics and gunfights in alleys. Experts estimate that 90% of an officer's day involves talking to citizens, doing paperwork and handling public relations. Many cops retire after sterling careers never having drawn their gun.

most
police
work
routine

As the job description expands beyond crime fighting into community service, <u>the growing presence of women may help ①burnish the tarnished image of police officers,</u> ②<u>improve community relations and ③foster a more flexible, and less violent, approach to keeping the peace. "Policing today requires considerable intelligence, communication, compassion and diplomacy,"</u> says Houston police chief Elizabeth Watson, the only female in the nation to head a major metropolitan force. <u>"Women tend to rely more on intellectual than physical prowess.</u> From that standpoint, policing is a natural match for them."

Elizabeth Watson,
only female police
chief of large city
(Houston)

<u>Such traits take on new value in police departments that have come under fire for the brutal treatment of suspects in their custody.</u> The videotaped beating of motorist Rodney King by four Los Angeles cops last year threw a spotlight on the use of excessive force by police. The number of reports continues to remain high across the country after the furor that followed that attack. <u>Female officers have been conspicuously absent from these charges;</u> the independent Christopher commission, which investigated the L.A.P.D. in the aftermath of the King beating, found that the 120 officers with the most use-of-force reports were all men. <u>Civilian complaints against women are also consistently lower.</u> In San Francisco, for example, female officers account for only 5% of complaints although

they make up 10% of the 1,839-person force. "And when you see a reference to a female," says Eileen Luna, former chief investigator for the San Francisco citizen review board, "it's often the positive effect she has had in taking control in a different way from male officers."

Though much of the evidence is anecdotal, experts in policing say <u>the verbal skills many women officers possess often have a calming effect that defuses potentially explosive situations.</u> "As a rule, they tend to be much more likely to go in and talk rather than try to get control in a way that makes everyone defensive," says Joanne Belknap, an associate professor of criminal justice at the University of Cincinnati. <u>Women cops</u>, she has found, <u>perceive themselves as peacekeepers and negotiators</u>. "We're like pacifiers in these situations," says Lieut. Helen DeWitte, a 21-year veteran of the Chicago force who was the first woman in the department to be shot in the line of duty. Having women partners for 14 years taught San Francisco sergeant Tim Foley to use a softer touch with suspects, instead of always opening with a shove. "It's nonthreatening and disarming," he says, "and in the long run, it is easier than struggling."

Exercise 11–1. Underlining

Directions: Using the suggestions listed above, underline and mark paragraphs 6 to 12 from Selection 11, reprinted below.

Such a measured style is especially effective in handling rape and domestic-violence calls, in which the victims are usually women. In 1985 a study of police officers' treatment of spousal-abuse cases by two University of Detroit professors concluded that female officers show more empathy and commitment to resolving these conflicts. While generalizations invite unfair stereotyping, male officers often tend not to take these calls as seriously, despite improved training and arrest policies in almost half of all states. "Men tend to come on with a stronger approach to quiet a recalcitrant male suspect," notes Baltimore County police chief Cornelius Behan, whose 1,580-member force includes 143 women. "It gets his macho up, and he wants to take on the cop."

Despite the research, the notion of "female" and "male" policing styles remains a controversial one. Individual temperament is more important than gender in the way cops perform, argues Edwin Delattre, author of *Character and Cops: Ethics in Policing.* Other experts contend that aggressiveness among officers is more a measure of a department's philosophy and the tone set by its top managers. "When cops are trained to think of themselves as fighters in a war against crime, they come to view the public as the enemy," observes James Fyfe, a criminal-justice professor at The American University.

Some female officers have qualms as well about highlighting gender-based differences in police work, especially women who have struggled for years to achieve equity in mostly male departments. The women fear that emphasizing their "people skills" will reinforce the charge that they don't have the heft or toughness to handle a crisis on the street. But while women generally lack upper-body strength, studies consistently show that in situations in which force is needed, they perform as effectively as their male counterparts by using alternatives, such as karate, twist locks or a baton instead of their fists.

Yet the harassment that persists in many precinct houses tempts female cops to try to blend in and be one of the boys. All too often that means enduring the lewd jokes transmitted over police-car radios and the sexist remarks in the halls. In most places it means wearing an uncomfortable uniform designed for a man, including bulletproof vests that have not been adapted to women's figures. The atmosphere is made worse because about

3% of supervisors over the rank of sergeant are women, in part owing to lack of senior-ity. Milwaukee police officer Kay Hanna remembers being reprimanded for going to the bathroom while on duty. Chicago Lieut. DeWitte found condoms and nude centerfolds in her mailbox when she started working patrol.

Women cops who have fought discrimination in court have fared well. Los Angeles officer Fanchon Blake settled a memorable lawsuit in 1980 that opened up the ranks above sergeant to women. Last May, New York City detective Kathleen Burke won a settlement of $85,000 and a public promotion to detective first-grade. In her suit she had alleged that her supervisor's demeaning comments about her performance and his unwillingness to give her more responsible assignments impeded her professional progress. He denied the charges. But many women still fear that complaining about such treatment carries its own risks. Beverly Harvard, deputy chief of administrative services in Atlanta, says a female officer would have to wonder "whether she would get a quick response to a call for backup later on."

Resistance toward women cops stems in part from the fact that they are still relative newcomers to the beat. In the years after 1910, when a Los Angeles social worker named Alice Stebbins Wells became the country's first full-fledged female police officer, women served mostly as radio dispatchers, matrons, and social workers for juveniles and female prison inmates. Not until 1968 did Indianapolis become the first force in the country to assign a woman to full-time field patrol. Since then, the numbers of women in policing have risen steadily, thanks largely to changes in federal antidiscrimination laws. Madison, Wis., boasts a 25% female force, the highest percentage of any department in the country.

Because female cops are still relatively few in number, a woman answering a police call often evokes a mixed response. Reno officer Judy Holloday recalls arriving at the scene of a crime and being asked, "Where's the real cop?" Detective Burke, who stands 5 ft. 2 in. and has weighed 100 lbs. for most of her 23 years on the force, says she made 2,000 felony arrests and was never handicapped by a lack of physical strength. Burke recalls subduing a 6-ft. 4-in., 240-lb. robbery suspect who was wildly ranting about Jesus Christ. She pulled out her rosary beads and told him God had sent her to make the arrest. "You use whatever you got," she says. When it looks as though a cop may be overpow-ered, the appropriate response for any officer—male or female—is to call for backup. "It's foolish for a cop of either sex to start dukin' it out," says Susan Martin, author of *On the Move: The Status of Women in Policing.*

Exercise 11–2. Underlining

Directions. Imagine you are taking a course in which you have been assigned to read the following passage from your textbook. Using the previously listed sugges-tions, underline and mark the passage.

Single-Parent Families

Single-parent families, in which there is only one parent present to care for the children, can hardly be viewed as a rarity in the United States. Because of continuing increases in the nation's rates of divorce and unwed motherhood, nearly half of today's children will be reared at least temporarily in single-parent families—90 percent of which are headed by women.

Whether judged in economic or emotional terms, the lives of single parents and their children are not inevitably more difficult than life in a traditional nuclear family. It is as inaccurate to assume that a single-parent family is necessarily "deprived" as it is to assume that a two-parent family is always secure and happy. Nevertheless, life in a single-parent family can be extremely stressful. Ronald Haskins, director of the Child Development Institute at the University of North Carolina, observes: "It's a big and risky undertaking when so many parents try to raise so many children alone."

There is a clear association between the increase in families headed by single mothers and the feminization of poverty. Families headed by divorced or never-married mothers represent the fastest-growing segment of the female poor. The economic problems of single mothers result from such factors as sex discrimination in the paid labor force, the high costs of child care, inadequate welfare benefits, and fathers' failure to pay court-ordered child support.

A family headed by a single mother faces especially difficult problems when the mother is a teenager. Currently, the United States has the highest teenage birthrate of any industrialized nation. The birthrate among unmarried teenagers tripled between 1960 and 1980. By 1981, there were more than 686,000 births to unwed mothers in the United States; of these, nearly 40 percent were to teenagers. Young single mothers commonly must drop out of school; as a consequence, most have few marketable skills and become dependent on family members or welfare benefits for financial support.

In 1982, about 800,000 fathers in the United States were bringing up sons and daughters without day-to-day assistance from a wife. Sociologist Kristine Rosenthal has studied the impact of sole custody on single fathers. One of her conclusions is that such fathers become less obsessed with their work and more "people-oriented." While an increasing number of women are entering jobs traditionally restricted to men, a growing number of men are adjusting to the social roles associated with single parenthood.

Many single parents complain that their lives are lonely. If the parent works outside of the home during the day—and then must prepare dinner and care for the child in the evening—there will be little time and energy left for socializing with adults or pursuing hobbies. As a result, single parents have banded together to form organizations such as Parents Without Partners which provide emotional support, social functions, and contacts for sharing of child care.[2]

Notetaking

Though helpful, underlining is still a relatively passive strategy. Taking notes from your readings is a more powerful strategy for several reasons:

- It forces you to think more actively about the material.
- Writing the important points provides stronger reinforcement than underlining.
- Notes are more useful for later study because they are more compact, and they show the organization of the material better than underlinings.

Of course, taking notes takes more time than underlining. For this reason, students are often reluctant to take notes from their reading assignments. Consider your goals for each assignment before you decide whether to take notes or merely underline. You may prefer to compromise by first underlining and then taking a limited set of notes on the most important points.

In any case, there will be times when you will have to take notes from your readings—for example, when you are working with a library book. College students should be able to take a good set of notes from their reading assignments.

Tips for Notetaking from Text

• *Read first.* As with underlining, read through a section first, then decide which points are noteworthy.

• *Paraphrase.* Avoid copying word for word from the text. Using some of your own words is a way of making sure that you understand what you have read. Paraphrasing also enables you to shorten and simplify the explanations in the book.

• *Word important points fully.* Use enough words so that your notes will be clear when you reread them.

• *Show the organization* of ideas by using an informal outlining procedure. Place major headings to the left, in capital letters; indent once for main points; and indent twice for details and examples.

```
HEADING
    Main Idea
        Detail
        Detail
    Main Idea
        Detail
    Main Idea
        Detail
        Detail
        Detail
```

• *Let your notes reflect the passage's pattern of organization.* For example, if enumeration is used in the passage, number the key points in your notes.

When you have finished taking your notes, read them over immediately to make sure they are clear to you. The following example illustrates effective notes from the first five paragraphs of Selection 11.

Are Women Better Cops?

Women have different and valuable skills to contribute to police work
    This may change public perception of police
    Only 9% of nation's cops are female
    Most police work does not involve violent confrontations
Women cops may help improve police image
    May help improve community relations
    Women use less violence
    Modern police work requires intelligence, communication, compassion & diplomacy
    Women cops rely more on intellect than physical strength
    (Elizabeth Watson, only female police chief in major US city—Houston)

Women's approach important today with all the complaints of police brutality
  Female cops have not been accused of brutality
  There are also fewer civilian complaints against female cops
Women cops are likely to use verbal skills in difficult situations
  They see themselves as peacemakers and negotiators

Exercise 11–3. Notetaking

Directions. Using the suggestions listed above, take an organized set of notes for paragraphs 6 to 12 from Selection 11 (on pages 242–243) that would be useful for later study.

_____

_____

_____

_____

_____

_____

_____

_____

_____

_____

_____

_____

_____

_____

_____

_____

_____

Exercise 11–4. Notetaking

Directions. Imagine you are taking a course in which you have been assigned to read the following passage from your textbook. In the space provided, take an organized set of notes from the passage that would be useful for later study.

The Male Role

The struggle to play the masculine role can be fraught with anxieties. The motives for acceptance and dependency are universal. So are the emotions that accompany them. Society's demand to suppress them is in effect a demand to "transcend your humanity." And efforts to do so can never completely succeed: "Since it is impossible to program out all emotions, even the most extreme he-man can only approximate" the masculine ideal. Thus every man—aware of the stirrings of the softer and weaker emotions he tries so dutifully to hide—is bound to worry about his own masculinity.

The Male Burden of Proof

Girls and women are considered feminine unless they display overwhelming evidence to the contrary—but boys and men have to win the right to be called masculine. They have to *prove* their masculinity; they have to face and succeed in all kinds of "financial, intellectual, sexual, and physical tests." The testing process starts early and continues throughout life. At different ages and in different environments, the requirements vary. Boys may have to prove themselves by being athletic or by being tough, men by making a lot of money or by being a man's man in whatever way this is defined by their associates. But the burden of proof is always present—and the burden is heavier than most people think:

> It is a strain for women to have to act weaker, more dependent and submissive, and less competent than they really are, but it's probably a greater strain to have to act tougher, stronger, more dominant, and more competent than one really feels inside. It is also a strain to have one's masculine status constantly dependent on success at work and providing well for a family of dependents.

The Burden of Being Superior

While women grow up with a tendency toward built-in inferiority complexes, men are sex-typed into thinking of themselves as superior. For all the secret self-doubts they may have, they have been taught that they are the better of the two sexes, destined by birth to be lord and master. This has its obvious advantages—yet it too can be a burden. Robert Seidenberg, a psychoanalyst, has made these observations:

> It is quite probable that men become victims of their own advantages. An unearned superiority is thrust on them. This places a constant burden of proof upon them which causes distortions of character and personality which are tragic to behold. The man is placed, often through no need or desire of his own, in a position of proving why he, of two people, should automatically be the standard bearer of the family. Often, to prove his doubtful superiority, he must resort to pseudo self-enhancement such as uncalled-for bravery, cunning, tricks, and outmoded feats of courage . . . Men ultimately suffer the corruption of unearned victories and ascendancy. Their personalities become warped by the myth of their own dominance and superiority.

And how is a man supposed to act toward a woman who is obviously as intelligent and well-educated as he is—perhaps even more so? A survey of Ivy League seniors showed that many of them felt extremely uncomfortable in such a situation. About 30 percent conceded that they had felt intellectually insecure or under strain. Some had simply decided to avoid such women. ("If a girl knows more than I do, I resent her." "I enjoy talking to more intelligent girls, but I have no desire for a deep relationship with them. I guess I still believe that the man should be more intelligent.") Others had mixed feelings. They wanted intellectual companionship with women but found it threatening. One of them admitted that it made him feel "nervous and humble."

It is perhaps as difficult to be automatically typed as superior as to be automatically typed as inferior. Men as well as women suffer anxieties over the way they are sex typed to perform—which may be totally at odds with their own motives and emotions, not to mention their physical strength and other capabilities. The traditional standards of masculinity and femininity may still serve a purpose or may have become obsolete—but as long as they continue to influence human behavior they will cause inner conflicts for both sexes, as well as some open conflicts between them.[3]

Mapping

As an alternative to traditional notetaking, you can take notes from your readings by mapping the important ideas. Mapping is a visual form of notetaking, a diagraming of ideas that shows their relationship to one another. To map notes, follow these steps:

1. Determine the main idea or main heading and write it inside a circle.
2. Draw lines branching out from the main idea for the major topics.
3. Branch out from the major topics to include corresponding details.

Figure 11–1 illustrates a typical map.

FIGURE 11–1   *Mapping Diagram*

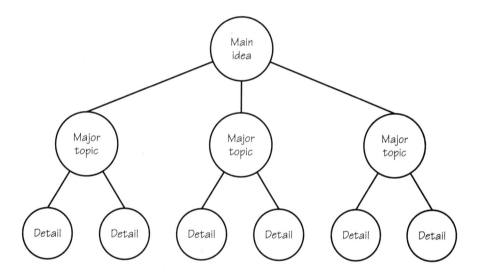

Figure 11–2 illustrates how we might map the first part of Selection 11.

There are no rules to mapping. You can map the ideas in whatever way seems most logical to you for learning the material. A successful map shows how the ideas in the passage are related. Figure 11–3 shows some possible mapping structures.

Mapping is a way of taking notes that especially appeals to visual learners (auditory learners sometimes like to record their notes on tape). If you have never tried this method, experiment with it to determine if you prefer it to traditional notetaking.

FIGURE 11–2   *Mapping Selection 11*

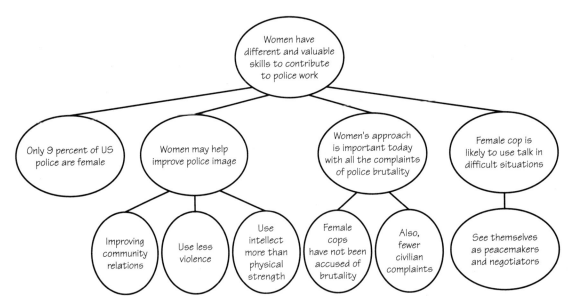

FIGURE 11–3 *Alternative Mapping Structures*

a. Simple main idea and details map.

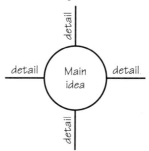

b. Map of sequence of events (or steps in a process).

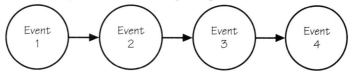

c. Map for comparison–contrast.

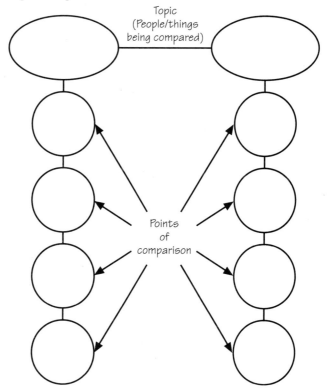

Exercise 11–5. Mapping

Directions. In the space below, map paragraphs 6 to 12 from Selection 11.

Exercise 11–6. Mapping

Directions. In the space below, map either "Single-Parent Families" or "The Male Role."

Exercise 11–7. Underlining and Notetaking

Directions.   Imagine you are taking a course called Marriage and Family and have been assigned to read the following passage from your textbook.

1. Underline and mark the passage.
2. Then, use either the traditional notetaking method or mapping to take a set of notes that would be useful for later study.

Functions of Modern Families

Many functions formerly performed within or by families are now shared with or provided by others. The production, preparation, and preservation of food are now Big Business. The education and religious training of children are now, to a large extent, entrusted to schools and churches. Protective services are provided by police and fire departments. Medical care is provided by doctors, nurses, and teams of technicians. What functions are left for the family to perform? What, indeed, but the most important of all—those that contribute to producing human beings capable of living competently in a world that their ancestors never knew. Contemporary families fulfill at least six important functions:

1. *Generating affection* between husband and wife, between parents and children, and among members of the generations. Love is a product of family living. Men and women in western societies usually marry for love and usually have children as an expression of their love for one another. Their children need to have love in an emotional climate of ongoing affection in order to thrive. The family in North America stays together through the years not because it has to, but because the members want to, out of enduring affection for one another. Ideally, both parents and children grow in a climate of mutual affection that contributes to their healthy development.

2. *Providing personal security and acceptance.* Most people look to the family for the security and acceptance they need to live lives of dignity and worth. Within the family, individuals can make mistakes and learn from them in an atmosphere of protective security. The family is one of the few remaining places where complementary rather than competitive relationships can be fostered and enjoyed. Thus the family provides a home base with stability that allows its members to develop naturally—in their own way, at their own pace.

3. *Giving satisfaction and a sense of purpose.* The family gives human beings a sense of basic satisfaction and worth that the world of work only occasionally provides. An unskilled laborer may derive only minimal satisfaction from a job, and the person in more challenging work may find it fraught with anxiety, conflict, and struggle. It is in the family setting that adults and children enjoy life and each other—in family gatherings and celebrations, around the family table, in family rituals, on family trips, and in many other activities that family members find satisfying. Parents often feel that they live for one another and for the children for whom they are responsible.

4. *Ensuring continuity of companionship.* Perhaps only within the family group can this need be met today. Friends, neighbors, colleagues, and others may or may not remain close by for more than a few years. Jobs change, neighborhoods shift, and people move on. In most cases family associations alone can be expected to endure. In ways not expected outside the family, the continuing presence of sym-

pathetic companions encourages family members to relate the happenings of the day and to share the disappointments and satisfactions of life as they occur. Who but members of one's own family can delight so fully in the flush of success or share so completely the burden of failure?

5. *Providing social placement and socialization.* In every society individuals learn what is expected of them and where they fit in the social hierarchy through their families. At birth a child automatically acquires his family's status by virtue of the genetic, physical, ethnic, national, religious, cultural, economic, political, and educational heritage unique to his parents and their kin. The family acts as the transmitter of the cultural heritage from one generation to the next. It performs the task of interpreting to its members the meaning of the many situations of which they are a part. Older family members serve as role models for the younger ones.

> It is also generally recognized that lifelong patterns of behavior, values, goals, and attitudes of children are strongly associated with the characteristics of their parents, especially as these are expressed in childbearing and family life styles. Although later experiences outside the home also have important influences on the developing child, the availability of these experiences to him and the ways in which he uses them are strongly affected by what he has learned in his home.

6. *Inculcating controls and a sense of what is right.* Within the family individual members first learn the rules, rights, obligations, and responsibilities characteristic of human societies. Family members feel free to criticize, to correct and to order, to praise or to blame, to reward or to punish, to entice or to threaten each other in ways that would be unthinkable elsewhere. "In all these ways, the family is an instrument or agent of the larger society; its failure to perform adequately means that the goals of the larger society may not be attained effectively." The kinds of praise and punishment experienced by children in their earliest years instill in them the sense of right and wrong that they will carry into adulthood in their moral values and in their definitions of the good, the right, and the worthy.

The family, functioning as a "choosing agency," evaluates and selects from among many ways of life—and so is a primary source of human values that spread outward into society as a whole.[4]

Notes: _____

_____

_____

_____

_____

_____

_____

_____

_____

_____

_____

_____

_____

_____

_____

_____

_____

_____

_____

_____

_____

_____

_____

Map:

Integrative Exercises

Exercise 11–8. Recognizing Organization

Directions.   Read each passage and answer the questions that follow it.

1. **Jung's Types**

    Unlike Hippocrates or Sheldon, Jung developed a theory of psychological types that avoids making connections between personality and physique. Jung developed the concepts of introvert and extravert as types. The *introvert* prefers to be alone and avoids people. He reacts to stress by crawling into his shell. The *extravert* is sociable and outgoing. He reacts to stress by seeking out others. Jung argued that every individual possesses innate mechanisms for both introversion and extraversion. In some circumstances, the mechanism for extraversion dominates and the individual behaves as an extravert; in other circumstances, the mechanism for introversion dominates and the individual behaves as an introvert. However, for some reason the dominance of one mechanism sometimes becomes chronic in some people. These people become types, either introverts or extraverts. Instead of displaying the normal variations in behavior that most people exhibit, these types behave in pretty much the same way in most situations.

    Jung's approach to psychological types is quite flexible compared, for example, to that of Hippocrates. According to Jung, people don't necessarily fit into one type or another. The mechanisms of introversion and extraversion are within us all, complementing and usually counterbalancing each other. A person becomes a "type" only when one of the mechanisms wins permanent dominance.[5]

_____ 1. The supporting material in this passage consists mainly of:
   a. An explanation of Jung's theory.
   b. Historical fact about Jung and his theory.
   c. Logic and emotion to persuade the reader that Jung's ideas are correct.
   d. Statistics and scientific fact to support Jung's theory.

_____ 2. The primary pattern of organization used in this passage is:
   a. Chronological order.
   b. Listing/enumeration.
   c. Comparison–contrast.
   d. Cause–effect.

_____ 3. We can tell from the passage that:
   a. Other theorists have classified people by their physical type.
   b. Jung's theory is widely accepted.
   c. Most psychologists prefer Hippocrates' approach to Jung's.
   d. Jung never knew of Sheldon's theory.

   4. Based on what you have read in the passage, would you classify yourself as an introvert or extravert? Explain your response.

_____

_____

2. **A Proposal for an Economic Bill of Rights**

    Should the Constitution Guarantee Fulfillment of People's Basic Needs?
    The nation celebrated the 200th anniversary of the Bill of Rights in 1991. The occasion
    should provide a timely opportunity to consider constitutional reform as a means for
    achieving what the political process has so far failed to accomplish: closing the widening
    gap between the rich and the poor and assuring every person the means with which to
    secure a quality of life worthy of human dignity. It is time to seriously consider adopting
    an economic Bill of Rights.
       This Bill of Human Rights and Services would include:
       • the right to a quality of life worthy of human dignity, including adequate nutrition,
    clothing, housing, public transportation, health care, and other social services necessary
    to satisfy basic human needs;
       • the right of familes to special protection, guaranteeing prenatal care, child care, and
    a reasonable period of leave for family illness or the birth of a child, and family planning
    assistance, including the right to choose an abortion;
       • the right to an education sufficient to prepare individuals for suitable occupations or
    professions of their own choosing and to enable them to participate in the cultural life of
    their communities;
       • the right to employment, with guaranteed public-sector jobs for those who cannot
    find work in the private sector, at fair and favorable wages, with equal pay for equal work;
       • the right to adequate income maintenance in the event of unemployment,
    illness, disability, or other lack of livelihood in circumstances beyond the control of
    the individual;
       • the right to clean air, clean water, and renewable sources of energy, with citizen
    plaintiffs granted standing to represent the interests of an endangered planet;
       • the right to economic and social security for future generations of older Americans.
       How a new Bill of Rights should be enacted—whether by constitutional amendment
    or, as some have suggested, by new civil rights legislation expanding the constitutional
    ideal of equality to include economic and social security, or by other means—is an issue
    that is likely to stir considerable controversy. What is essential is that a wide-ranging
    national debate begin and that we chart the road toward establishing an adequate standard
    of living as an entitlement of all Americans.[6]

_____ 1. The supporting material in this passage consists mainly of:
           a. Facts.
           b. Definitions.
           c. Research and the opinion of experts.
           d. Logical and emotional argument in support of the author's opinion.

_____ 2. The primary pattern of organization used in this passage is:
           a. Chronological order.
           b. Enumeration/listing.
           c. Comparison–contrast.
           d. Cause–effect.

_____ 3. The author believes that:
   a. The Constitution should not be changed.
   b. The old Bill of Rights is not relevant to modern life.
   c. The government should provide jobs for anyone who cannot find a job in the private sector.
   d. The most important right is the right to an education.

4. Do you agree with the author's proposal? Why or why not?

   _____

   _____

   _____

3. **Tell Me More: On the Fine Art of Listening**

I want to write about the great and powerful thing that listening is. And how we forget it. And how we don't listen to our children, or those we love. And least of all—which is so important too—to those we do not love. But we should. Because listening is a magnetic and strange thing, a creative force. Think how the friends that really listen to us are the ones we move toward, and we want to sit in their radius as though it did us good, like ultraviolet rays.

This is the reason: When we are listened to, it creates us, makes us unfold and expand. Ideas actually begin to grow within us and come to life. You know how if a person laughs at your jokes you become funnier and funnier, and if he does not, every tiny little joke in you weakens up and dies. Well, that is the principle of it. It makes people happy and free when they are listened to. And if you are a listener, it is the secret of having a good time in society (because everybody around you becomes lively and interesting), of comforting people, of doing them good.

Who are the people, for example, to whom you go for advice? Not to the hard, practical ones who can tell you exactly what to do, but to the listeners; that is, the kindest, least censorious, least bossy people that you know. It is because by pouring out your problem to them, you then know what to do about it yourself.

When we listen to people there is an alternating current, and this recharges us so that we never get tired of each other. We are constantly being re-created. Now there are brilliant people who cannot listen much. They have no ingoing wires on their apparatus. They are entertaining, but exhausting, too. I think it is because these lecturers, these brilliant performers, by not giving us a chance to talk, do not let us express our thoughts and expand; and it is this little creative fountain inside us that begins to spring and cast up new thoughts and unexpected laughter and wisdom. That is why, when someone has listened to you, you go home rested and lighthearted.

Now this little creative fountain is in us all. It is the spirit, or the intelligence, or the imagination—whatever you want to call it. If you are very tired, strained, have no solitude, run too many errands, talk to too many people, drink too many cocktails, this little fountain is muddied over and covered with a lot of debris. The result is you stop living from the center, the creative fountain, and you live from the periphery, from externals. That is, you go along on mere will power without imagination.

It is when people really listen to us, with quiet fascinated attention, that the little fountain begins to work again, to accelerate in the most surprising way.

I discovered all this about three years ago, and truly it made a revolutionary change in my life. Before that, when I went to a party I would think anxiously: "Now try hard. Be lively. Say bright things. Talk. Don't let down." And when tired, I would have to drink a lot of coffee to keep this up.

Now before going to a party, I just tell myself to listen with affection to anyone who talks to me, *to be in their shoes when they talk;* to try to know them without my mind pressing against theirs, or arguing, or changing the subject. No. My attitude is: "Tell me more. This person is showing me his soul. It is a little dry and meager and full of grinding talk just now, but presently he will begin to think, not just automatically to talk. He will show his true self. Then he will be wonderfully alive."[7]

_____ 1. The supporting material in this passage includes:
   a. Facts.
   b. Definitions.
   c. The author's personal experience.
   d. Explanation of theory and research findings.

_____ 2. The primary pattern of organization used in this passage is:
   a. Chronological order.
   b. Enumeration/listing.
   c. Comparison–contrast.
   d. Cause–effect.

_____ 3. The author's main point is that:
   a. Nobody listens anymore.
   b. Listening is a skill that requires a lot of practice.
   c. Listening has a powerful, positive effect.
   d. She learned to listen three years ago.

4. Name two people you know who are good listeners.

_____

_____

4. **Martin Luther King, Jr.**

The Early Civil Rights Movement

King's civil rights activities began with a protest of Montgomery's segregated bus system in 1955. That year, a black passenger named Rosa Parks was arrested for disobeying a city law that required blacks to sit or stand in the back of buses. Black leaders in Montgomery urged blacks to boycott (refuse to use) the city's buses. The leaders formed an organization to run the boycott, and asked King to serve as president. In his first speech as leader of the boycott, King told his black colleagues: "First and foremost, we are American citizens. . . . We are not here advocating violence. . . . The only weapon that we have . . . is the weapon of protest. . . . The great glory of American democracy is the right to protest for right."

Terrorists bombed King's home, but King continued to insist on nonviolent protests. Thousands of blacks boycotted the buses for over a year. In 1956, the U.S. Supreme Court ordered Montgomery to provide equal, integrated seating on public buses. The boycott success won King national fame and identified him as a symbol of Southern blacks' new efforts to fight racial injustice.

With other black ministers, King founded the Southern Christian Leadership Conference (SCLC) in 1957 to expand the nonviolent struggle against racism and discrimination. At the time, widespread segregation existed throughout the South in public schools, and in transportation, recreation, and such public facilities as hotels and restaurants. Many states also used various methods to deprive blacks of their voting rights. In 1960, King moved from Montgomery to Atlanta to devote more effort to SCLC's work. He became copastor of Ebenezer Baptist Church with his father.

The Growing Movement

In 1960, black college students across the South began sitting at lunch counters and entering other facilities that refused to serve blacks. Civil rights protests expanded further, including a major series of demonstrations in Albany, Ga. Also during the early 1960's, King became increasingly unhappy that President John F. Kennedy was doing little to advance civil rights. Early in 1963, King and his SCLC associates launched massive demonstrations to protest citywide racial discrimination in Birmingham, Ala., one of the South's most segregated cities. Birmingham police used dogs and fire hoses to drive back peaceful protesters, who included children. Heavy news coverage of the violence produced a national outcry against segregation. Soon afterward, Kennedy proposed a wide-ranging civil rights bill to Congress.

King and other civil rights leaders then organized a massive march in Washington, D.C. The event, called the March on Washington, was intended to highlight black unemployment and to urge Congress to pass Kennedy's bill. On Aug. 28, 1963, over 200,000 Americans, including many whites, gathered at the Lincoln Memorial in the capital. The high point of the rally was King's stirring "I Have a Dream" speech, which eloquently defined the moral basis of the civil rights movement.

The movement won a major victory in 1964, when Congress passed the civil rights bill that Kennedy and his successor, President Lyndon B. Johnson, had recommended. The Civil Rights Act of 1964 prohibited racial discrimination in public places and called for equal opportunity in employment and education. King later received the 1964 Nobel Peace Prize.[8]

_____ 1. The supporting material in this passage consists primarily of:
   a. Theory and research.
   b. The author's personal experiences.
   c. Historical fact.
   d. Logical argument.

_____ 2. The pattern of organization used in this passage is:
   a. Chronological order.
   b. Enumeration/listing.
   c. Comparison–contrast.
   d. Cause–effect.

_____ 3. We can tell from the passage that:
   a. Rosa Parks was an old woman.
   b. The Montgomery boycott was an important step in King's career.
   c. King was not afraid of the white terrorists.
   d. The main concern of the SCLC was to fight discrimination in the public schools.

4. Do you agree with King's philosophy of nonviolence? Or is it justifiable to use violence when your rights are denied? Briefly explain your opinion.

_____

_____

_____

Journal Entry

1. Are there some careers for which men are better suited than women? Are there some careers for which women are better suited than men? Explain your answer.

_____

_____

_____

_____

_____

_____

_____

_____

_____

_____

_____

_____

2. How good are your notetaking skills? What problems do you have underlining in your books and taking notes? In what ways can you improve on these skills?

_____

_____

_____

_____

_____

_____

_____

_____

_____

_____

_____

_____

12

INFERENCE

In Chapter 12, you will:

1. Preview and read a selection about nonverbal communication, underlining and marking the important points.
2. Answer comprehension questions on the selection to check your understanding and make a set of organized notes on the selection.
3. Learn what inference is and complete practice exercises to improve your inference skills.

SELECTION 12
NONVERBAL COMMUNICATION

Courtland Bovée and John Thill

Directions. Preview the passage and use the space below to write your preview and pre-thinking notes.

Preview Notes

_____

_____

_____

_____

Pre-thinking Notes

_____

_____

_____

_____

While You Read

Imagine you are in a business course and have been assigned the following selection from your textbook. You will need to learn and remember the important points from the passage.

Use the various strategies you have learned to gain a thorough understanding of the passage. Following the guidelines from Chapter 11, stop at the end of each section to underline and mark the important points before continuing on to the next section.

The most basic form of communication is nonverbal. Anthropologists theorize that long before human beings used words to talk things over, our ancestors communicated with one another by using their bodies. They gritted their teeth to show anger; they smiled and touched one another to indicate affection. Although we have come a
5   long way since those primitive times, we still use nonverbal cues to express superiority, dependence, dislike, respect, love, and other feelings.

Nonverbal communication differs from verbal communication in fundamental ways. For one thing, it is less structured, which makes it more difficult to study. A person cannot pick up a book on nonverbal language and master the vocabulary of
10   gestures, expressions, and inflections that are common in our culture. We don't really know how people learn nonverbal behavior. No one teaches a baby to cry or smile, yet these forms of self-expression are almost universal. Other types of nonverbal communication, such as the meaning of colors and certain gestures, vary from culture to culture.
15   Nonverbal communication also differs from verbal communication in terms of intent and spontaneity. We generally plan our words. When we say, "Please open the door," we have a conscious purpose. We think about the message, if only for a moment. But when we communicate nonverbally, we sometimes do so unconsciously. We don't mean to raise an eyebrow or blush. Those actions come naturally.
20   Without our consent, our emotions are written all over our faces.

Why Nonverbal Communication Is Important

Although nonverbal communication is often unplanned, it has more impact than verbal communication. Nonverbal cues are especially important in conveying feelings, accounting for 93 percent of the emotional meaning that is exchanged in any interaction.

25   One advantage of nonverbal communication is its reliability. Most people can deceive us much more easily with words than they can with their bodies. Words are relatively easy to control; body language, facial expressions, and vocal characteristics are not. By paying attention to these nonverbal cues, we can detect deception or affirm a speaker's honesty. Not surprisingly, we have more faith in

30 nonverbal cues than we do in verbal messages. If a person says one thing but transmits a conflicting message nonverbally, we almost invariably believe the nonverbal signal. To a great degree, then, an individual's credibility as a communicator depends on nonverbal messages.

     Nonverbal communication is important for another reason as well: It can be

35 efficient from both the sender's and the receiver's standpoint. You can transmit a nonverbal message without even thinking about it, and your audience can register the meaning unconsciously. By the same token, when you have a conscious purpose, you can often achieve it more economically with a gesture than you can with words. A wave of the hand, a pat on the back, a wink—all are streamlined expres-

40 sions of thought.

The Functions of Nonverbal Communication

Although nonverbal communication can stand alone, it frequently works hand in hand with speech. Our words carry part of the message, and nonverbal signals carry the rest. Together, the two modes of expression make a powerful team, augmenting, reinforcing, and clarifying each other.

45   For example, imagine that you are running a meeting. You might clear your throat and straighten up in your chair as you say, "I'd like to call the meeting to order now." Later you might hold up three fingers and say, "There are three things we need to decide today." As the meeting progresses, you might substitute gestures for comments—nodding your head and smiling to show approval, frowning to express reser-

50 vations. You might also use nonverbal communication to regulate the flow of conversation; by tilting your head, for example, you could invite a colleague to continue with a comment. Finally, you might hedge your bets by saying one thing but implying another nonverbally.

     Experts in nonverbal communication suggest that it has six specific functions:

55
- To provide information, either consciously or unconsciously
- To regulate the flow of conversation
- To express emotion
- To qualify, complement, contradict, or expand verbal messages
- To control or influence others
60
- To facilitate specific tasks, such as teaching a person to swing a golf club

     Nonverbal communication plays a role in business, too. For one thing, it helps establish credibility and leadership potential. If you can learn to manage the impression you create with your body language, facial characteristics, voice, and appearance, you can do a great deal to communicate that you are competent, trustworthy, and dynamic.

65   At the same time, if you can learn to read other people's nonverbal messages, you will be able to interpret their underlying attitudes and intentions more accurately. In dealing with co-workers, customers, and clients, watch carefully for small signs that reveal how the conversation is going. If you aren't having the effect you want, check your words; then, if your words are all right, try to be aware of the nonverbal

70   meanings you are transmitting. At the same time, stay tuned to the nonverbal signals that the other person is sending.

The Varieties of Nonverbal Communication

According to one estimate, there are over 700,000 different forms of nonverbal communication. For discussion purposes, however, these forms can be grouped into general categories, which include facial expressions and eye behavior, gestures and

75   postures, vocal characteristics, personal appearance, touching behavior, and use of time and space.

    Researchers have drawn some interesting conclusions about the meaning of certain nonverbal signals. But remember that the meaning of nonverbal communication is in the observer, who both reads the meaning of specific signals and interprets in the

80   context of the particular situation.

- *Facial expressions and eye behavior.* The face is a powerful source of nonverbal messages; it is the primary site for the expression of emotion, revealing both the type and the intensity of a person's feelings. A person's eyes are especially effective as a tool of communication. They can be used to indicate

85   attention and interest, to influence others, to regulate interaction, and to establish dominance. Although the eyes and the face are usually a reliable source of meaning, people sometimes manipulate their expressions to simulate an emotion they do not feel or to mask their true feelings.

- *Gestures and postures.* By moving their bodies, people can express both

90   specific and general messages, some of which are voluntary and some of which are involuntary. Many gestures—a wave of the hand, for example— have a specific and intentional meaning, such as "hello" or "goodbye." These movements clarify and supplement verbal communication. Other types of body movement are unintentional and express a more general

95   message. Slouching, leaning forward, fidgeting, and walking briskly all fall into this category. These unconscious signals reveal whether a person feels confident or nervous, friendly or hostile, assertive or passive, powerful or powerless.

- *Vocal characteristics.* Like body language, a person's voice carries both

100   intentional and unintentional messages. On a conscious level, we can use our voices to create different impressions. For example, consider the phrase "What have you been up to?" If you repeat that question four or five times, using a different tone of voice and stressing different words, you can convey quite different messages. However, your vocal characteristics also reveal

105   many things that you are unaware of. The tone and volume of your voice,

your accent and speaking pace, and all the little um's and ah's that creep into your speech say a lot about who you are, your relationship with the audience, and the emotions underlying your words.

- *Personal appearance.* An individual's appearance helps to establish his or her social identity. To a great degree, we are what we appear to be. People respond to us on the basis of our physical attractiveness. Some teachers, for example, expect nice-looking students to excel. Because we see ourselves as others see us, these expectations are often a self-fulfilling prophecy. When people think we're capable and attractive, we feel good about ourselves. We develop a positive outlook on life, and this affects our behavior, which in turn affects other people's perception of us. Although an individual's body type and facial features impose limitations, most of us are able to control our attractiveness to some degree. Our grooming, our clothing, our accessories, our "style"—all modify our appearance. Even without the gift of beauty, we can create a favorable impression, tailoring our physical appearance to send the message we want to convey.

- *Touching behavior.* Touch is an important vehicle for conveying warmth, comfort, and reassurance. Even the most casual contact can create positive feelings. This fact was revealed by an experiment in which librarians alternately touched and avoided the hands of students while returning their library cards. Although the contact lasted only half a second, the students who had been touched reported far more positive feelings about themselves and the library, even though many of them did not consciously remember being touched. Perhaps because it implies intimacy, touching behavior is governed by relatively strict customs that establish who can touch whom, and how, in various circumstances. The accepted norms vary, depending on the gender, age, relative status, and cultural background of the individuals involved. In business situations, touching suggests dominance, and so a higher-status person is more likely to touch a lower-status one than the other way around. Touching has become controversial, however, because it can sometimes be interpreted as sexual harassment.

- *Use of time and space.* Like touch, time and space can be used to assert authority. In many cultures, people demonstrate their importance by making other people wait; they show respect by being on time. However, attitudes toward punctuality are cultural. In North America, being on time is a mark of good manners; in other places it is more polite to be somewhat late. People can also assert their status by occupying the best space. In an organization, the person who wields power usually has the corner office and the prettiest view. Apart from serving as a symbol of status, space determines how comfortable people feel in talking with each other. When people stand too close or too far away, we feel ill at ease. In intimate conversation, North Americans typically stand 1½ to 4 feet apart: in business or social groups 4 to 12 feet; and in public, 12 to 25 feet. But in Latin America, people communicate more comfortably at closer range.[1]

Interest Rating.   Please rate the interest level of Selection 12 on the following 1–5 scale (circle one):

> 5—Very interesting
> 4—Fairly interesting
> 3—Mildly interesting
> 2—A little boring
> 1—Very boring

Difficulty Rating.   Please indicate how difficult Selection 12 was for you to understand on the following 1–5 scale (circle one):

> 5—Very difficult
> 4—Fairly difficult
> 3—Moderate
> 2—Fairly easy
> 1—Very easy

Comments: _____

_____

Notetaking Exercise

Directions.   Using either the informal outline or the mapping strategy described in Chapter 11, prepare a set of notes for Selection 12 that would be useful for later study.

Informal outline: _____

_____

_____

_____

_____

_____

_____

_____

_____

_____

_____

_____

Map:

Comprehension Questions

Directions. For questions 1–5, choose the answer that best completes the statement. For questions 6–10, write your response in the space provided. Base all answers on what you read in the selection (you may refer to the selection when necessary).

_____ 1. Supporting material consists largely of:
   a. Statistics.
   b. Examples.
   c. Definitions.
   d. The author's personal experience.

_____ 2. Compared to verbal communication, nonverbal communication is:
   a. Less important.
   b. More reliable.
   c. Less efficient.
   d. More controlled.

_____ 3. The meaning of nonverbal signals:
   a. Is the same from society to society.
   b. Is the same from person to person within a society.
   c. Depends on the person interpreting the signal.
   d. Cannot be studied.

_____ 4. We can tell from the passage that:
   a. Lying cannot be detected from nonverbal cues.
   b. Lying can always be detected from nonverbal cues.
   c. Honest people have more control over their body language than dishonest people.
   d. A skillful liar has good control over her nonverbal signals.

_____ 5. A person's emotions are most revealed in his:
   a. Personal appearance.
   b. Verbal messages.
   c. Vocal characteristics.
   d. Facial expressions and eye behavior.

6. Which pattern(s) of organization does the passage use (chronological order, enumeration/listing, comparison–contrast, cause–effect)? Explain your answer.

_____

_____

7. In a complete sentence of your own wording, express the main idea of paragraph 5 (lines 25–33).

_____

_____

8. According to the passage, why is nonverbal communication more difficult to study than verbal communication?

_____

_____

9. Name two advantages of nonverbal communication over verbal communication.

_____

_____

10. What nonverbal cues would show a teacher that a student is interested and motivated?

_____

_____

Vocabulary Exercise

Directions. Use a multistrategy approach to determine the meaning of each of the following words from the selection. Write your definition in the space provided.

1. anthropologists (1) _____

2. inflections (10) _____

3. universal (12) _____

4. invariably (31) _____

5. credibility (32) _____

6. augmenting (43) _____

7. dynamic (64) _____

8. site (82) _____

9. fidgeting (95) _____

10. wields (142) _____

Essay Question

Directions. On a separate sheet of paper, write a well-developed, half-page response to the following question:

Why is it important for business students to learn about nonverbal communication? In what other professions would an understanding of non-verbal communication be equally important?

Inference

Good comprehension includes understanding not only what is directly stated but also what is implied, or suggested. The process of interpreting implied ideas is called **inference.** In short, the writer *implies,* and the reader *infers.*

Read the two sentences below:

Timothy glanced nervously at his watch. Where was she? he wondered.

These two sentences tell us that Timothy has looked at his watch and that he is nervous. We may also begin to make inferences about Timothy and why he is nervous. We might infer that Timothy is waiting for someone he was supposed to meet and that she is late. We might even infer that he is waiting for his girlfriend or sister, although the sentences don't give enough information to be sure.

Webster's New World Dictionary defines the word *infer* as "to conclude or decide from something known or assumed; derive by reasoning, draw a conclusion." Inference is a thinking skill we use every day. Our inferences are based on the logic we apply to a given situation coupled with our own previous experiences. When we look at a cloudy sky and think "It's going to rain soon," we've made an inference. As Selection 12 suggested, we often make inferences about people based on their nonverbal messages. For example, what might you infer about a person who, during a job interview, was hesitant to make eye contact and used a lot of *um*s and *ah*s when answering questions?

Inference is an important part of reading comprehension. We must always interpret or "fill in the meaning" when we read. This process is sometimes called "reading between the lines." Good inference must be based on sound reasoning. Often as readers we are tempted to insert our own ideas and opinions into what we are reading, instead of logically interpreting the author's statements.

Inference skills must be used in virtually all reading situations. Whether you are reading a textbook, newspaper, novel, poem, or comic, you will use inference to gain a full understanding and appreciation of your material.

Inference and Humor

Inference often plays an important role in understanding a joke or comic. Look over the following comic strip:

Peanuts reprinted by permission of UFS, Inc.

PEANUTS

The humor in this cartoon is based on some simple inferences:

- How does the boy in the first frame feel about his sandcastle?
- Who is under the bucket in the second picture? How can you tell?
- How did the bucket get there? What is the girl's reaction?

Let's look at another example. Read the following humorous story, taken from the *Reader's Digest* column, "Campus Comedy."

> Realizing I had put off doing my laundry for too long, I stuffed all my clothes into a new laundry bag my mother had given me. On the way to the washers, I bumped into a friend who stopped to chat. Noticing letters stenciled on the bag, he straightened the material and read: "One more day and I'll be naked."
>   Looking back at me, he smiled and said, "I'll see you tomorrow."[2]

Contributed by Lori S.

To enjoy this story, we must again make a few simple inferences:

1. Is the narrator male or female? How do you know?
2. Why does it say, "One more day and I'll be naked" on the laundry bag?
3. Why is the young man smiling?

Inference and Poetry

Inference also plays an important role in understanding and interpreting fables, poems, and song lyrics. Read the song lyrics below and answer the questions that follow.

Teach Your Children

1	You who are on the road
2	Must have a code that you can live by
3	And so, become yourself
4	Because the past is just a goodbye
5	Teach your children well
6	Their father's hell did slowly go by
7	And, feed them on your dreams
8	The one they pick's the one you'll know by
9	And don't ever ask them why—if they tell you,
10	You'll just cry so, just look at them and sigh
11	And know they love you
12	And you of tender years
13	Can't know the fears that your elders grew by
14	And so, please help them with your years
15	They seek the truth before they can die
16	Teach your parents well
17	Their children's hell did slowly go by
18	And feed them on your dreams
19	The one they pick's the one you'll know by

20   And don't ever ask them why—if they tell you,
21   You'll just cry so, just look at them and sigh
22   And know they love you[3]
                              by Graham Nash

1. To whom is the author speaking in the first stanza (lines 1–4)? In other words, who is the "you" in the first line?

   _____

2. What road does he mean (line 1)?

   _____

3. In line 4, what point does the author want to make about the past?

   _____

4. What advice is the author giving to parents? Explain briefly in your own words.

   _____

   _____

5. What is the author's point about dreams (lines 7–8)?

   _____

   _____

6. What advice is the author giving to "you of tender years"? Explain briefly in your own words.

   _____

   _____

7. How can children teach their parents?

   _____

   _____

8. Is the message of this song positive or negative? Explain your answer.

   _____

   _____

Inference in Nonfiction Reading

When reading nonfiction material, our inferences are based on both the factual information presented by the author and the opinions she expresses. As in all reading, the inferences we make will reflect our own experiences as they compare with the author's ideas. Our goal, however, is to logically interpret the author's point of view.

It is also usually important to infer the author's *purpose* in writing the material. Is she trying to entertain the reader or make a serious point? Is she providing the reader with information or trying to win the reader over to her point of view?

Exercise 12–1. Inference in Short Passages

Directions. Read each passage and answer the questions that follow it. Base your answers on what is stated and implied in the passage.

Be prepared to discuss your answers in class.

1. **How Safe Are Over-the-Counter Drugs and Driving?**

   For years, you've read the dire statistics on drunk driving; fully half of all fatal collisions or crashes involve alcohol. But with all the publicity that drunk driving justifiably generates, one problem often goes virtually unnoticed—over-the-counter drugs* and driving.

   Statistics on the number of crashes or collisions involving over-the-counter drugs are hard to come by. "The law hasn't defined a category for it," says Charles Butler, AAA's manager of Driver Safety Services. "The information is not part of the standard collision report. These kinds of collisions are frequently attributed to fatigue, inattention, or 'unknown causes.'"

   However, experts agree that the effects of medications on driving performance cannot be overlooked. "There are some startling figures," says Dr. Art Kibbe, senior director of pharmacy affairs for the American Pharmaceutical Association. "One in every 10 people admitted to hospitals is admitted because they mismanaged their medications. And one in every four elderly patients is admitted for medication mismanagement. You have to ask yourself, 'How many car wrecks are due to some sort of problems with drugs?'"

   Of the more than 1,000 different ingredients in over 300,000 over-the-counter drugs available today, many have the same debilitating effect on your alertness, reaction time, and other driving skills that alcohol has. "Some over-the-counter drugs, like antihistamines with sedative qualities, can cause just as much drowsiness as alcohol or illegal drugs and can cause impairment to the point where you could easily cause an accident," says Los Angeles pharmacist Rory Richardson.[4]†

   1. Which over-the-counter drugs are more likely to contribute to automobile accidents?

      _____

      _____

   2. Why isn't more information available regarding the number of accidents caused by over-the-counter drugs?

      _____

      _____

---

*Drugs that may be purchased without a prescription.

†Copyright 1992 *AAA World* Magazine: reprinted with permission.

_____ 3. The author's primary purpose is to:
    a. Persuade the reader not to use over-the-counter drugs.
    b. Analyze the cause of automobile accidents.
    c. Inform the reader of the risks of using over-the-counter drugs while driving.
    d. Compare over-the-counter drugs with alcohol.

_____ 4. We can infer that the author:
    a. Has probably been arrested for drunk driving.
    b. Believes that the use of over-the-counter drugs sometimes contributes to car accidents.
    c. Has probably had an accident himself while using an over-the-counter drug.
    d. Feels that over-the-counter drugs cause more accidents than alcohol.

_____ 5. The author would be in favor of:
    a. Drivers being more cautious in their use of over-the-counter drugs.
    b. A ban on all over-the-counter drugs.
    c. A law against the use of over-the-counter drugs while driving.
    d. More research on the mismanagement of prescribed drugs by the elderly.

Directions. Read each sentence below. If the statement can be logically inferred from the passage, write Yes on the line before the statement. If the statement is not a logical inference based on the passage, write No.

_____ 1. The author feels that drunk driving gets too much publicity.

_____ 2. The cause of an automobile collision is always correctly determined.

_____ 3. One out of 10 automobile collisions is due to mismanaged medication.

_____ 4. Elderly people make more errors with medication than younger people.

_____ 5. Like alcohol, antihistamines can affect your alertness and speed of reaction.

2. **Winners and Losers**

Each human being is born as something new, something that never existed before. Each is born with the capacity to win at life. Each person has a unique way of seeing, hearing, touching, tasting, and thinking. Each has his or her own unique potentials—capabilities and limitations. Each can be a significant, thinking, aware, and creative being—a productive person, a winner.

The words "winner" and "loser" have many meanings. When we refer to a person as a winner, we do not mean one who makes someone else lose. To us, a winner is one who responds authentically by being credible, trustworthy, responsive, and genuine, both as an individual and as a member of a society. A loser is one who fails to respond authentically. Martin Buber makes this distinction as he retells the old story of the rabbi who, on his deathbed, is asked if he is ready for the world to come. The rabbi says yes. After all, he will not be asked, "Why were you not Moses?" He will only be asked, "Why were you not yourself?"

Few people are one hundred percent winners or one hundred percent losers. It's a matter of degree. However, once a person is on the road to being a winner, his or her chances are greater for becoming even more so.[5]

1. What is the authors' definition of a winner? What is their definition of a loser?

   _____

   _____

   _____

2. What is your definition of a winner?

   _____

   _____

_____ 3. The authors' primary purpose is to:
   a. Entertain the reader with a philosophical story.
   b. Persuade the reader to be more honest.
   c. Explain why some people are winners and some are losers.
   d. Clarify their definitions of winner and loser.

_____ 4. The authors imply that:
   a. There is little difference between a winner and a loser.
   b. Everybody is a winner.
   c. Once a loser, always a loser.
   d. Anyone can become a winner.

_____ 5. Which of the following would the authors *most* likely consider a winner?
   a. A woman who has just won a tennis tournament.
   b. A politician who has just been elected to office.
   c. A friend who admits to being upset about another friend's remarks.
   d. A student who receives an *A* on a test.

Directions. Mark each of the following statements Yes or No, according to whether or not the statement may be logically inferred from the passage.

_____ 1. A loser is someone who is unable to compete with others.

_____ 2. One must be very well educated to be a winner.

_____ 3. Winners are more honest about their feelings than losers.

_____ 4. The story about the dying rabbi makes the point that it is important to imitate those you admire.

_____ 5. Once you have started to act authentically, you probably will continue to do so.

3.   **Childhood**

As I have discovered by examining my past, I started out as a child. Coincidentally, so did my brother. My mother didn't put all her eggs in one basket, so to speak: she gave me a younger brother named Russell, who taught me what was meant by "survival of the fittest."

I have always felt sorry for only children because they are deprived of the opportunity of being rolled out of bed by a relative. For me, the relative was Russell, with whom I was closer than I ever wanted to be. We slept in one bed in a two-bedroom apartment, where I also got close to music because my marbles kept rolling under the piano.

"Somebody's gonna kill himself on your marbles," my mother would say.

"Only somebody walkin' under the piano," I would reply, trying to show that all my marbles were accounted for.

"Well, don't come runnin' to *me* when your father falls on 'em an' then decides to fall on *you*."

"He falls okay without marbles," I said, thinking of certain Saturday nights.

To be fair to my father, the man spent many years wrestling with a question that no parent has ever been able to answer:

What's wrong with that boy?

For some reason, things that had been endearing when done by Huck Finn lost their charm when done by me. Mark Twain would have appreciated my putting a frog in my father's milk, but my father did not care for a breakfast of marine life.

"Ther's a *frog* in my milk," he noted one morning. "Bill, *you* know how a frog got into my milk?"

"They can really get around," I replied.

"And I wonder how *you'll* be getting around," he said meaningfully.

No matter what threat my father ever made or carried out, I loved him very much, even though he didn't understand me. He did not, for example, understand why one day I painted four butterflies on his boxer shorts. But a child today who decorated Dad's drawers would at once be enrolled in a class in abstract art, and the child's mother would be stopping strangers to say, "My Andrew is an absolute genius at underwear impressionism. He just did a jock strap that belongs in the Louvre!"[6]

1.   What clues first signal the reader that the passage will be humorous?

_____

_____

2.   Does the passage make any serious points about childhood?

_____

_____

_____   3.   The author's primary purpose is to:

    a. Amuse the reader with anecdotes from his childhood.

    b. Let the reader know how difficult it is to have a younger brother.

    c. Explain how children are perceived by adults.

    d. Persuade the reader to become a caring parent.

_____ 4. Cosby implies that his father:

      a. Had no sense of humor.

      b. Sometimes drank on Saturday nights.

      c. Did not like art.

      d. Did not really love him.

_____ 5. Cosby implies that children today:

      a. Are sometimes taken too seriously.

      b. Are better artists than children of the past.

      c. Are better understood than children of the past.

      d. Do not respect their parents.

Directions. Mark each of the following statements Yes or No, according to whether it can be logically inferred from the passage.

_____ 1. As a child, Bill Cosby enjoyed playing the piano.

_____ 2. There are advantages to being an only child.

_____ 3. The Cosby family was wealthy.

_____ 4. Huck Finn liked to play practical jokes.

_____ 5. Cosby's father did not know how the frog got into his milk.

4. Identity Crisis in the Barrios

Social scientists have long been concerned with the plight of the bicultural person in our society, the person caught between the merciless demands of two cultures. Because of his inability to comply with the requirements of both groups, the bicultural individual often fails to identify with either. The two different demands on his loyalty keep him under constant stress. His conflicting values give him an uncomfortable sense of insecurity, instability and disorientation. He usually attempts to resolve the conflict by choosing one group and rejecting the other. Neither choice is entirely satisfactory.

    The Mexican-American is one of the many ethnic groups in the United States that is caught in this cultural dilemma. The Anglos pressure him to abandon the mother culture and emulate Anglo behavior. The members of his group who do not admire the Anglo ways encourage him to ignore them and retain the traditional folk culture. Most Mexican-Americans faced with these conflicts find it necessary to become either Identifiers (remaining loyal to their ethnic group and rejecting Anglo ways) or Anglicized (accepting Anglo ways and rejecting their identification with their ethnic group).[7]

1. What other ethnic groups in the United States (in addition to Mexican-Americans) face problems similar to those described in the passage?

_____

_____

2. Why is it difficult for a bicultural person to choose between the two cultures?

_____

_____

_____ 3. The author's primary purpose is to:
   a. Criticize American society.
   b. Reveal difficulties faced by the bicultural person.
   c. Persuade Mexican-Americans to become more Anglicized.
   d. Explain how the bicultural person can resolve his dilemma.

_____ 4. The bicultural person is:
   a. Often a social scientist.
   b. Faced with two conflicting value systems.
   c. Usually happy and well adjusted.
   d. Better off than the person who has only one cultural background.

_____ 5. We can conclude from the passage that:
   a. Some Mexican-Americans do not become either Identifiers or Anglicized.
   b. Most Mexican-Americans reject Anglo ways.
   c. Identifiers are more common among other ethnic groups.
   d. Most ethnic groups in the United States do not face similar conflicts.

Directions. Mark each of the following statements Yes or No, according to whether it can be logically inferred from the passage.

_____ 1. The problems of the bicultural person have only recently been recognized.

_____ 2. The bicultural person feels no loyalty to either group.

_____ 3. Identifiers are happier than those who become Anglicized.

_____ 4. A bicultural person sometimes does not identify with either of his two cultures.

_____ 5. Once a person has chosen to accept one culture and reject the other, he is free of tension and conflict.

5. **The Growth of Environmentalism**

In their rush to give consumers throughout the world what they want and need, managers must be careful that they cause minimal damage to the environment by their behavior. Business and government leaders throughout the 1990s will be discussing issues such as acid rain, global warming, the potential benefits and hazards of nuclear power, recycling, the management of forests throughout the world, the ethical treatment of animals, and the protection of the air we breathe and the water we drink. Construction giant Fluor Daniel is predicting that U.S. spending on pollution control alone will reach $100 billion in some years this decade.

European business schools are leading the way in focusing on environmentalism. For example, the European Business School in Germany has set up an Institute for Environmental Management. Some feel that environmentalism will be as influential as globalization before the end of the 1990s.

Environmentalism must not be a social cause of a few; it must be a major focus of everyone, and it is becoming increasingly so. In 1986 only 38 percent of American consumers thought plastics posed a serious environmental threat. In 1989, the concern rose to 59 percent. More than half of the consumers recently surveyed reported that they would change their buying habits if foods and beverages were sold in recyclable containers. Many decisions that consumers and businesspeople make in the 1990s will affect the environment.[8]

1. What is environmentalism?

   _____

2. How do consumers' decisions affect the environment?

   _____

   _____

_____ 3. The authors' primary purpose is to:
   a. Discourage consumers from buying products that are environmentally unsound.
   b. Convince government leaders to pass stricter environmental protection laws.
   c. Explain the importance of environmentalism to business today.
   d. Compare environmental issues of the past with environmental issues of the future.

_____ 4. In this passage, "managers," in the first sentence, refers to:
   a. Business managers.
   b. Sports team managers.
   c. Consumers.
   d. Government officials.

_____ 5. We can infer from the passage that American business schools:
   a. Do not teach anything about environmental issues.
   b. All agree on the importance of environmentalism.
   c. Are not focusing on environmental issues as much as European business schools.
   d. Are primarily concerned with globalization.

Directions. Mark each of the following statements Yes or No, according to whether it can be logically inferred from the passage.

_____ 1. During the 1980s, Americans became more aware of environmental issues.

_____ 2. Environmental considerations will become less important once the 90s are over.

_____ 3. Globalization will be an important aspect of business in the 90s.

_____ 4. If consumers were not concerned with the environment, businesses would have no reason to be concerned with the environment.

_____ 5. The authors feel that all consumers should be concerned with the environment.

Integrative Exercise

Exercise 12–2. Underlining and Notetaking

Directions. Imagine you are in a criminal justice course and have been assigned to read the following passage from your textbook.

1. Read and mark the passage.
2. Using either the informal outline or mapping technique, take a set of notes that would be useful for later study.

Components of the Criminal Justice System

The criminal justice system consists of three major components—law enforcement, courts, and corrections—and the specialized auxiliary services of probation, parole, and the juvenile justice system. In many cases, probation and parole are grouped under the corrections component because, as alternatives to incarceration, these programs seek to "correct" the offender. The juvenile justice system has been established to deal with offenders below a prescribed statutory age.

All of the components of the criminal justice system share certain common goals. For example, they collectively exist to protect society, to maintain order, and to prevent crime. But they also contribute individually to these goals in their own special way. In the discussion of the component functions that follow, you should pay careful attention to the system's overall goals as well as the individual contributions of each component.

Functions of the Major Components

There are three major components of the criminal justice system: law enforcement, the courts, and corrections.

Law enforcement

Law enforcement is the first component. It consists of all police agencies at the federal, state, county, and municipal levels. These agencies fulfill the following functions:

1. *To prevent criminal behavior.* Prevention involves all the efforts directed toward eliminating the causes of crimes. Among these efforts might be such activities as delinquency prevention programs and citizen education efforts. The purpose of the first is to reduce the likelihood of youths engaging in criminal activities. The second might counsel citizens on ways to avoid being victims of crime and what to do should they be victims of crime.

2. *To reduce crime.* Crime reduction essentially means eliminating and reducing opportunities for criminal behavior. Such police programs as preventive and conspicuous patrol activity; intelligence and information gathering on crime-producing situations and known criminals; and target-hardening strategies that attempt to make certain physical sites less vulnerable to criminals are examples of police crime reduction efforts.

3. *To apprehend and arrest offenders.* The police engage in criminal investigations; the gathering of evidence; presenting this evidence in the courtroom; and testifying before the courts against those who violate the criminal law.

4. *To protect life and property.* Protecting life and property includes the full range of police services in such areas as crime prevention, crime reduction, and investigation and apprehension strategies designed to protect society. It also includes the provision of specialized services designed to assure public safety.

5. *To regulate noncriminal conduct.* Every day the police are involved in efforts to ensure compliance by regulatory means with laws of public safety and security. This function includes activities such as traffic regulation and crowd control.

Courts
The courts include those judicial agencies at all levels of government that perform the following functions in the administration of criminal justice.

1. *To protect the rights of the accused.* The courts are responsible for reviewing the actions of law enforcement agencies to ensure that the police have not violated the legal rights of the accused. Similarly, the courts are given the authority and responsibility to review the actions of other agencies of criminal justice to ensure that their actions do not violate the rights of the convicted offender.
2. *To determine by all available legal means whether a person is guilty of a crime.* Review of all evidence presented by the police or private citizens to determine its relevance and admissibility according to established guidelines of acceptability. The court also examines the circumstances that surround the crime as it relates to the issues it must adjudicate.
3. *To dispose properly of those convicted of crimes.* The courts have the responsibility to examine the background of the accused and the circumstances of the crime. From this information and according to existing and applicable laws, the court considers possible sentencing alternatives and then selects the most proper form of disposition of the convicted offender.
4. *To protect society.* After the accused has been found guilty and after consideration of all factors, the court must determine if the offender should be removed from society and incarcerated in order to protect the safety of life and property.
5. *To prevent and reduce criminal behavior.* This is the task of imposing proper penalties and sanctions that will serve to deter future criminal acts by the offender and also serve as an example and a deterrent to others who would commit criminal acts or threaten public safety.

Corrections
Corrections consist of those executive agencies at all levels of government that are responsible both directly and indirectly for the following functions:

1. *To maintain institutions.* The correctional component is responsible for maintaining prisons, jails, halfway houses, and other institutional facilities to receive convicted offenders sentenced to a period of incarceration by the courts.
2. *To protect law-abiding members of society.* Corrections is responsible for providing custody and security in order to keep sentenced offenders from preying on other members of society through the further commission of crimes.
3. *To reform offenders.* During their period of incarceration in a correctional institution, corrections is given the function of developing and providing services to assist incarcerated offenders to reform. Additionally, corrections is responsible for developing programs that will assist the offender in returning to society upon his or her release and to lead a noncriminal life.
4. *To deter crimes.* Corrections is responsible for encouraging incarcerated and potential offenders to lead law-abiding lives through the experience of prison and the denial of liberty.[9‡]

‡Reprinted with the permission of Macmillan College Publishing Company from INTRODUCTION TO CRIMINAL JUSTICE, Third Edition by Robert D. Pursley. Copyright © 1984 by Macmillan College Publishing Company, Inc.

Informal outline: _____

_____

_____

_____

_____

_____

_____

_____

_____

_____

_____

_____

_____

_____

_____

_____

_____

Map:

Journal Entry

1. In your opinion, is nonverbal communication more important than verbal communication? Explain your answer.

_____

_____

_____

_____

_____

_____

_____

_____

_____

_____

_____

2. Did underlining and taking notes from Selection 12 help you learn and remember the important points better? Why or why not?

_____

_____

_____

_____

_____

_____

_____

_____

_____

_____

_____

_____

13

STRATEGIES USED
AFTER READING

In Chapter 13, you will:

1. Read a selection about the Los Angeles barrios, marking important points and using your inference skills to enhance your understanding of the selection.
2. Answer comprehension questions on the selection to check your understanding.
3. Learn strategies for reviewing and reacting to what you read.
4. Learn strategies for evaluating what you read and learn to distinguish fact from opinion.

SELECTION 13
IN THE BARRIOS OF THE CITY OF ANGELS

Stan Steiner

Selection 13 is from the book *La Raza: The Mexican-Americans,* by Stan Steiner, published in 1970. In this excerpt, Steiner describes the barrios of Los Angeles and the people who live there.

Directions. Preview the passage and use the space below to write your preview and pre-thinking notes.

Preview Notes

_____

_____

Pre-thinking Notes

_____

_____

_____

_____

While You Read

1. Use your inference skills to create a mental picture of the LA barrios of 1970.

2. Interrupt your reading from time to time to mark the important points.

The Urban Villages

On the hills of the City of Our Lady of the Angels there are tiers of little houses, like the strings of villages on the sea coasts of Spain or Italy or Mexico. The houses are painted in dime-store shades of yellow and white and lavender and pink. In between the houses are fig trees, and cypress, and cedars, and old cars and palms rise like questioning fingers out of the flower beds of poverty in between freeways. The sky is blue as the Mediterranean, or gray as a dirty window when the smog does not stay downtown where it belongs.

"Wonder at this scene of many-colored houses! The houses of our city make us, who are miserable, see light among the flowers and songs and see beauty. Where it gleams forth in fourfold rays, where the fragrant flowers bud, there live the Mexicans, the youth." So a poet wrote of the capital of the Aztecs, hundreds of years ago.

In the barrios of Los Angeles the modern descendants of the Aztecs have built a suburb of that ancient city. The metropolis is a paradox composed of oldest Mexico and the newest technological gadgetry in the United States.

Signs of that paradox are on the walls of the barrios: "VIVA KENNEDY!" "ABAJO DODGERS!" "GO, DODGERS, GO!" "EL BAZAAR DE MEXICO": a dry-goods store that sells workclothes and bikinis. "ROPA USADA": the secondhand clothing store with a surfboard and a pair of water skis in the window, besides used brassieres. "VOTE FOR REAGAN!" "GRINGO, GO HOME!" "THE JOKER'S DEN": the hamburger joint with "FINE MEXICAN FOOD." Tacos and Cokes. "TORTILLERIA": Wholesale and Retail. "JOIN THE U.S. MARINES." "CHICANO POWER."

Old women in black mantillas and floral dresses from Sears buy bananas from an open fruit stall. Across the street, in Spanish, the sign in the real-estate office entices the old women: "Naturalization Papers" and "Income Taxes Prepared."

Here is the religious store: *Artículos Religiosos, Herbas.* Candles to the Virgen de Guadalupe. Candles to the Infant of Prague. Candles to Christ. Candles to "Papa Julius." And candles to a huge, ominous Indian chief in blood-red wax.

Here is the secular shrine: the storefront mission of the Remedial Education and
30 Cultural Opportunity for the Rurally Deprived (RECORD, let's call it), where a Berlin café skit by Bertolt Brecht is advertised in Pachuco slang, underneath a plastic piñata made by the Sunset Years Club of retired farm workers.

Here is the "Extermino La Cucaracha" sign in every drugstore window. In sunny California the cockroaches grow healthy and strong. Exterminating cockroaches is
35 the main sport of the barrios' hunters. Who remembers that "La Cucaracha" was the anthem of the Mexican Revolution?

The barrios of Los Angeles are the third largest Mexican city in the world. Guadalajara and Mexico City alone have greater populations. No one knows for certain, but barrio leaders say that from 800,000 to 1,000,000 Mexicans live in Los
40 Angeles. Either population is larger than the population of Washington, D.C., or Cleveland, Ohio. The people of La Raza in the city, by themselves, constitute one of the ten largest cities in the United States.

Los Angeles is the capitol of La Raza. It is to the Mexicans what Boston has been to the Irish and New York City has been to the Jews.

45 Many people are extremely poor. And yet there is a beauty in the barrios. Roses entwine the junked cars in the backyards, much as the tropical flowers cover the poorest Indian hut in Mexico. In one of the cities in the San Joaquin Valley, there is a Community Poverty Council that has a eucalyptus tree on its front lawn, a lemon tree at its back door, and roses blooming on the window sill of the "welfare lady's" office,
50 where the poor come for their alms. The poverty of a rural home is not visible from outside, especially when the home is in a city.

Ever since the Aztecs built the City of Mexico the people of La Raza have been people of the cities. The conquistadors thought their city as magnificent as any in Europe. Bernal Díaz del Castillo, the chronicler of Cortés, wrote: "Some of the sol-
55 diers among us who have been in many parts of the world, in Constantinople and in Rome, said that so large a market place and so full of people and so well regulated and arranged, they had never beheld before." And Spaniards, too, were of the city: "The civilization of Spain is an urban thing," one historian says. "In America it is the one city that symbolizes the role of Spain," another writes. It is not surprising, then,
60 that 85.4 percent of the Chicanos of California live in urban areas.

In the Southwest the number of city dwellers is but slightly less; only in New Mexico are the urban Chicanos a minority—little more than one-third of the state. The population of La Raza in urban areas from Arizona to Texas ranges from 69.3 to 78.6 percent. The Chicano population of Los Angeles, Denver, and Phoenix is 10 to
65 20 percent of the city; in Albuquerque it is 25 percent; in San Antonio and El Paso 40 to 50 percent; in Laredo 85 percent.

Even so, the barrios of the Chicanos are not like the gray tenement tombs of the ghetto. The barrios sprawl over the hills and into the arroyos and valleys, amid the weeds and flowers, like wandering Indian villages. They are a paradox that defies
70 easy comparisons.

Ghettos are the refuse dumps of the industrial city.

"Who creates the ghetto?" asks Eliezer Risco, the editor of *La Raza,* the newspaper of the barrios of East Los Angeles. "The ghetto is where you are forced to live by housing discrimination. But La Raza has been living in the barrios for hundreds

75 of years. No one has forced us. The barrios are not ghettos, although we do have ghettos in the barrios. There are suburbs and there are skidrows; there are ghettos of the poor and there are neighborhoods of the rich. We have everything here that you have in the larger city, but one thing—you, in the larger city, govern us. We do not run our own lives because you do not let us. You run the barrios and you don't

80 know how."

"Barrio" is a Spanish word that simply means "neighborhood." In the colonial era of Mexico the Spanish rulers subtly changed the meaning by using barrio to designate the "native quarter," where the Indians lived. It was a word of contempt. The word barrio, as it is used in the United States to designate the Mexican or "Spanish"

85 neighborhood, is a modern version of that colonial term; except that today the Chicanos have once more changed the demeaning meaning of the old colonial word to one of pride.

It is a city within a city within a city. Wherever the outsider sees one barrio, there are not one but many barrios within the boundaries of family ties, origins

90 in Mexico, or simply street-map geography. Each barrio has its own loyalties, churches, local shrines, shopkeepers, gangs of boys, customs, history, and old village patriarchs.

"Urban villages" may be a better definition of "barrios." In these communities the Chicanos try to live in the best of both worlds: those of the village and those of

95 the city.

"Why do you still live in East Los Angeles?" a man on the street is asked by *La Voz,* the newspaper of the Community Service Organization. "Just a matter of being in a place something like the old country," one man replies. Incongruous? Where in Los Angeles is Mexico? He feels it is in the barrios.

100 Men and women who come from the rugged mountain towns of northern Mexico and the rural valleys of the Southwest to seek jobs in the city do so warily. In self-protection they bring their village ways with them. The rural feeling of independence, the little gardens, the religious ecstasies, the large and comforting family loves, the communal ways of life—all of these give the urban

105 villages and villagers a resilience that resists the numbing conformity of the concrete streets. None of these human exuberances fit within the confines of gray ghetto walls.

In the old days a goat and a vegetable garden were more of a necessity for the survival of a barrio family than a car port. Some of the barrios are still derisively

110 referred to by outsiders as "Goat Hill."

"Years ago Los Angeles was rural. It was all farms," says Eduardo Pérez, a barrio leader. He remembers that it was just one generation ago. "Where I was born, in East Los Angeles, there were Japanese farmers. Hundreds of vegetable farms. In World War II the Japanese farmers were put in concentration camps. And their land

115 was confiscated. Up to then the Mexican people used to come to Los Angeles to work on the farms."

It was not simply out of migrant camps that the barrios grew. The people of the Sonoran deserts and mountains on both sides of the border could have moved into the ghetto tenements, but they would have been suffocated. "We need open sky," Pérez
120   says, "or we would die."

"Our people in northern Mexico are rural people," Pérez says. "We're in the mess we're in partly because of that. Mexicans coming to this country head for the countryside. We're always going to the rural towns first to work in the fields, to do stoop labor. We're being displaced by automation on the farms. So we go to the cities. In
125   the barrios we know our countrymen will help us. We're desperate. Where else can we go?"[1]

Interest Rating.   Please rate the interest level of Selection 13 on the following 1–5 scale (circle one):

     5—Very interesting

     4—Fairly interesting

     3—Mildly interesting

     2—A little boring

     1—Very boring

Difficulty Rating.   Please indicate how difficult Selection 13 was for you to understand on the following 1–5 scale (circle one):

     5—Very difficult

     4—Fairly difficult

     3—Moderate

     2—Fairly easy

     1—Very easy

Comments: _____

Comprehension Questions

Directions.   For questions 1–5, choose the answer that best completes the statement. For questions 6–10, write your response in the space provided. Base all answers on what you read in the selection (you may refer to the selection when necessary).

_____ 1. The primary purpose of the selection is to:

     a. Describe the barrios and their residents.

     b. Explain why Mexican-Americans live in Los Angeles.

     c. Compare city life with country life.

     d. Show how discrimination has affected Mexican-Americans.

_____ 2. We can tell from the passage that the Spanish conquistadors were very impressed with:
  a. Los Angeles.
  b. Mexico City.
  c. Aztec civilization.
  d. The Aztec language.

_____ 3. The author uses statistical evidence to show that:
  a. Barrios are different from ghettos.
  b. The barrios are a paradox.
  c. Rural Mexicans prefer Los Angeles to other cities.
  d. Many Chicanos live in urban areas.

_____ 4. The word *barrio:*
  a. Was originally an Aztec word.
  b. Is difficult to define.
  c. Has been used with both positive and negative associations.
  d. Is used in the United States to refer to any urban village.

_____ 5. One complaint of barrio leaders, mentioned in the passage, is that:
  a. They are not allowed to govern themselves.
  b. The government does not fund enough programs in the barrios.
  c. There are not enough jobs.
  d. Older Mexicans are unwilling to adapt to modern American life.

6. Briefly describe the barrios of Los Angeles. What do they look like? What do they contain?

  _____

  _____

  _____

  _____

7. In this passage, the author points out several paradoxes of barrio life. Explain the paradox that he describes in paragraphs 3 and 4 (lines 12–22).

  _____

  _____

  _____

8. Write one complete sentence of your own wording to express the main idea of paragraph 11 (lines 45–51).

  _____

  _____

  _____

9. The author compares and contrasts the barrio and the ghetto. How are they similar? How are they different?

_____

_____

_____

10. Why do some Mexican-Americans retain their old ways of life?

_____

_____

_____

Inference Exercise

Directions. Mark each of the following statements Yes or No. Write Yes if the statement is directly or indirectly supported by the passage. Write No if the statement cannot be supported by what you've read.

_____ 1. The barrios of Los Angeles are dull, barren, and colorless.

_____ 2. Los Angeles is an old city built by the Aztecs.

_____ 3. Teenagers in the barrios like hunting cockroaches more than they like playing baseball or soccer.

_____ 4. More than a million people live in Washington, DC.

_____ 5. Many Irish people live in Boston.

_____ 6. Very few Mexican-Americans live in cities.

_____ 7. Not everyone who lives in the barrios is poor.

_____ 8. Many residents of the barrios take pride in their community.

_____ 9. People moving into the Los Angeles barrios from Mexico must give up all the customs of the old country.

_____10. "Goat Hill" is a humorous but complimentary nickname for the barrios.

Vocabulary Exercise

Directions. Use a multistrategy approach to determine the meaning of each of the following words. Write your definition in the space provided.

1. paradox (13) _____

2. rurally (30) _____

3. chronicler (54) _____

4. tenement (67) _____

5. refuse (71) _____

6. subtly (82) _____

7. contempt (83) _____

8. warily (100) _____

9. resilience (103) _____

10. derisively (107) _____

Essay Question

Directions. On a separate sheet of paper write a well-developed, half-page response to the following question:

Discuss both the positive and negative features of the LA barrios. Which does the author emphasize?

Strategies to Use after Reading

The study-reading process is not finished when you have reached the last page of your reading assignment. The final step in the process, which is just as important as the first step, is to review the material, react to it, and evaluate it.

Reviewing

If you want to remember what you've read, it is important to review the assignment immediately after you've read it. Immediate review allows you to clarify the important points while the material is still fresh in your mind. Make a habit of at least briefly reviewing every important reading assignment.

There are several review strategies you can use. In most textbooks, review material is provided at the end of each chapter in the form of questions and lists of terms. Sometimes students review by reading over their notes or underlinings. If you have taken effective notes or underlinings, you have already identified the most important points of the chapter. You can now use your notes or underlinings to reinforce what you have learned and transfer your knowledge to long-term memory.

Two of the most effective strategies for reviewing are self-testing and summarizing. Both of these strategies encourage you to become actively involved in the review process.

Self-testing requires you to ask yourself questions about the important points of the passage and then answer them. If you have written good goal questions while you were reading, you can use them as a starting point for self-testing. Also, use your underlinings and notes to identify the important topics from the passage, and then formulate questions from them. Headings within the passage may furnish cues for questions as well. Imagine you are the teacher; what questions would you ask if you were making up a test on the passage?

When testing yourself, first attempt to answer your questions without looking back at the material. If you are unable to answer a question, refer to the passage to locate the answer and review the material. Then test yourself again to make sure you have retained the information.

Here are some possible review questions for Selection 13. Can you answer them? What other questions might you ask?

What do the barrios look like?

How are the barrios different from ghettos?

Why do people come to the barrios to live?

Why do they stay?

Summarizing requires you to write a paragraph that restates the main points of the passage. You may choose to use summarizing instead of outlining, especially for material whose organization is not made clear by headings and subheadings. A written summary helps you review the main points and is also a useful aid for later study.

How to Write a Summary

1. Start with a general, introductory statement (if possible, state the article's thesis).
2. Following the order of the article or chapter, state its main points. Refer to your notes and/or underlinings to identify these main points. Avoid details and examples unless they seem of particular importance. Express the ideas in your own words as much as possible.
3. End with a concluding statement.
4. Your summary should be short—approximately 1 page for every 5 to 10 pages of text.
5. When finished, read over your summary to be sure you're satisfied with it. Check to see that you've included the most important points and that you've stated them accurately.
6. Keep your summary with your other study materials.

Here is a summary of Selection 11, "Are Women Better Cops?"

Though only 9% of the country's cops are women, they bring different and valuable skills to police work. Women cops may help improve police image and community relations. Police work today requires intelligence and sensitivity; women cops are likely to use brain rather than muscle. This approach is especially important now with all the complaints of police brutality. Women cops see themselves as peacekeepers and will use talk to deal with difficult situations. They are especially effective in handling cases of rape and domestic violence. However, not everyone believes that there is a significant difference in male and female policing styles. Female cops themselves are concerned about being viewed as unable to use force when necessary.

Female cops sometimes must deal with harassment and prejudice from male cops. Though they have been successful in court cases, they are still concerned about the attitudes of their male colleagues. Part of the problem is that women are newcomers to patrol work and few in number, and the public expects cops to be male. But with police work becoming more community-oriented, the skills of women cops are needed. The ideal police force today recognizes the value of gender balance.

Exercise 13–1. Self-Testing

Directions. Make up five or more review questions for Selection 12, "Nonverbal Communication" (pp. 265–269), and then write down their answers.

_____

_____

_____

_____

_____

_____

_____

_____

_____

Exercise 13–2. Summarizing

Directions. Following the guidelines listed above, write a summary of Selection 13, "In the Barrios of the City of Angels."

_____

_____

_____

_____

_____

_____

_____

_____

_____

Exercise 13–3. Reviewing

Directions. Read the following passage on daydreams and write a summary of its main points. Then make up five review questions for the passage.

Daydreaming

Frank is driving to a job interview. He wants the job very badly, and as he weaves in and out of the busy early morning traffic, he considers the upcoming conversation. In the midst of organizing his presentation, he has an image of the interviewer making fun of him and virtually laughing him out of the office. The image is gone as quickly as it came, and if you were to ask Frank about it later he would probably say he has no memory of it.

Janet has received a C+ on her sociology paper. She had worked hard on the paper and really thought she'd get an A. As she rereads the paper and goes over her professor's comments, Janet imagines herself storming into the teacher's office, hurling the paper on the teacher's desk, and telling the woman just what she thinks of her. This fantasy passes in a moment.

Lou is in Janet's sociology class and got an A− on his paper. He's quite excited. As he walks to his car, he starts to think about graduate school for the first time and wonders what it's like to be a professor. He imagines himself sitting in a cluttered office, surrounded by adoring students who are taking notes as he outlines his latest research project.

Frank, Janet, and Lou are daydreamers. Like most of the rest of us, their days are made up of more than looking, touching, responding. As they move through their varied activities, their behavior is accompanied by a private stream of consciousness. The total stream of consciousness includes the information they process, the events they remember, the plans they make. But a part of that stream is daydreaming, and it is as much a part of most people's lives as eating.

For most of this century, psychology has been committed to studying only observable behavior. This situation has left the realm of daydreaming—like other aspects of consciousness—largely neglected. But in recent years Jerome L. Singer of Yale University has addressed himself to the phenomenon of daydreaming, examining such questions as: Does everyone daydream? What types of daydreams are most common? And why do we daydream at all?

After questioning hundreds of people about their daydreams, Singer has concluded that virtually everyone daydreams, and he has identified three different types of daydreamers. The first type, like Frank, typically has rather anxious daydreams, often centered on fears of failure. These daydreams are unorganized, fleeting, and vague. The second type of daydreamer, like Janet, is given to self-criticism and self-doubt and is most likely to have hostile fantasies. The third type, whom Singer calls the "happy daydreamer," has positive fantasies, like Lou's. These daydreams usually include clear visual images and reflect self-acceptance. Not surprisingly, people in the third group enjoy daydreaming the most.

Women and men daydream equally often and in similar ways. However, women are slightly more likely to have personal, passive, and body-oriented fantasies, while men more frequently fantasize about athletic or heroic achievement. People seem to daydream less and less as they get older. Those who were "happy daydreamers" in their youth are the most likely to continue fantasizing in old age.

Our daydreams and night dreams are probably related to each other. Anxious or hostile daydreamers tend to have anxious or hostile night dreams; happier daydreamers have correspondingly positive night dreams. Daydreaming appears to peak every 90 minutes or so (similar to night dreaming), and this peak is associated with reduced eye movement and a particular type of brain wave. Thus it is possible that some of the same brain mechanisms are involved in both daydreaming and night dreaming.

But there are important differences between daydreaming and night dreaming. Night dreaming is associated with rapid eye movements—our eyes move during dreams as if we were watching a movie behind our closed lids. While we daydream, however, we tend to move our eyes much less than usual, as if we were staring at some far off point in space.

Why do we daydream? Singer speculates that daydreaming is necessary for optimum intellectual functioning, self-control, and a peaceful inner life. Our fantasies can keep us from going bananas when performing boring tasks and can provide periodic relaxation when doing demanding intellectual work.

Daydreaming can also provide us with the rewards we need when the world around us fails to do so. Singer suggests that for people with limited internal lives the external world becomes especially compelling. "For them, the social and physical environment seems to say, 'Eat me! Drink me! Touch me! Kiss me!' and they simply can't resist these appeals." In the absence of an inner world, rich in images and interest, nondaydreamers may respond to the demands of the external world in nonadaptive ways, such as crime, overeating, or drug abuse. Singer found, for example, that delinquent adolescent boys daydreamed very little.

Of course, the absence of daydreaming does not necessarily produce delinquents or drug addicts. But daydreaming does appear to be important to psychological well-being. The thread of daydreaming woven through our fabric of thought may serve an important function in tying the rest of consciousness together.[2]

Summary: _____

_____

_____

_____

_____

_____

_____

_____

_____

_____

_____

_____

_____

_____

_____

_____

_____

_____

_____

_____

_____

_____

_____

_____

_____

_____

_____

_____

_____

_____

Review questions: _____

_____

_____

_____

_____

_____

_____

_____

_____

_____

_____

_____

_____

_____

_____

Exercise 13–4. Reviewing

Directions.   Read the following passage on rap music and write a summary of its main points. Then make up five review questions for the passage.

Rap: The Poetry of the Streets

Every culture needs its poets. And yet, with notable exceptions—Lucille Clifton, Alice Walker, Maya Angelou, Rita Dove—there are virtually no prominent black poets with books published by major presses.

Still, there are scores of young black poets, and more developing every day. They just don't publish books. They press their art into the grooves of slamming beats stolen from wherever they can get them.

It's called rap. Music you can dance or nod your head to. It's a chaotic mixture that challenges the listener to suffer the poetic.

Yes, rap has at least two faces. One is superficial, defined by its reputation for being racist and sexist, and for promoting violence. And in certain instances this reputation is deserved. But the other face, which begins with recognizing each rap song as a poetic expression, leads to a deeper recognition of rap's cultural and artistic significance.

I know there is a fair amount of rap that gives us virtually nothing except the beat that carries it to our ears. But you don't have to listen very long before you discover the literary genius just below the beat.

To be a legitimate poet of the people, a writer must speak the language. And, at least since the Black Arts Movement of the 1960s, black poets have largely been a collection of honest and angry voices.

Chuck D of Public Enemy has called rap "black America's CNN." He proves his point with the words to *Hazy Shade of Criminal,* from the latest Public Enemy disc:

> *Never understood why the 'hood half of who's in da joint*

Perhaps he read the recent statistics showing that 56 percent of black men in Baltimore between 18 and 35 are behind bars, on parole, being pursued by the police or in some other way in the criminal justice system. And for Washington, D.C., the number was 42 percent.

In the same poem, to demonstrate his ability to communicate irony, Chuck D writes:

> *Jeffrey Dahmer enter the room without cuffs*
> *how the hell do we get stuffed*
> *in da back of a cell*
> *on an isle*
> *ain't it wild*
> *what's a criminal?*

Or we can go back to Ice-T, much under siege for his song *Cop Killer,* which is more rock than rap. But Ice-T drops deft social commentary into *The House*:

> *You know the house down the street*
> *where the kids are*
> *and every day they seem to have a new scar*
> *something strange is going on*
> *and everybody knows*
> *doors always shut*

windows always closed
the little girl had a burn
the boy was black and blue
they said it came from play
you know that s—- ain't true
the boy's arm's broke
girl's scared to speak
their parents drink all day
couple of deadbeats . . .
act like you give a damn
won't someone save these kids
do something, call a cop
the other night I heard gunshots!

This is the voice of a socially responsible poet, not a cop killer. Therein lies one of the complexities of rap poetry: It offers the flesh, the blood, the ideas, the shame, the beauty of the inner city. The struggling, angry, glorious world of besieged African Americans. A world that was waiting for hip-hop—a broader term for rap culture—to arrive. Hip-hop is the messenger that carries the poetry.

As in the Beat poetry of the late '50s and early '60s, slang and wordplay are everything. Rap poets create language. And while it may come to the uninitiated listener as alien, it actually is a hyperactive, mutating version of the slang that I grew up with. "Cool" is now "def" or "hype." We used to "scream on" people to put them down. Now we "dis" them. It's the same urban language system; we just didn't have a multimillion-dollar industry pumping it up.

And within the body of a rap poem we have all the elements of poetry. We can find rap poems in iambic pentameter with an almost classical construction. And newer rap poets are engaged in a range of structural experiments, playing with line length, mixing rhyming patterns for frenetic rhythms.

In 1992 there was an explosion of diversity in the rap community. Of course, there always has been diversity among rappers. The poetry of the gifted and prophetic Ice Cube always has been different from Big Daddy Kane's. There always has been a division between what is popularly considered "hard-core"—poetry that is totally uncompromising in language and story selection—and "soft"—poetry that is more accessible and more acceptable to the middle class.

In the past year, the growth in poetic styles has been pronounced. Added to the voices of the continuing poets are more recent ones like Kris Kross, TLC, Arrested Development, X-Clan, the Disposable Heroes of Hiphoprisy, Pete Rock & CL Smooth, P.M. Dawn, Das EFX, Naughty by Nature, House of Pain, Cypress Hill and many more.

While it's true that rap groups come and go with the speed of sound bites, the best tend to survive. This is true in all good art. And the beauty in this diversity is what we do not have in the traditional literary arts: It's always one "flavor of the year" for black authors, but there is a rich variety of rap poets.

Unfortunately, within the context of this pressure, the history of black storytelling and their relative youth, rap poets often indulge their sexual insecurities and their proclivities for aggression in their poems. Their characterization of women is particularly troubling. Women are routinely referred to as "ho's," bitches or "skinz." What is new is that increasingly they are answered by female rappers like TLC, Salt-N-Pepa, Queen Latifah, Yo-Yo and MC Lyte who are rising in power and popularity.

From Queen Latifah's *Fly Girl*:

Tell me why is it when I walk past the guys
I always hear "Yo, baby,"
I mean like what's the big idea
I'm a queen, nuff respect
treat me like a lady,
and no, my name ain't yo, and I ain't got your baby
I'm looking for a guy who's sincere
one with class and savoir faire
I'm looking for someone who has to be
perfect for the queen
Latifah, me*

Effective rap poets are engaged in three-way dialogue among themselves, their communities and white America. In this poetic dialogue lies all kinds of dangers. The main danger is that, in the process of telling the truth about their environment, they also reveal the failures of social and economic policies. They reveal the attraction of gangs and sexism, and the roots of homophobia and anger toward the police. It is society's lack of effective attention to these issues and an inadequate education that scream back from rap poems. The poets only tell the stories of their people.

When I heard Pete Rock & CL Smooth's *They Reminisce Over You*, I knew that rap was growing. Here was a poem about the silent, invisible black men of the inner city who work hard all of their lives but go unremembered, uncelebrated.

When I think back
I recall a man
off the family tree
my right hand
Papa Doc I see
took me from a boy to a man
so I always had a father
when my biological didn't bother

Then, later in the poem:

but only you saw
what took many times to see
I dedicate this to you
For believin in me

One of 1992's best collections of rap comes from Arrested Development. From *Raining Revolution, Tennessee* and *People Everyday* to the astoundingly moral *Mr. Wendal*, Arrested Development proves rap poets are taking seriously their role in the education of young people.

Here have a dollar, in fact, naw, brotherman here, have two.
Two dollars is a snack for me,
but it means a big deal to you.

Be strong, serve God only that if you do
beautiful heaven awaits.
That's the poem I wrote for the first time.
I saw a man with no clothes, no money, no plate.
Mr. Wendal, that's his name
no one ever knew his name
cuz he's a know one
never thought twice about spending on an ole bum
until I had a chance to really get to know one!
Now that I know 'em
to give him money isn't charity,
he gives me some knowledge
I buy him some food.
And to think blacks spend all that money on big colleges still
most of y'awll come out confused[t]

Rap continues to thrive. This is because, in spite of its reputation and the white noise of controversy that swirls around it, rap is art. In fact, rap poetry is the emergent African-American literary form of the postmodern age. It is all the more sweet that the Grammys have been forced, to a degree, to reckon with rap music. Black poets making money and winning awards—who would've thunk it?[3]

---

[t]*Mr. Wendal* © Copyright 1992 EMI Blackwood Music Inc. and Arrested Development.

Summary: _____

_____

_____

_____

_____

_____

_____

_____

_____

_____

_____

_____

_____

_____

_____

_____

_____

_____

_____

_____

_____

_____

_____

_____

_____

_____

_____

_____

_____

_____

Review questions: _____

_____

_____

_____

_____

_____

_____

_____

_____

_____

_____

_____

_____

_____

_____

_____

_____

Reacting

After you have read an assignment (and sometimes while you are reading it), you react to the material. On one level, your reaction is personal and subjective. Ask yourself the following questions:

Did I enjoy reading the assignment?

Did I learn something interesting from it?

Do I agree with the author's ideas?

Are the author's ideas consistent with my own experiences and previous knowledge?

On another level, you react more objectively to what you've read. Ask yourself:

How well has the author explained and supported his point of view?

Is the information useful and valuable?

Is the author objective, or is he providing only one point of view?

It is important to be conscious of your reactions to your reading material. Clarifying your reactions will help you become more interested and involved with what you read, whether it is material you have chosen for yourself or material that has been assigned. Awareness of your own reactions also enables you to evaluate what you read in a more objective manner.

Exercise 13–5. Reacting

1. Using the preceding questions as guidelines, write your reaction to Selection 13.

   _____

   _____

   _____

2. Using the preceding questions as guidelines, write your reaction to the article "Daydreaming."

   _____

   _____

   _____

3. Using the preceding questions as guidelines, write your reaction to the article "Rap: The Poetry of the Streets."

   _____

   _____

   _____

Evaluating

In our complex, modern world, we are bombarded with all sorts of information and advice:

> "Use Ultra-brite toothpaste to have a sexier smile."
>
> "Drive an Escort, America's favorite car."
>
> "Come to our school for the best education money can buy."

Ultimately, each of us must decide for ourselves what to believe, and the decisions we make in our lives—whether it's choosing a toothpaste, car, or school—will be based on our beliefs.

Similarly, you, as a reader, decide what you will accept from your reading and determine how the author's ideas and information can be most useful to you. But you may, at times, fail to question and evaluate what you read. You may assume that what you've read is true—just because it said so in the book (or newspaper or magazine).

Evaluating what you read is a complex process. You need to recognize the author's purpose and judge how effectively that purpose was accomplished. It is important to compare your own reactions with the author's point of view, but do not discount the author's ideas simply because they are different from your own.

Distinguishing Fact from Opinion.   An important first step in evaluating what you read is to distinguish fact from opinion. Since you are not usually in a position to verify the author's facts, you may treat them as correct—as long as the source is reliable and there is no reason to suspect the author's motives. You should, however, be much more cautious in accepting an author's opinions, especially when reading persuasive material (material intended to influence our thinking and behavior).

Facts.   What is a fact? The word *fact* is usually used to refer to something that is considered real or true. But facts are not always easy to determine. For example, consider an apparently simple fact—the amount you weigh. Do you know how much you weigh? Are you sure? Is that how much you weigh right now or how much you weighed last week? What scale did you use? How do you know the scale was accurate? Perhaps you really weigh .2 pound more and your scale rounded off to the nearest whole pound. Facts are not always as clear and simple as we would like them to be.

In any case, most readers do not usually take the trouble to verify an author's facts. When evaluating what you read, you can consider a statement to be factual as long as the statement is *capable* of proof or disproof. In other words, a *factual statement* is one that can be determined to be correct or incorrect—either by direct observation, experimentation, or referral to other sources of information. Thus, the statement that 85.4 percent of the Chicanos of California live in urban areas is a factual statement—not because you know it to be true but because you know that the statement can be either verified or disproved.

Examples of factual statements include:

Drawing Conclusions.   Drawing conclusions is another important aspect of critical reading. When evaluating what you read, you can note what conclusions the author draws. Are his conclusions logical? Are they supported by the facts he has presented?

You will also draw your own conclusions from the passage, which may help you judge the merits of the author's ideas. The conclusions you draw may lead you to agree or disagree with the author's point of view. Sometimes, the author's ideas will stimulate you to formulate valuable new conclusions or insights of your own.

For example, the author of the passage on rap music concludes that rap music is popular because it is a form of art. The reader may agree with this conclusion, challenge it, or form new conclusions of her own.

Exercise 13–7. Reacting and Evaluating

Directions.   Read each passage and answer the questions that follow it. The questions will require you to evaluate the author's ideas and to discuss your own reactions to the passage.

1. **Car Sick**

Our children's children will live in a world without oil. The world's growing car population will make sure of that.

Cars are getting better mileage, but there are more of them. World oil consumption continues to rise, topping 225 billion gallons this year [1990], an eightfold increase since 1950. At current levels of consumption, optimistic oil industry analysts expect oil to last another 45 years. But if consumption increases, as seems likely, this forecast will have to be shortened.

We rely far too much on the car. When the growing world car population consumes the resources that fuel it, then we will learn just how much we depend on it. The coming crisis will bring an end to the auto age. The issue, for the world, is not *whether* it will end, but when, and how, and at what cost.[4]

1. What is the author's opinion regarding the future of the automobile?

The auto age will end because we have run out of oil

2. What facts in the passage support the author's opinion?

3. Is the conclusion stated in the last sentence supported by the passage? Explain.

4. Using the questions on page 307 as guidelines, discuss your reaction to the passages and explain why you agree or disagree with the author's ideas.

_____

_____

_____

_____

2. **The Infinite Wonder of the Human Brain**

Not even the universe, with its countless billions of galaxies, represents greater wonder or complexity than the human brain. The human brain is a mirror to infinity. There is no limit to its range, scope, or capacity for creative growth. It makes possible new perceptions and new perspectives, just as it clears the way for brighter prospects in human affairs.

If the brain of an average fifty-year-old person could be fully emptied of all the impressions and memories it has stored, and recorded on tape, the length of the tape would reach to the moon and back several times. Indeed, it is possible that the memory contents of the human brain could never be fully inventoried; new impressions would come in faster than the old ones could be identified. Much has been said about the memory capability of computers, but the computer has not been devised that can match the potential capacity of the human brain. Silicon chips and semiconductors have been hailed as the supreme achievement of technology, but these chips are far inferior to the neurons of the human brain in terms of function.

The human brain presides over the biological wonderland that is the human body. The average brain weighs approximately three pounds, accounting for about 2 percent of the body's total weight yet consuming more than 20 percent of its oxygen.[5]

1. What is the author's opinion of the human brain?

_____

_____

_____

2. What facts in the passage support the author's opinion?

_____

_____

_____

3. What conclusions about the brain can be drawn from this passage?

_____

_____

4. Using the questions on page 307 as guidelines, discuss your reaction to the passage and explain why you agree or disagree with the author's ideas.

_____

_____

_____

_____

3. **The Search for Extraterrestrial Intelligence**

From a distance, at twilight, you might almost mistake them for human. I suspect they'll have their heads on top, as we do, and walk upright, but I hope that intelligent extraterrestrials have four arms instead of two. Two aren't enough, in my opinion.

My scientific colleagues raise their eyebrows when I speculate on details of appearance, but 99.9 percent of them agree that other intelligent life forms exist—and that large populations of them may infiltrate the universe.

Personally, I find nothing more tantalizing than the thought that radio messages from alien civilizations in space are passing through our offices and homes, right now, like a whisper we can't quite hear.

I have tracked those radio signals for more than 30 years in the search for extraterrestrial intelligence (SETI). I engineered the first modern search in 1960 at the National Radio Astronomy Observatory in Green Bank, West Virginia. I named it "Project Ozma." For two months I used what we now consider crude equipment to listen for intelligent signals from two nearby stars.

Project Ozma failed to detect extraterrestrial intelligence but succeeded in demonstrating our group's commitment to SETI. It also portrayed SETI as a legitimate, do-able, scientific endeavor. And it stimulated activity among others who shared our interest but had lacked the means to search.

According to the Drake Equation, approximately 10,000 advanced extraterrestrial civilizations share our Milky Way galaxy. Any one of them should have something of supreme importance to tell us.[6]

1. What is the author's opinion regarding the possibility of intelligent life in other parts of the universe?

_____

_____

_____

2. What facts in the passage support the author's opinion?

_____

_____

_____

3. Do you agree with the conclusion reached in the passage's last sentence? Why or why not?

_____

_____

4. Using the questions on page 307 as guidelines, discuss your reaction to the passage and explain why you agree or disagree with the author's ideas.

_____

_____

_____

_____

4. **Baseball's Enduring Hold on America**

Because of its ability to create lasting memories, baseball always has held a special place in the hearts of Americans. "I think baseball's attraction, in part, is the fact that it establishes a kind of clarity in the game between the players," indicates Benjamin Rader, a University of Nebraska-Lincoln history professor and author of *Baseball: A History of America's Game.* "They're separated from each other in a vast green expanse, so it's much easier to remember what happened in a baseball game clearly; it etches memories very sharply."

Rader points out that things other than the rules have remained constant in baseball. Problems that plague today's game also hindered it in the past, such as player behavior and the use of drugs, which he likens to alcohol use in the 19th and early 20th centuries. Moreover, players holding out for more money is nothing new. In fact, many—including Ruth—threatened to hold out for entire seasons in order to get pay raises. "I'm inclined to doubt there has been as much change in player attitudes as we might think. Today, there is more focus on the athletes because of modern journalism. Now we know how much the players make; we know everything about their personal lives."

He points out that players were better known and more respected in the past. Lou Gehrig, Rogers Hornsby, and Joe DiMaggio had huge followings and were, in their eras, among the most well-known people in the world. Modern day stars aren't as highly regarded.

However, Rader sees today's ball players possessing far superior athletic skills than their predecessors. "My belief is that athletes overall in the big leagues today simply have to be better by and large. And they are better despite the crying you hear from sportswriters and others."

Larry Gerlach, who teaches a history of baseball class at Utah State University and is author of *The Men in Blue: A Conversation with Baseball Umpires,* disagrees. While noting that today's players are bigger, faster, and stronger, he believes that in no way are they more skilled than they once were. In fact, he claims, the technical level of the game has declined greatly. "When you watch baseball today and see the poor execution of fundamentals, the purists, who enjoy sport as a performance art, cringe. Now, a lot of people will go to a ballgame and enjoy all the action going on, when in fact it's a lousy baseball game."

No matter, baseball always has and likely will continue to be considered America's favorite pastime. Though the game has changed little over the decades, it has created a history unprecedented by other sports.[7]

1. What is Rader's opinion as to why baseball has remained so popular in America?

_____

_____

_____

2. On what point do Rader and Gerlach disagree?

_____

_____

3. What conclusions about baseball does the author draw in the last paragraph?

_____

_____

_____

4. Using the questions on page 307 as guidelines, discuss your reaction to the passage and explain why you agree or disagree with the author's ideas.

_____

_____

_____

_____

5. **Which College Is Best for Me?**

The trend in higher education is for students to start out in community colleges. In 1990, an estimated 45 percent of all postsecondary students taking courses for college credit were enrolled in community, technical, and junior colleges. This compares to just 37.4 percent in 1980. Over half of all first-time students taking credit classes are enrolled in two-year colleges. Accessibility is cited as one of the big advantages of community colleges. Accessibility includes location, time, and money. Tuition, for example, averaged $884 versus $1,808 at public four-year colleges and $9,391 at private four-year colleges. Every indication is that growth in community colleges will exceed that in four-year schools for the foreseeable future.

When students complete their associate degrees at community colleges, they usually perform well at four-year colleges. Community colleges have a teaching focus which helps students get a firm foundation. Community colleges are especially attractive to adult students who want to upgrade their skills, especially in technical areas such as computers. Community colleges are often uniquely able to handle such students because they often offer evening courses and weekend programs geared to the part-time student. Community colleges also can develop close working relationships with local businesses so that graduates can be educated to fit the needs of the local community. Community colleges are especially good at preparing students for jobs that don't require a bachelor's degree, such as nursing, technical specialties, and police work.

About 39 percent of community college students plan to transfer to four-year colleges. There are advantages to four-year colleges as well. Some careers call for a bachelor's degree or more. Some students like to move away from the local community for various reasons. One of the benefits of education in the United States is the diversity available in colleges. Some students prefer a religious institution, others want the opportunity to play on nationally ranked athletic teams, and others seek the camaraderie of fraternities and sororities.

To find the best school for you, you should visit a variety of schools and attend some classes in each. Talk to the students and faculty, get a feel for the campus, and look over the curricula.[8]

1. What is the authors' opinion of community colleges?

   _____

   _____

   _____

2. What facts support the authors' opinion?

   _____

   _____

   _____

3. What conclusion do the authors reach in the last paragraph regarding choosing a school?

   _____

   _____

4. Using the questions on page 307 as guidelines, discuss your reaction to the passage and explain why you agree or disagree with the authors' ideas.

   _____

   _____

   _____

   _____

Integrative Exercise

Exercise 13–8. Critical Reading

Directions.   Read each passage and answer the questions that follow it.

1. **Gun Control**

Even though the U.S. has many more gun-control laws than any other nation, Americans are more likely to be victims of gun-related violence. We have no hope of greatly improving this situation as long as we continue to construct gun-control policy on a weak foundation of facts.

Since the 1960s some social and behavioral scientists have been investigating how violence is related to firearms. But their conclusions have largely been ignored. Neither supporters nor opponents of gun control laws have felt any great need to cite facts. Strong emotions have kept the conflicting parties at each other's throats.

Recent congressional debates on gun control have also relied on undocumented assertions. The Brady bill aims to reduce the violence associated with guns by making handgun purchases subject to waiting periods and police notification. The congressional debate over these issues is no more informed than it was during the deliberations that led to the Gun Control Act of 1968. A distaste for facts is also evident in the emphasis Americans have placed on research: much more money is spent on newspaper advertisements about gun control than on research about firearms and violence.[9]

Inference.   Mark each statement Yes or No, according to whether it can be logically inferred from the passage.

_____   1. The author believes that gun control laws accomplish nothing.

_____   2. The Brady bill establishes a waiting period for the purchase of a handgun.

_____   3. There is more gun-related violence in the United States than in any other country.

_____   4. The author would like to see more money spent on research about gun-related violence.

_____   5. Those who favor gun control laws have relied largely on emotional arguments rather than facts.

Fact and Opinion

1. What is the author's opinion of American gun control policy?

_____

_____

2. What facts in the passage support the author's opinion?

_____

_____

_____

3. Do you agree with the author's opinion? Why or why not?

_____

_____

_____

2. **There's Protein in Them There Bugs**

House flies, crickets, aphids and honey bees are more than just garden variety insects to Gordon Plague: to him, they're the new low-cholesterol, protein rich snack food of the '90s.

"It's animal protein, so it's good for you and it's readily available," Plague said.

To demonstrate his point, Plague, an assistant naturalist at the Science Center of New Hampshire, served up a few treats to a recent audience. On the menu were deviled eggs, topped with garlic sauteed mealworms, a bread containing ground crickets, a salad made with rice, olives, pimentos and crickets, and shortbread cookies with a wax moth filling.

But Plague, who literally has had butterflies in his stomach, says the Monarch variety should be avoided, because it contains a chemical that can cause rapid heartbeat.

Plague believes insects can help alleviate the world food dilemma, because they can be mass-produced. A female aphid can produce 1,500 sextillion offspring a year. A cow in comparison takes a year to produce a single calf, he said.

Plague says insects are cleaner than some animals people eat, and adds they are likely to be the most reliable source of animal food for anyone lost in the woods.

He also said the exo-skeletons of insects and shellfish can be ground up to produce a byproduct that can be used in medicine. Skin grafts and wounds can be treated with the substance, which is breathable, but prevents bacteria from passing through it, he said.[10]

Inference.   Mark each statement Yes or No, according to whether it can be logically inferred from the passage.

_____ 1. Plague has eaten insects himself.

_____ 2. Plague runs a small restaurant.

_____ 3. Insects have several advantages over other animals as a food source.

_____ 4. The author has eaten insects.

_____ 5. The primary intention of this article is to persuade the reader to include insects in his or her diet.

Fact and Opinion

1. What is Plague's opinion about insects as food?

_____

_____

_____

2. What facts in the passage support Plague's opinion?

_____

_____

_____

3. In your opinion, are insects a good food source? Should this passage be taken seriously? Why or why not?

_____

_____

_____

3. **The Exercise of the Eggs**

The eggs had been given into the care of the teacher, while the boy, who was the father of the eggs, delivered a note to the office. It was not an unusual occurrence. No one paid much attention to the eggs resting together in their small, criblike basket on the corner of the teacher's desk, each egg half-covered with a tiny blanket, its infant face staring up at the ceiling. There were many eggs in the class, all of them in their baskets, tucked in, cosseted by their parents, as eggs must be. In one basket the eggs were identical twins. In some baskets there was only one egg, which lay alone. There was something sad about those baskets with only one egg; the eggs in them appeared forlorn, abandoned. In all the baskets with only one egg a sense of loss was somehow said, tragedy was implied. And in one basket there were no eggs at all. But there had been eggs; the form of them was impressed upon the tiny blanket; there were signs in the stiffness of the bedding that something terrible had occurred, as final as a death.

All day and all night the eggs stayed with their child parents. Every night, at three AM, the parents of the eggs awakened to the rudeness of an alarm clock, as if the bell or buzz were the voice of an infant child crying. At the lunch hour the parents of the eggs had to find babysitters for their delicate wards or they could not go to lunch. Day after day, night after night, the eggs exacted their demands upon their eleven- or twelve-year-old parents, relentless, delicate, and as irreparable as Humpty Dumpty.

The teachers at Coral Way Elementary think the exercise of the eggs will teach their students something about the responsibilities of parenting. They have instituted the program because their students first begin to get pregnant in the sixth grade, and the teachers think it is the responsibility of pedagogues to educate children in the world. In this work they are as unforgiving as reality; the eggs in the baskets have not been cooked—if one should fall, its tiny face shatters and the yellow heart and clear, viscous body ooze through the wounds to die in the unrelenting world. The manicured pedagogues of Coral Way teach the tragic view of life, they give lessons in death.[11]

Inference. Mark each statement Yes or No, according to whether it can be logically inferred from the passage.

_____ 1. The eggs represent babies.

_____ 2. The teachers use the exercise with the eggs to help children who have irresponsible parents.

_____ 3. All of the students with eggs have real children of their own.

_____ 4. Sometimes the children are not successful in protecting their eggs.

_____ 5. Children who break or lose their eggs are punished.

Fact and Opinion

1. What facts are contained in the passage?

_____

_____

_____

_____

2. Does the author express any opinions? If so, what are they?

_____

_____

_____

3. What is your opinion of this experiment?

_____

_____

_____

4. **Grizzly Bears**

In nonscientific terms, grizzly bears tend to come in two types. I call type I grizzlies human-distant. They get as far away from people as they can as fast as they can. Through either good sense or a bad experience, they have wisely chosen to avoid two-legged, furless critters like the plague. Now, park management likes this type of bear, and you can't fault the National Park Service for that. Nothing ruins a chief ranger's day more than the news that some Yellowstone grizzly has eaten a camper, even though such an event is extraordinarily rare.

Type II grizzlies are what I call human-close. They seem to enjoy human-bear social encounters—at least, they enjoy the food that people tend to serve at such receptions. Bears—and grizzlies are no exception—are notorious gluttons; they'll eat anything. They are energy conservers, and some of them realize that they can save a lot of energy by showing up along roadways or wherever else humans congregate and taking the handouts that invariably are offered despite park prohibitions. It sure is a lot easier than catching a swift elk calf whose mama is not happy about your trying to eat her baby. Bears also have a sweet tooth, and jelly doughnuts and peanut butter sandwiches taste a lot better than a month-old winter-killed mule deer.[12]

Inference. Mark each statement Yes or No, according to whether it can be logically inferred from the passage.

_____ 1. All bears can be divided into two categories.

_____ 2. Bears never harm people.

_____ 3. Type I grizzlies are more intelligent than type II grizzlies.

_____ 4. A type II grizzly could become a type I grizzly.

_____ 5. Park rangers would prefer for campers not to feed the grizzly bears.

Fact and Opinion

1. What facts about grizzly bears are contained in the passage?

_____

_____

_____

2. Does the author express any opinions? If so, what are they?

_____

_____

_____

3. In your opinion, which type of bear is better off?

_____

_____

_____

5. **Sexual Harassment**

Early in the 1990s, sexual harassment became the third most critical employment issue, behind benefits and job security. Publicity over the Anita Hill/Clarence Thomas hearings led to an expectation of many more such claims in the 1990s. Sexual harassment refers to unwelcome sexual advances, requests for sexual favors, and other conduct of a sexual nature (verbal or physical). Such conduct becomes illegal when: (1) an employee's submission to such conduct is made either explicitly or implicitly a term or condition of employment, (2) an employee's submission to or rejection of such conduct is used as the basis for employment decisions affecting the worker's status, or (3) the conduct unreasonably interferes with a worker's job performance or creates an intimidating, hostile, or offensive working environment. There is no question that managers and workers are much more sensitive to comments and behavior of a sexual nature now. Nonetheless, this is likely to remain an important issue throughout the 1990s.[13]

Inference.   Mark each statement Yes or No, according to whether it can be logically inferred from the passage.

_____ 1. Sexual harassment is more common today than it was a decade ago.

_____ 2. Sexual harassment will become more common in the second half of the 1990s.

_____ 3. Benefits and job security are the two most important employment issues.

_____ 4. A verbal statement alone cannot be considered an act of sexual harassment.

_____ 5. The Anita Hill/Clarence Thomas hearings have made Americans more aware of the issue of sexual harassment, creating the expectation that fewer sexual harassment claims will be filed in the 1990s.

Fact and Opinion

1. What important facts about sexual harassment are included in this passage?

   _____

   _____

   _____

2. Does the author express any opinions about sexual harassment? If so, what are they?

   _____

   _____

   _____

3. In your opinion, is sexual harassment an important issue today? Why or why not?

   _____

   _____

   _____

Journal Entry

1. Have you ever moved to a new area? Discuss the changes you encountered in your new community and how you adapted to them. If you have lived in the same area all your life, discuss any other major change that has occurred in your life.

_____

_____

_____

_____

_____

_____

_____

_____

_____

_____

_____

2. Which of the after-reading strategies discussed in this chapter will be most useful to you? Why?

_____

_____

_____

_____

_____

_____

_____

_____

_____

_____

_____

_____

14 | APPLYING YOUR SKILLS

In Chapter 14, you will:

1. Read a selection about crime and violence in America, using all the strategies you've learned to gain a full understanding of the selection.
2. Answer comprehension questions on the selection to check your understanding.
3. Review the various comprehension and vocabulary strategies you have learned from this textbook.
4. Complete practice exercises for reviewing, evaluating, and reacting to what you read.

SELECTION 14
BITING THE BULLET

Vicki Kemper

Directions. Preview the passage and use the following space to write your preview and pre-thinking notes.

Previewing Notes

_____

_____

_____

_____

Pre-thinking Notes

_____

_____

_____

_____

While You Read

Directions.   Use all of the strategies you've learned this term to maximize your comprehension of the passage. Underline or make note of important points. The exercises following the selection will ask you to review the main points, react to the author's ideas, and evaluate what you have read.

After 28 years on the Washington, D.C., police force, after locking up tens of thousands of drug dealers and murderers, after putting more cops on the street and implementing new methods of policing, and—after all that—seeing still more years of record-breaking murder totals, Isaac Fulwood called it quits. The District of Colum-
5   bia chief of police saw all around him a growing culture of violence, and he feared that additional thousands of lives would be shattered and wasted.

The most powerful law enforcement officer in the nation's capital traded in his badge for what he believed would be a more effective anti-crime tool. Explaining that he wants to prevent crime rather than merely respond to it, and emphasizing the
10   importance of creating "better opportunities for our children," Fulwood became director of the District's nascent youth anti-crime programs. (At the time we went to press, a conflict between Washington's mayor Sharon Pratt Kelly and the city council about Fulwood's salary was unresolved.)

The time has come, Fulwood says, for politicians and society alike to bite the
15   bullet, to trade easy responses for real solutions, to get angry enough and compassionate enough and smart enough to address the causes of violent crime: poverty, guns, drugs, and "a value system that is totally out of kilter."

While many of the programs Fulwood advocates are new, his emphasis on the need for social and economic action is not; presidential commissions and federal laws
20   sounded a similar call in the late 1960s. But the sense of political urgency spawned by Watts, Detroit, and other urban riots soon faded; the War on Poverty approach to social problems fell into disrepute in the '70s. By the '80s, the federal government had switched gears completely, making drastic cuts in aid to cities and states and fostering wide income gaps between rich and poor. The Reagan and Bush administra-
25   tions adopted a short-term anti-crime policy, waging "war" on drug dealers and emphasizing more police, more arrests, more prisons, and stiffer sentences, including executions.

The conventional wisdom during the Reagan era was that social programs failed to make a dent in crime rates. Many criminologists argued, however, that the
30   prevention approach has never been given a fair chance. The riots in Los Angeles

last year seemed to reawaken the country—at least momentarily—to the needs
of the nation's cities and the desperation of many young people. But calls for job-
training programs, enterprise zones, and other measures soon were lost in election-
year politics.

35 For all Bill Clinton's talk of change, his approach is not much different from Reagan's and Bush's. He wants to put 100,000 new police officers on the streets and create "prisons that work," and he maintains his support for capital punishment. He does,
however, support a waiting period for handgun purchases, programs to make schools
and public housing projects safer, and the granting of federal funds to cities that estab-
40 lish community-based policing programs and expanded drug treatment services.

At the other end of Pennsylvania Avenue, members of Congress often see anti-
crime bills that emphasize prisons and more frequent use of the death penalty as good
vote-getters back home. Crime prevention programs, on the other hand, take time to
work, cost money, and usually are seen as social programs.

45 Voters put the politician in the position of championing policies that don't work.
Fulwood says, "Everybody says, 'Hey, you better stand up and talk tough about crime
and violence or we're not going to re-elect you.' " As a result, short-term "lock 'em
up" laws win out and "nothing happens. The problem continues on and on."

"We need to redefine the crime problem," says James Fyfe, a professor of crim-
50 inal justice and senior research fellow at Temple University who was a New York
City cop for 16 years. "It's an inner-city problem. It's a problem of young black kids
killing each other. It's a problem of poverty; the problem of kids being born to young,
single, uneducated parents; kids growing up without love or affection, without knowing what it is to be close to another person; kids growing up without beliefs, with no
55 value for life.

"Kids raised in the ghetto in effect are being raised in a crime factory," Fyfe continues. "To do something about crime over the long haul, we have to do something
about the conditions of the inner city."

For politicians and comfortable citizens who feel what happens in the impover-
60 ished inner cities doesn't involve them, Fulwood has a message: "You can't run far
enough, because it will get you, too." It might get you as an actual victim of crime,
or scare you into moving or buying a gun or investing in expensive alarm systems.
Or the increased costs of law enforcement and prisons could threaten to bankrupt your
local government.

65 Conservatives are fond of saying that liberal solutions to crime have failed. But
now we've had 12 years of aggressive conservative anti-crime policies. From fiscal
years 1981 to 1992, the Justice Department's budget increased more than 345 percent, while the Federal Bureau of Prisons' budget was bolstered 470 percent. Since
1989 the Justice Department has hired more than 800 additional FBI agents, 700 drug
70 enforcement agents, and 1,200 federal prosecutors. Since 1988, federal prison capacity has increased 62 percent and is "on its way to a 228 percent increase," noted Attorney General William Barr proudly in a 1992 memo to George Bush.

Yet according to the FBI, the national rate for violent crime reached an all-time
high in 1991, an increase of 24 percent since 1987. For the second year in a row the
75 United States also set a new murder record with an estimated 24,020 violent deaths.

Homicide was the nation's 10th leading cause of death, according to Surgeon General Antonia Novello.

For juveniles the violent crime rate is even worse. Gun murders among black males 15 to 19 years old increased 71 percent from 1987 to 1989, according to the
80   Centers for Disease Control, and since 1965 the arrest rate for juveniles charged with violent crimes has more than tripled. The FBI reports that homicide now is the leading cause of death among young black men.

If success is measured in the numbers of people behind bars, the attorney general was right to boast. Due largely to the "war on drugs," the number of inmates in
85   the nation's prisons and jails increased 143 percent from 1980 to 1991, according to the Bureau of Justice Statistics.

With more than 1.2 million citizens behind bars, the United States now has the highest incarceration rate of any industrialized nation; South Africa ranks second. The country spends some $24 billion a year to operate its prisons and jails, according
90   to the Sentencing Project, which promotes alternatives to incarceration. And with most prisons severely overcrowded, $10 billion in new prison construction is on the drawing boards.

This "short-sighted policy of incarceration . . . and tough law enforcement against street [drug] addicts . . . makes the world safe for politicians, but it doesn't
95   address the problems of community violence," says Barry Krisberg, president of the National Council on Crime and Delinquency in San Francisco.

"The current strategy is like trying to deal with AIDS by building more hospices," says ex-cop James Fyfe.

Krisberg and others expect violent crime to increase over the next several years
100   because of current "voodoo criminology" policies; a larger population of children entering the crime-prone teen years; a generation of teenagers raised in poverty; a dramatic increase in domestic violence; and the increasing availability of high-caliber guns.

"I've designed more lock-up programs than probably most [police] chiefs in this
105   country," Fulwood says, "and I know that they just don't necessarily work." Referring to an anti-drug program called Operation Clean Sweep that netted some 50,000 arrests in two years in the late '80s, Fulwood says, "You know, it didn't have a long-term impact. The homicide rate continued to escalate."

Guns are the biggest culprit, Fulwood and others say. In the District of Colum-
110   bia, guns are so much a part of the street culture that T-shirts featuring handguns, some complete with real or designer bullet holes, became the fashion rage among junior high and high school students last fall.

Fulwood speaks with horror of Washington, D.C., kids who have become so desensitized by everyday life in their neighborhoods that "when they see people with
115   their brains blown out they can laugh about it."

This plague of guns and violence is not unique to the District. The *Los Angeles Times* called 1991 "the year of the gun" in Southern California, and one out of four U.S. high school students carried a gun to class at least once during a recent month, according to the Centers for Disease Control. The *Journal of the American Medical*
120   *Association* declared gun violence a public health emergency.

The medical profession, criminologists, educators, community activists, and members of every major law enforcement organization have sounded the alarm: The violence will continue unchecked until the nation does something to control guns. Opinion polls show that 95 percent of Americans support some form of gun control,

125   and at least 26 states and scores of cities and counties have imposed waiting periods on some gun purchases, banned the sale of assault weapons, or both.

Yet Congress still refuses to pass some form of national gun control, and without it many state and local laws can't work. While gun sales are illegal in the District, for example, weapons can be purchased easily in neighboring Maryland and Virginia.

130   The Brady Bill, which would impose a waiting period on handgun purchases, was buried in the omnibus crime bill that in early October was defeated by threats of a Republican filibuster.*

To break the cycle of violence and crime, experts argue, we must—through our families, churches, and community organizations, as well as local, state, and federal

135   governments—move to protect children from the ravages of inner-city life. It is those children who are hit hardest by increasing rates of poverty, domestic abuse, urban decay, and job loss and a popular culture that continues to glorify and glamorize violence.

Crime prevention, youth education, and training programs cost money. While

140   roughly $1.5 billion a year would put more police officers on the streets and expand drug treatment in prisons, a comprehensive effort to educate and train inner-city children would cost $10 billion a year. But proponents argue that the money will be spent one way or another: It can be invested in programs that will enrich society and keep youth out of crime, or governments will be forced to spend even more—about $24

145   billion in 1992—to keep criminals off the streets.

"If we took half the money it costs to incarcerate people," Fulwood says, "and committed it to quality education and health care and decent housing for people, the benefit would be enormous, we'd turn the money over five times in every neighborhood."

150   As director of the District's new Youth Initiatives Office, Fulwood will oversee programs that target children at younger ages than ever before, programs that also reach out to families and single mothers and offer more health care services to the poor. Drug treatment and job-training programs will be expanded and targeted at younger residents, and a whole array of self-esteem, pregnancy prevention, conflict

155   mediation, and job-training programs designed for high-risk children ages 10 to 15.

"My fundamental goal is to try to get kids turned around and to get them to believe in themselves," Fulwood says, "to reinvest in the dream that they can make a difference, that their lives mean something and to get them to adopt different values: the value of education, the value of caring and giving back."

160   Ellen O'Connor, D.C.'s chief financial officer, notes that the District's $40 million budget for youth initiatives is virtually the same amount it spends on juvenile detention services.

---

*The Brady Bill has been enacted since the time of this writing.

"We're spending $39 million on only 1,800 kids [in detention facilities]," she says, and for $40 million they could reach most of the District's young children. The District spends roughly $252 million on its 4,700-member police force and more than $255 million to operate its prisons and jails, according to budget analysts.

While the District's programs are a step in the right direction, Fulwood and others say that much, much more must be done. Day care for children of single mothers, better health care for inner-city children, improved schools, support for families, mentoring, after-school programs, and job-training opportunities all are key, experts say.

Clinton's plan to put 100,000 new police officers on the nation's streets leaves Fulwood and many criminologists unimpressed.

"The absence of crime is not because of a heavy police presence," says ex-New York City cop James Fyfe, "but because people have a sense of community, a sense of ownership. They have things to lose. You see heavy street crime in places where people have nothing to lose."

Young people must also be given something to hope for, Barry Krisberg says, and jobs and the prospect of life outside the ghetto are at the top of the list. Providing decent employment opportunities for teenagers, who now resort to drug dealing and other crimes, could go a long way toward resolving some of their frustrations and lowering the crime rate, he says. Krisberg also points to the violence in rap music, music videos, movies, and television as a trigger for violent crime. Popular culture desensitizes children to violence, teaches them to brutalize women, and leaves them with no realistic understanding of what violence does to people, Fulwood adds.

Krisberg and others foresee several years of increasing violence on the nation's streets. There has been a dramatic increase in what studies show to be one of the most accurate predictors of violent behavior: violence suffered or observed by children. From 1981 to 1991 the number of reported child abuse cases increased 120 percent, according to figures from the American Humane Association and the National Committee for Prevention of Child Abuse. The nation's top priority, Krisberg says, should be a "massive national campaign on the prevention and reduction of family violence."

Meanwhile, citizens who have had enough of fear and horror are working to take their neighborhoods back. Whether they're patrolling their streets in bright orange caps or marching to city hall, community groups are demanding safety and prevention.

And this heartens Ike Fulwood, "I don't want to be viewed as a mushy person," says the burly former police chief, but it's easy to "feel defeated, to feel overwhelmed by crime and violence. We've gotta energize people to believe that we can in fact make a difference."[1]

Interest Rating.   Please rate the interest level of Selection 14 on the following 1–5 scale (circle one):

5—Very interesting

4—Fairly interesting

3—Mildly interesting

2—A little boring

1—Very boring

Difficulty Rating. Please indicate how difficult Selection 14 was for you to understand on the following 1–5 scale (circle one):

5—Very difficult

4—Fairly difficult

3—Moderate

2—Fairly easy

1—Very easy

Comments: _____

_____

Comprehension Questions

Directions. For questions 1–5, choose the answer that best completes the statement. For questions 6–10, write your response in the space provided. Base all answers on what you read in the selection (you may refer to the selection when necessary).

_____ 1. The primary purpose of Selection 14 is to:
  a. Explain why Isaac Fulwood quit his job as Washington DC police chief.
  b. Criticize Bush and Clinton for doing too little about crime.
  c. Argue for more effective approaches to crime and violence.
  d. Show why more police and prisons are needed.

_____ 2. Supporting evidence consists mainly of:
  a. Statistics and quotes.
  b. Explanation of theory and research findings.
  c. The author's personal experience and examples.
  d. Research findings and emotional appeals to the reader.

_____ 3. The author suggests that the prevention approach to crime, emphasizing social programs:
  a. Has been tried and has failed.
  b. Was advocated by Presidents Reagan and Bush.
  c. Has not been given enough of a chance.
  d. Led to the Los Angeles riots.

_____ 4. During the 1980s, the number of Americans in prison:
  a. Decreased.
  b. Remained approximately the same.
  c. Increased slightly.
  d. More than doubled.

_____ 5. Some experts suspect that in the near future violence in our society will:
  a. Decrease.
  b. Increase.
  c. Stay the same.
  d. Depend on the number of police on the streets.

6. Which is the principal pattern of organization used in Selection 14 (chronological order, enumeration/listing, comparison–contrast, or cause–effect)? Explain your choice.

_____

_____

7. Why did Isaac Fulwood quit his job as DC chief of police?

_____

_____

8. According to the article, what are the main sources of crime and violence in our society?

_____

_____

9. Briefly explain the difference between the conservative and liberal approaches to crime prevention.

_____

_____

_____

10. Is the conclusion of the article optimistic or pessimistic? Explain your answer.

_____

_____

_____

_____

_____

_____

_____

_____

_____

_____

_____

_____

Review Exercise

Directions. Write a half-page summary of Selection 14 (refer to the guidelines for writing a summary on page 297). Then write five review questions for the passage.

Summary: _____

_____

_____

_____

_____

_____

_____

_____

_____

_____

_____

_____

Review questions: _____

_____

_____

_____

Reacting and Evaluating Exercise

1. *a.* What is the author's opinion regarding gun control (see lines 109–132)?

_____

_____

   b. What facts in the passage support the author's opinion?

_____

_____

_____

c. Do you agree with the author's opinion? Why or why not?

_____

_____

_____

2. What facts does the author use to show that conservative anticrime policies have not been successful (see lines 65–92)?

_____

_____

3. What does the author believe is the best approach to the prevention of violent crime?

_____

_____

4. Write your reaction to the article. Do you agree with the author's ideas about crime prevention? What, in your opinion, would be the most effective way to deal with crime and violence in our society?

_____

_____

_____

_____

Vocabulary Exercise

Directions. Use a multistrategy approach to determine the meaning of each of the following words. Write your definition in the space provided.

1. nascent (11) _____

2. disrepute (22) _____

3. impoverished (59) _____

4. fiscal (66) _____

5. incarceration (93) _____

6. hospices (97) _____

7. desensitized (114) _____

8. filibuster (132) _____

9. ravages (135) _____

10. mediation (155) _____

Strategies Review

You have now learned the key reading and vocabulary strategies needed for success in college, and you have been practicing them for a term. It is important that you continue to use these strategies next term and throughout your college career. The more you use the strategies, the more you will retain from your reading and the stronger your reading habits will become. The process model illustrating the comprehension strategies is shown in Figure 14–1.

Exercise 14–1. Review of Comprehension Strategies

Directions. Imagine you are teaching a friend to use the comprehension strategies you have learned this term. In the space below, explain how and why each of the following strategies is used:

1. Previewing

How: _____

_____

Why: _____

_____

FIGURE 14–1 *Study Reading Process Model*

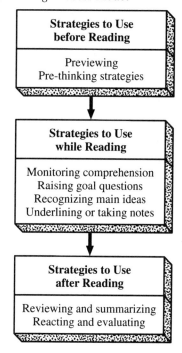

2. Pre-thinking

   How: _____

   _____

   Why: _____

   _____

3. Goal questions

   How: _____

   _____

   Why: _____

   _____

4. Identifying main ideas

   How: _____

   _____

   Why: _____

   _____

5. Marking the text and taking notes

   How: _____

   _____

   Why: _____

   _____

6. Reviewing

   How: _____

   _____

   Why: _____

   _____

7. Reacting and evaluating

   How: _____

   _____

   Why: _____

   _____

Exercise 14–2. Review of Vocabulary Strategies

Directions. Use your knowledge of vocabulary strategies to fill in the blanks in the following passage.

When encountering an unfamiliar word, the first step is usually to study the _____.

Next, the reader should probably consult the _____. If you are unsure of the

word's pronunciation, break the word into _____ or check the _____

in the dictionary.

Word parts are often valuable clues to the meaning of an unfamiliar word. The main

part of a word is called its _____. A part attached at the beginning of a word is

a _____; a part attached at the end of a word is a _____.

If you are having trouble remembering the meaning of a word you are learning, try

making up an _____, which will link the new word with something

you already know.

Exercise 14–3. Review, React, and Evaluate

Directions. Read each passage and answer the questions that follow it.

1. **Poverty Haunts College Students**

   Angel Ortiz studies literature and political theory at Amherst College, but his thoughts often dwell on gunshots, food stamps, welfare, and where to find cash for his next trip home.

   Like many children of poverty who have climbed to the upper echelons of American education, Ortiz remains bound by the economic and emotional chains of his youth. Indeed, educators and advocates say wealth and social disparities still make higher education an unequal opportunity in the 1990s—even at top schools with deep pockets and fierce commitments to fairness.

   "The reality of the Bronx is my reality," Ortiz said. "I am grateful to be here, but in a lot of ways I feel I shouldn't be. My mind tells me I should be home helping my family. I should be working. I should be dead."

   Ortiz' burdens at home are not unique. According to the U.S. Census Bureau, 9.4 percent of U.S. families had incomes less than $10,000 in 1990.

   His academic success, though, sets him apart. Only 6 percent of freshmen at private, four-year colleges in 1991 came from families earning less than $10,000. Low-income freshmen represented only 2.8 percent of the student body at private universities.

   Ortiz could easily have missed their ranks. The 21-year-old senior grew up amid the squalor and gang violence of a housing project in New York City. His father often was without work. Ortiz' family survived on food stamps.

   His mother, now separated from his father, still lives on welfare with six of Ortiz' seven brothers and sisters.

He took the first step out of poverty when, as a talented public school student, he caught the eye of Prep for Prep, a private group that funnels low-income students to top schools. With its help, Ortiz gained a scholarship at a private high school in Manhattan and later enrolled at Amherst, one of the country's top liberal arts colleges.

"I think a lot of young people like Angel end up at community colleges or not going past high school," said Gary Simons, a former Bronx elementary school teacher who now directs Prep for Prep. "Some of them unfortunately get pulled into the negative stuff that goes on in the neighborhood."

It has taken tens of thousands of dollars, in addition to Ortiz' own exceptional talents and commitment, to propel him.

Like many other disadvantaged students at leading schools, Ortiz receives nearly all his tuition—about $17,000 this year—in scholarship from the college. He uses nearly $4,000 in state and federal grants for low-income students to cover room, board, books and living expenses.

Still, he finds himself without ready money for trips home in emergencies, like when his brother was beaten up or his mother got sick with cancer. He has worn the same pair of sneakers for years.

Despite his intellectual growth and B average, Ortiz says he has always felt out of place in the rolling hills, cloistered classrooms, and the old-money affluence of this campus in western Massachusetts. He worries about finances every day. "Even if I become a millionaire, I will always be poor because . . . I will always have a fear," he said.

Many low-income students are intimidated even by the prospect of applying to top colleges, given their astronomical costs. Total expenses for a year of schooling at Amherst are estimated at $21,545. At nearby Smith College, they are $21,870.

"Just saying that is so forbidding," said Maureen Hoyler, an official at the National Council of Educational Opportunity Associations. "It's so otherworldish that you just don't go out and say, 'I'm going to Amherst.'"

If they do apply, low-income students are forced to borrow ever-greater sums to make up the difference between quickly rising costs and slowly rising federal and state grants, according to Ann Wright, dean of enrollment at Smith College.

"With low-income, disadvantaged students . . . student loans are not viewed as a positive factor," said Dallas Martin, president of the National Association of Student Financial Aid Administrators. "Many of these students' families, if they've had any credit experience at all, it has not been a positive experience."

Martin and other advocates want Pell grants, federal aid to low-income students, transformed into an entitlement program pegged to inflation.

Yet the hurdles go beyond money. Social alienation—even racism and other prejudice—can haunt students like Ortiz.

"Here are kids hopping on a plane or train and going home for the weekend. Here are kids going to Boston or to New York . . . to Broadway and the theater. It's a totally different world," said William H. Gray, president of the United Negro College Fund.

For Ortiz, Amherst represents, in part, a way of sharing that world's bounty.

"I'm banking—I use the word 'banking' purposely—that it will come around," he said. "First and foremost, I hope it pays financially."

But in the next breath, he says he hopes someday to go to law school and work as a prosecutor—preferably in the Bronx.[2]

1. Write a brief summary of the main points of the passage.

_____

_____

_____

_____

2. Is the passage mostly fact or opinion? Explain your answer.

_____

_____

_____

3. What conclusions does the writer of this article want the reader to draw?

_____

_____

_____

4. Discuss your reaction to the passage.

_____

_____

_____

2. **Two-Income Families**

Several factors have led to a dramatic growth in two-income families. The high cost of housing and the maintenance of a comfortable lifestyle have made it difficult if not impossible for many households to live on just one income. Furthermore, many women today simply want a career outside of the home.

One result of this trend is a whole host of programs that companies are implementing to assist two-income families. IBM and Procter & Gamble, for example, have implemented pregnancy benefits, parental leaves, flexible work schedules, and eldercare programs. Some companies offer referral services that provide counseling to parents in search of child care or eldercare. Such trends create many new opportunities for graduates in human resource management.

Many employers provide child-care benefits of some type; some of these programs are on-site. Such centers are expensive to operate and often cause resentment from employees who do not use the benefits. The resentment has led companies to offer "cafeteria benefits" packages, which enable families to choose from a "menu" of benefits. A couple may choose day care instead of a dental plan, for instance.

Many companies are increasing the number of part-time workers to enable mothers and fathers to stay home with children and still earn some income. The net result of all these trends is increased opportunity for men and women to both enhance their standard of living and raise a family. It also creates many job opportunities in day care, counseling, and other related fields.[3]

1. Write three review questions for the passage.

_____

_____

_____

2. Is the passage mostly fact or opinion? Explain your answer.

_____

_____

_____

3. What conclusions might you draw from this passage regarding the future of two-income families?

_____

_____

_____

4. Write your reaction to the passage.

_____

_____

_____

3. **Motivation**

Everything we do is the result of motivation. It may be positive or negative, intentional or unintentional, a little or a lot. Motivation can be learned or developed—we don't have to be born with it. Motivation is a force that moves us to action, and it springs from inside us.

It has often been thought that motivation, like gasoline to a car, can be pumped in from the outside through pep talks, rallies, or sermons. These can provide encouragement or inspiration for a person to act, but the person has to have the *desire*. Lasting change can happen only when the individual understands and feels the need inside. The person must want the reward in order to become motivated.

Motivation moves you in the direction of goals you have set. Even in the face of mistakes, discouragement, and setbacks, your positive inner drive keeps you moving ahead. Motivation is an emotional state. The great physical and mental motivations are survival, hunger, thirst, revenge, and love. Two strong emotions that are opposites of one another are part of motivation: fear and desire.

Fear is one of the most powerful emotions that can affect motivation in a negative way. Fear makes you panic, often needlessly, and it can defeat goals. The opposite emotion, desire, is like a strong positive magnet. It attracts and encourages plans and goals. Fear and desire are far apart and lead to opposite destinies. Fear looks to the past. Desire looks to the future. Fear remembers past pain, disappointment, failure, and unpleasantness and reminds us that these experiences can be repeated. Desire triggers memories of pleasure and success and excites the need to create new Winning experiences.

The fearful person says, "I have to," "I can't," "I see risk," and "I wish." The person with desire says, "I want to," "I can," "I see opportunity," and "I will." Desire is the emotional state between where you are and where you want to be. Winners have desire. They are not content with the way things are now. They want change for the better.[4]

1. Write a brief summary of the main points of the passage.

   _____

   _____

   _____

2. Is the passage mostly fact or opinion? Explain your answer.

   _____

   _____

   _____

3. What conclusions might be drawn from this passage regarding the effects of motivation on student achievement?

   _____

   _____

   _____

4. Discuss your reaction to the passage.

   _____

   _____

   _____

Journal Entry

1. Please comment on the journal assignments. Have they been interesting? Have you enjoyed them? In what ways have they helped you become a more effective reader and student?

_____

_____

_____

_____

_____

_____

_____

_____

_____

_____

_____

2. In what ways have your reading and study habits improved this semester? In what areas do you need further improvement?

_____

_____

_____

_____

_____

_____

_____

_____

_____

_____

_____

_____

ADDITIONAL READINGS

READING 1

tâm lý học, khái niệm về tâm lý

[sai kɔləʤi]

PSYCHOLOGY OF SELF-AWARENESS

Denis Waitley

Reading 1 is taken from the book *Psychology of Success: Developing Your Self-Esteem,* by Denis Waitley. Dr. Waitley is a widely respected expert on human performance and potential. He is the author of several books, including *The Psychology of Winning.* In this excerpt, Dr. Waitley discusses some of the components of self-awareness and their importance to personal growth.

Directions. Before you read the selection, answer these questions:

1. Have you ever read anything before about self-awareness or self-esteem?

   No , I haven't

2. What is your definition of success?

   making a best result

3. How do you usually react in stressful situations?

   take walking or listen to music

4. Who or what in your life has most positively contributed to the development of your self-esteem?

What Is Self-Awareness?

One of the most important elements of success is Self-Awareness. *Self-awareness* is the ability to step back from the canvas of life and take a good look at yourself as you relate to your environmental, physical, and mental worlds. It is the ability to accept yourself as a unique, changing, imperfect, and growing individual. It's the ability to
5   recognize your potential as well as your limitations.

Self-awareness is self-honesty: seeing yourself, your strengths, and your weaknesses clearly. It is knowing what you have to offer and recognizing that time and effort will be necessary for top achievement. Winners can look in the mirror and see what lies behind their own eyes. You are a Winner when what you think, how you
10   feel, and what you do all fit together.

Environmental Self-Awareness

Winners display an Environmental Self-Awareness. They are aware of how little they really know about anything in their world. They know that what they do know is shaded by their own heredity and environment. Winners are able to accept what is happening around them, and this contributes to their self-awareness. This awareness
15   includes being concerned about the needs of others.

Are you open-minded? Do you look at life through your parents' eyes? Are your prejudices inherited from your parents, or are they your own? Environmental self-awareness means realizing that each human being on earth is a person with the equal right to fulfill his or her own potential in life. It is realizing that skin
20   color, religion, birthplace, financial status, or intelligence do not determine a person's worth or value. Environmental self-awareness is accepting the fact that every human being is a unique individual. No two people are exactly alike—not even identical twins.

Have you ever heard someone say, "We're not on the same wavelength"? This
25   translates to: "You don't think as I do," or "I don't understand why you think the way you do." It's easy to see why there is so much misunderstanding and fighting in the world, within families and among nations. Everyone sees life through a different camera lens and "hears a different drummer."

Empathy

Empathy is the awareness of, and sensitivity to, the feelings, thoughts, and experi-
30   ences of others. It is seeing life through other persons' eyes—experiencing their pain, their curiosity, their hopes, their fears. It is watching marathon runners at the 20-mile mark and feeling your own legs ache.

You can feel empathy with anyone—whether that person is of a different generation, a citizen of another country, or simply someone with a different point of
35   view. Instead of being quick to criticize or judge other persons, try to see the situation through their eyes. How do they feel? What are they afraid of? What concerns them most?

Perform this "Empathy Checkup" on yourself by changing places with someone else:

40
- *If I were my husband/wife, how would I like to have a partner like me?*
Would I think I was supportive? Independent? Interesting? Understanding?
An equal partner?

- *If I were my child, how would I like to have a parent like me?* Would I think I
was patient? Encouraging? Positive? Supportive? Nonjudgmental?

45
- *If I were my instructor, how would I like to have a student like me?* Would I
think I showed a lot of effort? A lot of interest? Curiosity? Discipline? Concern for others in class?

- *If I were my boss, how would I like to have an employee like me?* Would I
think I was a good worker? Productive? Reliable? Responsible? Nice to work

50
with?

- *How would it feel to be an immigrant just arrived in America?* Would I feel
isolated? Frightened? Unsure of whom to trust? Challenged? Optimistic?
Hopeful?

- *How does the world appear through the eyes of a child?* Big? Confusing?

55
Exciting? Scary? Hard to understand? Fun?

Adapting

Does it bother you to discover that there are so many people around that are different from you? Do you think you might seem strange or different to other people?
We need to understand what being human is all about. To be human is to be a
changing, growing, imperfect, but amazing living creation. Winners know that they

60
will come across many different people, places, and experiences in their lifetimes. A
lot of those people, places, and experiences will seem very strange and unfamiliar.
How can you learn to enjoy all the different and unusual things that you come across
in life?

The answer is to *adapt*. Adapting means being flexible and open to the actions

65
of others. Because Winners are self-aware and have empathy for others, they do not
allow others to ruin their day or rain on their parade. Adapting to our environment
means being flexible and changing with the times as we need to.

Physical Self-Awareness

Our next step is to develop our Physical Self-Awareness. This means understanding
that our bodies are machines whose performance depends on good health. We must

70
each treat our body as our one and only transportation vehicle for life. We must care
for it with the fuel of good nutrition, activity, and health care. If we are fat and slug-
gish or thin and nervous because we smoke, drink, eat poorly, or don't exercise, we

cannot trade in our bodies for new models. If we abuse them we won't be able to use them as long or as well. You can *do* well only if you *feel* well.

Stress

75   *Stress is* any physical, emotional, or chemical effect that causes tension. It can even be a factor in causing disease. Earl Nightingale, a well-known motivational speaker, told the story of a trip taken with his son to the Great Barrier Reef, which stretches 1,800 miles from New Guinea to Australia. He noticed that the coral growing on the inside of the reef, where the sea was peaceful and quiet in the lagoon, looked pale and
80   lifeless. But the coral on the outside of the reef, constantly beaten by the powerful waves, looked healthy and brightly colored. Earl asked the guide why this was so. "It's very simple," came the reply. "The coral on the lagoon side dies rapidly with no challenge for growth and survival, while the coral facing the open sea thrives and multiplies because it is challenged and tested every day."
85   And so it is with all living things on earth. If we never challenge ourselves, we never have the opportunity to succeed. We can choose to just sit back and wither on the vine. Or we can use the failures and setbacks in our lives to strengthen us and help us guard against anxiety, depression, and other negative responses to stress.

Not much has changed since the days of our early ancestors when, at the first sign
90   of danger, the body got ready for "fight or flight." A person would either fight to defend himself against danger or run the other way. Nowadays, we experience at least one or two unpleasant surprises almost every day, and we have to make the decision to fight or walk the other way.

Anger

How many complete strangers got you upset and ready to risk your life on the road
95   today? Winners don't overreact to what is happening as the cave dwellers did. They are not quick to anger, with their blood pressures jumping, heart rates quickening, and adrenalin pumping. Every annoying situation is not a struggle for survival, and there are not always tigers ready to pounce.

Winners don't let this daily stress destroy their mental and physical health. They
100   don't drink more, smoke more, or pop more pills to escape or cope with the stress. They don't take their anger out on other people. They control their negative feelings and express them in a constructive way. When Winners feel angry or upset they jog around the block, take a long walk, or listen to some soothing music—anything that will relieve their negative feelings in a healthy way. Self-awareness is an important
105   part of the victory over stress. Winners learn how to relax and cope with the ups and downs of everyday life.

Expressing joy, love, compassion, and excitement is healthy. But openly expressing hostility, anger, depression, loneliness, or anxiety may not be healthy for us. The only healthy expression of the "fight or flight" response is in the face
110   of a life or death situation. But in most of our daily situations, stress and anger can be dealt with by deep breathing, relaxation, and exercise such as running, aerobics, or basketball.

115   Dr. Hans Selye, one of the first people to study stress, divides people into two categories: racehorses and turtles. A racehorse loves to run and will die from exhaustion if it is corralled or confined in a small space. A turtle will die from exhaustion if forced to run on a treadmill, moving too fast for its slow nature. We each have to find our own healthy stress level, somewhere between that of the racehorse and the turtle.

Mental Self-Awareness

120   An important part of positive self-awareness is Mental Self-Awareness. This is knowing the potential within our own minds that is just waiting to be challenged. We must ask ourselves, "What is my mental outlook toward life? Do I sell myself short or am I overconfident in my abilities?"

   Truth and honesty are necessary for any real and lasting success. We must ask ourselves: "Is this true? Is this honest?" If we can answer yes, or if we can seek out the truth with the help of someone else, we can move ahead and take action.

125   Attitude is the key to healthy self-awareness. In order to feel well and accomplish things in your life, you'll need to develop positive attitudes and positive responses to the pressures in life. The more honest and self-aware you become, the more ways you'll find to Win. Find a new way to Win today![1]

Interest Rating.   Please rate the interest level of Reading 1 on the following 1–5 scale (circle one):

   5 — Very interesting
   4 — Fairly interesting
   3 — Mildly interesting
   2 — A little boring
   1 — Very boring

Difficulty Rating.   Please indicate how difficult Reading 1 was for you to understand on the following 1–5 scale (circle one):

   5 — Very difficult
   4 — Fairly difficult
   3 — Moderate
   2 — Fairly easy
   1 — Very easy

Comments: _____

_____

Comprehension Questions

Directions.   For questions 1–5, choose the answer that best completes the statement. For questions 6–10, write your response in the space provided. Base all answers on what you read in Reading 1 (you may refer to the reading when you are not sure of an answer).

_____ 1. The author believes that it is important to:
- *a.* Criticize yourself.
- *b.* Appreciate people who are different from you.
- *c.* Avoid stress.
- (*d.*) Learn whether you are a racehorse or a turtle.

_____ 2. Which of the following is *not* a characteristic of a winner?
- *a.* Readiness to defend yourself at all times.
- *b.* The ability to empathize with others.
- (*c.*) Integrating your thoughts, feelings, and behaviors.
- *d.* Self-awareness.

_____ 3. The author suggests that:
- *a.* Heredity is more important than environment.
- *b.* Environment is more important than heredity.
- *c.* Environmental self-awareness is learned from our parents.
- (*d.*) Both heredity and environment contribute to self-awareness.

_____ 4. Regarding stress, the author believes that:
- (*a.*) The level of stress that is desirable varies from person to person.
- *b.* Turtles adapt better to stress than racehorses.
- *c.* The less stress in life the better.
- *d.* Fighting and running away are the best ways to cope with most stressful situations.

_____ 5. The author uses questions to:
- (*a.*) Make the point that many questions in life have no real answers.
- *b.* Show that he doesn't have all the answers.
- *c.* Encourage the reader to ask questions.
- *d.* Encourage the reader's self-awareness.

6. What is environmental self-awareness? Why is it important?

   <u>understanding what around environmental</u>

   _____

7. What is physical self-awareness? Why is it important?

   _____

   _____

8. The example of the coral reef (lines 74–82) is used to make what point about stress?

   _____

   _____

9. Are you a racehorse or a turtle? Explain.

_____

_____

10. Answer the questions on the "Empathy Checkup" (p. 347) for any *two* of the individuals listed.

_____

_____

_____

_____

_____

_____

Vocabulary Exercise

Directions. Each statement below is taken from Reading 1. Use the context to determine the meaning of the underlined word in each statement. Write a synonym (another word with the same meaning) for the word or express the definition in several words.

1. Self-awareness is the ability to step back from the canvas of life and take a good look at yourself as you relate to your <u>environmental</u>, physical, and mental worlds. (3)

_____

2. It is the ability to accept yourself as a <u>unique</u>, changing, imperfect, and growing individual. (4)

_____

3. It's the ability to recognize your potential as well as your <u>limitations</u>. (5)

_____

4. They know that what they do know is shaded by their own <u>heredity</u> and environment. (13)

_____

5. <u>Empathy</u> is the awareness of, and sensitivity to, the feelings, thoughts, and experiences of others. (29)

_____

6. If we are fat and <u>sluggish</u> or thin and nervous because we smoke, drink, eat poorly, or don't exercise, we cannot trade in our bodies for new models. (71)

_____

7. The coral on the lagoon side dies rapidly with no challenge for growth and survival, while the coral facing the open sea <u>thrives</u> and multiplies because it is challenged and tested every day. (83)

_____

8. We can choose to just sit back and <u>wither</u> on the vine. (86)

_____

9. They [winners] control their negative feelings and express them in a <u>constructive</u> way. (102)

_____

10. A racehorse loves to run and will die from exhaustion if it is corralled or <u>confined</u> in a small space. (115)

_____

READING 2

THE POWER TO CHANGE

Les Brown

Les Brown, now a popular public speaker and TV commentator, grew up in the poorest sections of Miami, Florida. Raised by his single mother, he faced many childhood difficulties. His mother's strength and the encouragement of one of his high school teachers helped him turn his life around. In Reading 2, an excerpt from his book *Live Your Dreams*, Brown recounts a school experience that had a profound impact on his life and discusses the lessons he learned from it.

Directions.　Before you read the selection, answer these questions:

1. Have you ever been unfairly punished? How did you react? How did it affect you?

   _____

   _____

2. What do you remember about your experiences in the 5th grade? Were they positive or negative? How did they affect you?

   _____

   _____

3. Do you believe that hurtful memories can inhibit your personal growth? Why or why not?

   _____

   _____

I know of no more encouraging fact than the unquestionable ability of man to elevate his life by conscious endeavor.

Henry David Thoreau

I will never forget the day the principal came into my fifth-grade classroom while we were clowning around, throwing paper, running, turning chairs over, acting wild. The teacher had left the room unattended and the class went crazy. Until the principal showed up.

She was outraged. Trouble had been brewing for several of us for some time. And it was at this moment that the principal made a decision that was to have a powerful impact on my life. In her anger, she began pointing at the most troublesome students and calling us names. "These students are stupid, dumb, retarded. They don't need to be here," she said. *"They need to be put back."*

"I want that one, that one and that one." She pointed at about six students. Including me. I remember the look on her face, the anger and the disgust her expression held. She was set on teaching us a lesson, on punishing us and making us pay. I remember the fear and hurt welling up inside me.

I said, "No, you are making a mistake! I'm not stupid!"

With that, they took us out of the fifth-grade class and put us back in the fourth grade as special-education students. I was kept in that category all through high school. It has taken me a long time to escape that label.

And in adulthood, much of my drive to succeed has been fueled by the devastating memory of that day in class when I was judged to be "slow" and without much promise. That memory has fueled my hunger to be somebody. It is a memory that still pricks at me, a memory that for a time shamed and stunted me but now drives me always to reaffirm my sense of who I am.

Later, the principal told my mother that they had put me back a grade for my own good. She said they were trying to help me. She was very courteous and persuasive. My mother, who had little formal schooling herself, went along. She felt she had no choice.

The Dodo Ward

Most people do not realize how detrimental negative labels can be; they become self-fulfilling prophecies. I began to believe that I couldn't do certain things and if I encountered any classroom difficulty, I would stop.

Actually, there were few difficulties or demands once I was relegated to the "dodo ward," as other students called it. Not much was expected of us dodos. School became a breeze. I would laugh at the students who had to do algebra or trigonometry. I rarely even had homework assigned. The last laugh was on me, of course.

In my naïveté, I thought I was getting off easy, but in fact, I spent many years of my adulthood trying to catch up. I still have problems with some basic mathematics. I have a mental block about taking written tests. I probably am restricted or damaged in ways that I am not even aware of.

Hurtful memories can stifle your development and growth. How do we break through this insidious mental conditioning? How do we grow and develop beyond hurtful episodes that bury themselves in our subconscious and influence our lives? How do we change and grow so that we can live our dreams?

The first step is to break the hold of these inhibiting influences from the past. Recognize them and then either get rid of them or turn them into a positive force that pushes you ahead rather than holds you back.

Identify these inhibiting memories in your life so that you control *them* rather than allowing them to control *you.* Did someone hurt your feelings? Forgive them and forget it. Move on. Did someone punish you unfairly? It's over. It's done. Go on.

Here are a few of the most common emotions that burrow into the subconscious and impede our growth as individuals:

- *Anger.* This is a natural response to a perceived attack or injury. It makes energy flow. But when allowed to simmer, it depletes energy that could be used to improve your life. If you hold your anger for more than a week, it is only hurting you. Make yourself let go. Envision yourself throwing it out. Ease your mind. Transform your anger into positive motivation. Don't get mad, get motivated.
- *Revenge.* The first cousin of anger. It also robs you of strength in the long run. The person who has injured you has probably gone on with life; so should you. Don't let the injury hurt you further by inhibiting your growth. Lose it or use it. Instead of saying, "I'll get them," say, "*I'll show them. I'LL BE SOMEBODY!*"
- *Sadness.* This is more crippling than anger because it drains you from the start, sapping your will to go on. You probably will have to let this drain away slowly at its own pace. Time heals, but if the sadness seems to linger, consciously force it out. Seek out things that make you laugh and feel positive about life. Realize that feeling sad will not change anything. Seek peace of mind as your right.
- *Resentment.* Life is not always fair. It is unrealistic to feel any other way, and holding on to resentment is no way to fight back. Drop it and get back into the battle.
- *Guilt* is another emotion that stands between you and your dreams. All of us have done things we feel bad about and regret. Things we would do differently. Many of us carry that guilt around and it keeps us from moving forward. Don't let people put you on a guilt trip. Say to yourself when someone is putting you on the defensive, "*No matter what you do or say to me, I am still a worthwhile person.*"

To rid yourself of these past emotions, put them in a perspective that is positive rather than negative and thereby cut off their painful roots in your subconscious. Reinterpret the past with these methods:

- *Get better, not bitter.* Find a quiet, comfortable place. Sit back and relax. Think about something or someone who caused you pain or disappointment. Now take a mental step back from that feeling and the situation. Assess it. Did the emotions that resulted make you stronger? Did they give you determination? Can you use those memories to empower you rather than drain you? Why let them hurt you further?
- *Envision those hurtful emotions as a sword held by an enemy.* In your mind, see yourself snatching the sword away and using it to cut away the emotional snares that have tied you up.
- *Get rid of regret.* If you are burdened by something you did, analyze it. Was it a business failure? Was it something foolish you said or did that hurt someone you

care about? If so, apologize. That often clears the air, but use discretion if you think it might make matters worse. If you owe money to someone, pay them. Or tell them
90   you intend to pay them a little at a time.

Whatever the cost, it is worth it to clear away burdensome emotions. If you have feelings of unworthiness because of something you did, let them go. Realize that we usually do the best we can according to our level of consciousness at the time. If you would not do the same thing again, you have changed. You are no longer the same
95   person. That person is gone, so forgive yourself.

Love yourself unconditionally, just as you love those closest to you despite their faults. *Let it go so you can grow.* You have the power to change.[2]

Interest Rating.   Please rate the interest level of Reading 2 on the following 1–5 scale (circle one):

> 5 —Very interesting
>
> 4 —Fairly interesting
>
> 3 —Mildly interesting
>
> 2 —A little boring
>
> 1 —Very boring

Difficulty Rating.   Please indicate how difficult Reading 2 was for you to understand on the following 1–5 scale (circle one):

> 5 —Very difficult
>
> 4 —Fairly difficult
>
> 3 —Moderate
>
> 2 —Fairly easy
>
> 1 —Very easy

Comments: _____

_____

Comprehension Questions

Directions.   For questions 1–5, choose the answer that best completes the statement. For questions 6–10, write your response in the space provided. Base your answers on what you read in Reading 2 (you may refer to the reading when you are not sure of an answer).

_____ 1. The author was put back a grade because:
> *a.* He did not keep up with his work.
>
> *b.* The principal had a grudge against him.
>
> *c.* He was a troublemaker.
>
> *d.* The principal wanted to help him.

_____ 2. The author's attitude toward his school experience is:
   a. Bitter.
   b. Philosophical.
   c. Sorrowful.
   d. Vengeful.

_____ 3. The author feels that as a result of this school experience:
   a. He is unable to learn.
   b. He received a better education.
   c. He became completely disinterested in learning.
   d. He has been motivated to succeed as an adult.

_____ 4. In regard to revenge, the author suggests that:
   a. You can use revenge to motivate yourself.
   b. Vengeful feelings should always be expressed.
   c. Revenge is the most difficult emotion to deal with.
   d. Revenge and anger are unrelated.

_____ 5. To deal with past emotions, the author recommends:
   a. Ignoring them or forgetting about them.
   b. Experiencing each negative emotion in order to release it.
   c. Seeking professional help.
   d. Analyzing, assessing, and reinterpreting them.

6. Why was being put on the "dodo ward" harmful to the author?

_____

_____

7. How was being put on the "dodo ward" beneficial to the author?

_____

_____

8. Why did the author's mother go along with the principal's decision?

_____

9. The author states that negative labels can become "self-fulfilling prophecies." What does he mean?

_____

_____

10. Which of the author's suggestions for dealing with past emotions do you think is most valuable? Why?

_____

_____

Vocabulary Exercise

Directions.   Each statement below is taken from Reading 2. Use the context to determine the meaning of the underlined word in each statement. Write a synonym (another word with the same meaning) for the word, or express the definition in several words.

1. Most people do not realize how <u>detrimental</u> negative labels can be. (30)

   _____

2. Not much was expected of us <u>dodos</u>. (34)

   _____

3. In my <u>naivete</u>, I thought I was getting off easy, but in fact, I spent many years of my adulthood trying to catch up. (38)

   _____

4. I probably am <u>restricted</u> or damaged in ways that I am not even aware of. (40)

   _____

5. Hurtful memories can <u>stifle</u> your development and growth. (42)

   _____

6. Here are a few of the most common emotions that burrow into the subconscious and <u>impede</u> our growth as individuals. (53)

   _____

7. But when allowed to simmer, it [anger] <u>depletes</u> energy that could be used to improve your life. (55)

   _____

8. Time heals, but if sadness seems to <u>linger</u>, consciously force it out. (65)

   _____

9. To get rid of these past emotions, put them in a <u>perspective</u> that is positive rather than negative. (75)

   _____

10. That often clears the air, but use <u>discretion</u> if you think it might make matters worse. (88)

    _____

READING 3

ALL STRESSED OUT

Deborah Beroset Diamond

Stress is one of the most widely discussed topics today. Read the following selection to discover why stress is a major concern of modern life and what you can do about it.

Previewing Exercise

Directions.   Preview the passage and answer the following questions.

1. What aspects of stress will be discussed in this selection?

   _____

   _____

2. Does the author view stress as positive or negative? How can you tell?

   _____

   _____

3. What are some of the author's suggestions for coping with stress?

   _____

   _____

Pre-thinking Exercise

1. What have you previously read or learned about stress?

   _____

   _____

2. What are some of the chief causes of stress in your own life?

_____

_____

3. Write three questions about stress.

_____

_____

_____

Last year was the most wonderful—and worrisome—of times for Mike and Angie Rooney, of St. Louis, Missouri. The Rooneys, both twenty-nine, were thrilled to learn they were expecting their first child. But when Angie, an accountant, was four months pregnant, her firm laid her off. "I'd worked sixty- and seventy-hour weeks during tax
5   time and was up for a promotion," she recalls. "My boss told me I was laid off for economic reasons, but I think it was because they found out I was pregnant."

After that, Angie's self-esteem plunged. She and Mike feared that his position as an engineer might also be in jeopardy, because his company was laying off large numbers of employees. Angie spent the next few months searching for a job, but most com-
10   panies were unwilling to hire someone who'd be going on maternity leave almost immediately. "I had one door after another slammed in my face," she says. She watched apprehensively as their savings diminished, while their pile of unpaid bills grew.

What should have been a joyful time for the parents-to-be was fraught with tension. The Rooneys began to argue a lot—especially about money—and Angie wor-
15   ried that her irritability might be harming the baby. "I was concerned, with all the stress I was under," she says. "I felt like I had no control. I'd think, Here I am without a job, you may lose your job, we bought this house based on two incomes, and we're going to have a baby soon. It was an *extremely* stressful time."

A Nation under Pressure

Stress has always been with us, of course, but today it's straining families as never
20   before. According to a 1991 study by Northwestern National Life Insurance Company, almost half the working population feels highly stressed, and it's making one in four of us sick—with everything from exhaustion and headaches, to ulcers and hypertension. That's double what a government survey of the general population found six years ago.
25   Why are we so tense now? As the Rooneys know firsthand, the recession has ratcheted the pressure higher than ever, with growing numbers of people either unemployed or about to be. Time seems to be shrinking, too; we simply can't find enough of it to do our jobs plus our errands plus the self-improvement we're supposed to be practicing. Parents worry about steering their children safely through a world blighted
30   by crack, AIDS and crime. Kids have their own concerns about school, sex, drugs and peer pressure.

At home, this anxiety tends to have a domino effect. "Stress is a family disease," says Peter A. Wish, Ph.D., a clinical psychologist and director of the New England Institute of Family Relations, in Framingham, Massachusetts. "If a husband loses his
35   job, for example, the tension hits everybody."

A Constant Balancing Act

One of the main causes of stress, experts agree, is a lack of control. In order to withstand tension, says cardiologist Robert S. Eliot, M.D., director of the Institute of Stress Medicine, in Denver, a person must feel that she is in charge of the events in her life. "The problem is, this society increasingly gives people *less* control," he says.
40   Some of our command slipped away with the buy-now-pay-later mentality of the eighties. In our rush to get ahead, we sacrificed personal and family time, and spent ourselves into debt, says Raymond Flannery, Jr., Ph.D., a clinical psychologist at Harvard Medical School at Cambridge Hospital, and author of *Becoming Stress-Resistant* (Continuum Press, 1990).
45   Now, in the no-nonsense nineties, we're struggling to regain some balance. It won't be easy. According to John P. Robinson, Ph.D., who directs a major time-study project at the University of Maryland, at College Park, Americans today actually have slightly more free time—hours when they're not working or sleeping—than they did twenty years ago. But they *feel* more harried, because society has created new
50   demands to fill every spare minute.

"I work such irregular shifts, sometimes I don't get to see my son for twenty-four hours or more," says Karen Bowersox, a thirty-year-old nurse who lives with her husband, Tom, and twenty-two-month-old Alex, in Des Moines, Iowa. "My dream is to be able to stay home with Alex, but we couldn't survive on one income."
55   Not surprisingly, women—especially working mothers like Karen—tend to feel the most frazzled. Take the case of Elizabeth Young, forty-one, a mother of two preschoolers and a designer of computer software in Los Angeles, California. She describes her life as a carefully choreographed routine in which getting the family up, fed, dressed and to preschool and work requires the precision of a NASA lift off. "If
60   one little thing goes wrong, it throws everything," she says. "Our day-to-day lives require an incredible amount of organization. We just barely keep it under control."

In the 1991 Hilton Time Values Survey, which Robinson worked on for Hilton Hotels, mothers were almost twice as likely as fathers to report feeling constantly under stress. No wonder—moms devote twice as much weekend time to housecleaning as dads do, and spend more time running errands. Nearly half reported that they
65   cut back on sleep in order to get everything done. Says Wish, "If you were to plug all that into a computer, the circuits would blow. It's too much."

Paying the Price

Sooner or later, human circuitry burns out, too. At first, says psychologist Flannery, "There's a loss of well-being. It's not as pleasant to get up in the morning. Then, you
70   feel jittery and worry a lot, or you have no energy."

New research also shows that high levels of stress can almost double your chances of catching a cold. And the consequences can be far more serious—like the

stress-related heart attack cardiologist Robert Eliot had at forty-four. "When people go out of control," says Eliot, now recovered, "they literally burn a dollar's worth of
75   energy for a dime's worth of trouble. The toll it takes on their bodies is something we've never seen before."

Stress exacts an emotional toll as well. The Bowersoxes notice they squabble more when their schedules are especially hectic. "We both work full-time, we're both tired a lot, and sometimes it's hard to deal with the things toddlers do," Karen says.
80   "When we're under stress, we're more touchy and quick-tempered."

As parents get more and more squeezed, they tend to dole out discipline that's arbitrary and erratic, says Charles Figley, Ph.D., director of the Marriage and Family Therapy Center at Florida State University, in Tallahassee. Children react by becoming agitated or withdrawn, getting into trouble and doing poorly at school.
85   To compound matters, most of us seek the wrong kinds of relief, says psychologist Wish. "There are all kinds of misguided ways of handling stress: overeating, spending too much, smoking, drinking, gambling. There are kids drinking and doing drugs in elementary school. People do these things to distract themselves from stressful situations, but in the long run, they produce more stress."

The Right Way to Cope

90   But there are a number of steps that every family member can take to avoid stress. And while we can't change our lives overnight, we can ease up on ourselves—as the Rooneys of St. Louis learned. Instead of feeling angry about being laid off, for instance, Angie took action—she filed a job-discrimination complaint against her former employer with the Equal Employment Opportunity Commission. And to make
95   sure they had enough to weather their next rainy day, the Rooneys continued to cut costs—even after their healthy baby daughter was born and Angie landed another good job.

By changing your perspective and reducing some of the stress points in your life, you, too, can feel relaxed and in control. Below are some practical and proven tech-
100   niques from the experts to help you de-stress—both in the long-term and on a day-to-day basis.

Adjust your Attitude

• *Keep your expectations reasonable.* Most of us push ourselves to do too much at work and at home. Instead of planning to get six major household projects done every weekend, concentrate on smaller goals. And don't ask for the
105   impossible from your children—encourage them to do their best and praise them for what they achieve, says Michael Fortino, a time-management consultant in San Francisco.

• *Don't be so hard on yourself.* All too often we tell ourselves that everything has to be perfect—office work has to be done just so, dinner has to be a gourmet feast.
110   Cut yourself some slack: Tell yourself that "good enough" is okay, and learn to live with imperfection.

• *Keep sight of what's important.* Instead of all those shoulds and have-tos, decide which activities mean the most to you—whether it's spending more time with your family or taking a class to get your degree. Make these your top priorities from
115   now on.

Day-to-Day Family Stressbusters

• *Get organized.* Most of us squander too many hours on unnecessary tasks, such as waiting in line, says time-management expert Fortino. Make realistic to-do lists and prioritize—ask yourself, Does this really need to be done *today*? And just in case you *do* wind up with a long wait, carry a good magazine or book to enjoy.

120   • *Put your financial house in order.* Many of our pressures come from over-spending. Before you buy something, stop and consider whether putting another charge on your credit card is worth the knotted stomach come bill-paying time.

• *Don't take your anger out on the wrong person.* A lot of family stress is actu-ally generated outside the home. For instance, say your boss is giving you a hard time
125   at work. You get uptight, but instead of talking to him about it, you go home and yell at your husband and kids. Not only does this create tension for the whole family, it teaches your children to take out their stress on other people. Rather than displacing your anger, talk over the problem with the person who upset you.

• *Open the lines of communication.* Establish regular family conferences to dis-
130   cuss matters such as vacation plans, rules, family problems and housework, advises psychologist Wish. "One of the major causes of stress in families is not feeling heard or acknowledged," he says. "Parents should have the final say, but it's important to give kids input in the decision-making process."

Be sure to tell children about the family schedule, so they'll know what to expect
135   each day, adds Lawrence Balter, Ph.D., a professor of applied psychology at New York University, the author of *Who's In Control?* (Simon & Schuster, 1989). For instance, if you'll be working late, inform your kids and explain how it will affect them: "Dad will pick you up from the baby-sitter's; I'll be home before you go to bed." Says Balter, "Kids need to know what's going to happen and not just be shut-
140   tled here and there, which can lead to a lot of stress."

• *Enjoy the ones you love.* "Don't give up those things that have been a source of enjoyment for the family because you feel there isn't time now," says Ray Guarendi, Ph.D., a clinical psychologist in Canton, Ohio, and author of *Back to the Family: Proven Advice on Building a Stronger, Healthier, Happier Family* (Simon
145   & Schuster/Fireside Books, 1991). And save time for your spouse. "There are even physical benefits," Flannery says. "Your immune system, your capacity to fight dis-ease is enhanced when you're in a loving relationship."

Minute-to-Minute Crisis Cures

When stress does strike, try one of these easy antidotes:

• *Take a few minutes to cool off.* At home, go into your bedroom; at work, shut
150   your office door. For total solitude, turn off the phone.

- *Catch your breath.* Sit in a comfortable position, close your eyes and breathe in deeply. Exhale slowly. Repeat for several minutes. It will calm you down and help clear your mind.

155
- *Meditate.* Close your eyes and visualize a relaxing, pleasant scene—lying on a beach, for instance. Make the picture come alive in your mind: Smell the salty ocean air, hear the lapping of the waves. Focus on this image for at least ten minutes. Then, slowly open your eyes, stretch and return to the real world, relaxed and refreshed.

- *Ease muscle strain.* If your neck and shoulders feel stiff, tense and then release them. Or try the neck roll: Lean your head forward, then slowly rotate it clockwise,
160 to the right, to the back, to the left, then forward. Repeat in the opposite direction.

- *Get outdoors.* Take a leisurely walk. A change of scenery—and a few minutes away from a tense situation—will reduce anxiety.

- *Get extra support.* Call your husband or a friend—just talking about the problem will make you feel better.

165
- *Smile,* or if you can manage it, laugh. Research indicates that it can cause chemical changes in the body that can actually increase your sense of well-being.[3]

For More Information:

The American Institute of Stress is a clearinghouse for information on the subject. Write them at: 124 Park Avenue, Dept. L, Yonkers, NY 10703.

The National Mental Health Association offers free brochures on stress, tension and depression. Write: National Mental Health Information Center, 1021 Prince Street, Alexandria, VA 22314-2971.

Interest Rating.   Please rate the interest level of Reading 3 on the following 1–5 scale (circle one):

5—Very interesting

4—Fairly interesting

3—Mildly interesting

2—A little boring

1—Very boring

Difficulty Rating.   Please indicate how difficult Reading 3 was for you to understand on the following 1–5 scale (circle one):

5—Very difficult

4—Fairly difficult

3—Moderate

2—Fairly easy

1—Very easy

Comments: _____

_____

Comprehension Questions

Directions. For questions 1–5, choose the answer that best completes the statement. For questions 6–10, write your response in the space provided. Base all answers on what you read in Reading 3 (you may refer to the reading when you are not sure of an answer).

_____ 1. Which of the following is *not* mentioned as a reason why people feel especially stressed nowadays?
   a. Economics.
   b. Lack of time.
   c. Lack of control.
   d. Lack of family support.

_____ 2. In comparing the 1980s with the 1990s, the author suggests that:
   a. People were more serious in the 80s.
   b. People were more stressed in the 80s.
   c. People overspent in the 80s.
   d. People have less free time in the 90s.

_____ 3. According to the article, the person within the family likely to feel most stressed is:
   a. The father.
   b. The mother.
   c. A teenager.
   d. A young child.

_____ 4. The Rooneys found an effective way to cope with their stress when they:
   a. Found new jobs.
   b. Filed a job discrimination complaint.
   c. Had their first baby.
   d. Took a family vacation.

_____ 5. The author recommends all of the following approaches to stress management *except*:
   a. Limiting your goals and expectations.
   b. Setting priorities.
   c. Seeking a professional family counselor.
   d. Visualizing pleasant scenes.

6. What are some of the consequences of stress?

   _____

   _____

7. What are some of the wrong ways to cope with stress?

   _____

   _____

8. What are some things parents can do to reduce their children's stress?

_____

_____

9. Which of the author's suggestions for managing stress do you feel is most valuable? Why?

_____

_____

_____

10. Do you think that life in the United States 50 or 100 years ago was less stressful than life today? Discuss.

_____

_____

_____

_____

Vocabulary Exercise

Directions.   Use the context clues and your dictionary to determine the meaning of each of the following words. Write your definition in the space provided.

1. jeopardy (8) _____

2. apprehensively (12) _____

3. fraught (13) _____

4. ratcheted (26) _____

5. blighted (29) _____

6. cardiologist (37) _____

7. choreographed (58) _____

8. arbitrary (82) _____

9. erratic (82) _____

10. antidotes (148) _____

READING 4

WHAT IS BUSINESS?

Joseph Straub and Stan Kossen

Reading 4 is taken from the first chapter of a business textbook. The selection discusses the importance of business in today's society and explains some basic business concepts. Read the selection to learn what business is and why it is central to the American economy.

Previewing Exercise

Directions.   Preview the passage and answer the following questions.

1. What is a business?

   _____

   _____

2. What other key terms are defined in this selection?

   _____

   _____

3. What does the graph on page 369 show?

   _____

   _____

Pre-thinking Exercise

1. Have you ever taken a business course or studied business?

   _____

   _____

2. What do you know about business from your own experience?

   _____

   _____

   _____

3. Writes three questions about business.

   _____

   _____

   _____

Down in Alabama there was an old man with a rowboat. He made his living ferrying
passengers across the river. He was asked, "How many times a day do you do this?"
and he said, "As many times as I can, because the more I go, the more I get. And if I
don't go, I don't get." That's the spirit of free enterprise I hope each one of you will
5   have throughout your lives.

C. M. Kittrell
Executive vice president, Phillips Petroleum Company

Business is everywhere in America, and everyone is a part of it. The pizza you eat,
the jeans you wear, the car you drive, the television you watch—all are produced, dis-
10   tributed, and sold by businesses. To be able to buy these things, you earn money
working in a business. The bank where you keep that money is a business.

Products you buy are created by the work of many businesses. Think of a loaf of
bread: first a farmer grew the wheat with the help of fertilizer supplied by a chemical
company; when it was ripe, he harvested it using a machine he bought (with the help
15   of a bank) from a manufacturer. He trucked the wheat to a mill, which ground it into
flour and sold it to a bakery. That company brought the flour by train to its plant,
where it was combined with other ingredients bought from other suppliers to make
bread. The bakery then wrapped the bread in plastic bought from yet another company. Using the trucks it bought from a truck manufacturer, the bakery transported
20   the bread to a retail store, where you were able to purchase it.

This example shows the complexity of American business—people have been
making bread for thousands of years, but the involvement of so many different companies is a recent development. And our example still does not show the whole picture of American business: it leaves out the variety. The companies that contribute to
25   that loaf of bread could be small operations or giant corporations. The bakery could
be a giant food-processing company that also produces dairy products, or it could be
a small local bakery. The retail store could be part of a supermarket chain or a corner
"mom-and-pop" store.

The Business of Business

Despite the variation in size and in activity, each of these companies is a **business**
30   because each one is *an organization engaged in providing goods or services in order
to make a profit.* Many people erroneously think of business as only providing
goods—*commodities that have physical presence*—like bread or cars or televisions.
But some businesses provide **services,** *actions that benefit consumers or other businesses,* rather than tangible goods. The farmer's wheat is a good; transporting flour
35   from mill to bakery is a service. The baked loaf of bread is a good; by offering it to
you in a convenient place, the retail store provides a service.

Economists use this distinction to divide the American economy into two large
segments. Goods-producing firms include mining, construction, and manufacturing
companies, which employ just over a quarter of all nonagricultural workers. (See Fig-
40   ure 1.1.) Service-producing firms, which employ more than two-thirds of the working population (again excluding farmers and farm workers), include transportation
companies; wholesale and retail firms; finance, insurance, and real estate firms; and
what are called service firms, such diverse businesses as accounting, beauty parlors,
appliance repair shops, health services, and television stations.

45   The service sector includes one other important employment group: local, state,
and federal government employees. Governments combine to employ about 16 million Americans, 17.5 percent of the more than 91 million people in the **work force,**
which is defined as *all people sixteen years of age or over who either are employed*

FIGURE 1.1

*Nonagricultural
Employment in
Goods-Producing
and Services-
Producing
Industries, 1981*

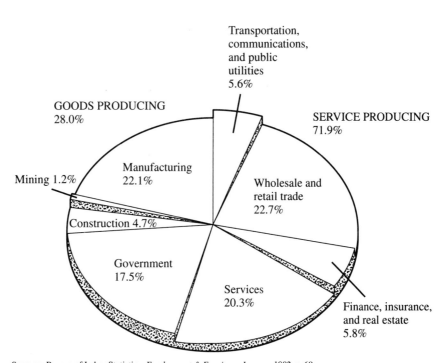

Source: Bureau of Labor Statistics, *Employment & Earnings: January 1982,* p. 69.

50 *or are unemployed but actively seeking work.* While this is a sizable portion of the work force, we will not be studying the agencies, bureaus, and departments of government because they are not businesses: those organizations do provide services, but not in order to make a profit.

Profit, then, defines business. But what is it? Simply, **profit** is *the difference between a business's total revenues or sales receipts and the total of its production*
55 *costs, operating expenses, and taxes.* Go back to our bread example. The bakery has to pay for its raw materials (flour, butter or shortening, yeast, salt), equipment (mixers, ovens, wrapping machines), employees, and the energy it uses. When the bakery sells the bread to the supermarket, it charges more than the cost of making the bread. That extra part of the selling price is profit.

60 Why do businesses want profit? Each person who runs a business is risking money. The bakery does not know that people will buy its bread; by spending money on the possibility that people will, it is taking a chance, a risk. The desire for profit is the desire for a reward for taking that chance. Were there no profits, it would not be worth the bakery's while to risk its money. Now you can see why
65 profit is so important to the economy: it is the goal that businesses pursue in producing goods or services.[4]

Interest Rating.   Please rate the interest level of Reading 4 on the following 1–5 scale (circle one):

5 — Very interesting
4 — Fairly interesting
3 — Mildly interesting
2 — A little boring
1 — Very boring

Difficulty Rating.   Please indicate how difficult Reading 4 was for you to understand on the following 1–5 scale (circle one):

5 — Very difficult
4 — Fairly difficult
3 — Moderate
2 — Fairly easy
1 — Very easy

Comments: _____

_____

Comprehension Questions

Directions.   For questions 1–5, choose the answer that best completes the statement. For questions 6–10, write your response in the space provided. Base all answers on what you read in Reading 4 (you may refer to the reading when you are not sure of an answer).

_____ 1. The author uses the example of a loaf of bread to show:
   a. The importance of profit-making.
   b. How small companies operate.
   c. How complex business is.
   d. How much business has changed.

_____ 2. Which of the following would the author *not* consider a business?
   a. A community college.
   b. A local restaurant.
   c. A dairy farm.
   d. An auto repair shop.

_____ 3. Profit is important to business because:
   a. It provides an incentive for taking risks.
   b. It is needed for the business to expand.
   c. A business must be able to reward its employees.
   d. Revenues must exceed costs.

_____ 4. We can tell from the graph that:
   a. Agricultural employment plays a minor role in today's economy.
   b. Goods-producing industries account for one-fourth of all US employment.
   c. Approximately the same number of Americans are employed by the government as by trade industries.
   d. Excluding farming, more than twice as many Americans work in service-producing industries than in goods-producing industries.

_____ 5. How is profit defined?
   a. The combination of costs and revenue.
   b. Sales receipts minus operating expenses.
   c. Total revenue minus cost, expenses, and taxes.
   d. Revenue plus sales receipts minus total production costs and taxes.

6. What point is made in the introductory quote by C M Kittrell?

   _____

   _____

7. Explain the difference between goods and services.

   _____

   _____

   _____

8. Why don't the authors consider government agencies to be businesses?

_____

_____

9. List several businesses that might be involved in the production and sale of the clothes you are wearing.

_____

_____

_____

10. If you ran a pizza shop, what factors would influence the amount of profit you earned?

_____

_____

_____

Vocabulary Exercise

Directions.   Use the context clues and your dictionary to determine the meaning of each of the following words. Write your definition in the space provided.

1. erroneously (31) _____

2. commodities (32) _____

3. tangible (34) _____

4. distinction (37) _____

5. nonagricultural (39) _____

6. utilities (see Figure 1.1) _____

7. wholesale (42) _____

8. diverse (43) _____

9. sector (45) _____

10. revenues (54) _____

READING 5

APPEALING TO BUYING MOTIVES

Joseph Straub and Stan Kossen

Reading 5, taken from a business textbook, discusses the various motives that affect consumer buying decisions. Read the passage to learn what these motives are and how they influence individual consumers and industrial buyers.

Previewing Exercise

Directions.   Preview the passage and answer the following questions.

1. What are the three main types of consumer buying motives?

    _____

2. List five industrial buying motives.

    _____

    _____

3. What information is provided in the passage's three tables?

    _____

    _____

Pre-thinking Exercise

1. Think of a recent purchase you made. Why did you buy that item? List all the factors that influenced your decision.

   _____

   _____

   _____

2. Where do you usually shop for clothes? Why?

   _____

   _____

3. Write three questions about consumers' buying motives.

   _____

   _____

   _____

Those who are involved in marketing promotion activities must understand why consumers buy the things they do. Have you, for example, ever thought about why you bought a particular product or service? What motivated you to pick one brand or model over the other? Did you make a rational buying decision, or did emotions influ-
5 ence your purchase? If you are like most consumers, your buying motives vary substantially depending on the particular product you buy and the mood you are in at the time you buy it.

    Marketers want to know what makes their customers buy a given product, because buying motives form the basis of effective promotional strategies. Industrial
10 buyers and final consumers have different buying motives.

Consumer Buying Motives

Consumer buying motives are *factors that cause someone to purchase a product for personal use.* They reflect the person's needs and wants, attitudes, and self-image. People buy things for emotional, rational, or patronage reasons, and sometimes for a blend of all three.

15 **Emotional Motives.**   Consumers are often unaware of the emotional motives that influence their buying decisions, but they are important motives for marketers to appeal to nonetheless. **Emotional motives** are *buying reasons that arise from impulse rather than careful thought and analysis.* Table 1 summarizes the most common emotional buying motives for various products and services. They do overlap, and sev-
20 eral of them may act simultaneously on a prospective buyer.

TABLE 1   **Emotional Buying Motives and Products or Services that Appeal to Them**

Emotional Buying Motive	*Products or Services*
Fear and safety	Smoke and burglar alarms
	Fire extinguishers
	Insurance
Love and social approval	Grooming aids
	Flowers
	Singing telegrams
Fun and excitement	Vacation tours
	Rock concerts
	Sporting goods
	Sports cars
Pride and prestige	Luxury cars
	Jewelry
	Maid service
Self-expression	Custom-painted murals on vans or trucks
	Personalized T-shirts
	Do-it-yourself books

Many products become successful by appealing to one or more emotional buying motives. Many people purchase designer jeans out of a desire to express themselves and seek social approval by being fashionable. Guitar manufacturers anticipate heavy sales when leading rock stars appear in concert playing their brand.
25 Amateur guitarists, combining emulation and self-expression motives, generate considerable demand.

Marketers work very hard to appeal to a buyer's self-image—a composite of the emotional motives listed in Table 1. Virginia Slims cigarettes, Adidas running shoes, and Stanley do-it-yourself kits are promoted through considerable and often subtle
30 appeals to self-image. In short, we sometimes buy products because they are promoted to the kind of person we believe or wish ourselves to be. While this is not logical behavior, it is extremely important that marketers take it into account.

Rational Motives.   Although the distinction between emotional and rational buying motives is not always clear, rational motives are easier for buyers to justify: they
35 make good sense. **Rational motives** are *buying reasons that arise from careful planning and analysis.* Home owners who install automatic lawn sprinkler systems want the assurance that their lawns will be watered regularly whether they are at home or away. Companies that pressure-clean houses appeal to the customer's rational motives by stating that regular cleaning prolongs the life of a shingled roof and takes
40 away the need to repaint by renewing the appearance of the exterior paint. Few consumers purchase goods for purely rational reasons. Examples of rational buying motives are summarized in Table 2.

TABLE 2   Rational Buying Motives and Products or Services that Appeal to Them

Rational Buying Motive	*Products or Services*
Economy and cost	Home freezers
	Auto repainting
	Freight-damaged items
Quality and dependability	Top quality watches
	Lifetime automobile batteries
	Service agreements on home appliances
Convenience	Fast-food restaurants
	Dry cleaning
	Dishwashers
	Remote control television sets

TABLE 3   Patronage Motives that Cause Customers to Shop Regularly at a Particular Store

Patronage Motives
Convenient location
Pleasant sales people
Positive public image or reputation
Cleanliness
Customer services (delivery, gift wrapping, advice on product installation and use)
Prices (high for status appeal, competitive or low to appeal to economy motives)
Variety of merchandise
An atmosphere of good will

Patronage Motives.   Another classification of motives, **patronage motives,** are *buying reasons based on the characteristics of a specific retail outlet or brand of* 45   *product.* Some of us are loyal to a particular brand or a specific store because of past satisfactions. Patronage motives make a given brand a specialty good to some buyers. Table 3 lists several reasons that have been given for regularly patronizing a firm. Do some of these factors cause you to buy repeatedly from the same retailer?

Industrial Buying Motives

Industrial buying motives are *factors that cause an industrial buyer to recognize a* 50   *logical need or want and make a purchase that satisfies it.* Business purchasers usually buy for rational reasons, and the most prevalent ones are depicted in Figure 1.

Profit.   Businesses cannot function for long without profit. Profit is, therefore, the governing motive for buying industrial goods. As a result, most marketing promotion efforts for industrial goods ultimately appeal to this motive.

FIGURE 1 *Industrial Buying Motives*

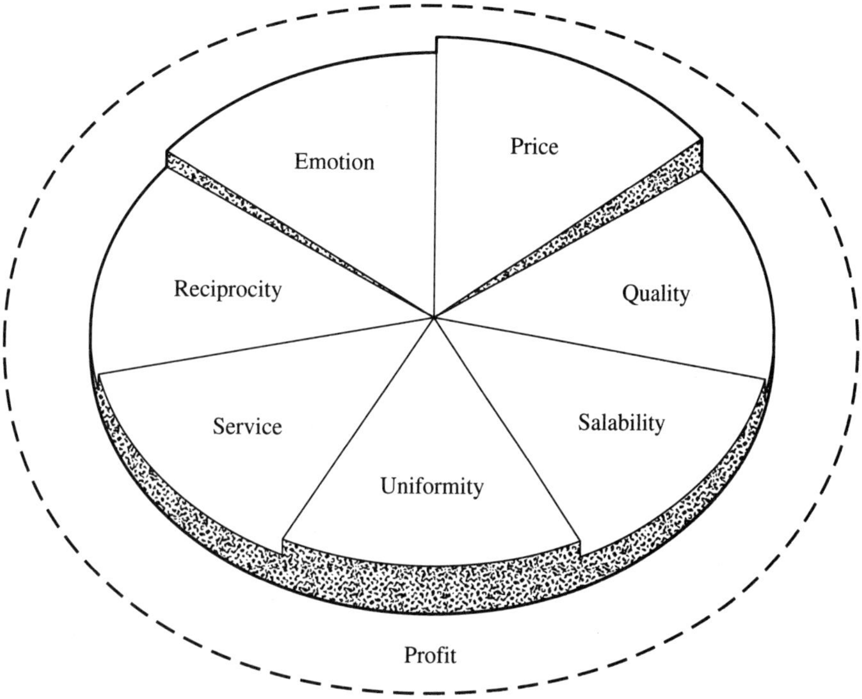

55   **Price.**   While price is important to budget-conscious industrial buyers, they may look beyond dollars to consider how the item can improve the finished product or help operations run more smoothly or efficiently. A firm may pay more to put steel-belted radial tires on its company cars, for example, because their longer wear and better gas mileage offset the higher cost. Although Sealed Air Corporation's protective air-

60   bubble packaging wrap costs more than excelsior or Styrofoam, firms that use it as a padding in shipping cartons may save more than its cost in lower postage expenses.

  Quality.   Quality is a significant industrial buying motive, but it must be reconciled with price. Firms do not want to buy more quality than they need. If you bought toilet tissue for employee rest rooms and for guest rooms at a chain of luxury hotels, for

65   example, would you buy the same quality for both? Probably not. An industrial buyer's quality standards must consider the final consumer's expectations, the company's image and reputation, and the budget for the product being produced. Manufacturers usually do not want to make the best product possible, because the cost and selling price would increase accordingly.

70   **Salability.**   Components and ingredients that make an end product more impressive to customers should be emphasized in marketing promotion. The paint used on a new Chevrolet Corvette, the silicone in Gillette Dry Idea deodorant, and the leather used in Nunn-Bush shoes, all make those products more salable. If an industrial product will make the finished consumer product look more attractive, perform better, or take

75 on a unique characteristic or function, that can influence an industrial customer's buying decision.

Uniformity.   An industrial product that makes finished items appear identical will appeal to many company buyers. An automatic bottling machine that is guaranteed to fill each container to within one–sixty-fourth of an inch of the same level, or an
80 automatic spray painting booth that applies paint of uniform thickness and finish to each unit, appeals to this uniformity motive.

Service.   Industrial buyers are concerned about service, because the failure of one key machine can stop an entire production line or damage dozens of units. For this reason, industrial customers demand assurance that the seller will maintain vital
85 equipment and repair defects quickly and correctly. This is a crucial factor, for example, in selling photocopying machines or computers. IBM Corporation, the world's leading computer manufacturer, attributes its success not only to high quality but also to its reputation for exceptional service.

Reciprocity.   In some instances firms observe **reciprocal buying,** *a practice*
90 *wherein two or more companies become mutual customers, buying each other's goods and services.* An auto repair shop, for example, may buy all of its parts from one auto parts store; the store, in turn, has its delivery fleet tuned up and repaired at the repair shop. Mutual sales mean mutual profits.

Emotion.   Despite the fact that industrial buyers purchase for their companies
95 (instead of themselves) and spend their firms' money (instead of their own), marketers of industrial goods should not ignore emotion as an industrial buying motive. A purchasing manager, for example, may like a salesperson enough to buy strictly on the basis of friendship. The owner of a copying-machine company enjoyed such exceptional rapport with one salesperson that he turned all competitors away auto-
100 matically. Or there may be other emotional motives—sometimes arbitrary ones. One materials buyer for a men's hat company would not buy anything from a hatless salesperson.[5]

Interest Rating.   Please rate the interest level of Reading 5 on the following 1–5 scale (circle one):

> 5—Very interesting
> 4—Fairly interesting
> 3—Mildly interesting
> 2—A little boring
> 1—Very boring

Difficulty Rating.   Please indicate how difficult Reading 5 was for you to understand on the following 1–5 scale (circle one):

5—Very difficult

4—Fairly difficult

3—Moderate

2—Fairly easy

1—Very easy

Comments: _____

_____

Comprehension Questions

Directions. For questions 1–5, choose the answer that best completes the statement. For questions 6–10, write your response in the space provided. Base all answers on what you read in Reading 5 (you may refer to the reading when you are not sure of an answer).

_____ 1. The passage is written primarily for:
  a. Private consumers.
  b. Industrial buyers.
  c. Marketers.
  d. Consumer protection agents.

_____ 2. A consumer is least likely to be aware of:
  a. A rational motive.
  b. A patronage motive.
  c. An emotional motive.
  d. A quality motive.

_____ 3. Which of the following is *not* an example of an emotional motive?
  a. Social approval.
  b. Emulation.
  c. Self-expression.
  d. Convenience.

_____ 4. Which statement is true regarding industrial buying motives?
  a. Most industrial buying motives are either emotional or patronage motives.
  b. The best quality product is not always desirable.
  c. Profit motives rarely affect purchase decisions.
  d. Service motives are of primary importance in most buying decisions.

_____ 5. A radio company decides to use better quality components in their radios. Which buying motive is probably involved?
  a. Price.
  b. Salability.
  c. Reciprocity.
  d. Service.

6. Explain the difference between emotional and rational buying motives.

_____

_____

_____

_____

7. What are patronage motives? How do they affect buying decisions?

_____

_____

_____

8. Explain how emotional, rational, and patronage motives might all be involved in the purchase of an automobile.

_____

_____

_____

_____

9. Which of the motives discussed in the passage influences you the most when you shop?

_____

_____

_____

10. Explain why price, quality, and salability motives are important in most industrial buying decisions.

_____

_____

_____

_____

Vocabulary Exercise

Directions. Use the context clues and your dictionary to determine the meaning of each of the following words. Write your definition in the space provided.

1. marketing (1) _____

2. simultaneously (20) _____

3. prospective (20) _____

4. emulation (25) _____

5. rational (33) _____

6. patronage (43) _____

7. prevalent (51) _____

8. ultimately (54) _____

9. crucial (85) _____

10. reciprocity (89) _____

READING 6

A NUTRITIONAL CHALLENGE TO EAT AT HOME

Susan Finn and Linda Stern Kass

Does your family sit down for meals together? Do you eat nutritious foods? Reading 6 discusses the value of family meals and the importance of a balanced diet. Read the selection to learn how you can improve your current eating habits.

Previewing Exercise

Directions. Preview the passage and answer the following questions.

1. What do the authors think about family meals?

   _____

   _____

2. What are some advantages of eating at home?

   _____

   _____

3. What will you learn from reading this article?

   _____

   _____

   _____

Pre-thinking Exercise

1. What have you previously read or learned about about nutrition?

_____

_____

_____

2. Do you eat a balanced diet? Describe your meals on a typical day.

_____

_____

_____

3. Write three questions about food and nutrition.

_____

_____

_____

Where is the traditional family meal heading? Sitting down to a meal with the family used to be a daily ritual that fed the soul as well as the body and provided a rhythm for the day. A family meal, for many, provided relief from stress.

5   To be sure, the family meal has always validated the importance of the family. It provided a forum for communication, a time when the kids could get the undivided attention of their parents, and vice versa. Mealtime offered everyone some sense of continuity and security. But the family meal hour is changing for at least some segments of the population.

The traditional American family of a homemaker-wife, a breadwinner-husband,
10   and 2.4 kids represents only 15 percent of all families today. One-fourth of all households are one-person households. Currently, nearly 60 percent of married women are employed outside the home. An interesting outgrowth of this lifestyle trend is that 52 percent of teenage girls spend two hours per week shopping for family groceries. Nearly half of all grocery shoppers are men, and most of them are shopping for the
15   family. The good news is that everyone is pitching in.

The bad news is that eating habits in this country have gone berserk, and some feel conventional meals are the biggest casualty. We often don't know where the next meal will come from, when or with whom. Breakfast may be a doughnut or a biscuit from a fast-food restaurant. Lunch is consumed off the dashboard or out of
20   the office candy machine. Dinner is often whatever can be grabbed from a store shelf at 6:00 P.M. "Grazing"—what snacking has been called for the last few years—has gone out of control. Today, sitting down to a meal no longer ranks with sleeping and bathing as a necessary daily routine. There has been a shift in attitudes in some segments about the role and importance of food. Yet to many, it is still

25   a family priority to break bread together—a priority that has become more challenging due to time constraints caused by Mom's lack of time to prepare dinner, the
children's early-evening activities, either parent's late night at the office, or all of
the above.

Regardless of what "family" is to you, a traditional family gathering at meal-
30   times, particularly dinner, is here to stay. Certainly, new technologies in the future
will allow the way we prepare food, as well as our specific choices of foods, to
change; but rest assured that the family dinner hour is not marked for extinction . . .

Balance, Moderation, and Variety

At home, you do have a head start. Home is where you have the most control over
eating what you want when you want it, the size of your portion, and the kinds of
35   foods and ingredients you use. In the last chapter, we discussed the Surgeon General's
Report on Nutrition and Health released in 1988. After reviewing all the scientific
evidence available, this landmark report gave us proof that dietary excesses and
imbalances do lead to chronic diseases. In fact, these diseases account for more than
two-thirds of all deaths in the United States.

40   In plain language, that means you need to look at all the foods you eat each day
and do your best to maintain a balanced diet, to eat all things in moderation, and
choose a variety of foods. Without this total diet approach, you are jeopardizing your
health. That is a fact. Proper nutrition, after all, is a matter of common sense. But, as
we have seen earlier, our reaction to food is often quite emotional. So when it comes
45   to nutrition, we can't assume common sense applies. Let's give you some tips now
on how to achieve balance, moderation, and variety in your diet.

Most of us fight a continual battle between self-control and self-indulgence. Balance lies somewhere in the middle. It shouldn't be feast or famine, all or none. Balance for some may be having low-fat cottage cheese and fruit, salads, and broiled
50   chicken or fish during the week, and splurging a bit on appetizers, sauces, and desserts
offered at weekend social gatherings. That's okay. Balance for others may be exer-
cising vigorously, then rationalizing the french fries, ice cream, and fudge brownies.
This has been called the work out/pig out syndrome. That's *not* okay.

Another aspect of balance in the diet has to do with the types of foods you eat
55   each day. A proper balance of protein, carbohydrates, and fat in your diet provides
you with the right amount of vitamins, minerals, and other nutrients that you need to
stay healthy. If you never eat any dairy products, chances are you're not getting
enough calcium. If you never eat any meat, fish, poultry, or vegetables, you probably
aren't getting enough iron. If you have juice and a muffin for breakfast, a salad for
60   lunch, and no dinner, you're short on nutrients and total calories for the day. The concept here is getting what you need—not too much and not too little.

You can achieve a balance in your diet by trading off one food item for another.
In other words, if you can't resist the candy machine at work at 3:00 P.M., pass on
dessert after dinner that night so you don't have too many calories or too much sugar
65   and fat that day. Don't have a three-egg cheese omelet for breakfast and an eight-
ounce cheeseburger for dinner—it's just too much fat and cholesterol in one day. But

you don't have to feel guilty every time you reach for a candy bar or enjoy your favorite cheeseburger. You can have your cake—just limit the amount you eat, and eat it on a day when you trade off other items that might be high in sugar, fat, and 70 calories. It's that easy.

Now let's take a look at how you can achieve moderation in your diet. Most important, you need to know what normal portions are. Here are some guidelines. A portion of milk is one cup, and the same goes for a portion of yogurt. Hard cheeses, on the other hand, are measured in one-ounce portions. The individually wrapped cheese slices are 75 generally 3/4 ounce per slice (or 1 1/3 slices per 1-ounce serving.) One portion of most vegetables is considered 1/2 cup, while fruit portions are more variable. Half a banana, one small apple, half a grapefruit, and half a cup of orange juice are each considered one portion. One slice of bread is considered one portion, as is 3/4 to 1 cup of ready-to-eat cereal. One serving of fat, in general, is 1 teaspoon whether it is butter, margarine, or oil.

80 A single portion of meat, poultry, or fish is usually three or four ounces, which is about the size of the palm of your hand. In fact, experts recommend no more than six ounces a day of animal protein; yet at restaurants you are often given at least twice that amount in one meal. In 1989, meat consumption averaged more than eight ounces of meat a day, according to an Agriculture Department report.

85 At home, you can control portion size. To get familiar with the portions mentioned, try to weigh and measure portion quantities until you are able to actually visualize what a portion looks like. Eating in moderation—eating normal-sized portions—allows you to eat more kinds of foods.

And eating a variety of foods is extremely critical to your health. You need about 90 forty different nutrients to stay healthy. While most foods contain more than one nutrient, no single food item supplies all the essential nutrients in the amounts that you need. So the greater the variety of your diet, the less likely you are to develop either a deficiency or an excess of any single nutrient. Furthermore, we still are not aware of all the properties in the foods we eat and all the nutritional requirements. To maintain the 95 proper variety, choose foods every day from each of the four major food groups: grains, milk and milk products, fruits and vegetables, meat, fish, and poultry, and meat alternatives, such as beans, tofu, and other vegetable proteins. Particular weight should be given to grains, and fruits and vegetables, to maintain the proper balance in your diet.[6]*

Interest Rating.   Please rate the interest level of Reading 6 on the following 1–5 scale (circle one):

   5—Very interesting
   4—Fairly interesting
   3—Mildly interesting
   2—A little boring
   1—Very boring

———————

Difficulty Rating. Please indicate how difficult Reading 6 was for you to understand on the following 1–5 scale (circle one):

5 — Very difficult

4 — Fairly difficult

3 — Moderate

2 — Fairly easy

1 — Very easy

Comments: _____

_____

Comprehension Questions

Directions. For questions 1–5, choose the answer that best completes the statement. For questions 6–10, write your response in the space provided. Base all answers on what you read in Reading 6 (you may refer to the reading when you are not sure of an answer).

_____ 1. The authors predict that:
    a. Traditional family meals will continue.
    b. The traditional family will continue to decline.
    c. Technology will eliminate the family meal.
    d. Teenagers and men will do more of the grocery shopping.

_____ 2. The authors are critical of:
    a. New cooking technologies.
    b. Skipping meals.
    c. Dairy foods.
    d. Dessert.

_____ 3. What would the authors be most likely to recommend to someone interested in losing weight?
    a. "Grazing" in place of regular meals.
    b. Avoidance of all high-calorie foods.
    c. A rigorous, intensive exercise program.
    d. A balanced and moderate diet.

_____ 4. The authors blame improper nutrition on all of the following except:
    a. Changes in Americans' eating habits.
    b. Emotional reactions to food.
    c. Self-indulgence.
    d. Lack of access to nutritious foods.

_____ 5. The best statement of the main idea of the last paragraph (lines 90–100) is:

    a. A balanced diet must include grains, fruits, and vegetables.

    b. Eating a variety of foods is essential to your health.

    c. No single food group provides all the essential nutrients.

    d. Family meals encourage balanced diets.

6. Why do the authors feel that family meals are important?

_____

_____

_____

7. What does a balanced diet consist of?

_____

_____

_____

8. What do the authors recommend to familiarize yourself with portion sizes?

_____

_____

_____

9. In a complete sentence of your own wording, write the main idea for the third paragraph on p. 385 (lines 40–46).

_____

_____

_____

10. What did you learn from the selection that you can apply to your own eating habits? Be specific.

_____

_____

_____

Vocabulary Exercise

Directions. Use the context clues and your dictionary to determine the meaning of each of the following words. Write your definition in the space provided.

    1. ritual (2) _____

    2. validated (4) _____

3. forum (5) _____

4. berserk (16) _____

5. casualty (17) _____

6. constraints (26) _____

7. excesses (27) _____

8. splurging (50) _____

9. syndrome (53) _____

10. nutrients (56) _____

READING 7

EDUCATION MYTHS

Richard Shenkman

Richard Shenkman is a historian who is interested in setting the record straight. His book *Legends, Lies and Cherished Myths of American History* lightheartedly exposes many of the myths Americans believe about our history. In this excerpt, Shenkman deals with myths concerning early American education.

Previewing Exercise

Directions. Preview the passage and answer the following questions.

1. What is the passage about?

   _____

2. What myths about education does the passage discuss?

   _____

   _____

3. Name one or two colleges that are mentioned in the passage.

   _____

4. Does the author believe that American schools were better in the past than they are today?

   _____

Pre-thinking Exercise

1. What do you know about American schools of the past? Have your parents ever discussed their schooling with you?

_____

_____

2. What do you think it would have been like to attend school 50 or 100 years ago?

_____

_____

3. Write three questions about American schools of the past.

_____

_____

_____

The popular belief that we currently don't educate our children very well but could if only we tried hard enough rests in part on a legend that once upon a time we did educate them well. People are a little vague about when this golden age existed—perhaps earlier in this century—but there's no doubt it did exist, whenever it was!

5   And how well we did the job! The school was so effective it could take the foreign language-speaking son of an immigrant peddler and in no time at all turn him into a happy, productive, English-speaking American professional. With a little luck the kid might even become a doctor or lawyer. It didn't matter what his ethnic background was, whether Irish, Italian, or Jewish; the school bestowed its blessings demo-

10   cratically, without regard to race, creed, or color. Neither caste nor class played a role; all were treated equally.

Yet we have it on good authority that the school of legend did not exist—at least not in the early decades of this century, when it was presumably doing so much to help immigrant children become good Americans. Colin Greer has established

15   that more students failed than succeeded in schools during just the time when the schools were supposedly doing such a crack job. Greer says that several studies conclusively show that most students in the schools of Chicago, New York, Boston, Detroit, Philadelphia, and Pittsburgh could not read, write, or do 'rithmetic at their grade levels.

20   A striking illustration of the failure of the schools was the dropout rate that prevailed in the 1920's and 1930's. A federal study of students across the country in that twenty-year period showed that only 56 percent graduated from high school. In individual cities the rate was often far lower. In New York City only 40 percent graduated. In the twenties in Philadelphia only 19 percent of those entering high school

25   managed to finish. Even in the 1940's things did not improve much; in Boston, for example, fully 50 percent of the ninth graders failed to complete high school.

Remarkable as these statistics are, it might take something more to persuade Americans that the early twentieth-century school was less effective than imagined. Perhaps a trip through time to a school in New York would do. What would we find? We would expect to see cleanly scrubbed children, quietly seated at neat rows of wooden desks equipped with filled inkwells. In truth, if we had chanced upon the hundreds of schools catering to the children of immigrants, say, at the turn of the century, we would find squalor equal to the worst tenements from which the children came. Like the tenements, the schools would be overcrowded. Worse, the stench and filth would be overpowering. A rat might even cross our path, though it would be hard to notice in such poorly lighted classrooms. If we happened along on the right day, we might run into Jacob Riis, the reformer, on one of his fact-collecting missions. The inner city school was high on the reformer's list of Things That Needed to Be Improved.

Whether the public school at the start of the century was better or worse than it had been previously is unclear. Things may have been worse. In the 1890's, according to the federal government, only slightly more than half the children in America entered school at all. Nonwhites in particular stayed away from school in droves; only 33 percent were ever enrolled.

Among institutions of learning, colleges, Harvard especially, also figure in myth. Harvard has for so much of this century demonstrated academic excellence that it is believed to have done so always. When Harvard celebrated its 350th anniversary in 1986, the rest of the country joined in; the university even found itself on the cover of *Time*. Harvardians naturally thought the attention well deserved. But why the rest of the country put up with the illusion that Harvard ought to be celebrating *all* of its 350 years is puzzling.

There is, for instance, the curious matter of the way Harvard ranked students during much of its history. While in the seventeenth century students were ranked according to academic standing, in the next century the college began ranking them according to family status, those at the top of the social heap placing at the top of the class. In the nineteenth century things improved, but not by much. Academic achievement again began to be taken into consideration, but rank was also determined by a student's behavior. Among other things, demerits affecting student rank were given for late attendance at prayers (sixteen points), lying on the grass (sixteen points), shouting from a window in the yard (sixteen points), playing a musical instrument in study period (sixteen points). Students interested in the academic side of college life frequently became demoralized since points for a good paper could easily be offset by demerits, say, for lounging. The result, predictably, as Edward Everett Hale complained, was that students became indifferent to college rank. Not until 1868 did the college agree (quoting a Harvard resolution) to keep "the scales of scholarship and conduct" distinct.

College rank aside, there is the question of the quality of teaching at Harvard. One assumes it was high. Yet the evidence suggests that even many of Harvard's own teachers thought it wasn't. Among other things, teachers regularly complained they were overwhelmed by the work load. This isn't an unusual complaint as far as college teachers are concerned, of course, but it seems to have been made with especially

good reason at Harvard in the last century. Even the great and learned Henry Adams complained he could not keep up with the demands. After he was hired, he was astonished to learn it would be up to him to teach all of Western history that fell between
75   the courses taught by two other professors, a period of about a thousand years. Even Adams was a bit daunted by the prospect, though he managed to retain his sense of humor. "There is a pleasing excitement," he wrote friends, "in having to lecture tomorrow on a period of history which I have not heard of till today . . . Thus far the only merit of my instruction has been its originality, one hundred youths at any rate
80   have learned facts and theories for which in after life they will hunt the authorities in vain, unless, as I trust, they forget all they have been told."

College teachers in general in the nineteenth century, by the way, were often inferior to their twentieth-century counterparts. When Charles William Eliot took over the presidency of Harvard in 1869, he complained that "very few Americans
85   of eminent ability" became college teachers. "The pay has been too low," he observed, "and there has been no gradual rise out of drudgery, such as may reasonably be expected in other callings." Henry Ward Beecher, putting the problem more colorfully, commented: "Who ever heard of a college professor that was not poor? They dry up in a pocket like springs after the wood is cut off from the hills. They
90   are apt to get very dry in other ways, too. A man that teaches cannot afford to know too much."

As for college students, they gave rise to a number of interesting myths, the most important of which may be the belief that students never engaged in major rebellions until the 1960's. History is replete with examples of student rebellions at
95   least as turbulent as the uprisings associated with the Vietnam War generation. In 1830 students at Yale revolted over a change in the teaching of mathematics in an incident dubbed the "Conic Section's Rebellion." Before it was over, forty-three students—about half of the class—had been expelled. In ensuing years tensions remained so high that some students came to school armed with dangerous
100   weapons. Earlier, in 1818 and again in 1828, Yale students revolted against the food; both times the situations became so severe the administration was forced to close the school down. One Christmas students became so destructive they went on a rampage, smashing windows in buildings across the campus. Professors in turn had to use axes to smash down the doors of several buildings which the students had
105   mischievously locked up.

Yale wasn't the only college in the nineteenth century to be struck by student violence. Historians say that at Princeton between 1800 and 1830 there were no fewer than six student insurrections. And at Harvard things got so bad several buildings were partially blown up; a Harvard leader observed that students frequently committed "crimes that were worthy of the penitentiary." At the University of Virginia in
110   1836 student militants, illegally armed with guns, engaged in mob violence so severe that the school had to ask for the help of armed soldiers. In 1840 a University of Virginia professor who angered his students was killed.[7]

Interest Rating. Please rate the interest level of Reading 7 on the following 1–5 scale (circle one):

5—Very interesting

4—Fairly interesting

3—Mildly interesting

2—A little boring

1—Very boring

Difficulty Rating.   Please indicate how difficult Reading 7 was for you to understand on the following 1–5 scale (circle one):

5—Very difficult

4—Fairly difficult

3—Moderate

2—Fairly easy

1—Very easy

Comments: _____

_____

Comprehension Questions

Directions.   For questions 1–5, choose the answer that best completes the statement. For questions 6–10, write your response in the space provided. Base all answers on what you read in Reading 7 (you may refer to the reading when you are not sure of an answer).

_____ 1. The author believes that public schools at the beginning of the twentieth century:
a. Were better than schools are today.
b. Were not as successful as many people think.
c. Successfully prepared many immigrant children to become professionals.
d. Were better in the city than in the country.

_____ 2. During the 1920s and 1930s, the percentage of students in the United States who did not graduate from high school was:
a. 56 percent.
b. 44 percent.
c. 50 percent.
d. 40 percent.

_____ 3. In the nineteenth century, student rank at Harvard was:
a. Influenced by the student's conduct.
b. Based solely on grades.
c. Determined by family status.
d. Not determined.

_____ 4. In the nineteenth century, college teachers:
   a. Were well paid.
   b. Had difficulty finding jobs.
   c. Were often not as qualified as today's college teachers.
   d. Frequently went on strike for higher pay.

_____ 5. The main point of the last paragraph (lines 106–114) is:
   a. Students at Harvard blew up buildings.
   b. Violence was not uncommon at nineteenth century universities.
   c. Students of today are less violent than students of the past.
   d. College students have always been violent.

6. Why might people want to believe that schools of the past were better than they really were?

_____

7. According to the author, what would we see if we could visit a public school in New York City in 1910?

_____

_____

8. What were some of the complaints of college professors in the nineteenth century?

_____

_____

9. In a complete sentence of your own wording, write the main idea for the passage's third paragraph (lines 12–19).

_____

_____

10. In your opinion, are schools today better than schools of the past? Explain.

_____

_____

Vocabulary Exercise

Directions.   Use the context clues and your dictionary to determine the meaning of each of the following words. Write your definition in the space provided.

1. ethnic (8) _____

2. caste (10) _____

3. squalor (33) _____

4. myth (45) _____

5. illusion (50) _____

6. overwhelmed (70) _____

7. eminent (85) _____

8. drudgery (86) _____

9. turbulent (95) _____

10. insurrection (108) _____

READING 8

MRS. CASSADORE AND APACHE STUDENTS

Mick Fedullo

Mick Fedullo is a writer and teacher. After accepting a teaching job in 1979 at a Pima Indian reservation in Arizona, he became interested in Native American culture. Traveling the Southwest and West, he taught Native American children and adolescents of several different tribes and recorded his experiences in his book *Light of the Feather.* In the following excerpt, Fedullo reports on a class discussion with Apache high school students on the subject of prejudice.

Pre-reading Exercises

Directions. Preview the passage and use the space below to write your preview and pre-thinking notes.

Preview Notes

_____

_____

_____

_____

Pre-thinking Notes

_____

_____

_____

_____

Elenore Cassadore, an elder of the San Carlos Apache, was employed in the bilingual program at the high school in Globe. Because she didn't drive, she rode with a
fellow aide each school day from San Carlos to Globe and back, a round trip of over
forty miles. I met Mrs. Cassadore at the beginning of a four-week stint working with
5   the Apache high school students. Because there was no high school on the reservation, the students were bused to Globe. Sometimes, when Mrs. Cassadore's ride was
unavailable, she joined the kids on the bus.

I knew from the moment I met her that I wanted to spend time talking with her;
I could learn much about the San Carlos Apaches from this intelligent and wise
10   woman. Mrs. Cassadore was of medium height and build, with salt-and-pepper hair.
Her weathered face looked quiet, firm, sad. I never saw her in anything but traditional,
ankle-length Apache camp dresses.

When I was first introduced to her, I explained what I hoped to accomplish with
the students. We would, I said, put together a manuscript of poems, stories, articles,
15   and drawings about Apache life, past and present—all composed by the students. I
would also conduct several sessions on "survival skills"—that is, comfortable or at
least practical ways for young Indian adults to get by in the non-Indian world. I added
that it would be an honor if she sat in on some of the classes.

Mrs. Cassadore nodded and said, "Sounds good."
20   I pressed: "I hope that you *will* be able to attend."

"In the morning classes," she answered. "Afternoons I'm busy in the office. But
the mornings are okay. Those two classes are the ones I sometimes teach anyway."

In my enthusiasm to develop an acquaintanceship, I said, "I would really enjoy
your company at dinner some evening. Maybe we could go to a restaurant. I'd like
25   to talk to you about the students and the bilingual program here. My treat." What
I really wanted was to talk to Mrs. Cassadore about her and her tribe. I had lied. A
white lie.

Mrs. Cassadore nodded and said nothing. I sensed that I had been too abrupt.

The following day, I saw Mrs. Cassadore walking down the hallway toward the
30   bilingual office. All the students were in class, and we were the only two people in
the oak-floored, echoey corridor.

"Excuse me, Mrs. Cassadore," I said. "Have you thought about that dinner? Is
any particular night best for you?"

"I've thought about it," she said. "There's nothing I can tell you over dinner that
35   I can't just as well tell you here at the school."

I staggered under the weight of this rejection. Forget it, she had told me. And
with a voice as soft and sweet as a mother's. If that quiet voice didn't echo in the hallway, it more than bounced around inside my skull.

"Oh," I said. Then, trying to regain my composure: "You're right, but the offer
40 still holds."

My own Anglo need to be immediately accepted had been thumped on, and,
ridiculously, it hurt. I spent that night repeatedly reliving the corridor scene, and
winced every time Mrs. Cassadore's words replayed in my mind.

My classes with the Apache students were both exciting and rewarding. Partic-
45 ularly interesting were the survival-skills sessions, since they involved more open
discussion. Each group I saw was composed of students from all four high school
grades, pooled from their English classes. Half of the students already knew and were
comfortable with me, since I had worked with them when they were seventh- and
eighth-graders at the elementary school on the reservation. At our initial meetings, as
50 I entered the classrooms, the freshmen and sophomores exclaimed, "It's Mick!" "All
right!" "You followed us to the high school!" The juniors and seniors, never having
seen me before, were quietly curious and suspicious of this white man's presence.

In the first class I conducted, Mrs. Cassadore sat at the back of the room on an
old pine chair pressed against the back wall, as far away from me as possible. In the
55 following weeks, she would attend most of my morning classes sitting in the same
distant spot. I was especially pleased, however, that she showed up at the beginning
of the classes and witnessed the students' welcoming cheers. If nothing else, this
would indicate to her the kind of rapport I developed with Indian students—with
Apache students.

60 I waited until the third week to begin the survival-skills sessions, giving the
older students time to become relaxed in my presence. The first and most important
rule of these classes was that, aside from me, no non-Indians were allowed in the
classroom. I wanted the Apache students to be open and honest about the problems
they perceived in their encounters with the Anglo world. I felt that my established
65 relationship with the younger students would make the discussions not only possible
but productive.

And I tried to keep realistic expectations. There was no way I could make survival in two different cultures easy. These Apache students, as well as Indian students
in general, had two major tasks challenging them: the maintenance of their own
70 Indian culture and the acquisition of skills that would enable them to function, when
they had to, in mainstream non-Indian society. What separated them from other
minorities, and made their task more difficult, was the fact that the nature of the differences between their culture and Anglo culture was so extreme. So, coping in the
Anglo world meant, as it does today, not a *reconciliation* of opposites, but an *adjust-*
75 *ment* to the very existence of profound opposites—an adjustment that must include
the development of behaviors that often seem strange to the young Indian. True bicul-
turalism also includes the maintenance of basic Indian cultural patterns and deep-
rooted beliefs. As difficult as this may be to accomplish, it remains for Indians a
realistic, attainable goal.

80 Subjects for our discussions ranged from Anglo "time" as a concept different
from Indian "time," to the analysis of Anglo behaviors the Apache students found odd
or intimidating. I constantly reinforced the idea that the students, in learning survival
skills, did not have to give up being Indian; they did not have to become *assimilated*.

The irony, of course, was that at the same time that I was conducting these
85 classes, I was also adjusting my own behaviors to conform to acceptable Indian ways

in my encounters with Mrs. Cassadore. Cross-cultural understanding is a two-way street. The non-Indian in contact with Indians has a responsibility to learn about their world and make the same adjustment to profound opposites that is expected of the Indian in reverse situations. When I talked to Mrs. Cassadore, usually in the bilingual
90   office, I kept my side of the conversations brief and to the point, spoke in a soft voice, and never tried to establish prolonged eye contact.

On Wednesday of the second week, I began the morning class by saying, "Today we're going to talk a little bit about racial prejudice toward Indians, toward you guys. Can anyone define what the word 'prejudice' means?"

95   Tom, a sophomore, said, "It's like when white people look at you funny 'cause they don't like Indians."

Marie, also a sophomore, chimed in, "They get suspicious of you, and some of them just hate us."

"Okay. Why don't we talk about ways that some white people act toward
100 Indians that might show prejudice, and how you can try to tell if those actions really do show prejudice. And we should talk about the ways you respond, and other possible responses. Someone tell me something that some whites do that might show prejudice."

"When they stare at us real long," offered an eleventh-grader named Sean. "You
105 look away, but every time you look back, they're still staring." The class stirred, the students nodding and mumbling in agreement.

Sean added, "It's like they don't even blink their eyes, kinda like snakes or some-thin'." Everyone chuckled.

This was a perfect start, I thought. The students had opened up quickly, and even
110 some humor had been injected; a relaxed but honest tone had been set. I said, "Star-ing. How about their expressions when they stare? Can you tell what they're feeling, like anger or hatred or, as Marie pointed out, suspicion?"

"Sometimes they look like they're mad."

"Or like they think you're gonna steal something."

115 "Usually just a stare, kinda blanklike."

More students were joining in. I said, "Okay, so let's talk about the situations in which staring occurs. When and where do whites stare?"

"Like last week," a tall, muscular senior said. "Me and my family were at a restaurant here in Globe. We was real quiet, like good Indians." He snickered as he
120 said this, and the class laughed again, acutely aware of the image many Indians believe they should project when in non-Indian public. "But this old white man and his wife just kept starin' at us. He even had to look partway over his shoulder to get a good view." More chuckles.

I said, "Let me tell you right off. Some white people like to stare, even though
125 it may be rude. Many times it *is* from prejudice. Sometimes it's not. Staring itself doesn't *always* indicate prejudice. Do you think those old people were staring because they were prejudiced, or could there have been some other reason?" This idea had obviously not occurred to most of the students. Several moments of silence passed as they considered it. Then I said, "Can you think of any kind of staring that's
130 really not prejudice?"

The muscular boy pulled his sunglasses down from the top of his head and over his eyes as he said, "Yeah. On the street, if it's a woman who's starin', it's 'cause she thinks I'm sexy." The whole class roared.

"Are you all laughing because white women get turned on when they see him, or
135 because so many white women are blind?" The volume of the laughter increased.

When the students settled, I said, "But there you have it. There's a reason why some whites stare at an Indian that's kind of the opposite of prejudice." I pointed to the boy; he was smiling from behind his sunglasses. "Just look at him," I said. "He's a handsome, sexy dude." The kids laughed again, but I knew they were getting the
140 point. "I'll bet every one of you has seen a white kid here at school that you thought was attractive. Maybe you even kind of stared at him or her. Maybe secretly. Maybe not so secretly." Little waves of giggles spread through the classroom. "Give me one good reason why a woman, any woman, wouldn't find this young man attractive. He may have been joking, but he was also right."

145 Our discussion lasted the full hour and would have to be continued the next day. The students had identified other situations in which staring clearly represented racial prejudice. The fierce, suspicion-filled glare of a store proprietor the minute a young Indian walks into a store—"It makes you feel like a criminal even though you wasn't gonna do nothin' wrong in the first place." The venomous stares of a group of
150 young whites on a street corner challenging a young Indian to some form of perverted, one-sided combat—"They scared the shit outta me." Concerning the old couple in the restaurant, the students concluded it was impossible to determine the motive for their rudeness. They might have been locals who disliked Indians, or they might as easily have been tourists from the hinterlands of the Midwest who had never laid eyes on a
155 real-honest-to-goodness "Injun."

During that first hour we had discussed the students' responses to their own individual situations; they had decided no *single* way of dealing with someone whose eyes are fixed on you suits every such encounter. In some cases, the students decided, it was better to ignore the stares. In others, they felt that staring back was justified, if
160 only to embarrass guilty eyes enough to turn them away. A few situations seemed to call for actual verbal or physical responses. One brassy young man told of an experience at a hardware store in which, when the clerk leveled her sights on her Apache target, he pulled out his wallet, raised his arms, looked back into the clerk's eyes, and said, "I got money, lady. I got money." This uncharacteristic response had been
165 applauded by the other students, but most of them, especially the young women, said they personally preferred to ignore stares altogether. We had also discussed at length the fact that different individuals, even of the same tribe, may react differently to similar situations. The important thing, we concluded, was to respond in a manner that felt as comfortable as possible, and at the same time maintain a sense of personal and
170 tribal dignity.

After the bell had sounded its old-fashioned clang, I stood at the doorway saying good-bye to the students individually as they filed out. We all looked forward to the next day's session. It was good, and rare, for these Apache students to have shared such personal experiences with an Anglo who was sympathetic and who could
175 offer legitimate, sometimes new, perspectives. It was good for *this* Anglo as well.

After the last student passed into the corridor, I took a deep breath, at once savoring the moment, giving the moment up, and readying myself to start the whole process over again with another group of kids. I felt exhilarated.

180   Then Mrs. Cassadore came from her usual spot at the back of the room. "That was good," she said. "We need more of that kind of thing."

"Thank you," I said, looking down.

Mrs. Cassadore had watched me interact with the Apache students for two-and-a-half weeks now. She had read their poems and articles. And she had just offered a compliment. I wondered if the time might be right to ask her to dinner

185   again. If she accepted, I would be delighted; if she turned me down, well, I could handle it gracefully and resign myself to knowing her only within the context of our high school meetings.

Looking down at the floor, I said, "You know, I would still enjoy your company for dinner some evening." I braced myself.

190   Mrs. Cassadore thought for a moment. I readied myself to say something like, "That's okay. It's not that important." Then I glanced up.

Mrs. Cassadore raised her head. In the same sweet voice she used with everyone, she said, "How about tonight?"[8]

Interest Rating.   Please rate the interest level of Reading 8 on the following 1–5 scale (circle one):

    5 — Very interesting

    4 — Fairly interesting

    3 — Mildly interesting

    2 — A little boring

    1 — Very boring

Difficulty Rating.   Please indicate how difficult Reading 8 was for you to understand on the following 1–5 scale (circle one):

    5 — Very difficult

    4 — Fairly difficult

    3 — Moderate

    2 — Fairly easy

    1 — Very easy

Comments: _____

_____

Comprehension Questions

Directions.   For questions 1–5, choose the answer that best completes the statement. For questions 6–10, write your response in the space provided. Base all answers on what you read in Reading 8 (you may refer to the reading when necessary).

_____ 1. Why does the author discuss his interactions with Mrs. Cassadore in the selection's introduction and conclusion?
   a. She is the most important character in the story.
   b. He likes her very much.
   c. To illustrate the complexity of Anglo-Indian relationships.
   d. To contrast her behavior with that of the Apache students.

_____ 2. At first, Mrs. Cassadore refuses to have dinner with the author because:
   a. She is married.
   b. He has not yet earned her trust.
   c. She is too busy with her job.
   d. She dislikes him because he is a stranger.

_____ 3. The primary goal of the survival skills discussions was to:
   a. Help Indian students assimilate into white society.
   b. Convince the Apache students that the white community was not prejudiced against them.
   c. Help the students get by in white society.
   d. Encourage the students to value their own heritage.

_____ 4. The students suggested all of the following explanations for whites staring at them except:
   a. Curiosity.
   b. Prejudice.
   c. Attractiveness.
   d. Suspicion.

_____ 5. Which pattern of organization is used in the passage?
   a. Chronological order.
   b. Listing/enumeration.
   c. Comparison–contrast.
   d. Cause–effect.

Explain your answer: _____

_____

6. Why is the author interested in having dinner with Mrs. Cassadore?

_____

_____

7. How do the Apache students feel about the author? How can you tell?

_____

_____

8. Explain this statement: "Cross-cultural understanding is a two-way street" (lines 85–86).

   _____

   _____

9. Why did Mrs. Cassadore change her mind and decide to have dinner with the author?

   _____

   _____

10. What did the students learn from their discussion with the author?

    _____

    _____

    _____

Vocabulary Exercise

Directions. Use a multistrategy approach to determine the meaning of each of the following words. Write your definition in the space provided.

1. elder (1) _____

2. bilingual (1) _____

3. abrupt (27) _____

4. composure (38) _____

5. acquisition (69) _____

6. attainable (78) _____

7. assimilated (82) _____

8. acutely (119) _____

9. proprietor (146) _____

10. venomous (148) _____

11. brassy (160) _____

12. exhilarated (177) _____

Essay Question

Directions. On a separate sheet of paper, write a well-developed, half-page response to the following question:

What causes prejudice between people of different traditions? What is the best way to respond to prejudice when you encounter it?

READING 9

THE NATURE OF LOVE

Valerian J Derlega and Louis H Janda

Love makes the world go round—or so they say. But what is love? Are there different types of love? Does love ensure a successful marriage? Read the following selection to learn about some interesting theories regarding love and marriage.

Pre-reading Exercises

Directions. Preview the passage and use the space below to write your preview and pre-thinking notes.

Preview Notes

_____

_____

_____

_____

Pre-thinking Notes

_____

_____

One view of love states that it is an intense physical or emotional attachment to another individual. It may take the form of an urgent desire for physical contact and sexual intercourse with someone or an intense need to be in the other's presence. This form of attachment, which can be identified as an extreme need for the other indi-
5   vidual, is similar to what the Greeks called **eros.**

Another view of love emphasizes giving and sharing or caring for another individual. In this approach, love is seen as an attempt to satisfy the needs of another. This view of love was called **agape** by the Greeks.

The view of love that depends on giving and caring for the needs of another first
10   became widely popular in twelfth-century Europe. It was called "courtly love." A man had this relationship with a woman who was not his wife. It did not usually involve sexual intercourse. Instead, it took the form of loyalty and dedication by a knight to a noble woman. It is interesting to note that medieval practitioners of courtly love felt that it was impossible to maintain love between a married couple. A law
15   passed by the "Court of Love" established by Marie, Countess of Champagne, in the twelfth century stated: "We declare and hold as firmly established that love cannot exert its powers between two people who are married to each other. For lovers give each other everything freely, under no compulsion of necessity, but married people are in duty bound to give in to each other's desires and deny themselves to each other
20   nothing." This view, which may be popular with many young persons, is contrary to a traditional idea that the need for intimacy can be fully satisfied only in marriage.

A third view of love emphasizes the character of the bond that exists between lovers. Social psychologist Zick Rubin calls this **intimacy** or closeness. It can be seen by individuals' willingness to disclose their feelings and thoughts. For
25   instance, a coed said that she knew her boyfriend loved her when he could share a secret with her:

> That time I knew he really cared about me. His father had died when he was 5 and he never talked about it. Even his mother said that she felt it would help him if he would talk about it. Then he told me all his memories. He got to the point of really crying. Of course he had
> 30   cried before, but that time made me feel he really cared about me, and I was so glad. I can't hold anything inside, and he had been holding so much inside.

Rubin constructed a scale that provides a useful way of measuring love as he defined it. This scale is composed of three dimensions: attachment (e.g., "If I were lonely, my first thought would be to seek _____ out"); caring (e.g., "I would
35   do almost anything for _____"); and intimacy (e.g., "I feel that I can confide in _____ about virtually everything"). A careful distinction must be made between measures of loving and liking. Liking reflects how we see individuals on task-oriented activities. People who are likable are respected because they are seen as intelligent, competent, or having good judgment. Loving reflects our feelings of
40   attachment, caring, and intimacy.

According to popular stereotypes, females are supposed to become more romantically involved than males. However, Rubin's research indicates that men may fall in love more easily than women and that women also fall out of love more easily than men.

45 In Rubin's sample, taken in the Boston area, men were more likely than women to agree with such statements about romantic love as: "A person should marry whomever he loves regardless of social position." Or, "As long as they at least love one another, two people should have no difficulty getting along together in marriage."

Romantic love has traditionally been considered an uncontrollable emotion that 50 happens at first sight. The couple wants to be with one another all the time, and partners think that the other person will satisfy their needs. Love, in this view, is not rational: People not only believe that they should marry for love but that love will insure happiness.

There have been many criticisms of romantic love as a basis for forming an inti- 55 mate relationship—or any kind of committed relationship. The idea that everyone will fall in love is not true. Belief in this idea can lead people to a frustrating search for someone to fall madly in love with.

Western culture is practically the only one that emphasizes falling in love as a basis for marriage. Other societies have developed techniques that control love, 60 including child marriage, physical segregation of men and women, or establishment of social taboos about who may be married and to whom. In some cases, family elders are given almost complete choice in the selection of mates. Besides considering marriage as a duty or a way of making social connections, children may believe that parents are more experienced and knowledgeable and can make a better decision about 65 a mate for them.

Some critics of romantic love say that an emphasis on romantic love encourages instability in marriage. European critic Denis de Rougemont argues that persons who fall in love will ignore considerations that affect the success of their relationship— factors such as similarity in ethnic, religious, and social backgrounds. A compatible 70 background is usually defined as one in which similarity of important characteristics promotes the success of the relationship. But the fact is that even in American culture, mating is not usually random. For instance, most couples share the same social class background and the same religion, race, and level of education. Parents are often able to exercise some control over a child's marriage partner by influencing social 75 contacts and by deciding what neighborhood the family will live in, what schools the child will attend, and so on.

A study of college students in the Boston area showed that similarity in age, educational plans, intelligence, and physical attractiveness is important in bringing couples together, even in a dating relationship. The couples in the study were also likely 80 to agree with each other on the importance of certain goals in their relationships, such as "finding a marriage partner" and "sexual activity."

A "refiltering model" may explain how couples consider whom they may marry. Early in a relationship, couples might use some sort of relatively "coarse filtering" mechanism. On a college campus, an individual might want to meet someone simi- 85 lar in intelligence and educational goals. When more important decisions are made about whether to continue dating and whom to marry, successively "finer filtering" may occur. As the relationship deepens and commitments are made, individuals may—and probably should—want even more similarity on whatever characteristics they consider important—intelligence, professional goals, physical attractiveness, and so on. Even when marriages occur between individuals who are not similar, other factors may operate to maintain the marriage. Couples with dissimilar religions, for instance, may find that their similar views about professional and personal goals are more important to them.

90

Love depends partly on seeing another as a person who will satisfy emotional and psychological needs. Today most persons view love as necessary for marriage. In a period of rapid social change, love probably has considerable value in maintaining relationships.[9]

95

Interest Rating.   Please rate the interest level of Reading 9 on the following 1–5 scale (circle one):

> 5—Very interesting
> 4—Fairly interesting
> 3—Mildly interesting
> 2—A little boring
> 1—Very boring

Difficulty Rating.   Please indicate how difficult Reading 9 was for you to understand on the following 1–5 scale (circle one):

> 5—Very difficult
> 4—Fairly difficult
> 3—Moderate
> 2—Fairly easy
> 1—Very easy

Comments: _____

_____

Comprehension Questions

Directions.   For questions 1–5, choose the answer that best completes the statement. For questions 6–10, write your response in the space provided. Base all answers on what you read in Reading 9 (you may refer to the reading when necessary).

_____   1. Medieval practitioners of courtly love believed that:
  a. Love was necessary for a successful marriage.
  b. The need for intimacy can be fully satisfied only in marriage.
  c. Love and marriage were contradictory.
  d. Love was incorruptible.

_____ 2. Rubin's view of love emphasizes:
   a. Romantic involvement.
   b. Similarities of background and education level.
   c. Intimacy and disclosure.
   d. Caring and sacrifice.

_____ 3. We can conclude from the article that:
   a. Marriage is more important for women than for men.
   b. Marriage partners usually have similar backgrounds.
   c. People of dissimilar backgrounds should not marry.
   d. Marriage partners usually have opposite temperaments.

_____ 4. Supporting material in the article consists primarily of:
   a. Personal experience and definitions.
   b. Explanation of theories.
   c. Examples and statistics.
   d. Emotional appeals and research results.

_____ 5. Which pattern of organization is used in the passage?
   a. Chronological order.
   b. Listing/enumeration.
   c. Comparison–contrast.
   d. Cause–effect.

Explain your answer: _____

_____

6. Explain the difference between eros and agape.

_____

_____

7. According to Rubin's research, how do men and women differ in their attitudes toward love and marriage?

_____

_____

_____

8. What are some of the criticisms of romantic love mentioned in the passage?

_____

_____

_____

9. According to the "refiltering model," how are marriage partners selected?

_____

_____

_____

10. In your opinion, what are the most important considerations in choosing a marriage partner?

_____

_____

_____

Vocabulary Exercise

Directions.   Use a multistrategy approach to determine the meaning of each of the following words. Write your definition in the space provided.

1. medieval (13) _____

2. exert (17) _____

3. compulsion (18) _____

4. dimensions (33) _____

5. virtually (36) _____

6. taboos (61) _____

7. instability (67) _____

8. compatible (69) _____

9. random (72) _____

10. filtering (83) _____

Essay Question

Directions.   On a separate sheet of paper, write a well-developed, half-page response to the following question:

What is love?

READING 10

Norms

Richard Schaeffer

Reading 10, taken from a sociology textbook, deals with an important social concept—norms. Read the selection to discover what norms are, how they operate, and how they affect our lives.

Pre-reading Exercises

Directions.   Preview the passage and use the following space to write your preview and pre-thinking notes.

Preview Notes

_____

_____

_____

_____

Pre-thinking Notes

_____

_____

All societies have particular ways of encouraging and enforcing what they view as appropriate behavior while discouraging and punishing what they consider to be improper conduct. "Put on some clean clothes for dinner" and "Thou shalt not kill" are both examples of norms found in American culture, just as respect for older peo-
5   ple is a norm of Japanese culture. *Norms* are established standards of behavior maintained by a society.

In order for a norm to become significant, it must be widely shared and understood. For example, when Americans go to the movies, we typically expect that people will be quiet while the film is showing. Because of this norm, an usher can tell a
10 member of the audience to stop talking so loudly. Of course, the application of this norm can vary, depending on the particular film and type of audience. People attending a serious artistic or political film will be more likely to insist on the norm of silence than those attending a slapstick comedy or horror movie.

Types of Norms.   Sociologists distinguish between norms in two ways. First,
15 norms are classified as either formal or informal. *Formal norms* have been written down and involve strict rules for punishment of violators. In American society, we often formalize norms into laws, which must be very precise in defining proper and improper behavior. In a political sense, *law* is the "body of rules, made by government for society, interpreted by the courts, and backed by the power of the
20 state." Laws are an example of formal norms, although not the only type. The requirements for a college major and the rules of a card game are also considered formal norms.

By contrast, *informal norms* are generally understood but are not precisely recorded. Rules of etiquette are a common example of informal norms. Our society
25 has no specific punishment or sanction for a person who eats peas with a knife. The most likely responses are stares and laughter.

Norms are also classified by their relative importance to society. *Mores* (pronounced "MOR-ays") are norms deemed highly necessary to the welfare of a society, often because they embody the most cherished principles of a people. Each
30 society demands obedience to its mores; violation can lead to severe penalties. Thus, American society has strong mores against murder, treason, and child abuse that have been institutionalized into formal norms. *Folkways* are norms governing everyday behavior whose violation raises comparatively little concern. Walking up a "down" escalator in a department store challenges our standards of appropriate behavior, but
35 it will not result in a fine or a jail sentence.

As Figure 1 illustrates, society is more likely to formalize mores than it is folkways. Nevertheless, folkways play an important role in shaping the daily behavior of members of a culture. Since they deal with so many facets of everyday life, it is impossible to offer a complete list of American folkways. Instead, let us look at one
40 fascinating example: the folkways which govern how far we should stand from people when interacting with them.

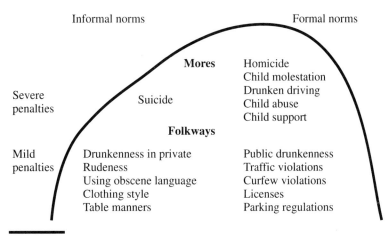

FIGURE 1

Penalties for Violation of Norms

Norms vary both in the degree to which they are formalized and in the severity of punishment when they are violated. In this figure, violation of norms at the top of the diagram leads to more harsh penalties than violation of norms at the bottom. Thus, people tend to receive more severe penalties for violating mores than folkways.

According to anthropologist Edward Hall, Americans and northern Europeans carry "bubbles" surrounding them. These invisible bubbles are actually cultural standards for appropriate distance between us and those with whom we communicate.

45 Hall suggests that we operate in four distance zones:

1. *Intimate distance*: Up to 18 inches. That is the distance of lovemaking and wrestling, comforting and protecting. It can also be an area of confrontation, as in "Get your face out of mine!" The use of this distance is not considered proper in public situations unless individuals are in a crowded environment, such as an elevator.

50 2. *Personal distance*: 18 inches to 4 feet. This is the conversational distance generally used with friends and acquaintances.

3. *Social distance*: 4 to 7 feet. Within this invisible bubble, we conduct impersonal business, such as purchasing products or interviewing strangers.

4. *Public distance*: 12 feet or more. This is viewed as proper distance for

55 public occasions. It will be used to separate a speaker or famous person from admiring fans.

It is important to note that these distances, while considered appropriate within American and northern European cultures, are not universally upheld in all cultures. Southern Europeans, Arabs, and Latin Americans stand closer together when con-

60 versing and are more likely to touch one another and maintain eye contact. This underscores the extent to which folkways (like mores) represent culturally learned patterns of behavior. If you were visiting another country and someone asked the correct time while standing only 15 inches away, you would be vividly reminded that American folkways are not shared by all peoples.

65   **Acceptance of Norms.**   Norms, whether mores or folkways, are not followed in all situations. In some cases, individuals evade a norm because they know it is weakly enforced. It is illegal in many states for teenagers to drink alcoholic beverages, yet underage drinking is common throughout the nation. In fact, teenage alcoholism is one of our country's serious social problems.

70   Interestingly, behavior that appears to violate society's norms may actually represent adherence to the norms of one's particular group. Teenage drinkers often break the laws of a state government in order to conform to the standards of a peer group. Similarly, a secret religious-criminal group in India known as the *Thugs* murdered and robbed travelers as a way of life. Members closely followed the norms of the reli-
75   gion—which dictated even how victims were to be killed—and believed that their behavior was commanded and approved by their sacred goddess, Kali.

          Norms are also violated in some instances because one norm conflicts with another. For example, suppose that you live in an apartment building and one night hear the screams of the woman next door, who is being beaten by her husband. If you
80   decide to intervene by ringing their doorbell or calling the police, your are *violating* the norm of "minding your own business" while, at the same time, *following* the norm of assisting a victim of violence.

          Even when norms do not conflict, there are always exceptions to any norm. The same action, under different circumstances, can cause one to be viewed either as a
85   hero or as a villain. Eavesdropping on telephone conversations is normally considered illegal and abhorrent. However, it can be done with a court order to obtain valid evidence for a criminal trial. A government agent who uses such methods to convict an organized crime baron may be praised for her or his actions. In our culture, even killing another human being is tolerated as a form of self-defense and is rewarded
90   in warfare.

          Some social norms are so widely accepted that they rarely need to be verbalized. They are implicitly taught by a society to its members, and there may be very little need to enforce them. An example of such a norm is the prohibition against cannibalism. It is unlikely that you can recall anyone telling you not to eat human
95   flesh. Nevertheless, as members of American society, we almost never consider doing so.

          Acceptance of norms is subject to change, as the political, economic, and social conditions of a culture are transformed. For example, under traditional American norms, a woman was expected to marry, raise children, and remain at home if her
100   husband could support the family without her assistance. However, these norms have been changing in recent decades, in part as a result of the contemporary feminist movement. As support for traditional norms weakens, individuals feel free to violate them more frequently and openly and are less likely to receive serious negative sanctions.[10]*

          Interest Rating.   Please rate the interest level of Reading 10 on the following 1–5 scale (circle one):

---

*Richard Schaeffer, *Sociology*, 2nd ed. (New York: McGraw-Hill, 1985), pp. 63–66. Used with the permission of McGraw-Hill.

5—Very interesting

4—Fairly interesting

3—Mildly interesting

2—A little boring

1—Very boring

Difficulty Rating.   Please indicate how difficult Reading 10 was for you to understand on the following 1–5 scale (circle one):

5—Very difficult

4—Fairly difficult

3—Moderate

2—Fairly easy

1—Very easy

Comments: _____

_____

Comprehension Questions

Directions.   For questions 1–5, choose the answer that best completes the statement. For questions 6–10, write your response in the space provided. Base all answers on what you read in Reading 10 (you may refer to the reading when necessary).

_____   1. The author's primary purpose is to:
   a. Explain what norms are and how they work.
   b. Explain why norms are followed.
   c. Persuade the reader that norms are important.
   d. Persuade the reader to follow norms.

_____   2. Supporting material in this passage includes:
   a. Definitions and examples.
   b. Personal experience and statistics.
   c. Statistics and research results.
   d. Quotes from experts and attempts at logical persuasion.

_____   3. If you violated a folkway, you would expect:
   a. A fine or jail sentence.
   b. Severe punishment.
   c. Mild disapproval.
   d. Praise.

_____   4. A conversation between a salesperson and a customer would probably occur at which distance zone?
   a. Intimate distance.
   b. Personal distance.
   c. Social distance.
   d. Public distance.

_____ 5. The author points out that:
- *a.* A norm has no effect if it is not verbalized.
- *b.* Formal norms are more important than informal norms.
- *c.* Norms controlling distance are the same in all cultures.
- *d.* All norms have exceptions.

6. Explain the difference between formal and informal norms.

_____

_____

_____

7. Explain the difference between folkways and mores.

_____

_____

_____

8. What two explanations does the author offer for teenage drinking?

_____

_____

_____

9. What is the main point of the concluding paragraph? Answer in a complete sentence of your own wording.

_____

_____

10. How do you feel when someone you are talking with stands too close? How might you react?

_____

_____

Vocabulary Exercise

Directions. Use a multistrategy approach to determine the meaning of each of the following words. Write your definition in the space provided.

1. sociologists (14) _____

2. formalize (17) _____

3. sanction (25) _____

4. facets (38) _____

5. vividly (63) _____

6. evade (66) _____

7. adherence (71) _____

8. intervene (80) _____

9. abhorrent (86) _____

10. contemporary (101) _____

Essay Question

Directions. On a separate sheet of paper, write a well-developed, half-page response to the following question:

Why are norms important? Why are they sometimes violated?

APPENDIXES

READING HABITS QUESTIONNAIRE

Directions. Answer each question honestly. Completing this questionnaire will make you more aware of your reading habits and interests and will provide information that will help your instructor work with you more effectively.

_____ 1. How often do you enjoy reading?
   a. Almost always.
   b. Often.
   c. Occasionally.
   d. Rarely or never.

_____ 2. Approximately how many hours a week do you read?
   a. None.
   b. 1–2.
   c. 3–6.
   d. 7–10.
   e. More than 10.

_____ 3. How frequently do you read the newspaper?
   a. Daily.
   b. Weekly.
   c. Occasionally.
   d. Rarely or never.

4. What newspaper(s) do you read?

_____

_____ 5. How often do you read magazines?
   a. Weekly.
   b. Monthly.
   c. Occasionally.
   d. Rarely or never.

6. List any magazines you read regularly.

_____

_____ 7. How often do you read and enjoy books?
    a. Frequently.
    b. Occasionally.
    c. Rarely or never.

_____ 8. How many books do you think you've read in your lifetime?
    a. None.
    b. 10 or less.
    c. 11–25.
    d. 26–50.
    e. 51–100.
    f. More than 100.

9. Name the last book you read and indicate when you read it.

_____

10. Name a book you especially enjoyed and would recommend to others. Include the author's name if you remember it.

_____

11. Which types of fiction reading do you enjoy? Check as many as apply:

_____ Mystery

_____ Science fiction

_____ Romance

_____ Thrillers

_____ Classics

_____ Historical novels

_____ Other (specify):

_____

12. Which of the following nonfiction subjects are of interest to you? Check as many as apply:

_____ Sports

_____ History

_____ Psychology

_____ Science

_____ Health/fitness

_____ Biography

_____ Other (specify):

_____

_____ 13. If you do not read much, what is the primary reason you don't
read more?
   a. I don't enjoy reading.
   b. I like to read but I'd rather do other things with my time.
   c. I have little free time.
   d. Other (specify):

_____

14. If you were to be assigned a research project on a subject of your
choice, what subject would you select?

_____

_____ 15. About how much television do you typically watch?
   a. None or very little.
   b. Several hours a week.
   c. 1–2 hours daily.
   d. More than 2 hours daily.

How to Preview a Book

The book preview is an essential first step toward effective use of your textbook or any other book you have been assigned to read. Previewing your text allows you to quickly discover what is in the book, how the material is organized, and how you can make best use of the book.

Follow these steps:

1. Note the *title*. What does the title suggest about the subject and emphasis of the book?
2. Note the *author's name, and* read any *background* information provided about the author.
3. Note the copyright *date*. How current is the book?
4. Read the *introduction* if it is short; skim it if it is long.
5. Study the *table of contents*. How many major sections does the book contain? How are chapters organized?
6. Determine if the book has a *glossary* and *index or other end material* that might be helpful to you.
7. Note any other *special features* of the book (e.g., review exercises, marginal summaries) by thumbing through one or two chapters.

C

PRONOUNCING UNFAMILIAR WORDS

When learning a new word, you should master its pronunciation as well as its meaning. Learning the pronunciation not only makes you more confident about using the word but also helps you remember the word more easily.

You can determine the pronunciation of an unfamiliar word from the dictionary's phonetic spelling. Normally, however, before looking up a word, we try to "sound it out" ourselves. Sometimes you may recognize a part of the word. For example, in the word *socioeconomic,* you recognize "economic"—and perhaps the "socio" as well.

Sometimes a new word may resemble other words you already know. For example, even if you have never seen the word *plight* before, you would guess that it rhymes with *light, night,* and *right,* because you are familiar with the *ight* pattern.

In this appendix, we will review three important strategies for determining the pronunciation of unfamiliar words: dividing words into syllables (syllabication), recognizing vowel sounds, and using the dictionary's pronunciation key.

Syllabication

Sometimes you have to sound a word out by breaking it down into syllables. In this section, we will review the syllabication rules. Though these rules are not foolproof, understanding them will enable you to approach new words with greater confidence.

What Is a Syllable?

The number of syllables in a word is equal to the number of vowel sounds in the word, which is equal to the number of times you open your mouth when pronouncing the word. A syllable, then, is a part of a word (or a whole word) that contains one and only one vowel sound. Every syllable must contain a vowel sound. A vowel sound may be spelled by the letters *a, e, i, o, u,* or *y,* or by a combination of two or three of these letters.

Pronounce the word *beautiful.* How many vowel sounds does it have? Notice that the first vowel sound is spelled by the letters *eau* (sounding like a long *u*). *Beautiful* has three vowel sounds—*beau-ti-ful*—and hence is a three-syllable word.

Study the following examples. Pronounce each word to yourself, noticing the location of the vowel sounds.

One-syllable words	plight, peak
Two-syllable words	exert, esteem
Three-syllable words	ruthlessness, vividly
Four-syllable words	motivation, originates

Exercise C–1. Syllable Count

Directions.   Pronounce each word to yourself (guess at the pronunciation if you are not sure) and write the number of syllables it contains.

1. Status   _____

2. affinity   _____

3. conditional   _____

4. warmth   _____

5. acceptance   _____

6. safety   _____

7. physiological   _____

8. stay   _____

9. pterodactyl   _____

10. photosensitivity _____

Syllabication Rules

Familiarize yourself with the following syllabication rules and complete each exercise as you come to it. Remember that the syllabication of a word reflects its pronunciation.

Rule 1.   Divide between double consonants.

Examples

esteem	es-teem
attain	at-tain

Rule 2.   Generally, divide before a single consonant. (Note that combinations like *ch, sh,* and *th* are treated as one consonant.)

Examples

enough	e-nough
motive	mo-tive
father	fa-ther

Exercise C–2. Syllabication

Directions. Rewrite each word in syllabicated form as shown in the examples above.

1. accept   _____
2. victims   _____
3. reason   _____
4. protect   _____
5. systems   _____
6. either   _____
7. adults   _____
8. order   _____
9. history   _____
10. gymnastic   _____
11. infrared   _____
12. confrontation   _____

Rule 3.   Divide after a single consonant when the vowel before it is short.

Examples

cabin	cab-in
level	lev-el

Exercise C–3. Syllabication

Directions.   Rewrite each word in syllabicated form.

1. never   _____
2. satisfy   _____
3. caper   _____
4. event   _____

    5. topic   _____

    6. silent   _____

    7. rapid   _____

    8. muscular   _____

    9. speculate   _____

   10. physical   _____

Rule 4.   Prefixes and suffixes are often divided as separate syllables.

Examples

    safety   <u>safe-ty</u>

    respect   <u>re-spect</u>

Rule 5.   Divide between the words that form a compound word (a compound word is a word formed by combining two smaller words).

Examples

    breakfast   <u>break-fast</u>

    classroom   <u>class-room</u>

Rule 6.   If a word ends with a consonant followed by *le,* divide before the consonant that is before the *le.* The consonant plus *le* form the last syllable of the word.

Examples

    puzzle   <u>puz-zle</u>

    able   <u>a-ble</u>

Exercise C–4. Syllabication

Directions.   Rewrite each word in syllabicated form.

    1. describe   _____

    2. vividly   _____

    3. lower   _____

    4. handle   _____

    5. nonsurvivors   _____

6. freedom   _____

7. maple   _____

8. undulate   _____

9. employees   _____

10. respond   _____

11. syllable   _____

12. predicament   _____

13. boathouse   _____

14. overhaul   _____

15. insoluble   _____

Rule 7.   When two neighboring vowels have distinct sounds, syllabication occurs between the vowels.

Examples

diet   _di-et_

Buick   _Bu-ick_

Exercise C–5. Syllabication

Directions.   Divide each word into syllables.

1. individual   _____

2. radio   _____

3. continuous   _____

4. dial   _____

5. hierarchy   _____

6. insomnia   _____

7. profound   _____

8. antagonize   _____

9. binomial   _____

10. spontaneous   _____

11. unusual   _____

12. genealogy   _____

Recognizing Vowel Sounds

When sounding out unfamiliar words, you must also guess at the vowel sounds. English vowels can be very confusing. You probably learned in elementary school about short and long vowels. Actually, there are over 20 vowel sounds in English. The dictionary shows four different sounds for the letter *a* alone.

In this section, we will review the English vowel sounds and the common vowel rules that help us predict the vowel sounds. Though there are many exceptions, understanding the vowel rules will enable you to make better predictions of the vowels in unfamiliar words and to use the dictionary more effectively when determining a word's pronunciation.

English Vowel Sounds

Speech is an alternation of vowel sounds and consonant sounds. The vowel sounds are continuable sounds made with the mouth open. Consonant sounds are made when the air is blocked by the lips, teeth, tongue, or throat.

The vowel letters are *a, e, i, o,* and *u.* The letter *y* may act as a vowel in some words. The letter *w* may be considered a vowel in combination with *a* or *o* (*aw, ow*). All words have at least one vowel.

English vowel sounds can be divided into five main groups: short vowels, long vowels, r-controlled vowels, vowel blends, and the weak vowel sound called the schwa.

Short Vowel Sounds.   The short vowel sounds are very common and should be learned. The short sound is the typical sound of the vowel when followed by a consonant within a syllable. A little curve over the vowel is the traditional symbol for the short vowel sound (ă, ĕ, ĭ, ŏ, ŭ).

Examples

short ă	at, ax, nap
short ĕ	end, egg, get
short ĭ	it, ill, bin, gym
short ŏ	ox, con, dot
short ŭ	up, cut, fun

Note that *y* often has the sound of *i* when it acts as a vowel.

You should learn the short vowel sounds if you do not already know them. The sentence "Fat Ed is not up" contains the five short vowel sounds.

Long Vowel Sounds.   The long vowel sound is the same as the name of the letter. A straight line over the vowel is the traditional symbol for the long vowel sound (ā, ē, ī, ō, ū).

Examples

long ā	ape, ace, wait
long ē	eve, sweet, ease
long ī	ice, bite, dine, sly
long ō	oak, hope, coat
long ū	use, cute, cube

R-Controlled Vowels. Vowels before *r* are usually neither short nor long but have a different sound, which blends with the *r*.

Examples

art, her, bird, torn, urge

Vowel Blends. Sometimes, two vowels blend together to form a special sound called a vowel blend or diphthong.

Examples

oi, oy	oil, toy
ou, ow	out, crown
au, aw	caught, law
oo	boot, cook

Note that *oo* has two slightly different sounds.

Schwa. Vowels in weak, unaccented, positions often have the schwa sound, which is the sound of *a* in *about*. Any vowel may have this sound. The dictionary uses this symbol (ə) for the schwa. The schwa is a very common vowel sound.

Examples

*a*lert, it*e*m, san*i*ty, c*o*nfess, alb*u*m

Silent Vowels. Sometimes a vowel has no sound. Usually, when one vowel in a syllable is silent, the other is long.

Examples

| ride | The *i* is long, the *e* is silent |
| steam | The *e* is long, the *a* is silent |

Vowel Rules

Study the following vowel rules and examples and complete the accompanying exercises. Use the rules when you are attacking an unfamiliar word.

The Short Vowel Rule

1. A single vowel at the beginning or middle of a syllable is usually short. (Another way to learn this is: a single vowel will be short if the syllable ends with a consonant.)

Examples

bŭzz, ăt-tĭc

Long Vowel Rules

2. A single vowel at the end of a syllable is often long.

Examples

trȳ, vē-tō

3. When in a syllable one vowel is followed by one consonant and an *e,* usually the first vowel is long and the *e* is silent.

Examples

slāve, dĭs-pūte

4. Sometimes, when two vowels are together in a syllable, the first is long and the second vowel is silent.

Examples

māin, swēet, bēad, cōat

Note that *ay* and *ow* may also produce a long vowel sound: swāy, lōw

Rules for Other Vowel Sounds

5. A vowel followed by *r* is usually not long or short.

Examples

cart, hurl

6. Sometimes, when two vowels are together in a syllable, they form a special sound called a vowel blend.

Examples

taught, saw
boil, toy

out, brown

boot, look

Note that we are considering *w* and *y* as vowels in these combinations.

7. A vowel in an unaccented position often has the schwa sound.

Examples

com-ply, fo-cus

Exercise C–6. Marking Vowel Sounds

Directions. Pronounce each word to yourself. Then mark the short and long vowel sounds in the word. Mark short vowels with a curve and long vowels with a straight line. Cross out silent vowels. Do not mark the other vowel sounds.

Examples

rē-lăx, wĭll-pow-er, tȳpe, glōat

1. ex-hib-it
2. vid-e-o-tapes
3. hyp-no-sis
4. do-main
5. ab-hor
6. por-tent
7. pro-found
8. sur-name
9. be-have
10. sim-u-late
11. in-duce
12. sym-bol-ic
13. spon-ta-ne-ous
14. ap-pre-hen-sion
15. val-id
16. bro-mide
17. hir-sute
18. cor-pu-lent

19. re-mu-ner-a-tion

20. de-void

Using the Dictionary's Pronunciation Key

You have now learned how to divide words into syllables and how to predict vowel sounds. When you analyze a new word, however, you cannot be sure of its pronunciation until you check the dictionary.

The dictionary shows the pronunciation of a word by spelling it phonetically. This means that the word is spelled exactly as it is pronounced with the accented syllables marked. The phonetic spelling is placed in parentheses immediately after the entry word.

pres-tige (prĕs tēzh´, -tēj´)

TABLE C–1   Phonetic Symbols

The following is a list of the symbols used by the *American Heritage Dictionary* to represent the sounds of the English language. Also provided are examples of common words that contain the sounds. Please remember that your dictionary may use different symbols for some of the sounds.

Symbol	Examples	Symbol	Examples
ă	pat	oi	noise
ā	pay	ŏŏ	took
âr	care	ōō	boot
ä	father	ou	out
b	bib	p	pop
ch	church	r	roar
d	deed, milled	s	sauce
ĕ	pet	sh	ship, dish
ē	bee	t	tight, stopped
f	fife, phase, rough	th	thin
g	gag	*th*	this
h	hat	ŭ	cut
hw	which	ûr	urge, term, firm, word, heard
ĭ	pit	v	valve
ī	pie	w	with
îr	pier	y	yes
j	judge	z	zebra, xylem
k	kick, cat, pique	zh	vision, pleasure, garage
l	lid, needle	ə	*a*bout, it*e*m, ed*i*ble, gall*o*p, circ*u*s
m	mum	ər	butter
n	no, sudden		
ng	thing		
ŏ	pot, horrid		
ō	toe, hoarse		
ô	caught, paw, for		

Note that there is one and only one sound for each symbol, though there may be several spellings for the same sound.

If you understand the phonetic code, you can learn the pronunciation of any word you find in the dictionary.

Each phonetic symbol has only one sound. Many of the phonetic symbols are the same as the actual letters, but some special symbols and markings are also used. It is usually the vowel markings that are less familiar to the average reader. Some dictionaries show the sound of each symbol at the bottom of each page; others include this information in the front of the dictionary (check your own dictionary to see where these symbols are located). The symbols are listed alphabetically, with each symbol followed by a word that contains that sound. Table C–1 shows the symbols used by the *American Heritage Dictionary* and many other dictionaries as well.

One of the phonetic symbols that you may not recognize is the schwa (ə). This symbol represents a weak vowel sound—the sound of *a* in *about*. The schwa is one of the most common vowel sounds in the English language. The schwa sound occurs only in weak, or unaccented, syllables.

The phonetic symbols are pretty much the same from dictionary to dictionary, but there are some minor differences. Familiarize yourself with the symbols used in your own dictionary and check the code when using a different dictionary. You do not need to memorize these symbols. However, you will become more confident about using them as they become more familiar to you. The exercises that follow will help you become better acquainted with phonetic spelling.

Exercise C–7. Recognizing Phonetic Spellings

Directions. Study the phonetic spelling to recognize each word below; then write the word, correctly spelled, in the adjoining space (you may use a dictionary or word book to check your spelling). Refer to Table C–1 as necessary. The first one is done as an example.

1. mŭn´ē   money
2. ə bŭv´   _____
3. fâr   _____
4. fär   _____
5. kro͞od   _____
6. bôt   _____
7. sho͝og´ ər   _____
8. kŏl´ ĭj   _____
9. kôrs   _____
10. ŭn´ yən   _____
11. pā´ shəns   _____

12. nŏl´ ĭj   _____

13. mĭs´ tə rē   _____

14. mĕzh´ ər   _____

15. sī kŏl´ ə jē   _____

16. ĭ lōō´ zhən   _____

17. ə tûr´ nē   _____

18. kŏn´ stə tōō´ shən   _____

19. sĕl´ ə fān   _____

20. skwäsh   _____

21. sûr´ kĭt   _____

22. ə brē´ vē ā´ shən   _____

23. kwäl´ ĭ tēs   _____

24. kŏn´ shəns   _____

25. ē fĭsh´ ənt   _____

Exercise C–8. Phonetic Writing

Directions.   Without consulting a dictionary, write the phonetic spelling for each of the following words. Carefully pronounce each word to yourself to determine the sounds you hear in it. When you are not sure of the phonetic symbol for a particular sound, refer to Table C–1.

1. love   _____

2. laugh   _____

3. car   _____

4. care   _____

5. enough   _____

6. chemist   _____

7. thought   _____

8. through   _____

9. machine   _____

10. echo   _____

Exercise C–9. Jokes in Phonetic Writing

Directions. The following jokes are written phonetically. Read them aloud or to yourself without skipping any words. If you are unsure of a phonetic symbol, refer to Table C–1.

1. Kär sĭknĭs ĭz thăt fēlĭng yōō gĕt ĕvrē mŭnth hwĕn thə pāmənt fôlz dōō.

2. Nouədāz thə fēlō hōō hăz thə härdĭst tīm stāĭng ĭn kŏlĭj ĭz thə kōch ŭv ə lōōzĭng tēm.

3. ə kŭstəmər wôkd ĭn tōō ə pĕt shŏp ănd spīd ə părət. Hē ămbəld ōvər tōō thə bûrd ănd sĕd, "Hā, stōōpĭd, kăn yōō tôk?"
   Thə bûrd ănsərd, "Yĕs, dŭmē, kăn yōō flī?"

4. Tōō dôgz wûr chāsĭng tōō răbĭts hwĕn wŭn răbĭt tûrnd tōō thə ŭthər ănd sĕd, "Lĕts stŏp hîr fôr ə fū mĭnĭts ănd outnŭmbər thĕm."

5. Wĭth mŏdərn mĕdĭsĭn dōōĭng sō wĕl ăt ĭnkrēsĭng our līf ĕkspĕctənsē, wēd bĕtər bē kârfəl əbout ădĭng tōō thə năshənəl dĕt—wē mīt hăv tōō pā ĭt ôf oursĕlvs, ĭnstĕd ŭv păsĭng ĭt ŏn.

Exercise C–10. Quotes in Phonetic Writing

Directions. The following quotes are written phonetically. Read them aloud or to yourself without skipping any words. If you are unsure of a phonetic symbol, refer to Table C–1.

1. Ū mŭst hăv lông-rānj gōlz tōō kēp ū frŭm bē´ ĭng frŭs´ trā tĭd bī shôrt-tûrm fāl´ yərz.—Charles C. Noble

2. Thə wā ī lōŏk ăt ĭt, ĭf ū wänt thə rān´ bō, ū gŏtə pŭt ŭp wĭth thə rān.—Dolly Parton

3. Ōn´ lē thē ĕj´ ōō kāt´ ĭd är frē.—Epictetus

4. Rēd´ ĭng fûr´ nĭsh əs our mīnd ōn´ lē wĭth mə tîr´ ē əlz ŭv năl´ ĭj; ĭt ĭs thĭnk´ ĭng māks hwŭt wē rēd ourz.—John Locke

5. Dōnt sā thə wûrld ōz ū ə lĭv´ ĭng; thə wûrld ōz ū nŭth´ ĭng; ĭt wŭz hîr fûrst.—Mark Twain

APPENDIX

D EXPANDED PREFIX LIST

This table lists 50 common prefixes. Prefixes in boldface type are discussed in Chapters 6 and 7.

Prefix	Meaning	Example Word
a, an	not, without	atypical, anarchy
ab	away	abduct
ad, at	toward	adhesive, attract
ambi	both	ambidextrous
ante	before	antedate
anti	against	antidote
auto	self	automobile
bi	two	bicycle
bene	good	benefit
cent(i)	hundred	century
circum	around	circumference
co, con, com, col, cor	with, together	cooperate, connect, company, collect, correlate
contra, counter	against	contradict, counterattack
de	down, from	descend
deci, deca	ten	decade
dia	through	diameter
dis	not, away	dissatisfied
equi, equa	equal	equidistant
ex, e	out	exhale, emit
extra	outside, beyond	extraordinary
hyper	excess, too much	hyperactive
in, im, il, ir	not	inactive, impossible, illegal, irregular
in, im, il, ir	in, into	invade, immigrate, illustrate, irrigate
inter	between	intermission

(continued)

Prefix	Meaning	Example Word
intra	within	intrastate
mal(e)	bad	malevolent
mega	large, great	megacycle
micro	small	microscope
mis	wrong	misjudge
mono	one	monotheism
multi	many	multivitamin
non	not	nonsense
oct	eight	octopus
omni	all	omnivorous
poly	many	polygon
post	after	postpone
pre	before	predict
pro	forward	progress
quad, quart	four	quadrant, quartet
re	again, back	repeat, reverse
retro	backward	retrospect
semi	half, partly	semicircle
sub	below	subway
super	over, above	supervise
syn, sym	with, together	synchronize, sympathy
tele	distant	telephone
trans	across	transport
tri	three	triangle
un	not	unknown
uni	one	university

E

EXPANDED LIST OF ROOTS

Roots in boldface type are discussed in Chapter 8.

Root	Meaning	Example Word
ann, enn	year	anniversary, perennial
arch	rule	monarchy
aqua	water	aquarium
astro, aster	star	astronaut, asteroid
aud, audit	hear	audible, auditorium
bio	life	biology
cap, cept	take, have	capture, reception
cess, cede	go	process, recede
chron	time	synchronize
cred	belief	credible
cur	run	current
dict	speak, say	predict
duct, duce	lead, carry	conductor, induce
fact, fic(t)	make, do	factory, fiction
fer	bear	transfer
geo	earth	geography
graph	write, draw	biography
gress, grad	step	progress, gradual
iatr(o)	medicine	pediatrician
ject	throw	eject
loc	place	location
loq	talk	eloquent
mater	mother	maternal
meter	measure	odometer
mit, miss	send	transmit, mission
mor(t)	die, death	immortal
mot, mob	move	motion, mobile
pater	father	paternal

(continued)

Root	Meaning	Example Word
path	feeling	sympathy
	disease	pathology
ped	children	pediatrician
ped, pod	foot	pedal, tripod
pel, puls	push	propel, propulsion
phon	sound	phonics
port	carry	transport
rupt	break	disrupt
scop(e)	look	telescope
scrib, script	write	inscribe, inscription
sect	cut	dissect
spect, spic	look	spectator
ten, tain	hold	retention, retain
terr	earth	territory
the(o)	god, religion	monotheism
tract	draw, pull	tractor
ven	come	convene
ver	truth	verdict
vert, verse	turn	invert, reverse
vis, vid	see	vision, video
viv, vit	life	survive, vital
voc, voke	call, voice	vocal, provoke
vor	eat	carnivorous

F

TEST–TAKING TIPS

This appendix provides suggestions to help you achieve better scores on tests. The suggestions will be divided into three sections: preparing for tests, taking tests, and reducing test anxiety.

Preparing for Tests

- *Develop regular study habits.* Preparation for a test begins the first day of class. Follow the suggestions made in Chapter 1 of this textbook to establish regular habits of study.
- *Review lecture notes frequently.* Reserve time each day to review and revise that day's notes and for selective review of notes taken in previous classes.
- *Use the reading strategies taught in this textbook* on all of your reading assignments. It is especially important that you use the suggestions made in Chapter 11 to develop strong skills in textbook underlining and notetaking.
- *Once a test is announced, plan your study time.* Identify the material to be covered and make up a study schedule. Plan more time than you believe you actually will need. Distribute your study time over several days to avoid cramming. Master your material section by section and review all of the material the night before the test.
- *Use active study methods.* Recite the material in your notes to yourself rather than just reading them over. Ask yourself questions and answer them. Record important points on index cards.
- *Choose study strategies that are consistent with your learning style.* If you are a visual learner, for example, you will benefit from outlines and charts (see the section on mapping in Chapter 11). If you are an auditory learner, you may wish to use tapes or to read study material aloud.
- *Use memory strategies.* When you have to memorize something, use memory techniques rather than rote memory. For example, you can use associations when you have to remember terms and their definitions.

• *Anticipate test questions.* Make up practice test questions that you think your instructor might ask and answer them.

• *When you believe you have learned your material, test yourself or have someone else test you.* Do not consider your preparation finished until you can demonstrate to yourself that you know all the material.

Taking Tests

• *Read and follow all directions carefully.* On most tests, you should answer all the questions. The only exception would be a test on which there is a penalty for wrong answers, such as the SAT.

• On *multiple-choice tests,* follow these steps:

   a. Read the stem of the question (the stem is the question itself before the answer choices). Make sure you are clear on the question before reading the answer choices. Paraphrase the stem (explain it to yourself) if it is long or complicated. You may also wish to underline key words and phrases within the stem.

   b. Always read all of the answer choices before selecting an answer.

   c. If the correct answer is not apparent, eliminate the least likely choices so you are left with the two most likely answers.

   d. Compare the two remaining answers, considering the emphasis in the stem of the question. Look for wording in one of the answers that may make it a weaker choice. For example, answers that say "always" or "never" are usually not correct.

   e. Once you have marked an answer, don't change it unless you have a definite reason to do so.

• On *essay tests,* follow these steps:

   a. Check the directions to be clear on how many of the questions you are to answer and see if the questions are equally weighted (worth the same number of points).

   b. Budget your time. If the questions are equally weighted, spend approximately the same amount of time on each question.

   c. Read each question twice to be sure you understand it clearly. Take a few seconds to mentally outline your answer before starting to write. If there is enough time, make a brief written outline of your answer or jot down some of the key points you want to include before writing out your response. Make sure you answer what the question asks. For example, if the question says "compare," be sure you do compare in your answer.

   d. Write as thorough an answer to each question as time allows.

   e. If time allows, read over your answers to be sure they are clearly and accurately worded.

Reducing Test Anxiety

It is normal to be a little anxious during a test. However, excessive anxiety can affect concentration and memory, causing errors that you would not normally make. If you get very anxious during tests and believe your anxiety is affecting your test performance, follow these suggestions:

• *Gain a thorough mastery of your test material.* The best defence sometimes is a good offense. The better you know the material, the less anxious you will be. Plan plenty of study time so that you can enter the test with the feeling that you have completely mastered the material.

• *Learn to use relaxation strategies.* Practice relaxation strategies (sometimes referred to as stress management techniques) on a regular basis. These include exercise, humor, meditation, visualization, and special breathing and muscle relaxation exercises (some of these techniques are discussed in Reading 3, "All Stressed Out"). Any good bookstore will have books and tapes that teach you how to use these techniques.

• *During the test, if you feel anxiety building, take a few long, slow, deep breaths and tell yourself "relax" or "I can do it."* Remind yourself that you are in control of the situation, that you know your material, and that you are going to do well on the test.

• *Tell yourself that it's OK to be anxious, but that you're not going to let your anxiety affect your thinking.* Return your concentration to the question at hand. If you are stuck on a particular question, skip over it and go on to the next one, returning to the more troublesome question at the end of the test.

Acknowledgments

Chapter 1

1. Reprinted with permission from Michelle Gagnon, "Learning Experience," *NECC Observer,* December 18, 1991, p. 2.
2. Les Brown, *Live Your Dreams* (New York: William Morrow & Co., Inc.), pp. 100–103. Copyright ©1992 by Les Brown Unlimited, Inc. By permission of William Morrow & Company, Inc.

Chapter 2

1. Excerpts from PSYCHOLOGY: AN INTRODUCTION, Fourth Edition, by Jerome Kagan and Ernest Havemann, copyright ©1980 by Harcourt Brace & Company, reprinted by permission by the publisher.

Chapter 3

1. Excerpts from PSYCHOLOGY: AN INTRODUCTION, Fourth Edition, by Jerome Kagan and Ernest Havemann, copyright ©1980 by Harcourt Brace & Company, reprinted by permission of the publisher.

Chapter 4

1. Reprinted with permission from the April 1989 Reader's Digest. ©1988 by Richard F. Graber, *Marathon World,* Issue 2, 1988, p. 16.
2. The dictionary entries in this chapter are from the *Webster's New World Dictionary* and the *American Heritage Dictionary of the English Language.*

Chapter 5

1. Muriel James and Dorothy Jongeward, *Born to Win,* Third Edition (pp. 179–183), ©1990 by Addison-Wesley Publishing Company, Inc. Reprinted by permission.

2. Jack Levin, "Riding the Rumor Mill," *Bostonia,* March–April 1990, p. 68. Used with permission.

3. Deborah Beroset Diamond, "All Stressed Out," *Ladies Home Journal,* November 1991. ©Copyright 1991, Meredith Corporation. All Rights Reserved. Reprinted from **Ladies' Home Journal** magazine.

4. Raymond Y. Chiao et al., "Faster than Light?" *Scientific American,* August 1993, p. 52.

5. William G. Nickels, James M. McHugh, and Susan M. McHugh, *Understanding Business,* 3rd ed. (Homewood, IL: Richard D. Irwin, 1993), pp. 108–9.

6. William Dement, *The Sleepwatchers* (Stanford, CA: Stanford Alumni Association, 1992), pp. 1–2.

7. Howard Zinn, *A People's History of the United States* (New York: Harper & Row, 1980), p. 124.

8. Jack Levin, "Sticks and Stones May Break . . . ," *Bostonia,* November–December 1989, p. 62. Used with permission.

9. The dictionary entries in this chapter are from the *Webster's New World Dictionary.*

Chapter 6

1. From PERSONAL ADJUSTMENT: *The Psychology of Everyday Life,* 3/e by Valerian J Derlega and Louis H Janda. Copyright ©1986, 1981 by Scott, Foresman and Company. Reprinted by permission of HarperCollins Publishers.

2. Richard Schaeffer, *Sociology* 2nd ed. (New York: McGraw-Hill, 1985), p. 176. Used with permission of McGraw-Hill.

3. "Milk," *The World Book Encyclopedia* (Chicago: World Book, Inc., 1993), Vol. 12, p. 460.

4. "Money." From *The World Book Encyclopedia.* ©1993 World Book, Inc. By permission of the publisher.

5. Migene Gonzalez-Wippler, *Dreams and What They Mean to You* (St. Paul: Llewellyn Publications, 1989), p. 22.

6. Thomas Gordon, *Teaching Children Self-Discipline* (New York: Times Books, 1989), p. 7.

7. Reprinted with the permission of Macmillan College Publishing Company from INTRODUCTION TO CRIMINAL JUSTICE, Third Edition by Robert D Pursley. Copyright ©1984 by Macmillan College Publishing Company, Inc.

8. Excerpts from PSYCHOLOGY: AN INTRODUCTION, Fourth Edition, by Jerome Kagan and Ernest Havemann, copyright ©1980 by Harcourt Brace & Company, reprinted by permission of the publisher.

9. Deborah Beroset Diamond, "All Stressed Out," *Ladies' Home Journal,* November 1991. ©Copyright 1991, Meredith Corporation. All Rights Reserved. Reprinted from **Ladies' Home Journal** magazine.

10. Maxine A Rock, *The Automobile and the Environment* (New York: Chelsea House Publishers, 1992), p. 25.

11. Thomas Gordon, *P.E.T.* (New York: New American Library, 1975), p. 13.

12. Mark McGee and David Wilson, *Psychology: Science and Application* (St. Paul: West Publishing, 1984), p. 108.

13. Dennis Wholey, *The Courage to Change* (Boston: Houghton Mifflin, 1984), p. 103.

14. From PERSONAL ADJUSTMENT: *The Psychology of Everyday Life,* 3/e by Valerian J Derlega and Louis H Janda. Copyright ©1986, 1981 by Scott, Foresman and Company. Reprinted by permission of HarperCollins Publishers.

Chapter 7

1. Zick Rubin and Elton B McNeil, *Psychology: Being Human.* Fourth Edition. Copyright ©1987. Used with permission of Houghton Mifflin Company.
2. From PERSONAL ADJUSTMENT: *The Psychology of Everyday Life,* 3/e by Valerian J Derlega and Louis H Janda. Copyright ©1986, 1981 by Scott, Foresman and Company. Reprinted by permission of HarperCollins Publishers.
3. Jack Halloran, *Applied Human Relations: An Organizational Approach,* 2nd ed. (Englewood Cliffs, NJ: Prentice Hall, 1983), p. 46.
4. Thomas Gordon, *P.E.T.* (New York: New American Library, 1975), p. xv.
5. "Home Street, USA: Living with Pollution," *Greenpeace Magazine,* November–December 1991, p. 10.
6. Carl Rogers, *On Becoming a Person* (Boston: Houghton Mifflin, 1961), p. 16.
7. Migene Gonzalez-Wippler, *Dreams and What They Mean to You* (St. Paul: Llewellyn Publications, 1989), p. 24.
8. Zick Rubin and Elton B McNeil, *Psychology: Being Human,* Fourth Edition. Copyright ©1987. Used with permission of Houghton Mifflin Company.
9. Tom McClellan et al., *Escape from Anxiety and Stress* (New York: Chelsea House Publishers, 1992), pp. 65–66. ©1992 by Chelsea House Publishers, a division of Main Line Book Co.
10. From PERSONAL ADJUSTMENT: *The Psychology of Everyday Life,* 3/e by Valerian J Derlega and Louis H Janda. Copyright ©1986, 1981 by Scott, Foresman and Company. Reprinted by permission of HarperCollins Publishers.
11. Excerpts from PSYCHOLOGY: AN INTRODUCTION, Fourth Edition, by Jerome Kagan and Ernest Havemann, copyright ©1980 by Harcourt Brace & Company, reprinted by permission of the publisher.
12. Migene Gonzalez-Wippler, *Dreams and What They Mean to You* (St. Paul: Llewellyn Publications, 1989), p. 21.
13. Cynthia A. Cutting, "Safer Driving at Any Age," *AAA World,* March–April 1993, p. 16.
14. Joseph T Straub and Stan Kossen, *Introduction to Business* (Boston: Kent Publishing Co., 1983), p. 319.
15. Tom McClellan et al., *Escape from Anxiety and Stress* (New York: Chelsea House Publishers, 1992). ©1992 by Chelsea House Publishers, a division of Main Line Book Co.
16. Joseph T Straub and Stan Kossen, *Introduction to Business* (Boston: Kent Publishing Co., 1983).
17. Clarence Lusane, *Pipedream Blues: Racism and the War on Drugs* (Boston: South End Press, 1991), p. 23.

Chapter 8

1. From PERSONAL ADJUSTMENT: *The Psychology of Everyday Life,* 3/e by Valerian J Derlega and Louis H Janda. Copyright ©1986, 1981 by Scott, Foresman and Company. Reprinted by permission of HarperCollins Publishers.
2. Excerpts from PSYCHOLOGY: AN INTRODUCTION, Fourth Edition, by Jerome Kagan and Ernest Havemann, copyright ©1980 by Harcourt Brace & Company, reprinted by permission of the publisher.
3. From PERSONAL ADJUSTMENT: *The Psychology of Everyday Life,* 3/e by Valerian J Derlega and Louis H Janda. Copyright ©1986, 1981 by Scott, Foresman and Company. Reprinted by permission of HarperCollins Publishers.

4. Richard Schaeffer, *Sociology,* 2nd ed. (New York: McGraw-Hill, 1985), pp. 235–36. Used with permission of McGraw-Hill.
5. From PERSONAL ADJUSTMENT: *The Psychology of Everyday Life,* 3/e by Valerian J Derlega and Louis H Janda. Copyright ©1986, 1981 by Scott, Foresman and Company. Reprinted by permission of HarperCollins Publishers.
6. Zick Rubin and Elton B McNeil, *Psychology: Being Human,* Fourth Edition. Copyright ©1987. Used with permission of Houghton Mifflin Company.
7. Walter Pauk, *How to Study in College,* 4th ed. (Boston: Houghton Mifflin, 1989), p. 11.
8. Jack Rettig, *Career Exploration and Decision* (Belmont, CA: David S. Lake Publishers, 1986).
9. From THE REAL LIFE NUTRITION BOOK by Susan Finn and Linda Stern Kass. Copyright ©1992 by Susan Finn and Linda Stern Kass. Used by permission of Viking Penguin, a division of Penguin Books USA Inc.
10. Jack Halloran, *Applied Human Relations: An Organizational Approach,* 2nd ed. (Englewood Cliffs, NJ: Prentice Hall, 1983), p. 45.
11. Richard Schaeffer, *Sociology,* 2nd ed. (New York: McGraw-Hill, 1985), p. 238. Used with permission of McGraw-Hill.
12. Robert Schaeffer, "Car Sick: Automobiles Ad Nauseum," *Greenpeace Magazine,* May–June 1990, p. 13.
13. Judy Christrup, "Sharks on the Line," *Greenpeace Magazine,* January–February 1991, p. 17.
14. David Rains Wallace, "The Forever Forests," *Greenpeace Magazine,* September–October 1990, p. 9. Used with permission.
15. Jared Diamond, "Playing Dice with Megadeath," *Discover,* April 1990, p. 57.
16. Jared Diamond, "Playing Dice with Megadeath," *Discover,* April 1990, p. 58.
17. Patricia Garfield, *Creative Dreaming* (New York: Ballantine Books, 1989), p. 11.
18. Patricia Garfield, *Creative Dreaming* (New York: Ballantine Books, 1989), p. 13.
19. Muriel James & Dorothy Jongeward, *Born to Win,* Third Edition (p. 47), ©1990 by Addison-Wesley Publishing Company, Inc. Reprinted by permission.
20. Jack Halloran, *Applied Human Relations: An Organizational Approach,* 2nd ed. (Englewood Cliffs, NJ: Prentice Hall, 1983), pp. 36–37.
21. Richard Schaeffer, *Sociology,* 2nd ed. (New York: McGraw-Hill, 1985), p. 254. Used with permission of McGraw-Hill.

Chapter 9

1. EXCERPTS from LOVE IS NEVER ENOUGH by AARON T BECK. Copyright ©1988 by Aaron T. Beck, MD. Reprinted by permission of HarperCollins Publishers, Inc.
2. John Langone, *Our Endangered Earth* (Boston: Little, Brown & Co., 1992), p. 56.
3. Jack Halloran, *Applied Human Relations: An Organizational Approach,* 2nd ed. (Englewood Cliffs, NJ: Prentice Hall, 1983), p. 37.
4. Thomas Gordon, *P.E.T.* (New York: New American Library, 1975), p. 92.
5. Richard Schaeffer, *Sociology,* 2nd ed. (New York: McGraw-Hill, 1985), p. 237. Used with permission of McGraw-Hill.

Chapter 10

1. From PERSONAL ADJUSTMENT: *The Psychology of Everyday Life,* 3/e by Valerian J Derlega and Louis H Janda. Copyright ©1986, 1981 by Scott, Foresman and Company. Reprinted by permission of HarperCollins Publishers.

2. Deborah Beroset Diamond, "All Stressed Out," *Ladies Home Journal,* November 1991. ©Copyright 1991, Meredith Corporation. All Rights Reserved. Reprinted from **Ladies' Home Journal** magazine.

3. Edgar Allan Poe, "A Dream Within a Dream," *Poe* (New York: Dell Publishing Co., Inc., 1959).

4. From THE REAL LIFE NUTRITION BOOK by Susan Finn and Linda Stern Kass. Copyright ©1992 by Susan Finn and Linda Stern Kass. Used by permission of Viking Penguin, a division of Penguin Books USA Inc.

5. Zick Rubin and Elton B McNeil, *Psychology: Being Human,* Fourth Edition. Copyright ©1987. Used with permission of Houghton Mifflin Company.

6. EXCERPTS from LOVE IS NEVER ENOUGH by AARON T BECK. Copyright ©1988 by Aaron T. Beck, MD. Reprinted by permission of HarperCollins Publishers, Inc.

7. Richard Schaeffer, *Sociology,* 2nd ed. (New York: McGraw-Hill, 1985), p. 222. Used with permission of McGraw-Hill.

8. Josie Hadley and Carol Staudacher, *Hypnosis for Change,* 2nd ed. (Oakland, Calif.: New Harbinger Publications, 1989), p. 11. Reprinted with permission.

9. Susan Terkel, *Should Drugs Be Legalized?* (New York: Franklin Watts, Inc., 1990), p. 25.

10. "Disappearing Ozone," publication of the Mineralogical and Geological Museum of Harvard University, 1991.

11. Laurence Morehouse and Leonard Gross, *Total Fitness in 30 Minutes a Week* (New York: Pocket Books, 1976), pp. 61–62. COPYRIGHT ©1975 by Laurence E Morehouse, PhD. Reprinted by permission of Simon & Schuster, Inc.

12. Richard Schaeffer, *Sociology,* 2nd ed. (New York: McGraw-Hill, 1985), p. 270. Used with permission of McGraw-Hill.

13. Tom McClellan et al., *Escape from Anxiety and Stress* (New York: Chelsea House Publishers, 1992), pp. 58–59. ©1992 by Chelsea House Publishers, a division of Main Line Book Co.

14. Richard Schaeffer, *Sociology,* 2nd ed. (New York: McGraw-Hill, 1985), p. 228. Used with permission of McGraw-Hill.

15. Richard Schaeffer, *Sociology,* 2nd ed. (New York: McGraw-Hill, 1985), pp. 174–75. Used with permission of McGraw-Hill.

16. Richard Schaeffer, *Sociology,* 2nd ed. (New York: McGraw-Hill, 1985), p. 248. Used with permission of McGraw-Hill.

Chapter 11

1. Jeanne McDowell, "Are Women Better Cops?" *Time,* February 17, 1992, pp. 70–72. Copyright 1992 Time Inc. Reprinted by permission.

2. Richard Schaeffer, *Sociology,* 2nd ed. (New York: McGraw-Hill, 1985), pp. 322–23. Used with permission of McGraw-Hill.

3. EXCERPTS from PSYCHOLOGY: AN INTRODUCTION, Fourth Edition, by Jerome Kagan and Ernest Havemann, copyright ©1980 by Harcourt Brace & Company, reprinted by permission of the publisher.

4. EXCERPT from MARRIAGE AND FAMILY DEVELOPMENT, 6TH ED. by EVELYN MILLIS DUVALL & BRENT C MILLER. Copyright ©1985 by Harper & Row, Publishers, Inc. Reprinted by permission of HarperCollins Publishers, Inc.

5. Zick Rubin and Elton B McNeil, *Psychology: Being Human,* Fourth Edition. Copyright ©1987. Used with permission of Houghton Mifflin Company.

6. Paul Savoy, "Time for a Second Bill of Rights," *The Nation* Magazine, June 17, 1991, pp. 813–15. This article is reprinted from *The Nation* magazine. ©The Nation Company, Inc. Used with permission.

7. Excerpts from "Tell Me More: The Art of Listening" by Brenda Ueland from *Strength to Your Sword Arm: Selected Writings* (Holy Cow! Press, 1993). Reprinted by permission of the publisher.

8. "Martin Luther King, Jr." From *The World Book Encyclopedia.* ©1993 World Book, Inc. By permission of the publisher.

Chapter 12

1. Courtland Bovée and John Thill, *Business Communications Today,* 2nd ed. (New York: McGraw-Hill, Inc., 1989), pp. 32–36. Reproduced with permission of McGraw-Hill.

2. Lori Smidt, from "Campus Comedy." Reprinted with permission from the August 1992 Reader's Digest. Copyright ©1992 by The Reader's Digest Assn., Inc.

3. ©Nash Notes—reprinted by permission. All rights reserved.

4. Wink Dulles, "How Safe Are Over-the-Counter Drugs and Driving?" *AAA World,* January–February 1992, pp. 6–7. Copyright 1992 *AAA World* magazine: reprinted with permission.

5. Muriel James & Dorothy Jongeward, *Born to Win,* Third Edition (p. 1), ©1990 by Addison-Wesley Publishing Company, Inc. Reprinted by permission.

6. Reprinted by permission of The Putnam Publishing Group from CHILDHOOD by Bill Cosby. Copyright ©1991 by William H. Cosby, Jr.

7. Manuel Ramirez, "Identity Crisis in the Barrios," from *The Chicano Today* (New York: New American Library, 1970), p. 57. ©May 1970 Music Educators Journal. Used by permission of Music Educators National Conference.

8. William G Nickels, James M McHugh, and Susan M McHugh, *Understanding Business,* 3rd ed. (Homewood, IL: Richard D. Irwin, 1993), p. 43.

9. Reprinted with the permission of Macmillan College Publishing Company from INTRODUCTION TO CRIMINAL JUSTICE, Third Edition by Robert D Pursley. Copyright ©1984 by Macmillan College Publishing Company, Inc.

Chapter 13

1. PAGES 140–144 from LA RAZA: THE MEXICAN AMERICANS by STAN STEINER. Copyright ©1969, 1970 by Stan Steiner. Reprinted by permission of HarperCollins Publishers, Inc.

2. Zick Rubin and Elton B McNeil, *Psychology: Being Human,* Fourth Edition. Copyright ©1987. Used with permission of Houghton Mifflin Company.

3. Alexs Pate, "Rap: The Poetry of the Streets," *USA Weekend,* February 5–7, 1993, pp. 19–20. Reprinted with permission.

4. Robert Schaeffer, "Car Sick: Automobiles Ad Nauseum," *Greenpeace Magazine,* May–June 1990, pp. 14–15.

5. From HEAD FIRST: THE BIOLOGY OF HOPE by Norman Cousins. Copyright ©1989 by Norman Cousins. Used by permission of Dutton Signet, a division of Penguin Books USA Inc.

6. Frank Drake and Dava Sobel, *Is Anyone Out There?* (New York: Dell/Delacorte Press, 1992), pp. xi–xii. Reprinted with permission of Dell, a division of Bantam, Doubleday, Dell Publishing Group, Inc.

7. Jim Ballard, "Baseball's Enduring Hold on America," *USA Today,* July 1992, pp. 20–21. Reprinted with permission.
8. William G Nickels, James M McHugh, and Susan M McHugh, *Understanding Business,* 3rd ed. (Homewood, IL: Richard D. Irwin, 1993), pp. 9–10.
9. Franklin E Zimring, "Firearms, Violence and Public Policy," *Scientific American,* November 1991, p. 48.
10. "There's Protein in Them There Bugs," Newburyport *Daily News,* May 19, 1993. Reprinted with permission of the Associated Press.
11. Reprinted from LATINOS, A Biography of the People by Earl Shorris, by permission of W. W. Norton & Company, Inc. Copyright ©1992 by Earl Shorris.
12. David K Wills, "Bear #134," *Humane Society of the United States News,* Spring 1991, p. 13. Reprinted from the *HSUS News,* published by The Humane Society of the United States, Washington, D.C. Used with permission.
13. William G Nickels, James M McHugh, and Susan M McHugh, *Understanding Business,* 3rd ed. (Homewood, IL: Richard D. Irwin, 1993), p. 613.

Chapter 14

1. Vicki Kemper, "Biting the Bullet," *Common Cause Magazine,* Winter 1992, pp. 16–22. Used with permission.
2. Jeff Donn, "Poverty Haunts College Students," Newburyport *Daily News,* March 23, 1992, p. A9. Reprinted with permission of the Associated Press.
3. William G Nickels, James M McHugh, and Susan M McHugh, *Understanding Business,* 3rd ed. (Homewood, IL: Richard D. Irwin, 1993), p. 41.
4. Denis Waitley, *Psychology of Success: Developing Your Self-Esteem* (Burr Ridge, IL: Richard D. Irwin, 1993), pp. 130–31. Reprinted with permission.

Additional Readings

1. Denis Waitley, *Psychology of Success,* 2nd ed. (Burr Ridge, IL: Richard D. Irwin, 1993), pp. 6–10. Reprinted with permission.
2. Les Brown, *Live Your Dreams* (New York: William Morrow & Co., Inc.), pp. 62–66. Copyright ©1992 by Les Brown Unlimited, Inc. By permission of William Morrow & Company, Inc.
3. Deborah Beroset Diamond, "All Stressed Out," *Ladies Home Journal,* November 1991. ©Copyright 1991, Meredith Corporation. All Rights Reserved. Reprinted from **Ladies' Home Journal** magazine. Used with permission.
4. Joseph Straub and Stan Kossen, *Introduction to Business* (Boston: Kent Publishing Co., 1983), pp. 7–9. Reprinted with permission.
5. Joseph Straub and Stan Kossen, *Introduction to Business* (Boston: Kent Publishing Co., 1983), pp. 265–70. Reprinted with permission.
6. From THE REAL LIFE NUTRITION BOOK by Susan Finn and Linda Stern Kass. Copyright ©1992 by Susan Finn and Linda Stern Kass. Used by permission of Viking Penguin, a division of Penguin Books USA Inc.
7. Richard Shenkman, *Legends, Lies and Cherished Myths of American History* (New York: William Morrow & Co., Inc., 1988), pp. 132–36. Copyright ©1988 by Richard Shenkman. By permission of William Morrow & Company.

8. Mick Fedullo, *Light of the Feather* (New York: William Morrow and Company, Inc., 1992), pp. 107–14. Copyright ©1992 by Mick Fedullo. By permission of William Morrow & Company.

9. From PERSONAL ADJUSTMENT: *The Psychology of Everyday Life,* 3/e by Valerian J Derlega and Louis H Janda. Copyright ©1986, 1981 by Scott, Foresman and Company. Reprinted by permission of HarperCollins Publishers.

10. Richard Schaeffer, *Sociology,* 2nd ed. (New York: McGraw-Hill, 1985), pp. 63–66. Used with permission of McGraw-Hill.

INDEX

AAA, 277
AAA World Magazine, 277
Acceptance needs, 94
Adams, Abigail, 223
Adams, John, 223
Alda, Alan, 88
Alive, 93
American Automobile Association;
    see AAA
American Heritage College
    Dictionary, 55, 439
American Humane Association, 330
American Pharmaceutical Associa-
    tion, 277
American University, 235, 242
Amherst College, 337, 338
Angelou, Maya, 302
Anthony, Susan B., 224
Are Women Better Cops (McDowell),
    233–37
Arrested Development, 303, 304
Aserinksy, 176
Assigned work, appearance of, 5
Associations, using, 201
Attitudes, 3–4

Barber, Theodore X., 120, 125
Barr, William, 327
In the Barrios of the City of Angels
    (Steiner), 289–93
Baseball: A History of America's Game
    (Rader), 314

Bayer Company, 210
Behan, Cornelius, 235, 242
Belknap, Joanne, 235, 242
Belushi, John, 205
Benetar, Pat, 88
Bias, Len, 205
Bill of Rights, 258
Biting the Bullet (Kemper), 325–30
Blake, Fanchon, 236, 243
Bliss, Ronald, 88
Body, 219–28
    patterns of organization, 220
    supporting material, 219–20
Boredom, overcoming, 4
Borker, Ruth, 190
Brady Bill, 329
Breaks, taking, 5
Brecht, Bertolt, 291
A Brief History of Drug Addiction in
    America (Wintner), 209–12
Brown, Les, 6–7
Bureau of Indian Affairs (BIA), 206
Bureau of Statistics, 328
Burke, Kathleen, 236, 243
Bush, George, 326, 327
Butler, Charles, 277

Cable Network News (CNN), 302
Career, decisions about, 146–48
Carroll, Lewis, 84
Cause-effect, 221
Centers for Disease Control (CDC), 328

Character and Cops: Ethics in Policing
    (Delattre), 235, 242
Child Development Institute, 244
Christopher commission, 235
Chronological order, 220–21
Cincinnati, University of, 235
Civil Rights Act of 1964, 261
Class
    attendance, 4
    preparation, 4
Clifton, Lucille, 302
Clinton, Bill, 327, 330
Coca-Cola, 211
Cold pressor response, 120, 124
College
    high school, 1–3
    suggestions for success, 3–6
Community Poverty Council, 291
Comparison-contrast, 221
Comprehension, 185
    monitoring, 82–86
Computers, and the workplace,
    150–51
Conclusions, drawing, 311–16
Contact hypothesis, 226
Context; *see also* Dictionary
    using, 45
Context clues
    direct, 24–25
    indirect, 25–27
    mixed practice, 27–28
    types of, 23–27
    using, 22–23

Contextual associations; *see* Word associations
Contrast clues, 23
Conversational etiquette, rules of, 192–95
Conversational styles, 190
Cop Killer, 302
Coral Way Elementary, 319
Cortes, 309
Couper, David, 237
Cross-references, 61–62
Cypress Hill, 303

D, Chuck, 302
Dahmer, Jeffrey, 302
Daniel, Fluor, 282
Das EFX, 303
de Beauvoir, Simone, 224
Declaration of Independence, 223
Definition clues, 23
Definitions, simplifying, 80–82
Delattre, Edwin, 235, 242
Delay, 51
del Castillo, Bernal Díaz, 291
Derived forms, 60
Detroit, University of, 235, 242
DeWitte, Helen, 235, 236, 242, 243
Dictionary, 54–70; *see also* Context
    choosing a definition, 62
    finding the word, 62–63
    phonetic symbols, 437
    practicing, 64–70
    pronunciation key, 437–39
    remembering the definition, 63–64
    unabridged, 56
    understanding the entry, 56–62
    using, 54–55
    when to use, 55
    which to use, 55–56
Dictionary entry, 56–62
    cross-references, 61
    derived forms, 60
    entry word, 56
    etymology, 58
    finding, 62–63
    homographs, 61
    idioms, 59
    parts of speech label, 57
    plurals and verb endings, 58–59
    pronunciation, 57
    synonyms, 60–61
    usage and subject labels, 59

DiMaggio, Joe, 314
Diplomacy, 194
Disagreement, 51
Disposable Heroes of Hiphoprisy, 303
Dissociation, 120
Dorchester District Court, 88
Dove, Rita, 302
Dracula, 88
Drake Equation, 313
Dreams, types of, 34–35
Dylan, Bob, 88

Ebenezer Baptist Church, 261
Eliot, Robert S. M.D., 84
Entry word, 56
Enumeration; *see* Listing
Esteem needs, 94
Etymology, 58
European Business School, 283
Exxon, *Valdez* disaster, 85
Eye behavior, 268

Facial expressions, 268
Fact and opinion, distinguishing, 308–10
FBI, 227, 327, 328
The Fed, 84–85
Federal Bureau of Investigation; *see* FBI
Federal Bureau of Prisons, 327
Federal Reserve Bank; *see* The Fed
Federal Reserve System, 84–85
The Feminine Mystique (Friedan), 224
Foley, Tim, 235, 242
Freud, Sigmund, 33, 34
Friedan, Betty, 224
Fulwood, Isaac, 326–30
Fyfe, James, 235, 242, 327, 328, 330

Gabor, Zsa Zsa, 89
Garland, Judy, 88, 205
Gehrig, Lou, 314
Gerlach, Larry, 314
Gestures, 268
Goal questions, 98–104
Goals
    setting, 6–7, 29
    solid, 7
Goals Get You Going (Brown), 6–7
Goldberg, Whoopie, 89
Gould, Elliot, 88
Gray, William H., 338

Habits, 4–6
Hanna, Kay, 236, 243
Harre, Rom, 88
Harrison Act, 211
Harvard, Beverly, 236, 243
Harvard University, 33
Haskins, Ronald, 244
Hazy Shade of Criminal, 302
Help, asking for, 5
Homographs, 61
Herman, Pee Wee, 89
Hilgard, Ernest, 119, 120, 126
Hilgard, Josephine, 119
Hippocrates, 257
Hobson, J Allan, 33
Holloday, Judy, 236, 243
Hornsby, Rogers, 314
The House, 302
House of Pain, 303
Hoyler, Maureen, 338
Hughes, Langston, 217
Hypnosis, 119, 218
    and pain reduction, 120
    susceptibility, 119
Hypnosis (Rubin and McNeil), 117–21
Hypnotic amnesia, 119, 162

Ice Cube, 303
Ice-T, 302
Idioms, 59
I Have a Dream (King), 261
Index crimes, 227
Inference
    and humor, 274–75
    and nonfiction reading, 276
    and poetry, 275–76
    and short passages, 277–84
Institute for Environmental Management, 283
Institute of Stress Medicine, 84
Interest inventory, 147
Interests, individual, 9–10
International Business Machines (IBM), 339
Interpreting Your Dreams (Wintner), 31–35
Interruptions, 193
Introduction, 215–19

James, William, 45
Job satisfaction, sources of, 148–50

Johnson, Ben, 205
Johnson, Lyndon B., 261
Joplin, Janis, 205
Jordan, Michael, 309
The Journal of American Medical Association, 328
Jung, Carl, 33, 34, 257
Justice Department, 327

Kane, Big Daddy, 303
Kelly, Sharon Pratt, 326
Kennedy, John F., 261
Kibbe, Dr. Art, 277
King, Dr. Martin Luther, 160, 260–61
King, Rodney, 235, 241
Kleitman, 176
Krisberg, Barry, 328, 330
Kriss Kross, 303

L.A.P.D., 235, 241
La Raza: The Mexican Americans (Steiner), 289
Learning style, 9–10, 184–85
    discovering, 5
Linehan, Marsha, 50–52
Listening signals, 193
Listing, 221
Los Angeles Police Department; *see* L.A.P.D.
Los Angeles Times, 328
Love Is Never Enough (Beck), 189–94
Low-frequency words, 201
Luna, Eileen, 235, 242

Main ideas
    and details, 154–62
    implied, 162–64
    reading for, 124–32
Maltz, Daniel, 190
Mapping, 249–53
March on Washington, 261
Martin, Dallas, 338
Martin, Susan, 236, 243
Maslow, Abraham, 92–95, 98–99
Maslow's self-actualized individual, 94–95, 98
Maslow's Theory of Human Needs (Derlega and Janda), 91–96
Matteson, David, 147

MC Lyte, 303
The Men in Blue: A Conversation with Baseball Umpires (Gerlach), 314
Merriam Webster's Collegiate Dictionary, 55
Mexican Revolution, 291
Mistakes, making, 4
Montaigne, 33
Mott, Lucretia, 224

NAACP, 160
Names and Identity (James and Jongeward), 73–76
National Association for the Advancement of Colored People; *see* NAACP
National Association of Student Financial Aid Administrators, 338
National Committee for Prevention of Child Abuse, 330
National Council of Educational Opportunity Associations, 338
National Council on Crime and Delinquency, 328
National Park Service, 320
National Radio Astronomy Observatory, 313
National Rifle Association (NRA), 227
National Transportation Safety Board, 85
Naughty by Nature, 303
Nebraska-Lincoln, University of, 314
Nicknames, 75–76
Nobel Peace Prize, 261
Nonverbal communication
    functions of, 267–68
    importance of, 266–67
    varieties of, 268–69
Nonverbal Communication (Bovée and Thill), 265–69
North Carolina, University of, 244
Notetaking, 244–48, 254–55
Novello, Antonia, 328

O'Connor, Ellen, 329
On the Move: The Status of Women in Policing (Martin), 236, 243
Operation Clean Sweep, 328
Opium Wars, 221
Organization, recognizing, 215

Orne, Martin, 121
Ortiz, Angel, 337–38
Outlaw, Darrel, 88
Overgeneralizing, 51

Paragraph
    practice, 140–41
    writing, 131–32
Parents Without Partners, 244
Parks, Rosa, 260
Partner's channel, tuning in, 192–93
Pearl, Minnie, 89
Pell grants, 338
Perez, Eduardo, 292–93
Personal appearance, 269
Pete Rock & CL Smooth, 303, 304
Phoenix, River, 89
Plurals, 57
P.M. Dawn, 303
Poe, Edgar Allan, 32, 216
Posthypnotic suggestion, 119, 162
Postures, 268
Prefixes, 105–11
    common, 132–38
    expanded list, 443–44
    list of common, 138
    negative, 105
    number, 108
    root and suffix, 104–5
Prep for Prep, 337, 338
Pre-reading strategies
    pre-thinking, 41–44
    previewing, 39–41, 427
Presley, Elvis, 119, 162, 167, 205
Prior knowledge, recalling, 42–43
Proctor & Gamble, 339
Pronunciation
    in dictionary, 57
    syllabication, 429–30
    syllabication rules, 430
    of unfamiliar words, 429–30
Psychological needs, 93, 98
Public Enemy, 302
Punctuation, 24
Pure Food and Drug Act, 211

Quality of work, improving, 151
Queen Latifah, 303
Questions
    asking, 193–94
    raising, 42–43

Rader, Benjamin, 314
Random House Dictionary, 55
Reader's Digest, 275
Reading strategies, 296–311
 evaluating, 308–16
 reacting, 307
 reviewing, 296–97, 299–300, 302–5
 self-testing, 298
 summarizing, 297–98, 298
Reagan, Ronald, 326, 327
Rewarding yourself, 6
Richardson, Rory, 277
Rogers, Carl, 113
Rogers, Don, 205
Roots, 164–74
 common, 165–66
 expanded list, 445–46
 list of common, 174
 and prefix and suffix, 104–5
Rosenthal, Kristine, 244
Ruth, Babe, 314

Safety needs, 93–94
Salt-N-Pepa, 303
Search for extraterrestrial intelligence
 (SETI), 313
The Second Sex (de Beauvoir), 224
Self-actualization needs, 94
Self-assessment, 8–9
 revisited, 183–84
Self-confidence, 4
Self-evaluation, use of, 185–86
Serious, Yahoo, 89
Shea, Kelly, 234, 241
Sheldon, 257
Simons, Gary, 338
Skills, applying, 186–87
Sleep
 need for, 17–18
 ordinary and paradoxical, 16–17
Sleep and Dreams (Kagan and Have-
 mann), 15–18
Smart, Robert, 88
Smirnoff, Yakov, 89
Smith College, 338
Southern Christian Leadership Confer-
 ence (SCLC), 160, 261
Space, use of, 269
Speakes, Larry, 88
Speech, parts of, 57
Stanford Hypnotic Susceptibility Scale,
 119, 126
Stanton, Elizabeth Cady, 224

State University of New York
 (SUNY), 88
Steil, Lyman, 205
Steiner, Stan, 289
Straightforward acceptance, 51
Study, habits, 5
Study-reading process, 38–39
Subject labels, 59
Suffixes, 104–5, 197–201
 learning, 199–201
 recognizing, 198–99
Summaries and Conclusions, 228–29
Sunset Years Club, 291
Surnames, 75
Syllabication, 429–30
 rules, 430–33
 syllable count, 430
Syllabication rules, 430–33
 compound words, 432
 divide before single consonant, 430
 divide between double conso-
 nants, 430
 neighboring vowels, 433
 prefixes and suffixes, 432
 short vowel, 431
 words ending with "le," 432
Synonyms, 60–61

T, Mr., 89
Tact, 194
Take the Sting Out of Criticism (Graber),
 49–52
Temple University, 327
Test-taking, tips on , 447–49
 preparing for, 5, 447–48
 reducing anxiety, 449
 taking, 448
Time
 planning, 5, 10–12
 use of, 269
Time management
 revisited, 179–80
 self-evaluation, 180–83
TLC, 303
Topic, and topic sentences, 127–29
Topic sentences, 127
 locating, 129–31
Torn, Rip, 89
Touching behavior, 269

Underlining, 254–55

Underlining—*Cont.*
 effective, 241–44
 tips for, 240–41
Unemployment, and mental
 health, 150
Uniform Crime Report, 227
United Negro College Fund, 338
United States Census Bureau, 337
United States Constitution, 204
United States Supreme Court, 260
Usage labels, 59
Utah State University, 314

Verb endings, 57
Verble, Margaret, 50–52
Vocabulary, building process, 20–22
Vocabulary strategies, 185
 integrating, 202–4
Vocal characteristics, 268
Vowel sounds, 434–37
 long vowel sounds, 434–35
 r-controlled vowels, 435
 schwa sounds, 435
 short vowel sounds, 434
 silent vowels, 435
 vowel blends, 435
Vowel rules, 435–36
 long vowel rules, 436
 rules for other vowels sounds, 436
 short vowel rule, 436

Walker, Alice, 302
Washington, University of, 50
Watson, Elizabeth, 241, 245
Webster's New World Dictionary, 55,
 81, 274
Wells, Alice Stebbins, 236, 243
Word associations, 201–2
Word roots; *see* Roots
Word structure, analyzing, 104–5
Work and Personal Adjustment (Derlega
 and Janda), 145–51
World War II, 227
Wright, Ann, 338

X, Malcolm, 160
X-Clan, 303
Yaroslavsky, Zev, 237
Youth Initiatives Office, 329
Yo-Yo, 303
Zappa, Moon Unit, 89